New Interpretat
in the 21st

Series Editor

Jennifer Jeffers
Cleveland State University
Department of English
Cleveland, Ohio
USA

Aim of the Series

As the leading literary figure to emerge from post-World War II Europe, Samuel Beckett's texts and his literary and intellectual legacy have yet to be fully appreciated by critics and scholars. The goal of New Interpretations of Beckett in the 21st Century is to stimulate new approaches and develop fresh perspectives on Beckett, his texts, and his legacy. The series will provide a forum for original and interdisciplinary interpretations concerning any aspect of Beckett's work or his influence upon subsequent writers, artists, and thinkers.

More information about this series at
http://www.springer.com/series/14737

David Addyman • Matthew Feldman • Erik Tonning
Editors

Samuel Beckett and BBC Radio

A Reassessment

Editors
David Addyman
University of Bergen
Bergen, Norway

Erik Tonning
University of Bergen
Bergen, Norway

Matthew Feldman
Teesside University
Middlesborough,
United Kingdom

New Interpretations of Beckett in the 21st Century
ISBN 978-1-349-95736-1   ISBN 978-1-137-54265-6 (eBook)
DOI 10.1057/978-1-137-54265-6

© The Editor(s) (if applicable) and The Author(s) 2017
Softcover reprint of the hardcover 1st edition 2017
This work is subject to copyright. All rights are solely and exclusively licensed by the Publisher, whether the whole or part of the material is concerned, specifically the rights of translation, reprinting, reuse of illustrations, recitation, broadcasting, reproduction on microfilms or in any other physical way, and transmission or information storage and retrieval, electronic adaptation, computer software, or by similar or dissimilar methodology now known or hereafter developed.
The use of general descriptive names, registered names, trademarks, service marks, etc. in this publication does not imply, even in the absence of a specific statement, that such names are exempt from the relevant protective laws and regulations and therefore free for general use.
The publisher, the authors and the editors are safe to assume that the advice and information in this book are believed to be true and accurate at the date of publication. Neither the publisher nor the authors or the editors give a warranty, express or implied, with respect to the material contained herein or for any errors or omissions that may have been made. The publisher remains neutral with regard to jurisdictional claims in published maps and institutional affiliations.

Cover image © University of Dundee The Peto Collection

Printed on acid-free paper

This Palgrave Macmillan imprint is published by Springer Nature
The registered company is Nature America Inc. New York
The registered company address is: 1 New York Plaza, New York, NY 10004, U.S.A.

"Beckett's experimentation with the medium played an important part in the growing awareness of the potential sound drama offered in relation to new directions in art, and it also had a lasting effect on his own future work."
"Beckett and the BBC Third Programme"

In memoriam
Julie Campbell

Acknowledgements

This volume appeared after several visits by the editors to BBC Written Archives Centre (WAC) in Caversham, Berkshire, UK. The editors are grateful to BBC WAC staff, led by Trish Hayes, for their assistance at various stages of this project.

Contributors were especially commissioned for this volume, and a symposium was held at Regent's Park College, University of Oxford. The editors are grateful to the college for their hospitality, and also thank Peter Fifield, Janet Wilson and David Tucker for their support. The editors are especially grateful to contributors for their forbearance and for their willingness to collaborate. Finally, we express our thanks to Jennifer M. Jeffers for inclusion of this project in the *New Interpretations of Samuel Beckett in the Twenty-first-Century* book series, and to Palgrave Macmillan for publishing *Samuel Beckett and BBC Radio: A Reappraisal*, in particular Ryan Jenkins and Paloma Yannakakis in Palgrave's New York office.

The editors duly acknowledge the University of Dundee archives for reproduction of the cover image, a copyrighted image of Samuel Beckett at the BBC Studios in January 1966 during the recording of *Eh Joe* (photograph by Michael Peto). We are also grateful to Julia and Francesca Bray for permission to cite from materials copyrighted to the Estate of Barbara Bray in this volume's Introduction, and chapters by Baroghel Chia, Rosignoli, Verhulst and Feldman; for the chapter "Beckett's 'Non-canonical' Radio Productions, 1957–1989," the latter would also like to extend his thanks for permission to reprint James Knowlson's 1976 BBC Radio 3 introduction to a reading of Beckett's "Drunken Boat" translation of Arthur Rimbaud's poem, "Le Bateau Ivre."

Contents

Introduction *David Addyman, Matthew Feldman, and Erik Tonning*	1
Beckett's "Non-canonical" Radio Productions, 1957–1989 *Matthew Feldman*	21
The BBC and Beckett's Non-radiogenic Plays in the 1950s *Dirk Van Hulle*	43
Mediating Modernism: The Third Programme, Samuel Beckett, and Mass Communication *Erik Tonning*	59
The BBC as "Commissioner" of Beckett's Radio Plays *Pim Verhulst*	81
Imagining Radio Sound: Interference and Collaboration in the BBC Radio Production of Beckett's *All That Fall* *Catherine Laws*	103

Author, Work and Trade: The Sociology of Samuel
Beckett's Texts in the Years of the Broadcasts for BBC Radio
(1957–89). Copyright and Moral Rights 139
Stefano Rosignoli

Changing My Tune: Beckett and the BBC
Third Programme (1957–1960) 169
John Pilling

"My God to Have to Murmur That": *Comment C'est/How
It Is* and the Issue of Performance 185
Elsa Baroghel

Fitting the Prose to Radio: The Case of *Lessness* 211
Paul Stewart

"My comforts! Be friends!": Words, Music
and Beckett's Poetry on the Third 229
Melissa Chia

Meditations and Monologues: Beckett's Mid-Late Prose
on the Radio 249
Steven Matthews

"None But the Simplest Words": Beckett's Listeners 269
Natalie Leeder

Bibliography 289

Index 301

Author Biographies

David Addyman is an independent scholar based in Oxford. He completed his Ph.D. on Beckett's relationship with space and place, and has published widely on this subject. He has also published on Beckett's postwar correspondence with Georges Duthuit, and recently acted as the Peder Sather Research Fellow at Bergen University.

Elsa Baroghel is completing her DPhil thesis on Samuel Beckett and the Marquis de Sade at the University of Oxford. She has published on the genesis of *Endgame* in *SBT/A* vol. 22 (2010) and on *Comment c'est* and Sade's *Les 120 journées de Sodome* (Samuel Beckett vol. 4, Brown (ed.), forthcoming (2016)).

Melissa Chia is completing her Ph.D. on Samuel Beckett and Sound at the University of Cambridge. She has reviewed for *The Journal of Beckett Studies* and has published as a Reuters journalist, a McGraw-Hill editor, a dramaturge with Cheek by Jowl, and a researcher for the Ministry of Education (Singapore).

Matthew Feldman is a professor in the Modern History of Ideas at Teesside University, where he co-directs the Centre for Fascism, Antifascism and Post-fascist Studies. He has published widely on Beckett, including *Beckett's Books* (paperback 2008) and his essay collection, *Falsifying Beckett* (2015). He is currently co-editing a transcription of Samuel Beckett's 'Philosophy Notes' for Oxford University Press.

Catherine Laws is a senior lecturer in Music at the University of York and a senior artistic research fellow at the Orpheus Research Centre in

Music, Ghent. She is the author of *Headaches Among the Overtones: Music in Beckett/Beckett in Music* (Editions Rodopi, 2013).

Natalie Leeder is a visiting lecturer at Royal Holloway, University of London. She is working on her first monograph and contributing three chapters to the forthcoming collection, *A Literary Heritage of the Natural World: The Pathetic Fallacy and Its Discontents*.

Steven Matthews is a professor of Modernism and Beckett Studies at the University of Reading. He is the author of various books on modernism, including *T.S. Eliot and Early Modern Literature*, which appeared from Oxford University Press in 2013. His volume of poetry, *Skying*, appeared from Waterloo Press in 2012.

John Pilling is an emeritus professor of English and European Literature at the University of Reading, UK. He is a former director of the Beckett International Foundation there, and a former editor of *The Journal of Beckett Studies*, and remains on the editorial board of *SBT/A*. He has written for over 40 years on almost every aspect of Beckett's life and work, having in recent times focused on the early fiction and on Beckett's poems. He is finishing a study of 'middle period' Beckett (1945–1953) provisionally titled *Shadows As Solid Things*.

Stefano Rosignoli received degrees in Modern Literature and Publishing at the University of Bologna. His Ph.D. at Trinity College, Dublin focuses on James Joyce, Samuel Beckett and ethics. Together with Mark Byron, he recently co-edited a dossier on "Beckett and the Middle Ages" for the *Journal of Beckett Studies* 25.1.

Paul Stewart is a professor of Literature at the University of Nicosia. He is the author of two books on Beckett: *Sex and Aesthetics in Samuel Beckett's Works* (Palgrave, 2011) and *Zone of Evaporation: Samuel Beckett's Disjunctions* (Rodopi, 2006), and the series editor for "Samuel Beckett in Company," published by Ibidem Press.

Erik Tonning is a professor of British Literature and Culture at the Department of Foreign Languages, University of Bergen. He is the author of *Samuel Beckett's Abstract Drama* (2007) and co-editor of *Broadcasting in the Modernist Era* (2014).

Dirk Van Hulle is a professor of English Literature at the University of Antwerp and co-director of the Beckett Digital Manuscript Project. He is the author of *Modern Manuscripts* (2014) and editor of the *New Cambridge Companion to Samuel Beckett* (2015).

Pim Verhulst is a postdoctoral researcher at the University of Antwerp's Centre for Manuscript Genetics. He is the author of The Making of Samuel Beckett's Radio Plays (2017, forthcoming) and an assistant editor of *The Journal of Beckett Studies*.

Introduction

David Addyman, Matthew Feldman, and Erik Tonning

Godot was not the only uncertain entity heralded in early-1950s Europe. Across the Channel, from the 5 January 1953 Théâtre de Babylone run that catapulted Samuel Beckett to global recognition, was another long-mooted arrival. In a recent volume that, like the present one, also centers upon the British Broadcasting Corporation's (hereafter BBC) extensive holdings of microfilm and files at its Written Archives Centre in Caversham (hereafter WAC), Finn Fordham identified this specter as television—haunting several passages by Beckett's one-time mentor, James Joyce.[1] In fact, on 17 March 1953—only three days before the passage of the UK's Television Act—the earliest-dated document in Samuel Beckett's detailed WAC archives records that the BBC's Parisian representative, Celia Reeves, had seen *Godot* in Paris together with the Features producer and novelist Rayner Heppenstall. Both recommended it for the Third Programme, the BBC's "highbrow" national radio service, although the broadcast failed to materialize in the 1950s on grounds that are explored in several chapters to follow. *Godot* would have to wait until

D. Addyman • M. Feldman (✉) • E. Tonning
Bergen and Teesside Universities, Middlesbrough and Bergen, UK and Norway

4 April 1960 to make his absence felt on the BBC—despite the aid of a narrator for radio.[2] The 1960 *Waiting for Godot*, moreover, was preceded by a number of other BBC radio "adaptations" of Beckett's work, including Patrick Magee's readings of "From an Abandoned Work," and excerpts from *Molloy, Malone Dies*, and *The Unnamable*.[3] As is highlighted across this volume, alongside Beckett's better known, "canonical" radio drama—*All That Fall, Embers, Words and Music,* and *Cascando*—these "non-canonical" broadcasts helped establish Beckett's Anglophone reputation and, as scholars have shown, also fuelled his creativity in later years.[4]

Mirroring the modernist avant-garde's public domestication only years after their initial appearance, the popular arrival in British households of what James Joyce characterized as "tellavicious" was indeed experienced as a potentially pernicious influence by some BBC executives in the 1950s.[5] Put bluntly, the rise of television threatened the "dumbing down" of British culture—and the BBC saw itself as that culture's leading light. Cuts to broadcasting hours, demoralized staff and fears about the rise of home television meant that the Third Programme's role became to some extent symbolic: it would continue to broadcast "high art" in an increasingly *This Is Your Life* celebrity culture. Responding to this challenge, BBC radio managers redoubled their search for high-quality original programming in the later 1950s, including Beckett, Harold Pinter, Eugene Ionesco, Arthur Adamov and other exponents of what Martin Esslin, one of those very BBC managers at the time, memorably dubbed "The Theatre of the Absurd." This introduction will examine some of these wider contexts below, before turning to a short survey of individual contributions that reassess the nature and scope of Beckett's relationship with BBC radio. Both here and in the ensuing chapters, special attention is given to the later 1950s and early 1960s, a time of key developments for home media use no less than for Beckett's work and international reception.

During these years, media consumption was changing markedly in Britain. By the later 1950s radio was being swiftly eclipsed by television, nearly 40 years on from the BBC's initial appearance as the British Broadcasting Company on 14 November 1922. Re-launched on New Year's Day 1927 with a Royal Charter, the Corporation's first Director-General, Sir John Reith, made no secret of its Arnoldian aim to educate the nation:

> [O]ur responsibility was to carry into the greatest possible number of homes everything that is best in every department of human knowledge, endeavour and achievement, and to avoid the things which are, or may be, hurtful.

> It is occasionally indicated to us that we are apparently setting out to give the public what we think they need—and not what they want, but few know what they want, and very few what they need.[6]

By the 1930s, BBC radio was overwhelmingly admired and emulated, and remained culturally ambitious in its output. Normal radio and television services were halted upon the outbreak of war in 1939, with the familiar Home and Light services from the 1930s only re-launched in June 1945. The BBC resumed television transmissions only 13 months later. Finally, the September 1946 launch of a third radio station was intended to be the vanguard of the BBC's most culturally highbrow output. Divided roughly equally between music and spoken-word programs, the Third Programme deliberately undertook challenging productions with a "consciously minority appeal." The Third Programme's unashamedly "small, satisfied and influential audience," continues Kate Whitehead, was "an important patron of creative writers" at this time, unafraid of undertaking many "avant-garde broadcasts," including championing the work of "late modernist" writers like David Jones, Dylan Thomas and Louis MacNeice.[7]

Revealing of just how far this golden age of radio "was to be shattered by the advent of competitive television" is Asa Briggs's panoramic study in five parts, *The History of Broadcasting in the United Kingdom*.[8] Dealing with the decade after World War II, his fourth volume is subtitled *Sound and Vision*. Underscoring the fundamental changes brought about by the rise of television in 1950s Britain, Briggs's final pages cite Sir Ian Jacob, the BBC's Director-General from 1952 to 1959, who was among the first to actively support television broadcasting:

> [T]hose engaged in sound broadcasting may have been wondering whether they would become a forgotten army, and whether in the intense struggle now taking place, they were going to be sacrificed in the demands for television.... Transfers of people and of resources were bound to take place, and many of them would be from sound to television. That was not surprising when it was remembered that originally sound broadcasting held the entire bank.[9]

This post-war epoch of the BBC's media monopoly lasted until the launch of *Competition* (the title of Briggs's fifth and final volume). This took the form, above all, of "independent" television, or ITV—commencing the same month as Beckett's first BBC radio "adaptation," a reading from

Watt in September 1955.[10] As with the vast majority of BBC productions of, and about, Beckett's work in the crucial period 1956–1964, these extracts from *Watt* were aired by the Third Programme: *the* principal vehicle for Beckett's public dissemination in Britain.

Talks, readings and radio drama—often with musical accompaniment—were the Third Programme's bread and butter throughout its 21-year existence. Yet the onset of television competition in the mid-to-late 1950s created a "paralysing anxiety" among Third Programme staff. Indeed, the whole of "the BBC was thrown into a state of panic," argues Humphrey Carpenter, for "the decline in radio listening had been hugely accelerated by the choice of television channels." The BBC's response was to initiate a top-down "reorganisation of radio." This entailed a "savage reduction in broadcasting hours" during 1957. In practice, it represented a 40 % reduction in the Third's hours between the transmission of *All That Fall* on 13 January 1957 and "From an Abandoned Work" on 10 December that same year.[11] In Whitehead's important survey of the Third Programme's literary output, the penultimate chapter, tellingly, is called "The Cut-backs of 1957," within a section entitled *The End*: "The 'streamlining' of 1957 had both cut the hours and undermined the ethos of the Third Programme, ending the sense of cultural 'mission' propounded by [Sir William] Haley which had motivated the network during its first ten years."[12]

As part of this revised strategy, a concerted effort to recruit "new talent" was undertaken, particularly for bespoke radio dramas. As Controller for the Third Programme at the time, John Morris had the unenviable task of overseeing severe broadcasting cuts while at the same time attempting to attract up-and-coming authors. His view, expressed in the Foreword to an anthology of Third Programme texts to celebrate its tenth anniversary in 1956, was that "any attempt to 'brighten-up' by 'talking down' to our listeners would inevitably have led to a general lowering of intellectual standards." Morris ruefully continued,

> I myself believe the days of 'experimental broadcasting' are long since past, but there is still much to do in solving the difficult problem of how to present abstract thought in such a way that it can be apprehended orally.[13]

Interestingly, this was the same man who went to Paris to meet Beckett and encourage the writing of *All That Fall*—he officially received the play on 29 September 1956—and oversaw a production so experimental that it led to the launch of the BBC Radiophonic workshop in 1958.[14]

From this point, the story of Beckett and the Third Programme is rather more familiar. It is touched upon in several of the chapters in this collection, and has been carefully assessed by the late, pioneering scholar of Beckett and the radio, Julie Campbell.[15] Less appreciated to date, however, is the level of perceived threat posed by television to radio's hegemony, during precisely the years of Beckett's closest and most fruitful relationship with the BBC. True, combined radio and television licenses had grown by more than 1.1 million per year between 1953 and 1966.[16] But it was the latter which was the driving force. In 1953, some 22 % of British households had television receivers; a decade later that figure had risen to 89 %. More troublingly for a once-dominant BBC radio, the quantity of listening dropped precipitously in these years: from 2 hours and 8 minutes in 1952, to 1 hour and 32 minutes in 1955 and only 1 hour and 14 minutes in 1963.[17] This, then, was the quickly changing landscape surrounding Beckett's turn to BBC radio.

***

It has become generally accepted that Beckett's multifaceted, *sui generis* works had to await their public until after the Second World War. Despite the recent scholarly attention given to Beckett's undoubtedly formative interwar writing, his "early" works received limited attention upon release: this applies to the award-winning poem "Whoroscope" (1930), the academic study *Proust* (1931), the short stories *More Pricks Than Kicks* (1934), his selected poems, *Echo's Bones* (1935) and the novel *Murphy* (1938). Written fitfully in wartime hiding from the Gestapo, *Watt* would await a publisher until after the appearance of the works that made Beckett's name, above all, "The Trilogy" of novels and the 1953 Parisian stage début of *En Attendant Godot*.[18] During his many "years of wandering," in the words of the 1934 poem "Gnome," engagements with radio either never came off—as in the case of the 1946 "Capital of the Ruins," apparently intended for Raidió Teilifís Éireann (RTÉ)—or were registered merely as personal annoyance, as with a 1938 complaint from Paris to his confidante, Thomas MacGreevy, Beckett's earliest-known remarks on radio:

> A terrible wireless has started next door. They turn it on when they get up, keep it on till they go out, & turn it on again when they come in. One morning it waked me at 7 am. I must put up with it.[19]

Around the time of Beckett's leap to widespread acclaim in the mid-1950s, he was, according to his biographers, sinking into a deep morass born of an inability to move beyond his post-war "frenzy of writing." Beckett was only too aware of his writer's block, lamenting with the characteristic (extra) gloominess of this period to Barney Rosset, his American publisher: "I think my writing days are over. *L'Innommable* finished me or expressed my finishedness."[20] Despite completing *Fin de Partie*, the English translation of *L'Innommable*, and his 13 *Texts for Nothing*, Beckett confessed to feeling that he was "dried up, with nothing left but self-translation."[21] It was here, fortuitously, that the BBC's increasing pursuit of Beckett bore fruit; providing, in James Knowlson's apt words, an "escape route" via a new medium: radio broadcasting.[22] Following the success of *All That Fall*, this was certainly the view cast by Donald McWhinnie, a BBC drama producer and later director of several Beckett's plays: "My impression is that if he is to write at all in the near future it will be for radio, which has captured his imagination."[23]

Naturally enough, scholarly explorations of Beckett's reception have tended to focus on his post-*Godot* publishing and stage drama, tracing the waves of a truly global expansion of both public and critical interest in Beckett's work.[24] According to Shane Weller, for instance, by 1961, "9,000 copies of *Molloy* had been printed [and] 24,000 copies of *Godot* had been printed" by Beckett's French publisher, *Les Éditions de Minuit*.[25] Many thousands were also seeing his plays, of course, in Europe and beyond. Yet the Third Programme catered to many *tens* of thousands, and played a crucial role in Beckett's Anglophone reception. To date, however, the extent of the BBC's embrace of Beckett has not received a full-length academic study—a key lacuna addressed by *Samuel Beckett and BBC Radio: A Reassessment*.

In terms of audience size, a striking example is the Royal Court Production of *Fin de Partie*, which opened on 3 April 1957 and seated 380 people per performance. One month later, the Third Programme broadcast a radio production (also in French). Like the London stage première, directed by Roger Blin, Michael Bakewell's radio production on 2 May 1957 included the same, celebrated cast (Blin, Jean Martin, Georges Adet and Christine Tsingos), but added a narrator (Jacques Brunius) to compensate for the "blind medium" of radio. Of these two performances of *Fin de Partie*, the latter would have been more widely received, a point stressed by P.H. Newby, Controller of the Third Programme between 1959 and 1967 (when the Third Programme was progressively absorbed into the new Radio 3 service):

> The range of drama we offer is enormously wider than anything offered by the London theatres. In any case, the mass of the population cannot get to

them. Any drama critic who took note of one of our new productions could do so in the knowledge that its audience would be nation-wide and big enough to fill the Royal Court Theatre for about nine months and that when it is repeated ten days or so later there will be another audience just as large.

Newby went on to stress that the Third Programme was "broadcasting Beckett's play *All that Fall* (it was commissioned by the Third Programme) for the seventh time early next year." By his calculations, this was the equivalent of more than four years of selling out the Royal Court Theatre.[26] Unlike the ensuing five "adaptations" of Beckett's work airing on the Third Programme, however, the theatrical *Fin de Partie* was not repeated for another 50,000 or more auditors. It seems quite likely, then, that a greater number of people in Britain were introduced to Beckett's work via BBC radio than those reading it or attending a live performance.

Added to the BBC's many performances *of* Beckett's work in Britain between the mid-1950s and mid-1960s, moreover, were a number of programs *about* Beckett as well. According to Raymond Federman and John Fletcher, *Waiting for Godot* was first reviewed for the Home Service on 21 August 1955—incidentally, some three weeks before Jack Holmstrom's reading of *Watt* excerpts on the Third Programme—and received comment for a second time the following week. This was followed by a review of *All That Fall* a week after its première. In the 1960s, the Home Service also reviewed *Happy Days*, *Words and Music*, *Play*, *Endgame* and *Waiting for Godot*.[27]

Yet once again it was the Third Programme that led the way in presenting, and even framing, Beckett's work. The following is a list of broadcasts on Beckett's contemporaneous works by the Third Programme in the decade following the 1957 transmission of *All That Fall*: Ronald Gray's Christian interpretation of *Waiting for Godot* (9 January 1957); G.S. Fraser's review of the recently broadcast *All That Fall* for the "Comment" segment (24 January 1957); J.J. Whiteman's theater review of *Fin de Partie* and *Acte sans paroles*, two days after its London première (4 April 1957); A.J. "Con" Leventhal's "Samuel Beckett: Poet and Pessimist" (30 April 1957); Patrick Bowles on translating *Molloy*, "A Master Work of Disillusion" (15 June 1958); Anthony Cronin's "The Unsayable," a discussion of "The Trilogy" (19 January 1959); Karl Miller for "Comment" on *Embers* and *All That Fall* broadcasts (25 June 1959); Barbara Bray for "Comment" on *Comment c'est* (2 February 1961); Peter Bull's radio documentary on *Waiting for Godot*, "Waiting for What?"

(14 April 1961); a "New Comment" roundtable discussion of Beckett's work (11 October 1961); Denis Donohue's "The Play of Words," partly on Beckett's drama (30 June 1962); Laurence Kitchin's general twentieth-century drama program, which included discussion of Beckett, called "Compressionism: The Cage and the Scream" (8 January 1963; with Kitchin later contributing to "New Comment" on *Play*, 14 April 1964); a "New Comment" installment on "Beckett's work from the actor's viewpoint" (2 June 1964, including interviews with Jack MacGowran and Patrick Magee); Christopher Ricks's "The Roots of Samuel Beckett" (18 November 1964); Eric Rhode for "New Comment" on *Waiting for Godot* at the Royal Court Theatre (6 January 1965); John Fletcher's "Beckett as Critic" on Beckett's non-fiction literary criticism (2 October 1965); and Barbara Bray on "Imagination Dead Imagine" for "New Comment" (9 March 1966).[28] Roughly half of these programs were repeated.[29]

Alongside this enormous dissemination, importantly, critics for the Third Programme advanced a number of abiding interpretative frameworks for Beckett's works. Even the advance billing for *All That Fall*, published in the BBC's house journal, *The Listener* (1929–1991), provides an early profile of the "mysterious author": "Figure, athletic; manner, decisive; a blend of extreme seriousness and twinkling good humour; modest; kind; and thoroughly good company." Published for a readership in excess of 130,000, this portrait was offered, fittingly, by Donald McWhinnie, later to direct television productions of *Waiting for Godot*, *Eh Joe* and *Ghost Trio*. McWhinnie summarized *All That Fall* in these terms:

> On the face of it, a simple, if unexpected, affair: an anecdote set in a rural community of Ireland. In fact, a careful synthesis of speech, sound and—as you might expect—silence; hectically funny and bitterly tragic; a story of the inadequacy of life and death, breathing an atmosphere of vitality and ruin, farce and suffocation.
>
> It is remarkable that Beckett shows such a clear grasp of the medium in his first work for radio; however, the problems he sets his producer cannot be solved by conventional means. Our meeting in his beloved Paris was all the more valuable; we worked over the text in detail, elucidating, modifying, adjusting even the tiniest of points of emphasis.[30]

A week later, on 9 January 1957, *The Listener* published Ronald Gray's "A Christian Interpretation of *Waiting for Godot*"—only four days before *All That Fall*—which elicited a lively correspondence over subsequent weeks.[31]

Of course, most radio broadcasts on Beckett did not later appear in *The Listener*. In this category his intimate friend and BBC correspondent Barbara Bray attempted, on 11 October 1961, "to consider how far the reading of Beckett's novels casts a useful light on his plays." Broadcast on the recently launched "New Comment" program, 23 minutes and 30 seconds were devoted to Beckett's work, with contributions by Martin Esslin, Patrick Magee and others.[32] Earlier that year, in another Third Programme broadcast not published in *The Listener*, Bray disputed the description of *Comment c'est* (1961) as a novel, comparing it instead to Dante's *Divine Comedy*—a text Beckett re-engaged when attempting to move beyond his creative impasse in the mid-1950s—in offering this homage:

> This a piece of 'total writing,' in which all the apparently contradictory powers, rational and irrational, of a uniquely rich and delicate sensibility and a uniquely piercing intelligence are brought together to give as pure a rendering of modern consciousness as words have yet been made to convey.

Upon receipt of the script the day after its broadcast, Beckett wrote that he liked it "very much—quite sincerely. You have 'understood' the book as no one so far."[33]

Barbara Bray was not the only commentator for the Third Programme drawn from among Beckett's network of friends (or family, in the case of BBC musical collaboration with his cousin John Beckett). Indeed, for Martin Esslin, who took over from Donald MacWhinnie in 1961 as Assistant Head of Radio Drama (Sound), "Beckett worked very much that way, with friendships. He wanted people whom he could trust and with whom he could work."[34] Personal connections were integral to Beckett during this pivotal period of "getting known," in the words of the radio-inspired *Krapp's Last Tape* from 1958. It is a pattern amply attested to in James Knowlson's masterful biography.[35] In a telling example related to radio, an old friend from Beckett's Dublin days, Con Leventhal, read "Samuel Beckett: Poet and Pessimist" for the Third Programme on 30 April 1957, only two days before the Francophone broadcast of *Fin de Partie*. Leventhal's talk then appeared in *The Listener* on 9 May, revealing a number of persisting tropes from Beckett's early prose and poetry to his 1950s plays. The piece compares Beckettian irony with that of the "dadaists and early surrealists," as a "jousting with words" and displaying an "erudition deeper, one suspects, than that of the Master"—James Joyce. Conducting an investigation of humanity's "via dolorosa," Beckett's was a world "barren of hope" for Levanthal.³⁶ Interestingly, two years before contributors to Ruby Cohn's influential special issue on Beckett for *Perspective* identified motion and rest as key themes in Beckett's early work—a collection often associated with launching Anglophone Beckett Studies in 1959—Leventhal identified the conception of movement-in-stasis and, in particular, the rocking chair, as a kind of "Beckett mascot."³⁷

Like Leventhal's contribution, many Third Programme commentaries on Beckett's work were clustered around broadcasts of radio productions of his prose and drama. Alongside periodic publication in *The Listener*—which would double or even triple the potential audience—this was clearly intended to increase British interest in, and knowledge of, Beckett's work. Emblematic of these commentaries is that by Beckett's co-translator for *Molloy*, Patrick Bowles, whose "*Molloy*: A Masterwork of Disillusion" aired three days before the broadcast of *Malone Dies*, and was printed as "How Samuel Beckett Sees the Universe" in *The Listener* the following day, 19 June 1958. Some 50 years before Beckett's proximity to European phenomenology was explored at length, Bowles found that *Molloy*, and "The Trilogy" of novels more generally, explores when "the distinction between the inner and outer world breaks down"; that is, the subject-object cleavage between "within and without": "What we perceive does not come to us cold, but is momentarily joined to us, object and subject in an unbreakable relationship."³⁸ This was in close keeping with Bowles's notes from meetings with Beckett in the middle 1950s—amidst the taxing translation of *Molloy*—in which he employs Husserlian terms to approach the "consciousness of consciousness. Not merely being the consciousness *of* some object, but the awareness of being *awake*, if you like."³⁹

Over and above the much wider circulation of Third Programme commentaries later appearing in *The Listener*—greatly inflating the potential audience with its six-figure print run—several early Beckett scholars advanced readings of Beckett's work. Six weeks after *Cascando* aired on 6 October 1964, Christopher Ricks, later of *Beckett's Dying Words* renown, contributed "The Roots of Samuel Beckett." This was only a month before an "unexpurgated" rendition of *Waiting for Godot* opened at the Royal Court Theatre, and four days before Beckett's Robert Pinget "translation," *The Old Tune* (first aired on the BBC on 23 August 1960) opened at London's Mercury Theatre).⁴⁰ In the ensuing publication of Ricks's Third Programme radio broadcast, he granted that "comparison and analysis," "the critic's usual tools," were difficult to apply to Beckett's "greatness and originality." Ricks placed Beckett in the tradition of Dante,

Bunyan, Swift, Dr Johnson and even Shakespeare's *King Lear*.[41] Similarly John Fletcher, having just published *The Novels of Samuel Beckett* and soon to release *Samuel Beckett's Art*—two paradigm-setting works in the nascent field of Beckett Studies—contributed an analysis of Beckett's criticism to the Third Programme, appearing as "Beckett as Critic" in *The Listener* on 25 November 1965; in other words, some five years before Lawrence Harvey's pioneering study, *Samuel Beckett: Poet and Critic*. Nearly as remarkable as the frequency of Beckett's work on the Third Programme, surely, is the space given there to early explications of that work (and, occasionally thereafter, in *The Listener*, which typically also ran notices on his recent radio productions).

Especially during the later 1950s and 1960s, there can be little doubt that the BBC doused its audience in programs by, and on, Samuel Beckett. Yet as several contributions here show, this was by no means restricted to these years. Beckett's 60th birthday was marked with a radio production of *Play* and two broadcasts on his poetry (both of the latter narrated by John Fletcher). Redoubling its coverage a decade later, what was now Radio 3 premièred *Rough for Radio II* on Beckett's 70th birthday; and the next day, 14 April 1976, Radio 3 repeated highlights from Jack MacGowran's 1966 poetry readings. The latter included then-virtually-unknown poems like "Whoroscope," "Serena I" and "Serena II," "Alba," "Echo's Bones," "Sanies I," and "Saint Lô."[42] Capping this extravaganza was what Radio 3 called "the first publication" of "For to End Yet Again" on 10 October 1976, just as "Beckett at 80" offered the first broadcast of *A Piece of Monologue*. There were many more productions besides these surprising "adaptations," as is presented in the "case-log" comprising Matthew Feldman's chapter "Beckett's 'Non-canonical' Radio Productions, 1957–1989." Before turning to a detailed overview of the present volume, however, a final word is in order on the corpus of materials to be reassessed.

***

From the BBC WAC's paper and microfilm collection, Beckett's radio productions are effectively split into two separately held categories. The first are microfiche production details and scripts for virtually all of the BBC radio "adaptations" listed in the so-called Play Library collection at Caversham. Also contained on microfiche are various programs about Beckett from the more general—and more disorganized—"Talks Library, 1922–1970" (as noted above, some of which also appeared in *The Listener*).[43]

Of greater interest still may be the second category of BBC WAC materials. Archived manuscript holdings for Beckett's BBC work (including television) are concentrated in the following files: "Samuel Beckett: Source File"; "Samuel Beckett: Copyright Files"; "Samuel Beckett: Drama Writer Files" (1960–1974 and 1975–1979); and finally and most relevantly here, the four-part "Samuel Beckett: Scriptwriter Files" (1953–1962; 1963–1967; 1968–1972; and 1973–1982). These materials shed light upon most BBC productions of Beckett's work over the last 33 years of his life. They are analyzed by contributors around several key themes, such as those dealing with degrees of collaboration intrinsic to radio production; as well as matters of contracts and payment; musical accompaniment and performers; the technicalities of broadcast transmission; and correspondence with, and more often about, Beckett among BBC staff. It is an expansive corpus of materials, comprising some 2,000 pages in total—making the BBC WAC holdings one of the most extensive Beckett-related caches to date, and receiving only limited scholarly treatment before now.

Erik Tonning's chapter "Mediating Modernism: The Third Programme, Samuel Beckett, and Mass Communication" sets out key elements of the Third's intellectual milieu. As Tonning has established elsewhere,[44] a kind of "Christian modernism" prevailed among a number of influential voices at the BBC, advocating "a more existentially reflected and artistically oriented culture" in post-war Britain. Ironically enough—and despite initially prevaricating over broadcasting *Waiting for Godot*—the Third Programme's "framing" of Beckett as a kind of tragi-comic moralizer helped to draw attention away from potential charges of blasphemy. It also showed the way in which the Third Programme "mediated" difficult modernist writers for a wider British public.

Yet in the next chapter, "The BBC and Beckett's Non-Radiogenic Plays in the 1950s," Dirk van Hulle makes clear the path was not a smooth one in the 1950s, even if the BBC would come to play a "substantial" role in Beckett's career. "The BBC and Beckett's Non-Radiogenic Plays in the 1950s" looks more closely at three 1950s Beckett plays with a very different relationship to broadcasting: *En Attendant Godot/Waiting for Godot* (1953), *Fin de Partie/Endgame* (1956) and *Krapp's Last Tape* (1958). Furthermore, the multiple formats Beckett was working in—writing theatrical and radio drama, self-translation and a return to prose with *Comment c'est*—reveal that radio was indeed "a catalyst for Beckett's work in the late 1950s." It may have taken time for the BBC to fully appreciate Beckett's "radiophonic potential," van Hulle asserts, but the Corporation would soon make up for lost time.

To be sure, the BBC collaborated with Beckett in various ways, from discussing initial ideas for radio outputs to helping to realize radio sound. But was Beckett actually "commissioned" by the BBC, in the words of P. H. Newby, above? Even if this was certainly not Martin Esslin's view, for Pim Verhulst, it was nevertheless accurate. In "The BBC as 'Commissioner' of Beckett's Radio Plays," Verhulst's attention is trained upon *Embers*—written in 1958, the same year he recently established as the most likely for the composition of *Pochade radiophonique*[45]—as well as *Words and Music, Cascando* and Beckett's translation of *Pochade*, broadcast on 13 April 1976 as *Rough for Radio II*. Even if this quasi-commissioning proved a "strain" for Beckett, Verhulst shows that Beckett let himself be "coaxed" by trusted colleagues like Donald MacWhinnie and later Martin Esslin.

BBC collaboration is also at the heart of Catherine Laws's chapter, "Imagining Radio Sound: Interference and Collaboration in the BBC Radio Production of Beckett's *All That Fall*." Sometimes working with his cousin, John Beckett, Beckett's growing familiarity with the medium of radio by the late 1950s allowed him to experiment with sound as a "character" in his radiogenic works. Drawing upon her recent monograph on Beckett's lifelong relationship with music, Laws examines Beckett's sophisticated "radio soundscapes" for the BBC, which has the effect "of collapsing the unity of time and space in an acoustic context" in *All That Fall*.[46] Like the preceding three chapters, Laws stresses the practical necessity, and yet surprising scope, of Samuel Beckett's collaborative work for radio. These opening chapters collectively attest that Beckett—often regarded as the apogee of an isolated, unaffiliated artist—could not do without the BBC's technical and professional advice for the successful realization of his radio productions, nor was he indifferent to the Third Programme's "wooing" of him, and the prospect of an unrivaled platform in Britain for his work.

As Stefano Rosignoli shows in his chapter, "Author, Work and Trade: The Sociology of Samuel Beckett's Texts in the Years of the Broadcasts for BBC Radio (1957-89)" the dozens of radio productions (and repeats) of Beckett's work aired on BBC radio were also comparably well paid. After years of penury, "Author, Work and Trade: The Sociology of Samuel Beckett's Texts in the Years of the Broadcasts for BBC Radio (1957–89)" reveals another side of Beckettian collaboration: the thorny matter of contracts and copyright. The extent to which Beckett was interested in wealth and fame has led to two very different perspectives. One picture, offered by Stephen Dilks, is of Beckett "salivating over his royalty statements" and cultivating a "hagiographic myth" of secular-saintliness. Mark Nixon paints a strikingly different picture of a Beckett willing to help friends and to donate manuscripts, emphasizing acts of charity among Beckett's growing circle.[47] Tending toward the latter of these positions, Rosignoli offers a portrait of Beckett's burgeoning income from publishing, theater and radio, on the one hand, and of his trying to keep such business questions at arm's length on the other. Nor does a clear pattern emerge for decisions like those in 1966, when Beckett firmly rejected a radio production of *Three Dialogues* (1949) but showed "a degree of flexibility" over allowing a radio "adaptation" of *Play* (1964). The latter, coming in at 18 minutes and four seconds, was aired by the Third Programme on 11 October and 30 October 1966, and then a third time by its successor, Radio 3, on 2 September 1967.

The ensuing three chapters then train this volume's attention upon specific texts, commencing with John Pilling's "Changing My Tune: Beckett and the BBC Third Programme (1957–1960)." While neither comfortably "canonical" nor "non-canonical," what "Changing My Tune: Beckett and the BBC Third Programme (1957-1960)" dubs Beckett's "expertly done" translation of Pinget's La Manivelle stresses the radiophonic importance in "the choice of an interpreter." For the Third Programme's 1960 broadcast, Jack MacGowran played Mr Cream, while Gorman was played by Patrick Magee, who had already performed "the trilogy" and "From an Abandoned Work" for the Third Programme by that time. "'My God to have to murmur that': Comment C'est/How It Is and the Issue of Performance," then examines Beckett's contemporaneous "novel" from 1961, which Beckett once referred to as a "microphone text." In the event, *How It Is* would never be broadcast on BBC radio—despite what Elsa Baroghel sees as a contribution to "Beckett's exploration of sound technique across genres in the late 1950s"—even if the composition of *Comment c'est* ultimately "helped inform Beckett's later radio plays." Indeed, as Paul Stewart demonstrates, not just radio plays but BBC radio "adaptations" also helped in this regard, as is stressed in "Fitting the Prose to Radio: The Case of 'Lessness'." Even if the outcome left Beckett "deeply dissatisfied," in the words of Martin Esslin, the latter nonetheless believed "Lessness" was "really for the radio." Thanks to Stewart's insight in "Fitting the Prose to Radio: The Case of 'Lessness'," it becomes clear just how a radio producer and literary artist might offer such different interpretations of Radio 3's broadcasts of "Lessness" on 25 February and 7 May 1971; ambitiously, the performance used six different actors (all Beckett "enthusiasts") to read a mathematical proportion of 60 sentences as voices A–F, collectively "meant to convey a single consciousness."[48]

In "'My Comforts! Be Friends!': Words, Music and Beckett's Poetry on the Third," Melissa Chia turns to Beckett's poetry on BBC radio, from the role of "Words" in *Words and Music*, broadcast on the Third Programme on 13 November 1962, to several programs dedicated to readings in 1966 and 1979. "'My comforts! Be friends!': Words, Music and Beckett's Poetry on the Third" then interrogates the role of literary critics on BBC radio, exemplified by Esslin and Fletcher in the 1960s, who championed Beckett's otherwise neglected poems—despite strong opposition from within the BBC. It may well have been Esslin's "energy, diligence, and persistence," as Steven Matthews notes in his contribution, that got such challenging works aired—like the 143-minute readings of all 13 *Texts for Nothing* read by Patrick Magee in 1975–1976. "Meditations and Monologues: Beckett's Mid-late Prose on the Radio" turns to these "meditations on being," as the Opening Announcement for these broadcasts for Radio 3 put it. Matthews's essay raises questions of intellectual "framing" and other forms of editorial input vis-à-vis Beckett's later work with BBC radio. It should be remembered that even in the middle 1970s, as Matthews notes, turning full circle to the longer-term context of a by-then cherished national institution, that the BBC was "an important mediator of Beckett's avant-garde practice to the broader UK public."

Consideration of the wider listening public in Britain animates the final chapter in this collection. In "'None but the Simplest Words': Beckett's Listeners," Natalie Leeder uses the BBC's scribal mouthpiece, *The Listener*, to return full-circle to the reception of Beckett's "canonical" radio plays—particularly in terms of their musicality. This is discussed in conjunction with the musical writings of Beckett's "one-time sparring-partner," Theodor W. Adorno, who, in these years of growing public recognition, was one of Beckett's best-known auditors. Leeder also raises the vital question of Beckett's audience—readership, viewership and listenership alike—as it began to increasingly intersect with popular culture. That BBC radio offered such rarefied access both (relatively) early and often was significant not only to his popularity in Britain and probably in the development of his poetics, but also, more widely, for thousands of Britons at turns amazed, perplexed and appalled—but rarely indifferent—to encountering broadcasts of Beckett's work. *Beckett in Popular Culture*, a collection of essays by P.J. Murphy and

Nick Pawliuk, testifies that this Anglophone public embrace has hardly abated, some six decades on. In terms of their innovative project no less than for the reassessment of Beckett's remarkably fruitful and longstanding relationship with BBC radio, their conclusion is a timely plea for continued research on Beckett's still-developing relationship with the mass media:

> We have only scratched the surface of this rich vein of material of all sorts in various genres, media, languages, and cultures.
>
> Feel free to post your own examples and accompanying comments on the website voxpopbeckett.ca.[49]

Notes

1. See Finn Fordham, "Early Television and Joyce's *Finnegans Wake*: New Technology and Flawed Power," in *Broadcasting in the Modernist Era*, eds. Matthew Feldman, Erik Tonning and Henry Mead (London: Bloomsbury, 2014).
2. Denys Hawthorne, who would later take part in two BBC poetry readings for the Third Programme, and was one of six voices performing "Lessness" on Radio 3 in 1971, performed the role of narrator.
3. For further discussion, see Matthew Feldman, "Beckett's 'Trilogy' on the Third," in *Samuel Beckett Today/Aujourd'hui* 26 (2015).
4. Key Anglophone works on Beckett and radio include Katharine Worth, "Beckett and the Radio Medium," in *British Radio Drama*, ed. John Drakakis (Cambridge: Cambridge University Press, 1981); Everett Frost, "Fundamental Sounds: Recording Samuel Beckett's Radio Plays," in *Theatre Journal* 43.3 (1991); Marjorie Perloff, "The Silence That Is Not Silence: Acoustic Art in Samuel Beckett's *Embers*"; and Stanley Richardson and Jane Alison Hale, "Working Wireless: Beckett's Radio Writing," both in *Samuel Beckett and the Arts: Music, Visual Arts, and Non-Print Media*, ed. Lois Oppenheim (New York: Garland Publishing, 1999); Barry McGovern, "Beckett and the Radio Voice," in *Samuel Beckett: 100 Years: Centenary Essays*, ed. Christopher Murray (Dublin: New Island, 2006); Kevin Branigan, *Radio Beckett: Musicality in the Radio Plays of Samuel Beckett* (Oxford: Peter Lang, 2008); Steven Connor, "I Switch Off: Beckett and the Ordeals of Radio," in *Broadcasting Modernism*, eds. Debra Rae Cohen, Michael Coyle and Jane Lewty (Gainesville: University of Florida Press, 2009), Jeffrey Lyn Porter, "Beckett and the Radiophonic Body: Beckett and the BBC," *Modern Drama* 53.4 (2010); Gaby Hartel, "Emerging out of a Silent Void: Some

Reverberations of Rudolf Arnheim's Radio Theory in Beckett's Radio Pieces," in *Journal of Beckett Studies* 19.2 (2010); Ulrika Maude, "Working on Radio," in *Samuel Beckett in Context*, ed. Anthony Uhlmann (Cambridge: Cambridge University Press, 2013); and most recently, Pim Verhulst, "'There are differences': Variants and Errors in the Texts of Beckett's Radio Plays," in *Journal of Beckett Studies* 24.1 (2015).

5. James Joyce, cited in Fordham, "Early Television and Joyce's *Finnegans Wake*," 46–7.
6. From Sir John Reith's 1924 *Broadcast Over Britain*, cited in Kevin Jackson, *Constellation of Genius, 1922: Modernism and all that Jazz* (London: Windmill Books, 2013), 386, 426.
7. Kate Whitehead, *The Third Programme: A Literary History* (Oxford: Clarendon Press, 1989), 1–2, 12.
8. Asa Briggs, *The History of Broadcasting in the United Kingdom, Volume 4: Sound and Vision* (Oxford: Oxford University Press, 1979), 520.
9. Sir Ian Jacob, internal BBC memorandum of 18 Oct. 1955, cited in ibid., 1023–4.
10. ITV launched on 22 Sep. 1955. Coincidentally; on the 9th of that month, Jack Holmstrom read selections from Beckett's *Watt*; see John Pilling, *A Samuel Beckett Chronology* (Basingstoke: Palgrave, 2006), 128.
11. These citations are drawn from Humphrey Carpenter, *The Envy of the World: Fifty Years of the BBC Third Programme and Radio 3* (London: Weidenfeld & Nicolson, 1997), 157–8, 166–8, 177.
12. Whitehead, *The Third Programme*, 227.
13. John Morris, "Foreword" to *From the Third Programme: A Ten-Years' Anthology. Imagination, Argument, Experience, Exposition* (London: BBC Publications, 1956), p. vi.
14. For further discussion on the establishment of the BBC's Radiophonic Workshop, see Louis Niebur, *Special Sound: The Creation and Legacy of the BBC Radiophonic Workshop* (Oxford: Oxford University Press, 2010), Chapter 1.
15. Julie Campbell, "Beckett and the BBC Third Programme," in *Samuel Beckett Today Aujourd'hui* 24 (2012).
16. Tom Burns, *The BBC: Public Institution and Private World* (London: Macmillan, 1977), 187.
17. Robert Silvey, *Who's Listening? The Story of BBC Audience Research* (London: Allen & Unwin, 1974), 164, 187, and 209.
18. For more on Beckett's post-war rise to global recognition, see Mark Nixon and Matthew Feldman, eds., *The International Reception of Samuel Beckett* (London: Bloomsbury, 2009).
19. Beckett to Thomas McGreevy, 26 May 1938, in *Letters I*, 626. For more on Beckett's "Capital of the Ruins," see Darren Gribben, "Beckett's Other

Revelation: 'The Capital of the Ruins,'" in *Irish University Review*, 38.2 (2008), with the original text reprinted online as "Samuel Beckett, 'Capital of the Ruins,'" available at: www.ricorso.net/rx/library/authors/classic/Beckett_S/St_Lo.htm. (all websites last accessed 22 Feb. 2016).
20. Beckett to Barney Rosset, 21 Aug. 1954, in *Letters II*, 497.
21. Beckett to Vivian Mercier, cited in Deidre Bair, *Samuel Beckett* (London: Vintage, 2002 [1978]), 499.
22. James Knowlson, *Damned to Fame: The Life of Samuel Beckett* (London: Bloomsbury, 1996), 431.
23. Donald McWhinnie, internal BBC memorandum of 21 Feb. 1957, cited in ibid.
24. For an incisive analysis, see Mary Bryden, "Beckett's Reception in Great Britain," in Nixon and Feldman, *The International Reception of Samuel Beckett*, Chapter 3.
25. Shane Weller, "Beckett's Last Chance: *Les Éditions de Minuit*," in *Publishing Samuel Beckett*, ed. Mark Nixon (London: The British Library, 2011), 119.
26. P.H. Newby, *The Third Programme* (London: BBC Publications, 1965), 14–15, 6.
27. J.W. Lambert, *Waiting for Godot*, 21 Aug. 1955; Lennox Milne, *Waiting for Godot*, 1 Aug. 1956; and Marie Budberg, *All That Fall*, 20 Jan. 1957, see Raymond Federman and John Fletcher, *Samuel Beckett: His Work and His Critics* (Berkeley: University of California Press, 1970), 307–8.
28. Ibid. 307–9.
29. See the BBC Genome Project for listings, available online at: http://genome.ch.bbc.co.uk.
30. Donald McWhinnie, *The Listener*, 9 Jan. 1957; viewing figures for the first half of the 1950s were about 135,000, see Briggs, vol. IV, 522. For developed readings of *All That Fall*'s "vitality and ruin," see Paul Stewart, "Sterile Reproduction: Beckett's Death of Species and Fictional Regeneration"; and Julie Campbell, "'A Voice Comes to One in the Dark. Imagine': Radio, the Listener, and the Dark Comedy of *All That Fall*," both in *Beckett and Death*, eds. Steven Barfield, Matthew Feldman and Philip Tew (London: Bloomsbury, 2009), Chapters 8 and 9.
31. See Ronald Gray, "A Christian Interpretation of *Waiting for Godot*," 16 Jan. 1957, followed by letters in *The Listener* on 31 Jan. and 7 Feb. 1957. For a more recent analysis of Beckett's "agon" with Christianity, see Erik Tonning, "Beckett's Unholy Dying: From Malone Dies to The Unnamable," in Barfield, Feldman and Tew, *Beckett and Death*, Chapter 6; and Tonning, "Samuel Beckett, Modernism and Christianity," in *Modernism and Christianity* (Basingstoke: Palgrave, 2013), Chapter 4.
32. See "New Comment," No. 41 for the Third Programme, 11 Oct. 1961, BBC WAC, "Talks Library, 1922–1970".

33. For Beckett's comments to Barbara Bray on 3 Feb. 1961, alongside excerpts from the latter's "Comment" script, see *Letters III*, 397–8. Beckett's return to Dante [i]n search of rest and relief' from the English translation of *L'Innommable* into English is recounted by Deirdre Bair, *Samuel Beckett: A Biography* (London: Vintage, 2002 [1978]), 526.
34. See "Martin Esslin on Beckett the Man," interview with James Knowlson, in *Beckett Remembering/Remembering Beckett: Uncollected Interviews with Samuel Becket & Memories of Those Who Knew Him*, eds. James and Elizabeth Knowlson (London: Bloomsbury, 2006), 149.
35. See Knowlson, *Damned to Fame*, especially Chapters 14–16.
36. See A.J. Leventhal's "Samuel Beckett: Poet and Pessimist," *The Listener*, 30 Apr. 1957.
37. See Samuel I. Mintz, "Beckett's *Murphy*: A Cartesian Novel"; and Hugh Kenner, "The Cartesian Centaur," both in *Perspective* 2.3 (1959). See also Richard N. Coe, "A Little Heap of Millet," in *Beckett* (London: Oliver and Boyd, 1964), Chapter 6; and more recently, Anthony Uhlmann, "The Cradle and the Rocking-Chair," in *Samuel Beckett and the Philosophical Image* (Cambridge: Cambridge University Press, 2006), 78ff.
38. Patrick Bowles, "How Samuel Beckett Sees the Universe," *The Listener*, 19 Jun. 1958. See also *Beckett and Phenomenology*, eds. Ulrika Maude and Matthew Feldman (London: Bloomsbury, 2009).
39. Patrick Bowles, "How to Fail," *PN Review* 96, 20.4 (1994); partially reprinted in *Beckett Remembering/Remembering Beckett*, 113.
40. Cited in Pilling, *A Samuel Beckett Chronology*, 151, 167.
41. See Christopher Ricks, "The Roots of Samuel Beckett," *The Listener*, 17 Dec. 1964. For Beckett's debts to Dante, see Daniella Caselli, *Beckett's Dantes: Intertextuality in the Fiction and Criticism* (Manchester: Manchester University Press, 2005); and on *King Lear*, see Steven Matthews, "Beckett's Late Style," in Barfield, Feldman and Tew, eds., Chapter 10. For Beckett's engagement with Samuel Johnson, see Emilie Morin, "Beckett, Samuel Johnson and the 'Vacuity of Life,'" *Beckett/Philosophy*, eds. Matthew Feldman and Karim Mamdani (Stuttgart: Ibidem/Columbia University Press, 2015); and on Swift and Bunyan see, respectively, Marjorie Perloff's "Beckett in the Country of the Houyhnhms: The Transformation of Swiftian Satire" and Julie Campbell's "Bunyan and Beckett: *The Legacy of Pilgrim's Progress* in *Mercier and Camier*," both in *Samuel Beckett: Debts and Legacies, SBT/A* 22 (2010), eds. Erik Tonning, Matthew Feldman, Matthijs Engelberts and Dirk van Hulle.
42. See the important text by James Knowlson, "Introduction to the Words of Samuel Beckett: A Discography," in *Recorded Sound: Journal of The British Library National Sound Archive* 85 (1984).

43. Also included are details of Beckett's television work for the BBC, which have been surveyed in Jonathan Bignell's *Beckett on Screen: The Television Plays* (Manchester: Manchester University Press, 2009), 10–11 and 88–89.
44. See Erik Tonning, "David Jones: Christian Modernism at the BBC," *Broadcasting in the Modernist Era*, eds. Matthew Feldman, Erik Tonning and Henry Mead (London: Bloomsbury, 2014), Chapter 6.
45. See Pim Verhulst, "Just howls from time to time: Dating *Pochade Radiophonique*," "*Beginning of the Murmur*," *SBT/A* 27, 143–57.
46. See, for instance, Catherine Laws, "'The fable of one with you in the dark': The Company of Schubert in *All That Fall*; Beckett and Schubert 1," *Headaches Among the Overtones: Music in Beckett/Beckett in Music* (Leiden: Brill, 2013), Chapter 4.
47. See Steven Dilks, *Samuel Beckett in the Literary Marketplace* (Syracuse: Syracuse University Press, 2011), 36–7, and Mark Nixon, "Beckett's Manuscripts in the Marketplace," *Modernism/Modernity* 18.3–4 (2011). The BBC WAC materials nuance this debate, as Feldman's overview of themes emerging from the Caversham archives has stressed; see, for example, "Beckett and the BBC Radio Revisited," in *Falsifying Beckett: Essays on Archives, Philosophy, and Methodology in Beckett Studies* (Stuttgart: Ibidem/Columbia University Press, 2015), 163–65.
48. For more on the composition of "Lessness," see Rosemary Pountney, *Theatre of Shadows: Samuel Beckett's Drama, 1956–1976: From All That Fall to Footfalls* (Gerrards Cross: Colin Smythe, 1988), especially 240–44.
49. P.J. Murphy and Nick Pawliuk, "Addenda: Beckett Cetera: A Pop Cultural Miscellany," *Beckett in Popular Culture: Essay on a Postmodern Icon*, eds. P.J. Murphy and Nick Pawliuk (Jefferson: McFarland & Company, 2016), 186.

Beckett's "Non-canonical" Radio Productions, 1957–1989

Matthew Feldman

Little is known of Samuel Beckett's "non-canonical" radio productions, despite their key role in his "getting known" in the Anglophone world. There were more than two dozen broadcasts of what may be seen, to varying degrees, as "adaptations" of Beckett's work that had first appeared on, or at least had been written for, either the page or stage. The following is the most complete account to date, covering programs recorded and first broadcast during Beckett's lifetime.[1] Accordingly, details largely derive from the BBC "Play Library" microfilm collection, held at the Written Archive Centre in Caversham, Berkshire. As is reflected below, the level of detail in these holdings varies greatly.

Additional material on Beckett's many radio productions includes, of course, the BBC WAC's substantial holdings on the writer's strictly radiogenic writing between 1956 and 1964: *All That Fall, Embers, Words and Music, Cascando, Rough for Radio I* and *II* and his Pinget translation, *The Old Tune*.[2] Also at the WAC, but excluded in this case-log, are entries on Beckett's television work for BBC2: *Eh Joe, … but the clouds …* and *Ghost Trio*.[3] Also excluded from the listings below are the "radiogenic" work *Rough for Radio II* (first broadcast by Radio 3, Tuesday, 13 April 1976)

M. Feldman (✉)
History Section, Teesside University, Middlesbrough, Tees Valley, UK

and reproductions of Beckett's plays, whether undertaken in his lifetime (as with the stereo performance of *All That Fall* on Sunday, 4 June 1972 for BBC Radio 3), or after Beckett's death in 1989.[4] As noted in the editorial introduction to this volume, traces of all of these works—as well as an uneven amount of information on their evolution, transmission and reception—are contained in the Caversham archives.[5] Supplementing these manuscripts are helpful listings for virtually all BBC radio transmissions, available online at the searchable BBC Genome Project.[6]

Chronological listing of BBC broadcasts of Samuel Beckett's "non-canonical" radio work (to Dec. 1989):

1)
Fin de Partie (87'43") [performance in French]
Producer: Michael Bakewell
Third Programme: Thursday, 2 May 1957, 20:50–22:20 pm
R.P. Reference No.: TLO 28115 (Narration recorded on 24 April 1957)
Recording Date: 5 April 1957
Cast:
Narrator .... Jacques Brunius
Hamm .... Roger Blin
Clov .... Jean Martin
Nagg .... Georges Adet
Nell .... Christine Tsingos

2)
An Extract from *Molloy* (59'14")
Third Programme: Tuesday, 10 December 1957, 21:45–22:45 pm
Third Programme Repeat: Friday, 13 December 1957, 20:15–21:15 pm
Producer: Donald McWhinnie
Speaker: Patrick Magee
Music by: John Beckett
Conductor: Bertold Goldschmidt
Opening: This is the BBC Third Programme. This week we are broadcasting two readings form the work of Samuel Beckett. Tonight's reading is an extract from his novel *Molloy* which has been translated from the French by Patrick Bowles in collaboration with the author. It is spoken by Patrick Magee, with music by John Beckett.

Closing: That was an extract from *Molloy*, the first of two readings, spoken by Patrick Magee, from the work of Samuel Beckett. *Molloy* was translated from the French by Patrick Bowles in collaboration with the author. The music was composed by John Beckett. The production was by Donald McWhinnie. This programme can be heard again on Friday at quarter past eight. The second reading, which is of an unpublished meditation, *From an Abandoned Work*, will be broadcast Saturday at a quarter to nine.[7]

3)
"From an Abandoned Work" (23′51″)
Third Programme: Saturday, 14 December 1957, 20:45–21:05 pm
Third Programme Repeat: Thursday, 19 December 1957, 22:35–22:55 pm
Producer: Donald McWhinnie
Speaker: Patrick Magee
Music by: John Beckett
Rehearsals: 4 December 1957, 10:30 am–5:30 pm in Studio PP4
5 December 1957, 10:30 am–5:30 pm in Studio PP4
Recording: 5 December 1957, 19:00–19:45 pm
R.P. Reference No.: TLO 44261
Opening: This is the BBC Third Programme. Tonight we are broadcasting the second of two readings from the work of Samuel Beckett, an unpublished meditation, *From an Abandoned Work*. It is spoken by Patrick Magee.
Closing: That was *From an Abandoned Work*—an unpublished meditation by Samuel Beckett. It was spoken by Patrick Magee and the production was by Donald McWhinnie. This programme will be broadcast again next Thursday at 10:35 pm.

4)
An Extract from *Malone Dies* (71′38″)[8]
Third Programme: Wednesday, 18 June 1958, 21:00–21:15 pm
Third Programme Repeat: Wednesday, 18 June 1958, 20:00–21:15 pm
Third Programme Repeat: Thursday, 19 June 1958, 21:30–22:45 pm
Third Programme Repeat: Wednesday, October 15 1958, 20:00–21:15 pm
Producer: Donald McWhinnie
Speaker: Patrick Magee
Music by: John Beckett
Conductor: Bernard Keeffe

5)
The Unnamable: Extracts from the novel (60′51″)[9]
Third Programme: Monday, 19 January 1959, 20:35–21:35 pm
Third Programme Repeat: Tuesday, 10 February 1959, 21:35–22:40 pm
Producer: Donald McWhinnie
Speaker: Patrick Magee
Music by: John Beckett
Conductor: Bernard Keeffe

6)
Waiting for Godot
Third Programme: Wednesday, 27 April 1960, 20:00–22:10 pm
Third Programme Repeat: Tuesday, 17 May 1960, 20:35–22:45 pm
Produced by: Donald McWhinnie
Rehearsals: Piccadilly Rehearsal Room 201
Wednesday, 23 March 10:30 am–17:30 pm
Thursday, 24 March 10:30 am–17:30 pm
Friday, 25 March 10:30 am–17:30 pm
Rehearsals in Grafton Studio:
26 March 1960, 10:30 am–17:30 pm
27 March 1960, 10:30 am–Recording
Recording: 27 March 1960, 18:30–21:30 pm in Grafton Studio
R.P. Reference: TLO 13400
Cast:
Estragon .... Wilfrid Brambell
Vladimir .... Patrick Magee
Lucky .... Donal Donnelly
Pozzo .... Felix Felton
A Boy .... Jeremy Ward
Narrator .... Denys Hawthorne

7)
"From the Fifties": *Waiting for Godot*
Home Service: Monday, 5 February 1962, 20:30–22:00 pm
Producer: Robin Midgley
Rehearsals:
27 January 1962: 10:30 am–17:30 pm in PP1
28 January 1962: 10:30 am–17:30 pm in Grafton

29 January 1962: 10:30 am–17:30 pm in Grafton
30 January 1962: 10:30 am–17:30 pm in Grafton
31 January 1962: 10:30 am–17:30 pm in Grafton
1 February 1962: 10:30 am–15:15 pm in Grafton
Recording: 1 February 1962, 15:15–17:30 pm in Grafton
R.P. Reference No.: TLO 75977
Editing: 2 February 1962, 14:30–16:00 pm in Grafton H.22
Playback: 5 February 1962, 15:15–17:30 pm in Grafton Room 5055
Cast:
Vladimir .... Nigel Stock
Estragon .... Kenneth Griffith
Pozzo .... Philip Leaver
Lucky .... Andrew Sachs
The Boy .... Terry Raven

8)
Endgame[10]
Third Programme: Tuesday, 22 May 1962, 20:40–22:10 pm
Third Programme Repeat: Friday, 15 June 1962, 20:00–21:30 pm
Producer: Michael Bakewell
Rehearsals:
16 May 1962, 10:30 am–17:30 pm in Grafton
17 May 1962: 10:30 am–17:30 pm in Grafton
18 May 1962: 10:30 am–17:30 pm in Grafton
19 May 1962: 10:30 am–17:30 pm in Grafton
20 May 1962: 10:30 am—Recording in Grafton
Recording: 20 May 1962, 14:00–17:30 pm in Grafton
R.P. Reference No.: TLO 83590
Cast:
Hamm .... Donald Wolfit
Clov .... Maurice Denham
Nagg .... Richard Goolden
Nell .... Mary O'Farrell
Narrator .... Haydn Jones

9)
Wrth Aros Godot [*Waiting for Godot*, Welsh version][11]
Welsh Home Service: Tuesday, 20 November 1962

10)
"Poems by Samuel Beckett"
Third Programme: Tuesday, 8 March 1966, 21:55–22:30 pm
Third Programme Repeat: Monday, 14 November 1966, 22:00–22:35 pm
Narrator: Dr. John Fletcher
Speakers: Jack McGowran and Denys Hawthorne
Producer: Martin Esslin
Recording date: Wednesday, 29 September 1965
Poems by Samuel Beckett:
"Whoroscope"
"Enueg I"
"Serena II"
"Malacoda"
"Alba"
"Cascando"
"Saint-Lo"
From *Collected Poems*: "My way is in the same flowing"
From *Collected Poems*: "What would I do without this world"
From *Collected Poems*: "I would like my love to die"

11)
Play (18′04″)
Third Programme: Tuesday, 11 October 1966, 20:00–20:30 pm
Third Programme Repeat: Sunday, 30 October 1966, 22:15–22:40 pm
Network Three Repeat: Saturday, 2 September 1967, 19:30–20:00 pm
Producer: Bennett Maxwell and Pauline Jameson
Studio Manager: Brian Hodgson
Cast:
M—Robert Stephens
W1—Pauline Jameson
W2—Billie Whitelaw

12)
"More Poems by Samuel Beckett"
Third Programme: Thursday, 24 November 1966, 22:40–23:00 pm
Narrator: Dr. John Fletcher
Speakers: Jack McGowran and Denys Hawthorne
Producer: Martin Esslin
Recording date: Wednesday, 10 August 1966

Poems by Samuel Beckett:
"The Vulture"
"Echo's Bones"
"Da Tagte Es"
"Serena I"
"Serena III"
"Sanies I"
"Who may tell the tale" [from *Watt*]
"Watt will not" [from *Watt*]
"Spent the years of learning" ["Gnome"]
"Age is when to a man" [from *Words and Music*]

13)
"Imagination Dead Imagine"
Third Programme: Saturday, 18 March 1967, 21:50–22:10 pm
Third Programme Repeat: Friday, 28 April 1967, 22:40–23:00 pm
Producer: Martin Esslin
Speaker: Jack MacGowran
Rehearsal: 9 February 1967, 14:30–16:30 pm in Studio 6c
Recording: 9 February 1967, 16:30–17:30 pm in Studio 6c
R.P. Ref No.: TLO 06/DA731D
Introduction by Barbara Bray: The gradual reduction that has taken place in Samuel Beckett's work has often been misunderstood. Starting off in MORE PRICKS THAN KICKS and MURPHY with the usual complement of limbs and organs, and more or less normal powers of locomotion etc., the characters of his fiction have come to lose almost all appurtenances, physical and social, and almost all possibility of movement, to end up like Pim in HOW IT IS, crawling naked through the mud, or Malone dying in bed telling himself stories. The books themselves used also to be of more or less conventional aspect: they had the same number of words as other novels, and a sort of plot with a beginning, middle and end. But form as well as content has become ever more stripped and quintessential.
This progression in Beckett has sometimes been mistaken for an obsession with mutilation. But that's the opposite of the truth. The gradual whittling away of externals, although of course like every element in Beckett has its comic aspects, is primarily a way of making, and marking, an approach to "being" itself, with everything extraneous, as far as possible, eliminated.

IMAGINATION DEAD IMAGINE, written last year, takes the process of intensification a considerable stage further. It is a piece of prose about a thousand words long in which, if you're looking for a plot, all you can say is that it tells how a vision of a tiny white rotunda three feet across and three feet high, with the recumbent figures of a man and woman inside, is discovered by chance in the midst of a surrounding, seemingly cosmic whiteness, lost, miraculously rediscovered, and finally lost again forever. While Pim in the mud and The Unnamable in his jar could still speak for themselves in the first person, here even the "I" has been got rid of, and the actions of the imaginer are conveyed by means of the imperative.

The writer is now approaching as near as can be got to imagination unalloyed. His creatures, with more loss of symbolism about them than ever, are shapes that are "the thing itself." The lifelong distillation, which might only have led to a clinical purity, has left Becket confronted with the deepest regions of his own being. And since he is what he is, and since the artist's function is to dream chaos into order, the resulting visions make our truth.

With incredibly narrow limits of space and time, Beckett, like Webern, creates outside the universe of phenomena another universe in which space and time become aspects of form.

But why this miniaturization?

First of all, it should be made clear that Beckett is not merely seeking brevity for its own sake. IMAGINATION DEAD IMAGINE, like some other more recent pieces, represents the residue of an attempt to find the motive-power for a sustained work which may well follow.

But whether it actually results in a short work or a long one, the delimitation of the imaginative space is now essential. Beckett's whole work may be seen as a groping after "being," to be expressed and perhaps even attained through a sort of adequation between the within and the without. The world of perception offered no commensurate object, the within makes its own without. At the time of MOLLOY each term of the relation was still rich, plethoric—"the big blooming buzzing confusion" already deplored in MURPHY. Now, although the reduction may still be far from complete, a certain amount of Occamisation or excision of unnecessaries has been achieved. The groping after being culminates in an apperception of extreme minuteness, and this acute sense of inward smallness (as of a microorganism), which wasn't there before, would remain definitively unrelated—unbearable—unless it produced its own term of relation. How to go on, how not to give up, was always the question with Beckett as a writer. Now the only way not to give up—the only way not to remain, in a sense, "alone," with this vision of minuteness—is to imagine a correlative minuteness.

In ordinary life Beckett is a great walker. In his work, imagination has always been a kind of place—a place where there's an imperative need to walk around. Just as someone whose physical faculties are failing may limit his movements to a house or a room or a little garden, which he knows and where he feels at home, so the poet, finding "given" space insupportable, must organize a special, autonomous space in which to move around.

How mysterious, though, that such minuteness should suggest such vastness, and that the mind voyaging through such strange seas of space should turn to us no "marble index," but one that as it grows more remote grows more moving.

Here is Jack MacGowran, reading IMAGINATION DEAD IMAGINE by Samuel Beckett.

14)
"Lessness"
Radio 3: Thursday, 25 February 1971, 22:05–22:40 pm
Radio 3 Repeat: Friday, 7 May 1971, 21:25–22:00 pm
Producer: Martin Esslin
Secretary: Esther Dunstone
Recorded: 7 Feb 1971, 10:00 am–13:00 pm in Studio B.10
R.P. Reference No.: TLN 06/DE262
Cast:
A—Nicol Williamson
B—Denys Hawthorne
C—Leonard Fenton
D—Harold Pinter
E—Patrick Magee
F—Donal Donnelly

ANNOUNCER: "Lessness" by Samuel Beckett. This reading of Samuel Beckett's latest work (by the voices of Nicol Williamson, Denys Hawthorne, Leonard Fenton, Harold Pinter, Patrick Magee and Donal Donnelly), is introduced by Martin Esslin.

ESSLIN: This short prose text originally appeared in French in the autumn of 1969 in a limited edition under the title *Sans*, S-a-n-s, (the French word for without). Beckett's own translation into English was published by the *New Statesman* in its issue of 1 May 1970. It has since also appeared in book form. A German translation by Elmar Tophoven, in collaboration with Samuel Beckett, which is contained in a volume of short prose pieces, *Residua*, has the title *Losigkeit*.

The syllables *lessness* are thus quite clearly shown to represent the suffix denoting "absence of" in such words as endlessness, changelessness which, in fact, occur in the text itself.

Lessness is not, as has been assumed in the press, a play. The misunderstanding was bound to arise when we announced the names of the distinguished actors taken part in the broadcast. On the other hand, "Lessness" is a text peculiarly suited to radio, and perhaps fully realizable only in radio. To explain why that is so I want to say a few words about its subject matter and form.

Thematically "Lessness" belongs to a group of short texts which have appeared in the last few years and which seem to form part of a larger whole, a work yet in progress. Imagination Dead Imagine of which Jack MacGowran gave a memorable reading on this wavelength in 1967 belongs to this group, so does the fragment Dans Le Labyrinthe which appeared in a French magazine in 1967, and two short texts only available in very expensive luxury editions Sejour and L'Issue, and finally Bing, translated by Beckett as Ping and accessible in the volume No's Knife. All these texts describe, as it were, landscapes of the soul. In Imagination Dead Imagine two bodies are contained in an enclosed, brightly lit space, a rotunda. In Dans Le Labyrinthe lost souls are trying to escape from a vast cylindrical structure by climbing ladders. Some have given up. The same search for an exit dominates Sejour and L'Issue. In Ping we are with one small figure in another severely enclosed space: "Light neat white floor one square yard never seen. White walls one yard by two white ceiling one square yard never seen." The small body darts around in this enclosed space and the title Ping refers to the click with which these sudden changes of location occur. "Bare white body fixed one yard ping fixed elsewhere."

"Lessness" seems to show the same little body at a later stage. The enclosed space has vanished—"fallen open," the white walls have "fallen over backwards." We are in a landscape of ruins—a featureless gray plain under a gray sky in which the little body is on the only thing still upright.

There can be no doubt that the larger work to which all these texts are related represents a new phase in Samuel Beckett's writing. In the great narrative trilogy and in Texts for Nothing as well as in the radio plays Words and Music and Cascando we were listening to an internal monologue, voices which emerged from the depths of consciousness telling us—and their narrator—stories. In the novel How it is it was still a voice, a panting voice, we were hearing, but the description it gave was already that of a landscape from a kind of Dante's Inferno.

In this latest group of texts the standpoint has I feel radically changed: the description has become objective, there is no longer the ceaseless flux of the never ending murmur of inner voices: we are in a world which seems fixed in its very moment.

In the play Comedie—Play is its title in English—Beckett tackled this theme in dramatic form: damned souls in eternity, eternally reliving their last moments on earth: eternity here expressed by the fact that the three heads protruding from urns (enclosed spaces these like the rotunda, or the square box of the later texts) were repeating the same fragments of speech twice over; and, when the lights faded, had begun to repeat them a third time—and no doubt on and on ad infinitum. The stage direction in the published version of Play after the text has been spoken for the first time is "Repeat play exactly."

But for the stage production, and later the radio production, Mr. Beckett provided a variation: each of the three characters still spoke exactly the same text but the order in which each character spoke was different. In other words: in eternity the same things occur in endless permutation, ever the same and yet ever changing: after all, in infinite time every combination, every change must recur an infinite number of times and a mind, capable of being aware of these all at once, would therefore see this infinite number of changes as a totally static, unchanging rigidity.

This, I think, is also the image which Lessness is designed to convey. When we were talking about a broadcast of the text, Mr. Beckett indicated how he wanted six voices to share in the reading. Not as different characters or persons, but as indicators of different groups of images. Lessness is a pattern of statements. Each statement occurs twice, in a different order, or rather disorder. And there are six groups of statements. Each group has its own dominant image: the ruins, the vastness of each and sky; the little body; the fact that the enclosed space is now forgotten, "all gone from mind"; a denial of past and future; and opposed to it an affirmation of the continued existence of past and future. These groups of statements are intricately interwoven in a rhythmic structure, and the different voices serve to bring out the pattern; each voice is a strand of color intertwining to form this web of sound and images. It is thus only by hearing Lessness that we can become fully aware of its structure and indeed of its full meaning which is expressed by its formal pattern.

ANNOUNCER: Lessness by Samuel Beckett. The voices—in the order in which they first appear, are those of Nicol Williamson, Denys Hawthorne, Leonard Fenton, Harold Pinter, Patrick Magee and Donal Donnelly. Lessness.

15)
"The Lost Ones" (57'17")
Radio 3: Tuesday, 2 January 1973, 21:30–10:30 pm
Radio 3 Repeat: Thursday 6 September 1973, 21:55–22:55 pm
Producer: Martin Esslin
Speaker: Patrick Magee
Rehearsal: 2 September 1972, 10:00 am–18:00 pm in Studio PP5
Recording: 3 September 1972, 10:00 am–18:00 pm in Studio PP5
Tape Reference No.: TLN36/DF854B
Assistant: Esther Dunstone
Announcer: Cormac Rigby

16)
"First Love" (56'47")
Radio 3: Saturday, 7 July 1973, 22:10–23:10 pm
Radio 3 Repeat: Tuesday, 4 June 1974, 20:50–21:50 pm
Producer: Martin Esslin
Secretary: Libby Spurrier
Rehearsal: 5 May 1973, 10:00 am–18:00 pm in Studio P.P.5
Recording: 6 May 1973, 10:00 am–18:00 pm in Studio P.P.5
Tape Reference No.: TLM 19 DC 771
Speaker: Patrick Magee

17)
Texts for Nothing by Samuel Beckett (158'29" for all four parts)
Produced by Martin Esslin
Radio 3: Texts I, II, III: Thursday, 12 June 1975, 21:35–22:15 pm
Radio 3: Texts IV, V, VI: Thursday, 19 June 1975, 21:20–22:00 pm
Radio 3: Texts VII, VIII, XI, X: Thursday, 26 June 1975, 21:35–22:25 pm
Radio 3: Texts XI, XII, XIII: Thursday, 3 July 1975, 21:30–22:10 pm
Studio Manager: Anthea Davies
Secretary: Barbara Crow
Rehearsal: 19 October 1974, 10:00 am–18:00 pm in Studio B.16
Recording: 20 October 1974, 10:00 am–18:00 pm in Studio B.16
Tape Reference No.: BLN43/DL293H

Texts for Nothing, I–III (43'40")
The first programme in four where Patrick Magee will read the whole of
   Beckett's 13 Texts for Nothing.

These prose poems are meditations on the nature of the self and the burden of being. The voice we hear has reached a state detached from a world which has become unreal. It is from this vantage point that the speaker looks back at existence.

R.P. Reference No.: BLN43/DL293B

Texts for Nothing, IV–VI (39'10")

Opening: We are now broadcasting the second programme in a series of four in which Patrick Magee reads Samuel Beckett's "Texts for Nothing." Beckett wrote this work after he had completed his trilogy Molloy, Malone Dies and The Unnamable, an exploration of man's self which had led to a point at which it seemed to the author that no more could be said, and that the resources of language were exhausted.

The 13 meditations of "Texts for Nothing" were thus an attempt by Beckett to find his way out of that dead end. In this programme Patrick Magee reads the fourth, fifth and sixth of Samuel Beckett's "Texts for Nothing."

"Texts for Nothing"—Four.

Closing: Patrick Magee read the fourth, fifth and sixth of Samuel Beckett's "Texts for Nothing." This was the second of four programmes in which he reads the complete work. The programme was produced by Martin Esslin.

R.P. Reference No.: BLN02/DL813B

Texts for Nothing, VII–X (46'07")

Opening: We are now broadcasting the third programme in a series of four in which Patrick Magee reads Samuel Beckett's "Texts for Nothing." Beckett wrote this work after he had completed his trilogy Molloy, Malone Dies and The Unnamable, an exploration of man's self which had led to a point at which it seemed to the author that no more could be said, and that the resources of language were exhausted.

The 13 meditations of "Texts for Nothing" were thus an attempt by Beckett to find his way out of that dead end. In this programme Patrick Magee reads the seventh, eighth, ninth and tenth of Samuel Beckett's "Texts for Nothing".

"Texts for Nothing"—Seven.

Closing: Patrick Magee read the seventh, eighth, ninth and tenth of Samuel Beckett's "Texts for Nothing." This was the third of four programmes in which he reads the complete work. The programme was produced by Martin Esslin.

R.P. Reference No.: BLN02/DL814B

Texts for Nothing, X–XIII (37'13")

Opening: We are now broadcasting the final programme in a series of four in which Patrick Magee reads Samuel Beckett's "Texts for Nothing." Beckett wrote this work after he had completed his trilogy Molloy, Malone Dies and The Unnamable, an exploration of man's self which had led to a point at which it seemed to the author that no more could be said, and that the resources of language were exhausted.
The 13 meditations of "Texts for Nothing" were thus an attempt by Beckett to find his way out of that dead end. In this programme Patrick Magee reads the eleventh, twelfth and thirteenth of Samuel Beckett's "Texts for Nothing."
"Texts for Nothing"—eleven.
R.P. Reference No.: BLN02/DL815B
Closing: Patrick Magee read the eleventh, twelfth and thirteenth of Samuel Beckett's "Texts for Nothing." This was the last of four programmes in which he read the complete work. The programme was produced by Martin Esslin.

18)
"MacGowran reads poems by Beckett" [taken from the March and November 1966 BBC Third Programme recordings]
Radio 3: Wednesday, 14 April 1976, 21:50–22:25 pm
Radio 3 Repeat: 5 June 1976, 22:15–22:45 pm
Produced by: Martin Esslin
Speaker: Jack MacGowran
Assistant: Barbara Crow
Announcer: Robin Holmes
Studio Manager: John Whitehall

19)
"For to end yet again" (11′30″)
Radio 3: Monday, 4 October 1976, 22:10–22:25 pm
Producer: Martin Esslin
Speaker: Patrick Magee
Opening: A reading of Samuel Beckett's latest short prose text, translated from the French by the author. This broadcast is the first publication of this text in English, which is to appear in book form towards the end of October.
Recording: 17 September 1976, 10:30 am–13:00 pm in Egton Studio
Studio Manager: Lloyd Silverthorne
Secretary: Barbara Crow
Tape Reference No.: BLN37/003Q415

20)
"The Drunken Boat" by Rimbaud, translated by Samuel Beckett (7'15")
(With an introductory talk by Dr. Jim Knowlson [7'43"])
Radio 3: Saturday, 12 March 1977, 23:10–23:25 pm
Radio 3 Repeat: Wednesday, 20 July 1977, 9:35–9:50 pm
Producer: Martin Esslin
Speaker: Ronald Pickup
Opening: Samuel Beckett's translation, which dates from the early thirties, had been thought to be lost but it has recently been rediscovered by Dr. James Knowlson, who introduces this first public reading of the poem by Ronald Pickup.
Circumstances of Composition and Publication (Knowlson):
Stage Manager: John Dixon
Secretary: Barbara Crow
Recorded: 22 December 1976, 21:00–22:00 pm in Studio B11
Tape Reference No.: BLN51/101L244
NB: *A slightly amended version of this text was first reprinted in the notes to* Samuel Beckett: Collected Poems in English and French *(London: Calder, 1977):, 145–147. Now out of print and expensive to obtain, only 200 copies of this edition were printed, with half bearing Beckett's signature. I am grateful to Professor Knowlson for this information, and for his permission to reprint the following transcription from the BBC WAC "Play Library".*
Introduction by Jim Knowlson: [with handwritten additions in brackets]: The circumstances in which Samuel Beckett's early unpublished translation of Arthur Rimbaud's Le Bateau ivre came to be written are in themselves of some interest. But the reasons why his original typescript has been preserved and the coincidence that has led to its eventual [rediscovery and] publication, more than forty years after it was written, are even more curious and worth relating.
At the end of December 1931, Beckett left Trinity College, Dublin, where he had been Lecturer in French for only four terms. He then traveled to Germany and resigned his academic appointment by post from Kassel. After a short stay in Germany, he moved [on] to Paris where he joined his friend and fellow Irishman, Thomas MacGreevy, with whom Beckett had been lecteur d'anglais at the Ecole Normale Superieure in the rue d'Ula in 1928, Beckett staying on alone for a further year. It was in 1932, while staying in the same hotel as MacGreevy, that Beckett was working on his first [still] unpublished novel Dream of fair to middling women.

Following the assassination of the President of the Republic, Paul Doumer, on 7 May 1932 by the White Russian Gorgulof, it was decided that a check should be made on the papers of all foreigners who where then living in Paris. Since Beckett did not possess a valid carte de sejour, he was forced to leave his hotel, and, as he could not legitimately register elsewhere, he spent several nights sleeping in the Studio Villa Seurat of the painter, Jean Lurcat, on the floor. In order to obtain money to leave the country, Beckett called on Edward Titus, the editor of the literary review, This Quarter, at his offices in the rue Delambre. Earlier, Titus had expressed interest in publishing an English translation of Rimbaud's poem, Le Bateau ivre, and it was with this in mind that Beckett now completed a translation of the poem, begun by him some time before. He had already produced several translations from the Italian of Montale, Franchi and Comisso, and Titus had published [him] in This Quarter in 1930; a little later Beckett had translated poems and prose by Breton, Eluard and Crevel for the special number on Surrealism which was to appear, edited by André Breton, in September 1932. Beckett had accepted this earlier work as a paid commission and in view of his difficult financial situation, he asked Titus for a thousand francs for Drunken boat. In the event, he was offered seven hundred francs for the poem, [and this] allowed him to travel to London and live there for a short time, staying near the Gray's Inn Road. It was during this stay in London that Beckett tried to organize for himself a career in literary journalism, but a call on Desmond McCarthy failed to bring the commissioned reviewing that he had hoped for. Soon after this the money paid to him by Titus ran out and Beckett was forced to return home to Dublin where he could stay for nothing in the family home in Foxrock. The following year his father died, leaving Samuel, his second son, a small annuity, intended as the equivalent of his share in the family business, which was continued by his brother, Frank Edward. The money enabled Beckett to travel further in Europe and eventually allowed him to settle in Paris in 1937.

It was Beckett's custom to type out three copies of anything that he wrote and there is no reason to suppose that he [acted any] differently with the translation, Drunken boat.

Nothing is known as to the whereabouts of Titus's typed copy, nor of the reason for his failure to publish the poem in This Quarter. The review continued however, only until the end of 1932, when publication was discontinued. Similarly there is no trace of the original manuscript or of the third copy. The top copy of the text was given by Beckett in the mid-1930s to an Irish friend, Nuala Costello, in whose private library it has been kept until last year.

It was while he was on a fox-hunting holiday in Ireland [a former colleague of mine], Felix Leakey, met, quite by chance, the owner of the typescript and spoke to her [about] the Samuel Beckett collection in the Reading University Library. She recalled that Beckett had gifted to her an early work that might well interest me as the founder of the Beckett Archive. This proved to be the typescript of the unpublished "spoof" lecture which Beckett had given to the Modern Language Society at Trinity College, Dublin [in the later 1920s]. This lecture which is referred to in the Beckett bibliography by Raymond Federman and John Fletcher, SAMUEL BECKETT: HIS WORKS AND HIS CRITICS, as "probably lost," is about an imaginary literary movement in France, entitled not as had been thought, "Le Convergisme" but "Le Concentrisme," whose exponent is said to be one Jean du Chas, the author of a "Discours de la Sortie"; the lecture is clever and extremely funny. This typescript, with some manuscript corrections in Beckett's hand, is now on permanent loan to Reading University Library. On a second visit to Ireland by Felix Leakey, the owner of "Le Contrentrisme" produced for him the typescript of [yet] another early piece by Beckett, also described in the Beckett bibliography as "probably lost." This was the present translation by Beckett of Rimbaud's LE BATEAU IVRE. The preservation of the typescript of DRUNKEN BOAT is even more surprising, since it survived a fire in the owner's house only because it had been folded away in her copy of THE OXFORD BOOK OF FRENCH VERSE, between the pages in which the original Rimbaud poem is printed. As the facsimile reproduction reveals, the pages of Beckett's typescript have been charred by fire. It is therefore as a result of a series of coincidences that Beckett's translation has found its way into the Beckett collection in Reading and that, thanks to the kindness of its owner and Samuel Beckett, we were able to publish the text for the first time. [Here then is Drunken Boat by Arthur Rimbaud, translated by Samuel Beckett and read by Ronald Pickup.][12]

21)
"Beckett at the National" (53'35")
Radio 3: Friday, 13 April 1979, 21:40–22:40 pm
Radio 3 Repeat: Thursday, 18 October 1979, 20:30–21:30 pm
Opening: Selected Readings from Beckett's work. To mark Samuel Beckett's birthday on Good Friday, 13th of April 1979, a programme of

his prose and poetry was recorded at the National Theatre. Selected by Jack Emery and Michael Kustow and read by Peggy Ashcroft, Kenneth Cranham, Gawn Grainger, Dennis Quilley, Struan Rodger and Philip Stone. Directed in the theater by Jack Emery and edited for radio by Ian Cotterell and Piers Plowright. Peggy Ashcroft is a National Theatre player.

Poems by Samuel Beckett:
"My Way Is In The Sand"
"Still"
"I Would Like My Love To Die"
Prose extracts by Samuel Beckett:
from *Malone Dies*
from "Dante and the Lobster" [in *More Pricks than Kicks*]
" *Murphy*
" *Watt*
" *The Unnamable*
" *Mercier and Camier*

22)
"From an Abandoned Work"
Radio 3: Monday, 20 August 1979, 20:20–20:40 pm
Radio 3 Repeat: Monday, 29 October 1979, 20:05–20:25 pm
Producer: David Warrilow
Speaker: Gawn Grainger
[Originally recorded at the National Theatre in 1976]

23)
Company
Radio 3: Monday, 14 July 1980 21:15–22:30 pm
Radio 3 Repeat: Sunday, 20 July 1980, 20:00–21:15 pm
Producer: Tom Sutcliffe
Speaker: Patrick Magee

24)
Ill Seen Ill Said (70'13")
Radio 3: Sunday, 31 October 1982, 19:00–20:10 pm
Radio 3 Repeat: Sunday, 20 March 1983, 19:50–21:00 pm
Director: Ronald Mason
Speaker: Patrick Magee

Ill Seen Ill Said: a monologue for radio: By recalling the last months of the life of an old lady encased in a frail body, we come to have a perception of the end of a life and the meaning of what has come and gone to bring us to this point. There emerges a fear that all our perception is ill seen and ill expressed.
Rehearsal: 26 February 1982, 10:30 am–18:00 pm in Broadcasting House 5124
Recorded: 1 March 1982, 10:00 am–18:00 pm in Studio B11
Programme Number: BDB418V242
Tape Reference No: TLN09/418V242
Announcer: Malcolm Ruthven
Studio Manager: Richard Beadsmore
Secretary: Julienne Hunger

25)
Worstward Ho (40'50")
Radio 3: Thursday, 4 August 1983, 21:35–22:20 pm
Radio 3 Repeat: Sunday, 26 August 1984, 18:45–19:30 pm
Producer and Director: Ronald Mason
Speaker: Norman Rodway
Recording: 19 February 1983
Tape Reference No: 475P519
Opening: What we are, whence we came, we see in half-light and so grope to find the words to express our perceptions of origin and function.

26)
"Beckett at 80: *A Piece of Monologue*" (15'15")
Radio 3: Friday, 18 April 1986, 21:10–21:25 pm
Director: Ronald Mason
Speaker: Ronald Pickup
Announcement: Nothing stirring anywhere. Nothing to be seen anywhere. Room once full of sounds. Faint sounds. Whence unknown. Fewer and fainter as time wore on. Nights wore on. None now.
Recorded: 4 March 1986, 14:30–14:45 pm in Broadcasting House B10
Rehearsal: 3 March 1986, 10:00 am–18:00 pm in Broadcasting House 5125
4 March, 1986, 10:00 am–18:00 pm in Broadcasting House 5125
Editing: 8 March 1986, 10:00 am–18:00 pm in Broadcasting House H55
Programme No.: BDA556W249

Announcer: Donald MacLeod
Stage Managers: Peter Harwood and Anne Marie Warmington
Secretary: Susan Westwood
Opening: We present A PIECE OF MONOLOGUE by Samuel Beckett with Ronald Pickup as the speaker. He observes a figure, white haired, white nightgown, white socks dimly perceived in the faint lamp light issued from a skull-sized glob. Behind [the figure] only just visible, the white foot of a pallet bed.

27)
"Beckett Double Bill" (with *A Piece of Monologue*)
"Stirrings Still" (18'30")
Radio 3: Saturday, 28 October 1989, 22:25–23:45 pm
Radio 3 Repeat: Friday, 2 March 1990, 23:00–23:20 pm
Producer: Peter Kavanagh
Speaker: Barry McGovern
One night or day then as he sat at his table head on hands he saw himself rise and go. First rise and stand clinging to the table. Then sit again ... .
Programme No: 89DA5515LBO
Recorded: 29 April 1989
Description of Programme: A character questions whether he should stir out one final time. For if he goes is it likely that he will return? Beckett's last published work is both foreboding of his imminent death and resume of the themes of much of his earlier writing, and as ever the mix of brooding pessimism and delicious cackling at the void. The piece marks the end of literary style, almost a genre of which Beckett was the undisputed master.
Artists: Barry McGovern (the reader) is considered to be the new interpreter of Beckett's work and has toured in Beckett productions worldwide (including the premier of this production in New York earlier this year). He is a friend of Beckett's and has visited him in Paris a number of times.

Notes

1. The two texts previously charting these works were Clas Zilliacus's *Beckett and Broadcasting* (Åbo: Åbo Akademi, 1976), 209ff—covering the years 1957 to 1973—followed by James Knowlson's "Introduction to the Words of Samuel Beckett: A Discography," in *Recorded Sound: Journal of*

The British Library National Sound Archive 85 (1984), which includes Beckett's radio "adaptations" from the following decade.
2. Beckett's radio plays (including his translation of Robert Pinget's *La Manivelle*) are collected in *Samuel Beckett: The Complete Dramatic Works* (Faber: London, 1990). Helpful works on these broadcasts include Ruby Cohn's *A Beckett Canon* (Ann Arbor: University of Michigan Press, 2001); John Pilling, *A Samuel Beckett Chronology* (Basingstoke: Palgrave, 2006), 132ff; and James Knowlson, *Damned to Fame: The Life of Samuel Beckett* (London: Bloomsbury, 1996), 427ff. For details of these productions see Knowlson, *Damned to Fame; A Samuel Beckett Chronology* and Ruby Cohn *A Beckett Canon* (Ann Arbor: University of Michigan Press, 2001), 232ff.
3. See Jonathan Bignell's *Beckett on Screen: The Television Plays* (Manchester: Manchester University Press, 2009), 10–11 and 88–89.
4. For an example of the latter, see Nicholas Johnson's comments on a stage adaptation of *All That Fall* for the Abbey Theatre in Dublin, "Samuel Beckett: Radio head," *The Irish Times*, 5 Feb. 2016, online at: www.irishtimes.com/culture/books/samuel-beckett-radio-head-1.2524127 (all websites last accessed 22 Feb. 2016).
5. For the only published overview of the BBC Written Archives Centre at Caversham, see Jacquie Kavanaugh, "BBC archives at Caversham," *Contemporary British History* 6:2 (1992), 341–49.
6. I am thankful to Dr Pim Verhulst for his assistance information on Beckett's radio productions. For a listing of performances also see the BBC Genome Project, available online at:http://genome.ch.bbc.co.uk/search/0/20?media=playable&adv=1.
7. See Matthew Feldman, Appendix to "Beckett's Trilogy on the Third," in *Revisiting the Trilogy*, eds. Mark Nixon, David Tucker and Dirk van Hulle, *Samuel Beckett Today/Aujourd'hui* 26 (2014), 53–55.
8. Ibid., 55–57.
9. Ibid., 57–58.
10. I am grateful to Dr Pim Verhulst for his assistance with this information.
11. For further details, see the Appendix to Mr. Stefano Rosignoli's contribution to this volume.
12. For both translation and further discussion, see Samuel Beckett, *The Collected Poems of Samuel Beckett: A Critical Edition*, eds Seán Lawlor and John Pilling (London: Faber, 2012), 64–68, with commentary at 358–61.

The BBC and Beckett's Non-radiogenic Plays in the 1950s

Dirk Van Hulle

The BBC has undeniably played a substantial part in Samuel Beckett's career, but it took a long time before it assumed this encouraging role. For several years, the Third Programme preferred to wait and see which way the wind was blowing, until it "missed the boat" and suddenly started compensating for its initial lack of initiative. This development in the early years of the BBC's hesitant engagement with Beckett's work is closely connected to the development of Beckett's dramatic, non-radiogenic works of the 1950s. This chapter investigates the BBC's role in Beckett's career as a playwright in the 1950s, from its "culpably unenterprising" sidelining of *Waiting for Godot* to its being sidelined as a mere source of inspiration for *Krapp's Last Tape*, itself unsuitable for broadcast. It seems appropriate to let the three-part structure (1. *Waiting for Godot*, 2. *Endgame*, 3. *Krapp's Last Tape*) be preceded by a prelude, following the example of Beckett himself, who wrote an opening statement to precede the first broadcast of his work.

The research leading to these results has received funding from the European Research Council under the European Union's Seventh Framework Programme (FP7/2007–2013)/ERC grant agreement no. 313609.

D. Van Hulle (✉)
Department of Literature, University of Antwerp, Antwerp, Belgium

© The Author(s) 2017
D. Addyman et al. (eds.), *Samuel Beckett and BBC Radio*,
New Interpretations of Beckett in the 21st Century,
DOI 10.1057/978-1-137-54265-6_3

Prelude: A Radiogenic Opening Statement

The story of Beckett's non-radiogenic plays and the radio did not start with the BBC. The British Broadcasting Corporation was much slower to recognize the radio potential of Beckett's work than their French colleagues at RTF (Radiodiffusion-Télévision française). Actually, the adjective "non-radiogenic" is perhaps not quite adequate, since the public life of Beckett's theatrical works paradoxically started on the radio. *En attendant Godot* (a selection of scenes from Act 1) was broadcast on 17 February 1952,[1] almost a year before the play's première on stage. The playwright Samuel Beckett thus made his entrance "on the air," on Michel Polac's aptly called program *Entrée des auteurs* (part of the RTF's Club d'Essai service, directed by Jean Tardieu) introducing new authors who had just received public grants for their first plays. Thanks to Roger Blin, Beckett's *En attendant Godot* had been awarded a government grant and was subsequently selected for the program, which typically consisted of a few opening remarks by Polac, an introduction by an expert, a statement by the author himself, and finally a selection of scenes from the play, recorded before a live audience at the Club d'Essai studio at 37, rue de l'Université in Paris. Angela Moorjani has thoroughly investigated this radio première, which lasted 31 minutes and 35 seconds. Toward the end of the eight minutes preceding the performance of the selected scenes (the opening of the play until Estragon's dream [8′05″] and the Pozzo and Lucky scene until the end of Act 1 [15′40″][2]), a short statement by the author was read, not by Beckett himself (who "refused to be present"[3]), but by Roger Blin.

En attendant Godot was not conceived as a play for the radio, yet it was paradoxically "born" in this medium, albeit only partially or—in the words Beckett frequently borrowed from Jung—"never entirely born" or "never properly born."[4] The short statement that preceded its pre-première broadcast, however, was entirely and properly born to be broadcast, while its content relates to theater: "Je n'ai pas d'idées sur le théâtre. Je n'y connais rien. Je n'y vais pas." ("I have no thoughts about the theatre. I know nothing about it. I don't go to the theatre." [trans. Angela Moorjani]) At the same time, theater seems to have been a pretext to use this statement as an opportunity for Beckett to officially formulate his poetics of ignorance and have it broadcast. The text consists of less than 30 sentences, organized in 13 short paragraphs, four of which open with the words "Je ne sais pas":

Je ne sais pas plus sur cette pièce que celui qui arrive à la lire avec attention.
Je ne sais pas dans quel esprit je l'ai écrit[e].
Je ne sais pas plus sur les personnages que ce qu'ils disent, ce qu'ils font et ce qui leur arrive. De leur aspect j'ai dû indiquer le peu que j'ai pu entrevoir ....
Je ne sais pas qui est Godot. Je ne sais même pas[, surtout pas,] s'il existe. Et je ne sais pas s'ils y croient ou non, les deux qui l'attendent.
(I know no more about this play than someone who manages to read it attentively.
I don't know in what mood I wrote it.
I know no more about the characters than what they say, what they do, and what happens to them. About their appearance I must have shown the little I could glimpse ....
I don't know who Godot is. I don't even know [above all not][5] if he exists. And I don't know if they believe in him or not, the two who are waiting for him.' [trans. Angela Moorjani])

The verb "entrevoir" ("to glimpse") is the same as in Beckett's last work, "Comment dire" / "what is the word": "folie que de vouloir croire entrevoir – / quoi – / comment dire –" ("folly for to need to seem to glimpse – / what – / what is the word –"), but there are also echoes with Beckett's earlier works. As Angela Moorjani indicates, the "cadenced protestations of unknowingness echo the opening paragraph of *Molloy*."[6] Although this is only a cursory remark in her discussion of Michel Polac's broadcast, it deserves some attention as it may offer us a key to an understanding of the tension between radio as a medium and the plays that were not written for this medium. The first-person narrator of *Molloy* opens by stating that he is in his mother's room: "I don't know how I got there." He claims that he works now, but "*I don't know how* to work any more," and he does not work for money. For what then? "*I don't k now*. The truth is *I don't know much*."[7] Although the rest of *Molloy*'s first part is also told by a first-person narrator, it is not impossible that it differs from the narrator of the opening paragraph.[8] The rest of part I is announced as "my beginning," whereas "now [in the opening paragraph] it's nearly the end."[9] And to the question "Is what I do now any better?" the narrator replies: "*I don't know*." If this is the "same" narrator, he is—not unlike Krapp in *Krapp's Last Tape*—clearly aware of the distance in time between his present self and his earlier self or selves.

Against this background, Beckett's statement preceding the broadcast of the abridged *Godot* in February 1952, read by another voice than his own, becomes a statement by yet another narrator, who takes his distance from his creation. Knowing full well that this will be broadcast, the narrator talks about *En attendant Godot* as a text rather than a performance, presented as something to be *read*: "I know no more about this play than someone who manages to *read* it attentively." My suggestion is that radio may have been, for Beckett, a medium that facilitated precisely this kind of attentive reading. And this kind of attentive reading, such as Patrick Magee's reading of *Molloy*, was in its turn a stimulus for further writing.

Waiting for Godot and the "Culpably Unenterprising" BBC

On 17 March 1953, relatively shortly after the première of *En attendant Godot*, the BBC's Paris representative Cecilia Reeves sent the play to the then Assistant Head of Drama, Donald McWhinnie, suggesting its potential for the Third Programme. On 8 April 1953, it was sent to E. J. King Bull, who—among many other things—notes that it would be "culpably unenterprising not to undertake the project."[10] Interestingly (given Beckett's future career as a bilingual author and self-translator), King Bull signals potential problems with the translation. In the P.S. he even notes that asking Beckett to translate or adapt his play himself might be "an embarrassing mistake," taking his work and "present standing" into account. Because of these misgivings, the Controller of the Third Programme, John Morris, was "reluctant to commit himself until he [knew] what complications [were] likely to arise in the making of an English version." Explicitly "without committing ourselves in any way at this stage," the BBC contacted the International Copyright Agency to ask for permission to make an English translation and radio adaption. In early August 1953, the BBC's Copyright Department received the message that it would be "quite all right" to broadcast the play, but only in Beckett's own translation, which was sent to the BBC on 23 September. A week later (30 September), McWhinnie received a note from Helena Wood, who evaluated the text: "This seems to me a perfectly workable translation although it has a few un-English turns of phrase and is slightly different in tone from Mr. King Bull's interpretation." In spite of the rather slow bureaucracy, everything seemed to be going well.

But on 20 October, half a year after Cecilia Reeves first drew the BBC's attention to Beckett's play, the wind seemed to be turning. Suddenly, Val Gielgud personally intervened in the matter, denouncing the play with the then fashionable Caulfieldian term "phoney": "I am left with the impression of something that is basically 'phoney.'" His advice to John Morris was to "drop" the project. Several months passed, until on 1 February 1954, J. Ormerod Greenwood wrote to McWhinnie, drawing attention again to the importance of the play. Two days later, McWhinnie replied, thanking Greenwood for his memo, but obediently repeating the same phrasing of the official standpoint that there was something "basically phoney" about the play and that they had accordingly "dropped it."

The sudden change of mind that partially caused Val Gielgud to condemn the piece was explained in a note from E. J. King Bull to Leslie Stokes, dated 24 May 1954. When he had read Beckett's own translation, he thought it was much less funny and racy than the French version. What's more, the British reviewer thought "one might seriously say" that the author had had "Irish inflections and idiom in his mind." The slander in the note gradually builds up. King Bull knew from hearsay that Beckett was "un sauvage"; collaboration with him would be "out of the question," but the Paris representative might perhaps receive permission "to tinker" with his translation.

In the midst of all this lukewarm half-heartedness, J. Ormerod Greenwood made another warm plea for the play on 1 June, four months after his previous note. This time he called it "altogether a 'must.'" But to no avail. Nothing happened, and on 5 May 1955 Barbara Bray, then Script Editor at the BBC "Sound," returned the script of *En attendant Godot* to the Paris representative Cecilia Reeves. After the BBC's more than two years of hesitating, it had 'now finally been decided against'. On the same day, she also returned the English translation to the International Copyright Agency, stating quite clearly that "the idea of producing it on Sound Radio has now been abandoned." That was that: after more than two years of toing and froing, Beckett was effectively sidelined by means of the judgment "basically phoney":

	1953	*1954*	*1955*	*1956*	*1957*	*1958*	*1959*	*1960*
Godot	…………	…………	….					

Still, the BBC had not given up on Beckett entirely. An extract from *Watt* was broadcast on 9 September, and less than two weeks later (20 September 1955)—one-and-a-half months after the opening of Peter Hall's production of *Waiting for Godot* at the Arts Centre in London and a week after its transfer to the Criterion Theatre[11]—the Head of Drama, Val Gielgud received another plea to broadcast *Waiting for Godot*, this time from Helena Wood. Her concluding judgment is highlighted with a double pencil mark: "there is so much significance, vitality and poetry in the dialogue and subtle music in the phrasing that it is obviously radio material. And the theme, though eternal, has a sharp immediacy. I feel this is a play we should be sorry not to have broadcast."

Val Gielgud subsequently gave instructions to Raymond Raikes to go and see *Waiting for Godot* at the Criterion Theatre on 28 September and report on his "impressions of its suitability for radio," which he sent the next day. In his opinion "it would be as vital in radio as it is on the stage." After stressing that he "would not advise a single cut," Raikes concludes that it was no less than a "minor tragedy" that the BBC had not been more enterprising in 1953 and his advice is to "record and broadcast this production as soon as possible lest it be said that the BBC has once again 'missed the boat.'" Subsequently, the copyright was cleared, but the audience of the Third Programme would still have to wait almost five years before the BBC finally broadcast *Waiting for Godot* (27 April 1960), seven years after Cecilia Reeves's initial suggestion:

	1953	1954	1955	1956	1957	1958	1959	1960
Godot	.....	.....	..–..	.....	.....	.....	.....	...|

Fin de partie/*Endgame*: 'Quite Unsuitable for Broadcasting'

In the meantime, John Morris sent a cutting from the *Sunday Times* (17 June 1956) to the Head of Drama, announcing two new plays by Beckett. The first work was the then still unnamed mime "Act Without Words." For obvious reasons, this mime was of no interest to the "Sound" department of BBC Drama, unlike the announcement of the second work, which is marked in the margins. The future title *Fin de partie* of this work was not definitive yet. Underneath Morris's memo, Val Gielgud has penciled: "We've asked Cecilia Reeves to get the script if she can." Reeves reacted immediately. Although she called Beckett an "elusive character," she apparently managed to persuade him to write something for radio—which is the beginning of a new chapter in Beckett's career, the genesis of the first of his radio plays. With regard to *Fin de partie*, Beckett wrote to her on 4 July 1956 that it seemed unlikely that his new—at that point still untitled—play would be performed at Marseille; that he did not wish to have it translated for some time; and that it was so visual that it was quite unsuitable for broadcasting. As Cecilia Reeves was on holiday, John Morris received a copy of Beckett's letter and was quick to let him know (11 July) he was "*extremely excited* to hear that you have had an idea which may lead to something in the Third Programme" (emphasis added). He asked to meet Beckett on Wednesday the 18th in Paris. That same day, Morris reported to the Head of Drama that Beckett had shown himself "extremely keen to write an original work for the Third Programme." And as to the possibility of broadcasting the "non-radiogenic" play *Fin de partie*, Beckett—according to Morris—did *not* after all think it was too visual for radio. On 27 September 1956, Beckett sent the script of *All That Fall* to Morris, and a few months later (13 January 1957) it was already broadcast. Morris congratulated Beckett on 15 January, and a week later the Paris Representative confirmed that Beckett "intend[ed] to write another broadcast" for the BBC, calling him "a most charming man." Clearly, the atmosphere had changed, and so had Beckett's image at the BBC—from "un sauvage" to an "elusive character" to "a most charming man."

Beckett sent a copy of *Fin de partie* to Morris, who thanked him for it on 11 February 1957 and expressed his wish to broadcast it. But Beckett repeated his original objections. He thought *Fin de Partie* would be unsuitable for radio and was not sure that he would be able to translate the play. He would talk it over with Donald McWhinnie, whom he was going to meet the next Tuesday. After this meeting, McWhinnie reported to his boss, Val Gielgud (21 February): "My impression is that if he is to write at all in the near future it will be for radio, which has captured his imagination." With regard to the possibility of broadcasting *En attendant Godot* or *Fin de partie*, Beckett had been very clear: "He is not in the least interested in 'adaptation' and would much prefer to write something new for the medium than to adapt 'Godot' or the new play." Nonetheless, Val Gielgud instructed Barbara Bray a few weeks later to do just that and make arrangements for an "adaptation" of *Fin de partie* in English translation. Barbara Bray even translated a few samples. In the meantime, the original French version was broadcast on 2 May 1957.

While Beckett insisted that his plays were not radiogenic, he suggested that his prose, on the contrary, *was* quite suitable for radio. Five days after the broadcast of *Fin de partie*, it was Beckett himself who came up with the idea to use *Molloy* as a text for radio. And on 30 June, when he had just finished a rough translation of *Fin de partie*, he even suggested another prose text, *Malone Dies*, as a possibility for radio broadcast. McWhinnie seems to have felt the need to curb Beckett's enthusiasm, writing on 3 July: "I think we had better stick to 'Molloy' in the first instance. If it comes off there is no reason why we should not experiment with the others." After McWhinnie's visit to Paris in November, the decision was made—in a very short period of time—to broadcast *From an Abandoned Work* (14 December) in the same week as *Molloy* (10 December).

On the last day of 1957, Donald McWhinnie wrote a long letter to Beckett, with all kinds of new suggestions, such as "What about doing a section from 'Murphy' sometime?" McWhinnie expressed his concern about the Lord Chancellor's censorship of "The bastard" in *Endgame*, but immediately saw another opportunity for the Third Programme: "The news about 'End Game' is very disturbing. If there is likely to be an indefinite theatrical postponement would you consider letting us do a broadcast." Beckett had mentioned to McWhinnie that he was writing something in English, to which McWhinnie did not fail to respond encouragingly. While he was probably referring to an early draft of *Embers*, the context of this writing in English also includes not only the translation of *Fin de partie* (which had already been completed in August), but also the translation of *L'Innommable*. After a first aborted attempt in 1956, and a long period of abandonment, Beckett had taken up the translation again on 22 October 1957 (indicated by a horizontal line in the first of the three notebooks of the English manuscript). The first page of the second notebook is dated "November 1957." On 22 November, he wrote to Ethna MacCarthy: "I am supposed to be translating L'Innommable, which is impossible"[12]; and on 11 December he told Mary Hutchinson that he had only managed to complete just over half of the first draft.[13]

His work on the translation was interrupted by what McWhinnie referred to as "writing in English again." On 18 December 1957, he wrote to Jacoba van Velde that he had started writing a radiophonic text in English, but that he was not doing it wholeheartedly. He clearly expressed his appreciation of Magee's readings—which he claimed would encourage him if he were encourageable.[14] This negative attitude is typical of the correspondence with Jacoba van Velde, and tends to present an overly bleak picture. He does seem to have been both encourageable and effectively encouraged by the broadcasts. What he was writing in English was most probably the first draft of *Embers*, in a notebook preserved at Harvard University's Houghton Library. A note in the manuscript of his translation of *L'Innommable* indicates that Beckett resumed his work on the translation on 21 January 1958: "Reprise 21.1.58 après échec de Henry et Ada" ("Taken up again 21.1.58 after failure of Henry and Ada").[15] This "échec" was not exactly a "failure," as it would eventually become *Embers*. Beckett told McWhinnie on 23 December that he preferred Magee's *Molloy* to his reading of *From an Abandoned Work*, and that he was trying to write in English,[16] which is most probably a reference to the draft in the Harvard notebook—a dialogue between Henry and Ada, referred to as "He" and "She," which opens without a title. The voice of "She" is described as low and remote throughout.[17] In order to create these voices, Beckett had interrupted his translation of *L'Innommable*, only a few pages after he had written "It must not be forgotten, sometimes I forget, that all is a question of voices."[18] If the Harvard manuscript is the trace of this "échec de Henry et Ada," the writing of *Embers* does seem to have been going rather smoothly, at least initially. The first three pages of the sketch are written in a fairly legible hand and without too many cancelations. It also suggests that Beckett had a pretty good idea of the radio play's structure, for although some parts of *Embers* do not feature yet in this draft, Beckett did already indicate the places where he wanted to insert them—such as the opening monologue, Addie's music lesson and her riding lesson.

But Beckett apparently put the sketch aside a few days after he had started it. On Boxing Day, he wrote to Barney Rosset: "Excited by Magee's readings I have been trying to write another radio script for the Third. It is not coming off. There is something in my English writing that infuriates me and I can't get rid of it. A kind of lack of brakes .... I have laid it aside for the moment."[19]

A chronology of the first years of Beckett's work for the BBC shows how long it took for the BBC to fully appreciate the radiophonic potential of Beckett's work. But once this happened, it led to a period of a concentrated succession of various works:

Waiting for Godot:
    17 March 1953: production in consideration
    5 May 1955: 'decided against'
    20 September 1955: idea taken up again
    27 April 1960: first BBC broadcast

Watt
    9 September 1955: first BBC broadcast

All That Fall
    27 September 1956: script sent to John Morris
    13 January 1957: first BBC broadcast

Fin de partie/Endgame
    11 February 1957: copy sent to Morris
    2 May 1957: first BBC broadcast (French version)
    22 May 1962: first BBC broadcast (English version)

Molloy
    10 December 1957: first BBC broadcast

From an Abandoned Work
    14 December 1957: first BBC broadcast

Malone Dies
    18 June 1958: first BBC broadcast

The Unnamable
    19 January 1959: first BBC broadcast

Embers
    November-December 1957: first draft
    21 January 1958: temporarily abandoned
    24 June 1959: first BBC broadcast

It is remarkable how many things were happening more or less simultaneously in this short period of time, especially in the Winter of 1957–58, as the following table visualizes (the dots represent the months of preparatory work, the vertical lines represent the broadcasts):

	1953	1954	1955	1956	1957	1958	1959	1960
Godot	....	....	....	....	....	....	....	...|
Fin de P. / *Endgame*				....	...|	....	....	....
ATFall				...	|||		|	
Molloy					........|			
FaAW					·||			
Malone					·	.....|||		
The Unn.			..		...	· ...	|	
Embers					·	....	.....|| |	

The intensity of Beckett's *"travail"* in this period (Winter 1957–58) is marked by the diversity of the media and genres in which Beckett was working:

- While he was translating *L'Innommable* and writing *Embers* in the winter of 1957–58, passages from *Molloy* and *From an Abandoned Work* were being broadcast.
- The censored words in *Endgame* were constantly on his mind throughout the month of January.
- On 13 January 1958, two weeks after McWhinnie's New Year's letter, Beckett typed a rather long letter to McWhinnie, mentioning that Devine had suggested he write a stage monologue for Magee; that he preferred not to be commissioned; and that what he had been writing was "with thought of" McWhinnie, Magee and the Third Programme.
- On 21 January, after the *"échec"* of *Embers*, Beckett resumed translating *L'Innommable*.
- On 15 February, Beckett could tell McWhinnie that he had "almost finished first draft" of the translation (*The Unnamable*) and that he would "return to the radio text [*Embers*] and see if there is anything to be saved from that wreck" once the translation of *L'Innommable* was completed.[20]
- On 20 February he started writing the Magee monologue (*Krapp's Last Tape*).[21]
- Three days later, Beckett finished his translation of *L'Innommable*. The end of the translation is marked in the manuscript: "23.2.1958 Ussy."[22]

In the meantime, at the BBC, the "prayer passage" in *Endgame* caused quite a fuss. The matter had to be examined by the "Assistant Director of Sound Broadcasting," who wrote a page-long report to the Director of Sound Broadcasting, L. Wellington on 29 January. The next day Wellington wrote a long note to the Director-General. From the Director-General it went to the Chairman of the BBC himself, who received a note on 3 February, to which he replied the same day: "I think he [Beckett] should be asked to find alternative for the word." From the top, the news trickled down again and on 12 February, the Controller of the Third Programme John Morris received a note from Wellington, saying that "the Chairman feels obliged to object to the use of the word 'bastard' on page 37—not to the play, or to the episode denying the existence of God, but to the word 'bastard.' Will you ask Beckett, when you see him in Paris, whether he would agree to change or omit the word for the purpose of broadcasting." Possibly by way of compensation, the Third Programme picked up on the idea, suggested earlier by Beckett, to broadcast passages from *Malone Dies*. McWhinnie suggested to Morris on 18 February that he "should like to ask John Beckett to write some music for the production of Samuel Beckett's 'Malone Dies.'" He must have decided that it was easier to discuss the affair on the telephone, for two days later he wrote to Beckett that "It was good to hear your voice again the other evening. I find the whole business of 'End Game' extremely upsetting." In the same letter, McWhinnie makes a few very concrete suggestions for sequences from *Malone Dies* to be read by Magee. The date of this letter is the same as the date of the first draft of *Krapp's Last Tape*.

KRAPP'S LAST TAPE: '(DEFNITELY NON-RADIO)'

On 26 February, Beckett replied to Donald McWhinnie, making suggestions for a revised sequence of passages from *Malone Dies*. After mentioning that he has just finished the first draft of his translation of *L'Innommable*, Beckett is uncharacteristically enthusiastic about his work: "I have an exciting idea for a short stage monologue for Magee," immediately adding a disclaimer: "But I know my exciting ideas and how depressing they can become."[23]

While he wrote the first draft of *Krapp's Last Tape*, he was still translating the last part of *L'Innommable* (until 23 February). And he had only recently been listening to the tapes with the broadcasts of *Molloy* and *From an Abandoned Work*. According to Michael Robinson, "It is almost certain that Beckett abandoned the novel in favour of the play."[24] It seems unlikely that Beckett abandoned the piece of prose *in order to* write the play *Krapp's Last Tape*, since *From an Abandoned Work* was probably written in 1954[25] and already published in *Trinity News* on 6 June 1956. But Robinson does have a point when he draws attention to the affinities, which according to him are "too great to be dismissed as coincidence": for instance "the same nostalgia for a lost past"; "Krapp also thinks back to his mother, in his case to remember her death in an obsessional mixture of guilt and sorrow"; and while Krapp keeps coming back to the "farewell to love" scene, the protagonist of *From an Abandoned Work* suggests "A good woman might have been the making of me."[26] Perhaps Beckett did not abandon the prose work "in favour of the play," but unearthing the text again and preparing it for the broadcast on 14 December and the repeat on 19 December may explain some of the affinities with *Krapp's Last Tape*.

The first drafts of *Krapp's Last Tape* were written in the so-called Eté 56 notebook. Apart from material for *Krapp's Last Tape*, this exercise book contains drafts of *Fin de partie*, *Comment c'est*, *All That Fall*, *Happy Days* and *Words and Music*. The notebook reflects the quasi-simultaneous development of various projects in the second half of the 1950s. The BBC's catalyzing role in this period also helps us date some of the notes and drafts in this notebook more precisely. The notes on *Fin de partie* start with a "Petit supplément" to the play, consisting of Nagg and Nell's dialogue regarding the sawdust or sand in their bins. The additions to *Fin de partie* are followed by the phrase "Arsy-versy" and other notes for the radio play *All That Fall*, including the biblical verse from which the radio play's title derives: "The Lord upholdeth all that fall and / raiseth up all those that be bowed down."[27] Page 03r can be dated rather precisely thanks to the BBC archive, since the passage at the bottom is a draft of the typed letter Beckett sent to John Morris on 27 September 1956:

> Dear Mr Morris,
> Herewith the script we spoke of in Paris.
> It calls for a rather special quality of bruitage, perhaps not quite clear from the text.
> I can let you have a note on this if you are interested in the script for the Third Programme.[28]

After a few other scenes for *Fin de partie*, such as the story of the tailor, Beckett wrote the first draft of *Krapp's Last Tape*, called "Magee Monologue" (20 February 1958). He alternated between making typescripts and writing in this copybook.[29] The manuscript versions of *Krapp's Last Tape* continue until page 21r. Again, it is thanks to the BBC archive that we can date this page rather precisely, because the facing verso (20v) contains the draft of a letter regarding a prospectus of a tape-recorder to be sent to Beckett in order for him to check up on the mechanics of it. This may be a draft of the letter to John Beckett, mentioned in Beckett's letter to Donald McWhinnie of 7 March 1958:

> I have written a short stage monologue for Magee (definitely non-radio). It involves a tape-recorder with the mechanics of which I am unfamiliar. I can't release it until I check up on some points. I have asked John B. to send me a book of the words (instructions for use). If he delays in doing so I may have to ask you to help me. Indeed if you happen to have such a thing handy you might send it along straight away. The monologue is rather a s[e]ntimental

affair in my best original English manner. Begin to understand why I write in French.[30]

So, while Beckett had told McWhinnie in January that what he was writing was "with thought of you and Magee and the Third" (see above), the thought of Magee had clearly gained the upper hand, and Beckett could not have been clearer about its unsuitability for broadcasting.

In conclusion, it seems fair to say that there is a sense of justice in Beckett's parenthesis "(definitely non-radio)": the BBC had been "culpably unenterprising" by sidelining *Waiting for Godot* when Beckett could have used the publicity in the first half of the 1950s; now, toward the end of the 1950s, Beckett—even if it can hardly have been his conscious intention—effectively sidelined the BBC as a mere source of inspiration for the *non*-radio play *Krapp's Last Tape*. Many critics have drawn attention to the moment(s) of inspiration when Beckett heard his own characters on tape at the BBC's Paris studio on Avenue Hoche, but it is good to realize that the BBC and Magee's voice as direct sources of inspiration had a precursor in the RTF, notably the recorded moment Roger Blin read Beckett's words preceding the first broadcast of scenes from *En attendant Godot*, lending a voice to this self-narrating author performing the role of someone who, like Krapp, is clearly aware of the distance in time between his present, unknowing self (claiming he "know[s] no more about the characters than what they say") and his earlier self or selves (showing "the little [he or they] could glimpse").

In many ways, radio and the BBC became catalysts for Beckett's work in the late 1950s. When he wrote to McWhinnie that he preferred not to be commissioned, Beckett seems to have been aware of the strange effect of the collaboration with the BBC on his creative production. What he was trying to write was "with thought of" McWhinnie, Magee and the Third Programme, but he did not say he was writing "for" the radio. The "thought of" the radio and the people involved in the *broadcasting* of his *prose* works seems to have been a paradoxical way of moving on with his *drama* in a *non-radiogenic* direction.

Notes

1. James Knowlson, *Damned to Fame* (London: Bloomsbury, 1996), 386.
2. Angela Moorjani, "*En attendant Godot* on Michel Polac's *Entrée des Auteurs*," *Samuel Beckett Today Aujourd'hui* 7 (1998), 50.

3. Ibid.
4. See David Melnyk, "Never been properly Jung," *Samuel Beckett Today/Aujourd'hui* 15 (2005), 355–62.
5. The words "surtout pas" feature in Roger Blin's version of the text.
6. Moorjani, "*En Attendant Godot*," 51.
7. Samuel Beckett, *Krapp's Last Tape and Other Shorter Plays* (London: Faber and Faber, 2009), 3.
8. Moorjani, "En attendant Godot," 40–43.
9. James Knowlson draws attention to a biographical correspondence, noting that Beckett "wrote the greater part of ... *Molloy*, which he had begun on 2 May, literally in '[his] mother's room' at New Place in Foxrock, although the very beginning of the novel seems to have been written last" (Knowlson, *Damned to Fame*, 367).
10. All the passages from BBC correspondence in this chapter are quoted from the BBC Written Archives Centre, Caversham, "Scriptwriter 1953–1962" folder. I owe a debt of gratitude to the editors of this volume for providing me with digital facsimiles of this correspondence. For further details on the BBC's proposed approach to translating and adapting *Waiting for Godot*, see Erik Tonning's Chapter in this volume.
11. Pilling, John, *A Samuel Beckett Chronology* (Houndmills, Basingstoke: Palgrave Macmillan, 2006), 128.
12. Quoted in Knowlson, *Damned to Fame*, 441.
13. See Pilling, *A Beckett Chronology*, 137.
14. Correspondence between Samuel Beckett and Jacoba van Velde, Bibliothèque nationale de France, NAF 19794, 204 ff.
15. HRC MS SB 5/9/2, 23v; quoted in Dirk Van Hulle and Shane Weller, *The Making of Samuel Beckett's* L'Innommable/The Unnamable (London: Bloomsbury, 2014), 40.
16. Pilling, *A Beckett Chronology*, 138.
17. Harvard University, Theatre Collection, mss Thr 70.3.
18. Samuel Beckett, *The Unnamable*, ed. Steven Connor (London: Faber and Faber, 2010), 59; HRC MS SB 5/9/2, 17r; quoted in Beckett Digital Manusript Project, *L'Innommable*/The Unnamable eds. Dirk Van Hulle, Shane Weller and Vincent Neyt, Brussels: University Press Antwerp, 2013, www.beckettarchive.org.
19. Beckett, quoted in Clas Zilliacus, *Beckett and Broadcasting: A Study of the Works of Samuel Beckett for and in Radio and Television* (Åbo: Åbo Akademi, 1976), 149.
20. Quoted in Knowlson, *Damned to Fame*, 790 n.1.
21. For a more detailed chronology and account of the genesis, see Beckett Digital Manuscript Project, vol. 3, *The Making of Samuel Beckett's* Krapp's Last Tape (London: Bloomsbury, 2015, forthcoming).

22. See Van Hulle and Weller, *The Making of Beckett's* L'Innommable (London: Bloomsbury, 2014), 48.
23. Beckett, *Letters III*, 111.
24. Michael Robinson, *The Long Sonata of the Dead: A Study of Samuel Beckett* (New York: Grove Press, 1969), 212.
25. Pilling, *A Beckett Chronology*, 122–3.
26. Robinson, *The Long Sonata of the Dead*, 212.
27. Ps 145.15.
28. Beckett, *Letters II*, 656.
29. Dirk Van Hulle, *The Making of Samuel Beckett's* Krapp's Last Tape/La Dernière Bande (London and Brussels: Bloomsbury and University Press Antwerp, 2015), 51.
30. Beckett, *Letters III*, 115.

Mediating Modernism: The Third Programme, Samuel Beckett, and Mass Communication

Erik Tonning

It was, T.S. Eliot said, a "massacre," "sheer vandalism," and a "plan to pander to the more moronic elements in our society."[1] The occasion for this invective, delivered at a meeting between an influential group of protestors and some of the governors and officials of the BBC in 1957, was the looming threat of a cut in the Third Programme's broadcasting hours, due to its limited audience and "specialized" content. The incident illustrates how much of a national cultural institution the Third Programme had become in the 11 years since its first broadcast on 29 September 1946. It also points to a recurring pattern in the long-running debate about its nature and viability. As Stefan Collini goes on to argue after quoting Eliot's words,

> the service has acted as something of a lightning rod for larger anxieties about "exclusiveness" versus "accessibility," along increasingly predictable lines: complaints build up about its "elitist" or "off-putting" character; the BBC proposes changes to make it more "accessible" and "inviting;" this provokes a chorus of protest about the "dilution" of quality and the "debasement" of standards; the BBC responds by emphasizing its duty to

---

E. Tonning (✉)
Department of Foreign Languages, University of Bergen, Bergen, Norway

the payers of the licence fee and the need to adapt to social change; the service is modified very much along the lines of the original proposal; the regular audience for the service remains tiny and predominantly middle-class and middle-aged; after a while the complaints about its "elitist" and "outdated" character reach a new crescendo; and so on.[2]

Yet when we turn from this general view of the cultural battlefield to the more specific role of the Third Programme in mediating *modernism* to the British public in those first decades of its existence, the picture becomes more complex. There can be no doubt that the self-conscious elitism and insistence on cultural "standards" within the Third was a precondition for its willingness to promote "difficult" modernist writing in the first place. Furthermore, the pressure not to seem "out of touch"—but to be discovering and promoting serious contemporary work alongside the diet of past classics—also drove the Third in this direction. However, vis-à-vis these modernist writers themselves, the Third could often appear, not as uncompromisingly elitist, but rather as an agent of popularization and perhaps unwelcome tampering: trying too hard to please its mass audience, and destroying the artistic integrity and autonomy of the modernist work in the process. And the Third did in fact see it as its duty to reach as broad a segment of the population as could benefit from its programs. The idea was to steadily try to broaden the Third's appeal as the "apex" of a cultural pyramid that should also connect with the broader "base," associated with the Home and Light services. Its ethos was educational, for the programs were meant to create wider interest in otherwise inaccessible high-quality content and to foster cultural betterment.

But this is not the only way in which mediating modernism could prove problematic for the Third. It also had to contend with the anti-Establishment, and specifically the anti-Christian impetus of some modernist writing. The general policy of the BBC on religious broadcasting was heavily weighted toward a Christian ethos. Although some more controversial programs—such as the famous 1948 debate between Bertrand Russell and Frederick Copleston on the existence of God, or Margaret Knight's 1955 broadcasts on "Morals without Religion" from a humanist viewpoint—were sparingly allowed, caution, *gravitas*, and a high moral tone were considered essential at all times.[3] Of course, when broadcasting fiction, poetry, or drama to a "thinking" audience, the Third was not necessarily subject to the exact same strictures; but anti-religious provocation and blatant blasphemy would be regarded as offensive, and would need to be policed by the producers to some extent. At the same time, as we shall see, the Third also drew on an influential intellectual tradition of "Christian modernism," represented by both Eliot, a figure much admired within the BBC, and Harman Grisewood, the Third's second Controller (1948–1952), a Catholic and a close friend of the poet, painter, and occasional cultural theorist David Jones.[4] For these men, an anti-Christian animus in a work of literature by no means sufficed to condemn it; on the contrary, such a work might challenge a complacent culture to fruitful existential self-examination; and Christianity should in any case be robust enough to withstand such attacks.

These two areas—artistic autonomy and anti-religious provocation—would on the face of it seem potentially troublesome in the encounter between the Third Programme and Samuel Beckett. The Beckett files in the BBC written archive at Caversham reveal that even Beckett's own agent and publisher, Jérôme Lindon, frankly considered him "'un sauvage,' with whom any sort of collaboration would be out of the question."[5] Yet in fact, the hurdles were in the end negotiated remarkably smoothly, and Beckett became one of the Third Programme's most valued assets. The BBC Written Archive files give unique insight into the give-and-take of that negotiation over many years, and Beckett's case may suggest broader implications for examining the shifting and complex "rules of engagement" between the Third and modernist writers more generally as well.

***

The Third's first encounter with Beckett was in the wake of the success of the first French *Godot* in 1953. Cecilia Reeves and Rayner Heppenstall went to see it, and came back impressed with the first half ("extraordinarily effective") but less so with the second: perhaps a radio presentation might make the piece more accessible?[6] E. J. King Bull was asked to review the script for a possible adaptation by the Third, and his three-page report (dated 15 April 1953[7]) speaks volumes about the Third's intended approach to this enigmatic text. Certainly, his overall conclusion is that it would be "culpably unenterprising not to undertake the project." There was a risk—"it might fail in effect"—but it "could scarcely fail in interest, because it is entirely novel to an English audience in almost every respect." This sense of "novelty" is double edged here, though: if the play can be made to work radiogenically, and be accepted by its audience, the Third might garner praise for an astute discovery of fresh Continental writing; whereas the feared, opposite reaction—neatly summarized in the heading of a review of the London stage *Godot* two years later—would be:

THE LEFT BANK CAN KEEP IT.[8] In other words, the deep-seated English resistance to "incomprehensible" French intellectuals is hovering in the background of this discussion. The feeling was made explicit in Val Gielgud's final rejection of the piece as "basically 'phoney'"[9]—a judgment in which even Donald McWhinnie, generally far more experimental than Gielgud and later a trusted collaborator of Beckett's, would on this occasion support him.[10] The implicit question for King Bull in his report is therefore: how can the play be put across on the Third so as to forestall that reaction?

A principal strategy is to assimilate Beckett's play to one of the BBC's most-loved comedy shows, *It's that man again*, ITMA for short, written by Ted Kavanagh in collaboration with its star, the comedian Tommy Handley. Known for its bizarre and rapid-fire repartee, broad type-based characters with names like Colonel Chinstrap, and its many catchphrases, this was the show that kept English morale up during the Second World War. A particular specialty, reflected in the name of the show itself (which derived from a newspaper heading about the Führer from 1939), was ridicule of Hitler. "It is," King Bull wrote, "very much for consideration whether production should be left to stand on flat comic dialogue, or treated in the full-dress surrealistic convention of Itma. It is, in fact, basically radiogenic provided the clowning can be somehow interpreted in that tradition."[11] The two principal characters are, he writes, "something like the Two Black Crows, [or] Claude and Cecil,"[12] the latter pair being ITMA standbys, and the former, a blackface comedy act popular in the 1920s and '30s. Throughout King Bull's report, the emphasis is on comic potential; the play might be "supremely funny," it returns to a central "gag" (colloquially translated here as "Let's move on / Got to wait for Godot"), yet it is not a question of a single extended joke, for "the actual dialogue is full of nonsensical humour and character."[13] While there may be, "on top of this," some "philosophic or even religious allegory, which is sure to make some people mention Kafka,"[14] this is very much by the way. The Kafka reference introduces a weighty intellectual, but noncommittally; it is all well and good if "some people" should be thus excited, and the play should accordingly be highbrow enough for the Third; but the heart of the matter, the comedy, will have wider appeal. As for religion, the play might even, King Bull suggests offhandedly, be translated as "Waiting for Nobodaddy"—harking back to William Blake's poem "To Nobadaddy" (c. 1793) addressing an anthropomorphic deity: "Why art thou silent and invisible?" I would suggest that this is intended to familiarize by associating the play with a great and acceptably "spiritual" English Romantic poet, but also to deflate any suggestion of the pretentious or the provocatively blasphemous, merely by invoking the quaint name of Nobodaddy.

In practical terms, King Bull outlines two stages for presenting the play in a style acceptable for the Third, translation and adaptation, a task he would be willing to undertake himself. While the "transliteration from the French" is "child's play,"[15] the real issue would be exploiting a variety of English accents and sociolects for comic effect, which should be thought of "in the same breath as casting": "Is one to think of Jimmy Edwards and Dick Bentley, or Tommy Handley and Deryck Guyler?"[16] The adaptation would then proceed along broadly ITMA-ish lines, with bits of the text in principle "available for total cutting, or additional dialogue."[17] King Bull notes that it might prove an "embarrassing mistake"[18] to ask the author himself to undertake the translation, for this would be to relinquish control over an important stage of the adaptation process itself.

In fact, it was Beckett's insistence on providing his own English translation of the play as the basis for any presentation by the Third that began to turn the tide of opinion against undertaking the project. James Knowlson reports that by June 1953 Beckett had produced a first-draft translation for his American backer Harold Oram, precisely because he was already worried "by the very sound of the word 'adaptation' and anxious about the quality of any resulting translation."[19] After sending an inquiry about translation and adaptation rights on 18 May, the BBC received the reply from the International Copyright Agency on 6 August that a broadcast was feasible, but that Beckett's own translation had to be used; the text itself was sent on 30 September.[20] We should not conclude from this that Beckett was inflexibly opposed to radio adaptation *per se* at this stage, for he did give his permission for a radio Godot; indeed, in 1960 he would even allow a *Godot* that included a narrator. His well-known letter to Barney Rosset (27 August 1957) refusing permission to stage *All That Fall* on the grounds that "[i]f we can't keep our genres more or less distinct, or extricate them from the confusion that has them where they are, we might as well go home and lie down"[21] should not, then, be taken as a hard and fast principle applying to his whole career, for Beckett seems to have worked on a case-by-case basis, especially where friends were involved. At this point, though, no personal contact had been made, and it is fair to assume that had Beckett known the Third's plans for his play in detail, he would have withdrawn in horror. But, serendipitously perhaps for future relations between Beckett and the BBC, the project was stopped in its tracks before he actually heard of those plans.

At first, King Bull, when confronted with Beckett's translation, was disposed to be flexible, even though, as Helena Wood pointed out in a memo, "it has a few un-English turns of phrase and is slightly different in tone from Mr King Bull's interpretation."[22] But he too would turn against it, as he explained in retrospect—after the project had already been dropped—on 24 May 1954:

> The reason for my change of front about this as a project …. is that on reading Beckett's own English version, it struck me as far less funny, and less racy, than in the original, and I think one might seriously say that Beckett has had Irish inflections and idiom in his mind.
>
> His agent and publisher, whom I saw in Paris, described him as "un sauvage," with whom any sort of collaboration would be out of the question, but it is possible that Cecilia Reeves might obtain, through the same channels, permission to tinker with his version. What is requisite is really nothing less than a free hand.[23]

But a free hand was what they were very unlikely to get; so better to drop it. This then is how the Third dealt with a promising new author who *might* turn out all right, but who was also associated with a potentially "phoney" leftbankishness. An adaptation would have to be done on their terms or not at all. But in 1955, after the London stage *Godot* had been famously lauded by Kenneth Tynan and Harold Hobson and the play had become the talk of the season, their attitude changed completely.

This change was perfectly natural, for Peter Hall's acclaimed production had done the job that the Third had originally envisaged undertaking from scratch: to successfully introduce Beckett to an English audience. In the Third's initial approach to Beckett we see caution winning out; we should recall here that the institution itself was always more or less under attack from different quarters, and their decision-making about individual authors therefore a constant balancing act. After the London production, the pressure was palpably off. Helena Wood, who had expressed polite skepticism about Beckett's translation not matching King Bull's interpretation in September 1953, now reported thus on the script:

> This is a morality play, a really contemporary morality play, inconsequent inconclusive, flippant and profoundly serious, concerned with man's relationship to man, his predicament on earth, his desperate need of something to give meaning to the hopeless nonsense of life…. For radio it is not without

dangers. The setting and the appearance of the tramps is essential, and will have somehow to be conveyed on the air. It is perhaps over-long and often irritatingly obscure, but there is so much significance, vitality and poetry in the dialogue and subtle music in the phrasing that it is obviously radio material. And the theme, though eternal, has a sharp immediacy. I feel this is a play we should be sorry not to have broadcast.[24]

We will return to the significance of invoking the medieval genre of the morality play, but for now the completely new emphasis is worth noting: the stress is on *seriousness* and the "eternal" themes, not clowning; and it is seen as radiogenic, not because of the potential for back-chat and repartee, but because of the "significance, vitality and poetry in the dialogue and subtle music in the phrasing"—reasons that indicate high respect for Beckett's craftsmanship, rather than viewing his text as available for chopping and changing. The worry about "obscurity" remains, but much less prominently. On 28 September, Raymond Raikes was dispatched to see the show at the Criterion:

I am quite sure that if the present company were asked to perform this play for the microphone, with only such radio production as would be necessary to transfer the play from the theatre to broadcasting, I believe that it would be as vital in radio as it is on the stage.[25]

Most of the actors, Raikes pointed out, "are experienced in our medium and would be capable of making the necessary changes in technique."[26] He praised the "brilliant direction of Peter Hall" including a radiogenically promising "studied control of the dialogue, with its extraordinary contrasts of rhythms and its compelling climaxes"[27]; this echoes Wood's report. In fact, Raikes would not want to make "a single cut" in the dialogue, though possibly adding "a few words for clarity in our non-visual medium."[28] He also liked the musical accompaniment added to the play by Peter Hall (which Beckett, incidentally, is on record as having loathed[29]), and suggests that this would be effective in a radio production. His conclusion is concerned—as are all these assessments, whether implicitly or explicitly—with the BBC's reputation:

May I suggest that we record and broadcast this production as soon as possible lest it be said that the BBC has once again "missed the boat." It seems to me a minor tragedy that on the strength of the report that this play obtained when it was first received from Paris in April 1953 (a report I have only now just read after seeing the play itself) it was not then given on the Third Programme.[30]

That was easy enough to say in retrospect. However, after Peter Hall's production Beckett was no longer an unknown quantity. His reputation as a writer had been established and his craftsmanship and haunting dialogue could now be safely admired. Furthermore, Hall's production had now done at least part of the job that the Third had wanted to do: we should recall that Beckett himself was critical of the fast-paced comedic style in which parts of it were played, as well as of the use of music and what he referred to as the "Anglican piety" of the ending.³¹ The play had, to some extent, been assimilated and conventionalized by Hall's company; so it is no wonder that Raikes found it fully packaged and presentable for the Third.

At this point, the BBC began actively to woo Beckett. The negotiations to secure adaptation rights for *Godot* were complicated by the fact that Donald Albery at the Criterion wanted the play to run for some months in the provinces after its London run, and no broadcast was allowed before this had taken place. While these negotiations dragged on, though, the BBC still had their eye on the ball. After seeing a notice in the *Sunday Times* (17 June 1956) saying that Beckett had written two new pieces in French for the Marseilles festival—a mime and a one-acter, at this stage called "Soif" (later *Acte sans paroles I*) and "La fin du Jeu" (*Fin de partie*)—they wrote to him, asking both for the text of the latter, and whether he would consider writing a radio play specially for the Third.³² Beckett was, Cecilia Reeves reported, an "elusive character," but there were signs of a thaw: "He has ... reacted amiably to a suggestion that his mime piece 'Soif' which is to be given at Marseille should be considered for Television so I imagine that his former rather hostile attitude to radio in general is improving."³³ They worked actively to overcome that "hostile attitude," not least through personal contact with Beckett, and succeeded spectacularly. In terms of *Fin de partie*, there is an interesting oscillation in Beckett's attitude: at first he reportedly tells the BBC that they can "certainly" have the text when it is finished;³⁴ then, in a letter dated 4 July to Cecilia Reeves,³⁵ he rows back and claims it is such a "visual affair" that it is "quite unsuitable for broadcasting;" but after personally meeting Beckett in Paris, John Morris, the Third Programme Controller, could report that "he himself, contrary to previous reports, does not necessarily think it will be too visual for sound radio."³⁶ The play was in fact broadcast on the Third, in April 1957—*in French*. Beckett's new prestige within the BBC is very clear from the fact that the Third were willing to present a new play by him in French if they had to, whereas three years ago they had turned down *Godot* largely because they could not have a free hand with the translation. It is also clear from the fact that John Morris himself was the one to seek out Beckett. For his new play written for the Third, he would be given the royal treatment, for the Third regarded netting Beckett as a major "scoop."[37] And—as his change of heart over *Fin de partie* already indicates—Beckett was not immune to this lavish attention.

At first Beckett had professed himself "doubtful of my ability to work in this medium," though he had to his own surprise had an idea "that may or may not lead to something."[38] The memo from Suzanne Poulain, composed before this letter was received, quotes Beckett as saying that "he has never written anything for radio before and he will probably need a little more persuasion from Miss Reeves before he actually starts working on it."[39] When he lunched with John Morris in Paris on July 18th, Beckett had already written the first few pages of his script. The two discussed radio technique, and Morris "got the impression that he has a very sound idea of the problems of writing for radio and that we can expect something pretty good."[40]

All That Fall was praised from the beginning by critics for its masterful and innovative use of sound as scene-painting, to produce comedy, and for intrusive and defamiliarizing effect. Beckett seems to have oriented himself very consciously toward the medium and the needs of the Third, and he remained willing to seek out and accept the advice of the professionals. Upon sending his script, he wrote to Morris that the soundscape he had in mind for the play "calls for a rather special quality of bruitage"[41]; if they wanted it, he could send a further note on this. In a later letter, Beckett expresses doubts whether this is "no more than an amateur's statement of what is common radio practice"; the best thing would be to "meet the bruiteur, before production, and talk it over."[42] Donald McWhinnie was thus promptly dispatched to Paris to discuss the details with Beckett, initiating a highly successful long-term collaboration. McWhinnie would go to great lengths to get the sound right for this play: as Julie Campbell has emphasized, his experimentation in this area led, in Martin Esslin's words, "directly to the establishment of the BBC's Radiophonic Workshop."[43] Beckett was also invited to London to take part in the production itself, but he was tied up with *Fin de partie* in Paris; however, he was quite sure his play was "in good hands in yours."[44] The result was lauded by all. Beckett himself wrote to thank McWhinnie and everyone involved warmly for an excellent job,[45] and also wrote to John Morris that he was "deeply touched by the welcome you have extended to my play and by the trouble you have taken over it," adding that he should "like nothing better than to be able to work again in such an atmosphere of friendliness and understanding."[46] Even the once-skeptical Val Gielgud himself glowed with praise:

> My warmest congratulations on your outstanding success with the Beckett play. I am more than aware what a tremendously difficult production job this was. Indeed, in my experience I cannot think of one presenting more difficulties. Your all over grasp of the problems involved, your exceptional casting, your ingenious use of effects, and your extreme sensitivity of approach, combined to do a fascinating script every sort of justice. Well done....[47]

The sense of happy conjunction between Beckett and the Third Programme over *All That Fall* is in fact so remarkable that it seems legitimate to consider the play for a moment in light of how extremely well it suited the Third's needs. To what extent did Beckett—that supposedly uncompromising and uncooperative modernist "sauvage"—in fact write with an idea of appealing to the Third's mass audience at least partly in mind?

This is of course complex territory, in so far as the initial inspiration from the play undoubtedly came from "boyhood memories," described in a letter to Aidan Higgins of 6 July 1956 as "feet dragging and breath short and cartwheels and imprecations from the Brighton Rd to Foxrock station and back, insentient old mares in foal being welted by the cottagers and the Devil tottered in the ditch."[48] Still, the play is markedly more plot-based and accessible than either *Waiting for Godot* or *Endgame*. It is perfectly lucid in its there-and-back-again structure of Maddie Rooney picking up her husband from the train station; it deploys broad and even rude comedy; and there is also, very unusually for Beckett, a detective-story-style mystery at the end, however unresolved. It has often been observed that the play sidesteps the overall tendency toward lessness and anti-plotting that characterizes Beckett's prose and drama at the same point in time. It does not, therefore, seem unreasonable to speculate that he deliberately set out to be clearer and more accessible. Perhaps one reason behind this choice was that he knew that the visual element which he had developed so brilliantly in the dominant stage metaphors of *Godot* and *Endgame* (and in his mime, too) would be missing, and a stronger sense of orientation was thus needed for the listener. We might even call this a kind of Beckettian pedagogy, introducing his characteristic preoccupations in a slightly more digestible form than usual.

The comedy—and the hyperbolical Irishness of the play—in particular serve to sweeten the pill. Thinking back to King Bull's report on *Godot*, we recall how he had felt that establishing a dominant and recognizable comedic convention from the outset would be crucial to putting the play across. The presence of a "philosophic or religious allegory" coming "on top of this" was not too much of a problem—in fact it could add a Third-worthy intellectual gravitas—so long as it did not seem pretentious or too explicitly blasphemous. By centring his play on a mad old hag of an Irishwoman and an entourage of eccentric villagers gushing blarney as they bump grumpily into one another, Beckett has in fact achieved a presentation that we can feel sure King Bull would have heartily approved. It is quite possible that, even though he grumbled about the overstated comedy in the London *Godot*, he also learned something about what would go over well with an English audience. These then are funny and bizarre Irish villagers, not to be taken quite seriously. So what if they are "cursing, under my breath, God and man, under my breath, and the wet Saturday afternoon of my conception," or breaking into hysterical laughter at the Psalm verse (Ps. 145), "The Lord upholdeth all that fall...?" But of course, for the serious listener, there is plenty to ponder; and for the reviewers, as the many notices collected in the BBC files indicate, there was plenty to discuss. This thinking person's comedy, then, was indeed positively "made for" the Third.

***

The BBC files surrounding *All That Fall* do not reveal any anxiety on the producers' part that the play would be perceived as provocatively blasphemous, despite such moments as those just quoted. One reason, as I have argued, is that these moments are ingeniously cloaked in broad comedy, and would therefore be less likely to give offense. Yet we do find an awareness from the beginning of the Third's dealing with Beckett of the potentially volatile impact of his work on its audience. The King Bull strategy was to bracket the "religious or philosophical allegory" with comedy, and keep things vague ("Waiting for Nobodaddy"). In some measure, Beckett himself had achieved a version of this on his own in *All That Fall*. However, there was also, as it were, a second-tier strategy available, reflected in Helena Wood's report on *Godot* as a "morality play" with a highly serious "eternal theme." The phrase "morality play" with regard to *Godot* has a familiar ring to all Beckettians: it was used some months later in G.S. Fraser's much-discussed and much-maligned *Times Literary Supplement(TLS)* article from 10 February 1956, which called it "a modern morality play on permanent Christian themes."[49] This sparked considerable debate in the letters pages, and it is hard to believe that the BBC's decision to revive this debate by broadcasting a talk by Professor Ronald Gray entitled "*Waiting for Godot*: A Christian Interpretation" on 9 January 1957—four days ahead of the first broadcast of *All That Fall*, which somewhat daringly fell on a Sunday[50]—was not a conscious attempt to frame the debate about Beckett's new radio play in advance.[51] Certainly, two of the reviews of *All That Fall* picked up on this framing, and discussed the play in terms of possible Christian themes. Both the *Irish Times* reviewer (18 January), G. A. Olden, and Roy Walker of *The Tribune* (n.d.) expressed skepticism about Gray's views, each of them leaning instead toward an existentialist interpretation of Beckett; however, they both endorsed the play itself as an "eloquent expression of a deep spiritual *malaise*" (Olden) and an "apotheosis of Irish paradoxical pessimism," so this hardly mattered.[52] What mattered was that the issue was framed as a serious debate about an open question, so that it was not possible to simply dismiss Beckett offhand as an outright blasphemer. Gray himself was challenged in the correspondence columns of *The Listener*, and his defense of his views (published 7 February 1957) significantly made extensive reference to *All That Fall* as well as to *Godot*:

> I agree with Mr. Houfe when he says that this play is "the portrayal of the hopeless condition of a Godless world ...." But I do not see why, because there is no solution offered at the end, the author need be as perplexed as the men he portrays. He may also be indifferent, or callous, or he may feel compassion as Maddy Rooney does in "All That Fall": "If you had my eyes you'd understand. The things they've seen and not looked away. This is nothing." As an artist he records what he sees, it is not his business to give messages, and what he does see is horrifying. My business as interpreter, it seemed to me, was to show that the point of view of the characters was not the only one represented in the play; that it had a positive sense as well as a negative one, much as the ordinary world has...

With considerable subtlety, Gray continues:

> Neither of Mr Beckett's plays is propagandist. Like his novel *Molloy*, which reads like the recollections of two souls in damnation, they enter into a Godless world and experience it from the inside, after the pattern of our Lord. But the fact that they bring no explicit Christian message does not

mean that they bring a message of despair either.... This objective form of presentation achieved its sharpest effect in the radio play, at the moment when the text was announced: "The Lord upholdeth all that fall, and raiseth up all those that be bowed down." The screeches of laughter that followed this suggested to one reviewer that the play was sardonic in intention. Certainly the laughter itself was sardonic. Yet it might equally well have been felt as a deep wound, and have brought home a realisation that this is in fact how such affirmations are greeted. It matters, whether a hearer reacts one way or the other, but Mr. Beckett does not impose an answer. What he does provide inescapably is something of the experience of helpless wretchedness, which nobody, Christian or not, has a right to exclude from his consciousness. I do not believe that the experience can be endured indefinitely without Christian faith.[53]

In Gray's account, Beckett's refusal to offer a "solution" or to "impose an answer" becomes the hook on which to hang a Christian reading. Significantly, from the Third's point of view, a quality that they had always worried about in presenting Beckett—his obscurity—could thus also be useful in guarding against any charges of direct blasphemy. In this respect, at least, the ambiguity and difficulty of his texts actually made them more acceptable for mass broadcasting.

I am not, however, suggesting that the Third's deployment of Gray as authorized interpreter of Beckett was merely strategic. In fact, Gray' approach accords well with the intellectual tradition of "Christian modernism" which was already a significant influence within the organization, especially through the figure of Harman Grisewood, the second Controller (1948–1952), who became Director of the Spoken Word in 1952, and finally Assistant to the Director-General. Two "Christian modernist" cultural theorists in particular, T. S. Eliot and David Jones, carried significant prestige within the BBC, and their ideas were cited in official documents and internal discussions about programming.[54]

Eliot's concept of the "Christian blasphemer"—which by the time of Fraser's *TLS* piece on Beckett could be alluded to as common knowledge[55]—focuses the issue neatly. As early as 1930, in his essay on Baudelaire, Eliot had maintained that "[g]enuine blasphemy, genuine in spirit and not purely verbal, is the product of partial belief, and is as impossible to the complete atheist as to the perfect Christian. It is a way of affirming belief."[56] Baudelaire is thus concerned

> not with demons, black masses, and romantic blasphemy, but with the real problem of good and evil.... In the middle of the nineteenth century, the age which (at its best) Goethe had prefigured, an age of bustle, programs, platforms, scientific progress, humanitarianism and revolutions which improved nothing, an age of progressive degradation, Baudelaire perceived that what really matters is Sin and Redemption.[57]

Eliot's idea is that a decadent age grown deaf to the Christian message might receive a beneficial cultural shock from being confronted with "genuine" blasphemy: it might even recover a sense of Sin and Redemption. Similarly, for David Jones, modern civilization in its emphasis on mere technology and utilitarian efficacy on every level of thought and practice has grown increasingly inhuman, to the point where "the utile is all [man] knows and his works take on something of the nature of the works of the termites;" indeed, "nothing could surpass the 'eccentricity' of the 'normal' life and works of megalopolitan man today—and tomorrow."[58] This is not a situation that any individual artist has the power to change, yet authentic art here necessarily becomes

> a contradiction, a fifth-column, within that civilization, and here it shares the honours of sabotage with the tradition of religion, for both are disruptive forces, both own allegiance to values in any event irritant, and easily becoming toxic to those values which of necessity dominate the present world-orders.[59]

Modernist art—even if ostensibly anti-Christian—can thus be an ally in disrupting cultural complacency and fostering a "rebellion," a drive toward a more existentially reflective and artistically oriented culture that could lay the basis for a new interest in Christianity. Fraser's and Gray's arguments about Beckett align themselves with this broader cultural view. Gray suggests that the laughter of Maddy and Dan at the psalm verse, while sardonic, may also "have been felt as a deep wound" at the very fact that "this is in fact how such affirmations are greeted" in the culture. Furthermore, Beckett's intense existential questioning and the "experience of helpless wretchedness" that his work conveys is something that no one, whether Christian or not, "has a right to exclude from his consciousness." But, once the defenses are down, that very experience can push a listener in the right direction: "I do not believe the experience can be endured indefinitely without Christian faith." Such a cultural project, it should be noted, necessarily has a curiously double relationship to the very idea of mass communication, and implicitly therefore to broadcasting. From one angle, there is a fear of mere entertainment used as a soporific against existential and religious awareness. Eliot's high-pitched attack on the impending "massacre" of the Third Programme and his accusation of pandering to the "moronic elements in our society" should be seen in this light: for him, the issue was not simply about broadcasting hours, it touched on an ultimately messianic cultural project. Yet on the other hand, precisely because of this missionary zeal, maintaining a mass *audience* for the kind of high culture (including modernist works) that could challenge and improve the dominant "mass culture" was still crucial.

It goes without saying that such rarefied views were by no means held by all of the Third's producers in the 1940s and '50s. The point here is simply that long before the Third came into contact with Beckett, there existed a strong intellectual tradition even among the Christians within its ranks that was both positive toward modernism, and prepared—within limits—to take a broad view of blasphemy and cultural "fifth column" activities by artists. This, then, would be at least part of the explanation as to why no hackles were raised about Beckett-as-blasphemer—until, that is, a direct challenge presented itself in 1958.

Endgame, Beckett's English translation of *Fin de partie*, had been denied a performance license by the Lord Chamberlain's Office, despite the fact that the play had been performed in French in London in 1957. The objection was that the mock-prayer scene—and in particular the line "The bastard! He doesn't exist"—was deemed blasphemous. Beckett, at this stage, was not willing to change the offending word. An additional complication was that the play had been broadcast in French on the Third by the original company. The BBC insisted that the Lord Chamberlain's decisions were not binding on broadcasting, and so they could not simply accept this verdict, but would need to make an independent editorial decision. If they were to drop the broadcast, they would look as though they were caving in to external pressure, and, furthermore, they would be in the faintly ridiculous position of having already broadcast in French but being somehow unable to stomach the English version. On the other hand, in several memos a fear of negative publicity in case of a broadcast is evident. The detailed arguments give fascinating insight into the way the issue of blasphemy was framed within the Third Programme and in the BBC generally at this time.

Two memos from the Assistant Director of Sound Broadcasting (29 January 1958) and the Director of Sound Broadcasting (the following day) both concluded in favor of broadcasting *Endgame*. The Assistant

Director, R. D'A Marriott, observed that while there must be "limits to the blasphemy or obscenity" which individual characters in a play may be allowed to utter on the air, in deciding what to allow the BBC must consider "the nature of the audience, the standing of the author and his seriousness of purpose."[60] The "particular world that we are trying to interest," he argues, will not "be offended by this passage or fail to understand that the purpose of the play is serious"—even if the audience for the English version should be "slightly larger" than for the French one.[61] Within that "world," he continues, "there may be two views about Beckett but there is no doubt about his significance and standing as a writer. He is not a religious writer in the ordinary sense of the word in that his philosophy, as I understand it, is one of despair but he is concerned with religion in the widest sense in that he was dealing with the meaning and purpose, or purposelessness, of life."[62] This latter point is reiterated in a memo by Lindsay Wellington, the Director, on the following day (30 January): it is clearly the official position on Beckett's writing in general, which is itself perfectly in line with the Third's previous efforts to frame Beckett's texts, examined above. The two reports also agree that the Third should look to the likely reaction of a serious intellectual audience, and not to the popular press, when making their decision. Marriott's memo belligerently pitches the "people whose respect for the intellectual integrity of the Third Programme we value"—and who might disapprove if there were no broadcast—against "the evil minded and pretendingly religious papers like the Sunday Express," likely to come up with a heading such as "the BBC supports blasphemy."[63] He also expresses distaste at being associated with the censorship of the Lord Chamberlain's Office, which is "considered by sensible people to be out of date" and had recently been "brought into public contempt" over the handling of Arthur Miller's play *View from the Bridge*.[64]

In Wellington's memo, another group is singled out for mild disdain: the Roman Catholics. Wellington cites their definition of blasphemy as anything "contumelious towards God," with a view to ridiculing it as rigid and old-fashioned.[65] By contrast, Wellington continues, an "intelligent Church of England Christian" such as Canon Roy McKay (the controversial Head of Religious Broadcasting from 1955 to 1963) did not need to "found himself on any authoritative and precise definition," and felt "the blasphemy is at most technical" and only objectionable in "Victorian" terms.[66]

The whole tenor of the BBC's internal discussion, then, was in favor of this controversial broadcast: yet the final answer was no. The explanation lies in the BBC's own policy, as summarized by Wellington: "I take it for granted that whatever license we give in practice to the Third Programme we do not extend that license to cover infringements of the Corporation's basic policy that it does not broadcast blasphemy, obscenity, or libel."[67] In the end, the word "bastard" with reference to God felt like too much of a provocation. The BBC Chairman, Arthur fforde had the last word, and argued that "in its context, it will cause real offence to a respectable number of intelligent people"—in other words, not just the hostile press, the Catholics and the "Victorians." Could Beckett be persuaded to change it? When a negative answer came back, the project was dropped on 18 March 1958. Yet in 1962, when the idea of performing the play on the Third was taken up again—Beckett having in the meantime made the change—a second consultation with the Chairman (who was on holiday) was not even felt to be necessary for approval. The decision really did boil down to a single word.

***

At least since John Carey's provocative study *The Intellectuals and the Masses* from 1992, a debate has raged about modernism's supposed disdain for "the masses."[68] Carey suggested that a hyper-experimental literary style designed for the few and a construction of the masses as subhuman went together for the modernists; they wrote, he claimed, specifically to exclude and belittle the masses. However, in a review of a later book by Carey, James Wood shrewdly retorted that "it is Carey who has decided that the masses can only understand simple realism; by contrast, it was Modernism that so anxiously desired (and feared) the reading public's comprehension of its new radical techniques."[69] Wood points out that "modern art was partly a rebellion against massification because the masses were believed to incarnate and enforce generalising conformities"; for Friedrich Nietzsche, for instance, the danger was in turning "free spirits" *into* a mass.[70] The modernists, in undermining such conformity, can also be read as wanting to offer its audience something more challenging and ultimately enabling; an approach that can imply respect for ordinary people's intelligence rather than disdain.

The study of the interaction between the Third and modernist writers such as Beckett sheds light on some of the tensions involved in mediating modernism itself to a "mass" audience. We have seen that despite his initial skepticism about broadcasting, and "adaptation" in particular, Beckett was willing to make concessions; while he insisted on his own translation of *Godot* being used, for example, he did not exclude adaptation altogether. Once the medium itself had caught his artistic imagination, he was also willing to provide a radio play that on some level functioned as a pedagogical introduction to his style and thematic concerns, with more orientation points for the listener than he was willing to supply in his contemporary theatrical aesthetic. Beckett would not submit his work to "massification" in the sense of having an alien and commercially digestible style imposed upon his work; but he did clearly wish to reach and communicate with a broad audience. Within these parameters, there was plenty of room for negotiation.

One reason why the collaboration between the Third and Beckett proved so successful is that the parties implicitly agreed on the importance of presenting an existentially challenging, serious and artistically satisfying work to the public. In this light, the fierce negativity, pessimism and anti-Christianity of Beckett's work hardly mattered; as we have seen, the Third could frame these elements as "religious" in a broad sense, and Beckett's stance of not explaining his own work meant that he would never contradict such efforts in public. Clearly, the Third worried over the potentially provocative or pretentious "philosophical or religious allegory" in Beckett from the start—yet the only time this in fact had clear practical consequences for broadcasting his work was over the *Endgame* blasphemy issue in 1958. Fundamentally, then, both Beckett and the BBC arguably shared the assumption that the audience remain "free spirits," capable of deciding for themselves how to respond to existential challenge.

Finally, studying the Third's mediation of modernism can also shed new light on the rather stale dichotomy of intellectual elitism versus "accessibility" that has framed so much of the debate surrounding this cultural institution. It is certainly true, as for instance Marriott's previously quoted memo shows, that the Third's producers cared deeply about the network's "intellectual integrity" and about approval from the "right" set of people. Yet this was just one of many shifting and complex considerations, mostly directed toward furthering the reputation of the Third Programme and the BBC, and preserving it from potential attacks. This explains the striking contrast in attitude toward Beckett as a relatively unknown writer whom the Third would have to take the chance of introducing to an English audience, and Beckett as a playwright of established reputation already successfully introduced. The initial worry over obscurity, pretentious allegory, and translation rights was substituted by serious appreciation of Beckett's craftsmanship and outright wooing. The Third had a *range* of strategies for presenting modernism to its audience, including a partial assimilation to already-popular genres from the Light Programme of the kind suggested by King Bull, the dedicated artistry and devotion to the author's text provided by McWhinnie, and the "framing" effort suggested by Gray's talk. Each of these reveals but one facet of the practical approach of an institution that, remarkably, was engaged for decades in the near-impossible balancing act of effectively mediating modernism to an audience wider than such works had ever before enjoyed, while somehow avoiding its "massification" as well.

Notes

1. Eliot, quoted in Stefan Collini, *Absent Minds: Intellectuals in Britain* (Oxford: Oxford University Press, 2006), 445.
2. Ibid., 445–6.
3. The standard account of religious broadcasting in this period is Asa Briggs, *The History of Broadcasting in the United Kingdom, Volume IV: Sound and Vision* (Oxford: Oxford University Press, 1979), 696–733.
4. See Erik Tonning, "David Jones: Christian Modernism at the BBC," in *Broadcasting in the Modernist Era*, eds. Matthew Feldman et al. (London: Bloomsbury Academic, 2014), 113–34; and, on Eliot, see Todd Avery, *Radio Modernism: Literature, Ethics and the BBC, 1922–1938* (London: Ashgate), 111–36, and Michael Coyle, "'T. S. Eliot on the Air': 'Culture' and the Challenges of Mass Communication," in *T. S. Eliot and Our Turning World*, ed. Jewel Spears Brooker (London: Macmillan, 2001), 141–54. Asa Briggs notes the general admiration for Eliot within the BBC in *The History of Broadcasting in the United Kingdom, Volume IV*, 698 n. 10. One direct personal link for Eliot would have been Eric Fenn, who was Assistant Director in the BBC Religion Department from 1939 to 1945 and later became part of its overseas religious broadcasting operation. Fenn acted as secretary for the elite clandestine Christian intellectual discussion group "The Moot," which, as has recently been argued, can be analyzed as an example of "Christian modernism" in so far as the group aimed for a Neo-Thomist "Christian revolution": see Jonas Kurlberg, "The Moot, the End of Civilisation and the Re-birth of Christendom," in *Modernism, Christianity and Apocalypse*, eds. Erik Tonning et al. (Leiden: Brill, 2015), 222–35.
5. Memo, 24 May 1954, in *SW 53-62*.
6. Memo 17 Mar. 1953, in *SW 53-62*.
7. In *SW 53-62*.
8. Cecil Wilson in the *Daily Mail*, 4 Aug. 1955, quoted in James Knowlson, *Damned to Fame: The Life of Samuel Beckett* (London: Bloomsbury, 1996), 445.

9. Memo, 20 Oct. 1953, in *SW 53-62*.
10. Memo, 3 Feb. 1954, in *SW 53-62*.
11. Report, 15 Apr. 1953, in *SW 53-62*.
12. Ibid.
13. Ibid.
14. Ibid.
15. Report, 15 Apr. 1953, in *SW 53-62*.
16. Ibid.
17. Ibid.
18. Ibid.
19. Knowlson, *Damned to Fame*, 398.
20. See *SW 53-62*.
21. Beckett, *Letters III*, 64.
22. 30 Sep. 1953, in *SW 53-62*.
23. *SW 53-62*.
24. Memo, 20 Sep. 1955, in *SW 53-62*.
25. Memo, in *SW 53-62*.
26. Ibid.
27. Ibid.
28. Ibid.
29. Knowlson, *Damned to Fame*, 417.
30. Ibid.
31. Ibid.
32. One memo by John Morris dated 18 Jun. 1956 stresses the importance of getting an option on the new play "before the rats get at it" (*SW 53-62*).
33. Memo, 21 Jun. 1956, in *SW 53-62*.
34. Memo from Suzanne Poulain, 4 Jul. 1956, in *SW 53-62*.
35. *SW 53-62*; *Letters II*, 632 n.5.
36. Memo, 18 Jul. 1956, in *SW 53-62*.
37. Memo 22 Oct. 1956, in *SW 53-62*. In this memo by Barbara Bray a point is made of paying Beckett the maximum possible fee.
38. Letter to Cecilia Reeves, 4 Jul. 1956, in *SW 53-62*.
39. 4 Jul. 1956, in *SW 53-62*.
40. Memo, 18 Jul. 1956 in *SW 53-62*.
41. 27 Sep. 1956, in *SW 53-62*; *Letters II*, 656.
42. 18 Oct. 1956, in *SW 53-62*; *Letters II*, 656, n. 3.
43. Esslin, *Mediations: Essays on Brecht, Beckett and the Media* (London: Abacus, 1983), 129; quoted in Julie Campbell, "Beckett and the Third Programme," *Samuel Beckett Today/Aujourd'hui* 25 (2013), 113. Campbell's fine piece also taps the BBC Written Archive, and contains much material that supplements my account here, including a review of the Audience Reports commissioned on Beckett broadcasts by the BBC.

44. Beckett to McWhinnie, 5 Dec. 1956, in *SW 53-62*.
45. Beckett, *Letters III*, 12–13.
46. Beckett to Morris, 17 Jan. 1957, in *SW 53-62*.
47. Memo to McWhinnie, 13 Jan. 1957 in *SW 53-62*.
48. Quoted in Knowlson, *Damned to Fame*, 428.
49. G. S. Fraser, "They Also Serve," *Times Literary Supplement*, 10 Feb. 1956, 84.
50. Although the BBC's so-called Reith Sunday (no broadcasts at all until after church hours, and only religious services, serious talks and classical music thereafter) had been abandoned by 1957, there was still a strong emphasis on religious and "serious" broadcasting on Sundays. It is telling therefore that Beckett's play was deemed appropriate for a Sunday slot.
51. My thanks to Matthew Feldman for this point, and for drawing the Gray text to my attention. Gray's talk was published in *The Listener* on 24 Jan. 1957. For more evidence of the BBC's attempts to frame Beckett's work in religious terms, see Stefano Rosignoli's contribution to the present volume.
52. These reviews are quoted from clippings in the BBC archive, filed under *SW 53-62*.
53. Ronald Gray, "Waiting for Godot" (letter to the editor), *The Listener* 57, 7 Feb. 1957, 239.
54. See note 4 above for documentation of "Christian modernism" at the BBC.
55. Thus Fraser on Beckett: "Even at his most nihilistic he will come under Mr Eliot's category of the Christian blasphemer." Quoted in Fraser, "They Also Serve," 84.
56. T. S. Eliot, "Baudelaire," in *Selected Essays* (London: Faber, 1999), 421.
57. Ibid., 427.
58. David Jones, "Religion and the Muses," in *Epoch and Artist* (London: Faber), 95.
59. Ibid., 100.
60. Memo, 29 Jan. 1958, in *SW 53-62*.
61. Ibid.
62. Ibid.
63. Memo, 29 Jan. 1958, in *SW 53-62*.
64. Ibid.
65. Memo, 30 Jan. 1958, in *SW 53-62*.
66. Ibid.
67. Memo, 30 Jan. 1958, in *SW 53-62*.
68. John Carey, *The Intellectuals and the Masses* (London: Faber, 1992).
69. James Wood, "Cold-Shouldered," *London Review of Books*, 8 Mar. 2001, 13.
70. Ibid.

The BBC as "Commissioner" of Beckett's Radio Plays

Pim Verhulst

Despite Martin Esslin's claim that Beckett "was, indeed, never commissioned by the BBC to write anything,"[1] three of his six radio plays—*All That Fall*, *Embers* and *Words and Music*—were written at their instigation. If it had not been for the British Broadcasting Corporation (BBC), Beckett might never have written for the medium at all, so it is impossible to overstate the importance of "the beeb" for his radiophonic output. While Esslin is right to emphasize that "[t]he real story of the genesis of these radio plays is far more complex and interesting,"[2] to say that Beckett never was "commissioned" in the official sense of the word is somewhat misleading. Not only did he allow himself to be engaged in this official sense at one point in his career, his own use of the term also reflects his changing relationship with the BBC throughout the late 1950s, the early 1960s and the mid-1970s, when his last script was aired.

This chapter investigates the role of the BBC as a "commissioner" of Beckett's radio plays, supplementing Esslin's canonized insider's account as a BBC employee, based on his own experience and his selection of material from the WAC, with a scholarly perspective that draws on the "grey canon" of Beckett's "letters, notebooks, manuscripts and

---

P. Verhulst (✉)
Department of English Literature, University of Antwerp, Antwerp, Belgium

the like."[3] By relating the WAC to other archival collections, such as Beckett's correspondence with former BBC Script Editor Barbara Bray held at Trinity College, Dublin, and the drafts of his radio plays in holding libraries worldwide, the multifaceted relationship between Beckett and the BBC as a "commissioner" of his radio scripts can finally be outlined in its full complexity.

THE 1950S

Beckett's initial contacts with the BBC between 1953 and 1955—over *En attendant Godot* and his English self-translation of the play as *Waiting for Godot*—were not exactly smooth, as Erik Tonning ("Mediating Modernism: The Third Programme, Samuel Beckett, and Mass Communication") and Dirk Van Hulle ("The BBC and Beckett's Non-radiogenic Plays in the 1950s") have shown in this volume. Nevertheless, a year later, Controller John Morris, with the help of BBC Paris Representative Cecilia Reeves, managed to interest Beckett in writing an original script for them, which became *All That Fall*. The genesis of Beckett's first radio play is a story often told already, so there is no need to dwell on it here, but his readiness to oblige was surprising given the BBC's recent—and somewhat discourteous—rejection of *Godot*. This, however, did not mean that Beckett was willing to let himself be "commissioned" as well. In the report of his Paris visit, John Morris referred to Beckett's "output" as "unpredictable": "sometimes he works slowly, at others very fast, but he does not wish to be tied down to any definite date but says he will keep in touch and let me have the script as soon as it is finished."[4] Whereas Morris refused to commit himself to *Godot* in 1953, and even requested permission to translate and adapt the play for radio without prior commitment,[5] it was now the BBC who tried to commit Beckett, and he who decided the terms. Even though the word "commission" is not mentioned in the memo, Morris is likely to have brought it up with Beckett, as "throughout the 1950s the Third Programme was desperately searching for more talent" and commissioning authors was one way of securing it.[6] Beckett, too, was careful to avoid the official term in his letters. Instead, he had been "asked" or "invited," leaving him free to opt out. Despite the BBC's elaborate pampering, in an attempt to make up for their mistake with *Godot*, Beckett's attitude would remain largely the same throughout the 1950s. But his developing friendships with Donald McWhinnie and Barbara Bray were beginning to challenge his artistic freedom, of which *Embers* is the best example.

EMBERS

In the same letter acknowledging the safe arrival of Beckett's *All That Fall* script at the BBC, on 5 October 1956—well before the radio play was put into production and broadcast on 13 January 1957—John Morris already expressed the firm hope that "this is only the beginning and that you will be interested to do some more for us."[7] A month later (16 November 1956) Morris repeated his request, which was not to be the last time: "I need hardly to tell you that I shall be delighted if you will do some more for us, and I hope you will let me know as soon as you have an idea for another piece for the Third Programme."[8] Morris had an idea of his own, recalling the author's passion for the sport, and pitched "a sort of cricketing Godot."[9] But Beckett suggested "something else for the Third Programme, possibly with my cousin John."[10] This was the seed of *Words and Music*, but it would not be written until 1961.

For the time being, all Beckett could offer were passages from *Molloy* and *From an Abandoned Work* with musical intermezzos, an experiment soon repeated for *Malone Dies* and *The Unnamable*.[11] The benefit was mutual: while the BBC continued to exploit Beckett's name and fame, he bought himself time to write a new script. The first real breakthrough occurred when he could at last hear *All That Fall* clearly, unhindered by static and other kinds of distortion. On Tuesday 19 February 1957, Donald McWhinnie visited Paris again, to listen with the author to a tape of the radio play at the BBC Studios in the Avenue Hoche, and evaluate the production together. While Beckett was on the whole pleased with the result, McWhinnie's report mentions that "he could improve on the text and is anxious to achieve a tighter and more integrated script next time."[12] The experience gave him a better idea of *All That Fall*'s shortcomings as a radio play, but it did not spark any concrete ideas for his next script. This changed shortly after McWhinnie's third visit to Paris, in late November 1957, to discuss the readings of his prose by Patrick Magee. Clas Zilliacus has argued that "Beckett's efforts to write another text specially for broadcasting grew directly out of his enthusiasm for the productions based on the trilogy."[13] But he actually started writing *Embers* before any of these prose fragments had been broadcast by the Third (*Molloy* on 10 December and *From an Abandoned Work* on 14 December 1957).

Some two weeks earlier, on 2 December 1957, Beckett told Barney Rosset he had taken a week off from his translation of *L'Innommable* to try and finish a new radio script.[14] So, the concept of *Embers* seems to have developed from *The Unnamable*, with the Magee readings fulfilling a more catalytic function. As Dirk Van Hulle and Shane Weller duly observe, "[i]t is perhaps no coincidence that Beckett should have written his first two *radio* plays during the period in which he was struggling to translate *L'Innommable*, a work in which 'c'est entièrement une question de voix, tout autre métaphore est impropre' ('it's entirely a matter of voices, no other metaphor is appropriate')."[15] Having also notified McWhinnie about a possible new script in December 1957, the producer tried, ever so gently, to formally enlist Beckett's services again: "If 'Molloy' has stimulated you to any thoughts of possible radio expression, I need hardly say that nothing would please us more than to commission you to do something for us, but the thought may be a terrible bore."[16] Beckett replied in the negative on 13 January 1958, quoting Bartleby, the Scrivener: "There is no need to commission me and I prefer not. What I have been trying to write is with thought of you and Magee and the Third."[17] Yet another week later, he logged the failure of *Embers* in an exceptional note halfway through the second notebook of *The Unnamable* and returned to the translation: "Reprise 21.1.58 après échec de Henry et Ada" ("Taken up again 21.1.58 after failure of Henry and Ada").[18]

At this point, circumstantial evidence suggests that Beckett had managed to compose a partial holograph of *Embers* in a notebook held at the Harvard Theatre Collection,[19] and a more advanced typescript held at the Harry Ransom Humanities Research Center,[20] yet still missing the two Addie lessons with her music and riding masters. On 15 February 1958, Beckett assured McWhinnie he would soon "return to the radio text and see if there is anything to be saved from that wreck," but first *L'Innommable* needed to be translated.[21] He promised the same to John Morris, with whom he had a late-February lunch in Paris,[22] and to Barbara Bray on 6 July 1958,[23] but his interest in *Embers* would not be rekindled for another four months. It seems that McWhinnie, who was directing *Krapp's Last Tape* at the Royal Court Theatre in London, again played an important role. Beckett attended rehearsals in early November.[24] To Ethna McCarthy he wrote that it was very exciting to work with McWhinnie and Magee, and that he wanted no other director in the future.[25] The prospect of extending the successful collaboration to *Embers* may have persuaded Beckett to give the "aborted" typescript of his radio play to the BBC producer, as he wrote to Barney Rosset on 23 November 1958.[26]

Six days later, on 29 November 1958, revision of the piece began when Beckett told Barbara Bray he would "change a few words and try to rewrite the Addie lessons."[27] A long correspondence followed about textual details—yielding two more typescripts,[28] as well as the final title of the radio play, which changed from "Ebb" to *Embers* after almost a dozen alternatives had been rejected. Beckett sent Bray the supposedly final version of the script on 2 March 1959,[29] but he was still making changes in mid-June, when he saw McWhinnie in Paris to prepare the recording.[30] In addition to late textual changes, like the addition of "Little book" at the end,[31] the final typescript of the radio play at The University of Reading has over 50 annotations in blue ink.[32] They mostly consist of expanded directions, never included in any publication of the text, for example that the sea should sound very stylized or that certain effects, like the hooves and the dripping, should be cut short. Some words are to be stressed in pronunciation, even spoken with relish, and Beckett distinguishes between a dialogue and a monologue tone in Henry's lines. The most striking textual change is the expansion of Ada's contractions, so that "they're" and "I'm" become "they are" and "I am," making her sound even more lifeless.

All pointers were followed in the BBC recording, broadcast on 24 June 1959, but in spite of these minute preparations, Beckett felt the result did not "come off." The reason was not the performance or the production, he confessed to Alan Schneider, but the text being "too difficult."[33] As early as 29 November 1958, Beckett had openly questioned the merits of his second radio play, writing to Barbara Bray: "It was really less much less for the Drama Department than for you and Donald personally to have your opinion on the Bolton-Holloway experiment. It is a very aborted and unsatisfactory text and I'd be just as glad if you never did it. But you may if you wish."[34] At the start of the new year, after some revision on the script, he was still not feeling confident about its broadcastability.[35] Nevertheless, by 13 February copyright had been cleared.[36] This not only shows the persistence of Bray and McWhinnie, but also the personal level to which Beckett had become involved with the BBC. He was no longer writing for a faceless corporation, but for a small group of close friends who were very difficult to refuse. Unfortunately, the fervor of McWhinnie and Bray was not shared by their colleagues.

According to Kate Whitehead, they "had great difficulty in persuading Gielgud and Third Programme planners to accept *Embers*."[37] There is no direct evidence of this in the WAC, but the fact that the broadcast was censored reveals the growing internal disagreement over Beckett's work and may have been a necessary compromise.[38] Even though *Embers* was entered for the Prix Italia competition—and won the less prestigious RAI prize instead[39]—the corporation-wide support for *All That Fall*, reflected by the plethora of congratulatory memos exchanged among staff around the time of its premiere, had all but diminished by the end of the 1950s, which was also, as we shall see, a sign of the times.

THE 1960S

In April 1957, John Morris asked Beckett—through Donald McWhinnie—if there was any chance of getting a new script from him to "open the new style Third Programme for October."[40] This was in fact a corporate euphemism. *All That Fall* had come at a propitious time, crowning the first ten years of the network, but in 1957 the Third was facing severe cutbacks in broadcasting time and budget, due to a "disproportionate spending on programmes that appealed to such a small minority."[41] Beckett knew about the situation and hoped, in his letter to Bray of 29 May 1957, that the reorganization was not too depressing for her and her colleagues.[42] One result of the network's restyling was a curbing of its freedom, as audience considerations now started to affect planning more deeply than it had before. A particularly knotty issue, according to an anonymous memo from early 1958, was "the general balance of programmes & the comment that we are doing too many gloomy plays in the minds of those concerned."[43] The remark pertains to *Endgame*, but Beckett's name in general was associated with this label among BBC staff. In just a few years' time, he had thus evolved from liability to attraction and back again, because of a changing context.

Another younger writer "too close in style and feeling to Beckett" was Harold Pinter, but McWhinnie—who made the remark—meant it as "a compliment."[44] He soon produced two of his scripts on the Third: *A Slight Ache* (29 July 1959) and *A Night Out* (25 February 1960). Working with Pinter in radio was so encouraging that McWhinnie agreed to direct his new stage play *The Caretaker* and even "left the BBC to work full time in the theatre."[45] His decision may also have been influenced by the difficult relationship between editors and producers on the one hand, and the Head of Drama on the other, who was "seen as extremely conservative and opposed to most forms of experiment."[46] The situation reached a low point with Pinter's third commissioned script, *The Dwarfs*, a radio adaptation from an unpublished novel. All staff members consulted were in favor of production, except Val Gielgud, who "expressed doubts about it" and dismissed the script as "incomprehensible."[47] In a desperate attempt to stifle peer pressure, Gielgud stubbornly maintained that *The Dwarfs* could only be effectively produced by Donald McWhinnie—who had left the BBC. When plans were made to bring him back at the Third's expense, Gielgud again boycotted the affair by unexpectedly putting Barbara Bray in charge of the production.[48] Being thus reduced to a pawn in a tactical power play must have been very unpleasant for Bray. She complained about it to Beckett, who responded sympathetically on 16 October 1960:

> I am so sorry to hear about all this office unpleasantness and hope by now you are feeling less upset. I suppose he is in a hurry to impose his taste on 3rd Drama, which will be unpleasant for Michael and others .... What do you expect of a man who was obviously always against what you & Donald were doing? Expressions of appreciation?[49]

Like McWhinnie, Bray soon left the BBC, to pursue a career as freelance translator-critic in Paris.

In Third Programme policy, Whitehead explains, "the importance of personal contact was stressed owing to the universal feeling amongst young writers that the BBC was a large organisation which was difficult to approach."[50] The efforts of both Cecilia Reeves and John Morris, but especially Donald McWhinnie and Barbara Bray, had indeed served to "cement" the relationship with Beckett, a term used by McWhinnie in his memo of 4 February 1957.[51] By the end of the 1950s, his communication with the BBC increasingly went through their private correspondence. But now that Beckett's two intimate contacts were seeking creative fulfillment elsewhere, the personal approach had become a potential threat. Beckett doubted if the Third would survive such a loss of talent, and even spoke of its probable end to Robert Pinget, who noted the remark in his unpublished memoir "Notre ami Sam."[52] His relationship with the BBC had come under stress at this time, but a first important provider of continuity was the Third's new Controller, P. H. Newby, who replaced John Morris at the end of 1958.

Newby was a broad-minded intellectual, without a university degree, who also wrote successful novels in his spare time. When he took up his post, Carpenter notes, Newby found the staff members "in a state of shock from the cuts, feeling that the BBC had no confidence in them."[53] He realized that it was necessary to "build up morale" and part of his plan was to encourage producers, who "tended to regard the Controller and his deputy as abominable no-men dedicated to turning down imaginative programme ideas," to come up with "suggestions and criticisms of all kinds."⁵⁴ Beckett agreed to meet Newby but he thought he "should know something of his novels beforehand," so Bray sent him *The Picnic at Sakkara* (1955) in April 1959.⁵⁵ While their first encounter did not take place until a year later, as Beckett's letter to Bray of 28 April 1960 reveals,⁵⁶ he seems to have liked Newby as much as John Morris.

Still more important for the continuation of Beckett's relationship with the BBC was the succession of Donald McWhinnie by Martin Esslin as Assistant Head of Drama (Sound). Esslin was a theater scholar who had written a book on Brecht and much admired Beckett as a proponent of what he would later call *The Theatre of the Absurd* (1961). They met for a few beers in late December 1960, Beckett telling Bray that Esslin was a pleasant and imaginative fellow, who nevertheless seemed nervous and troubled about succeeding McWhinnie in the wake of all the internal fuss at the Third.⁵⁷ When Esslin finally replaced Gielgud as the Head of Drama in 1963, appointing sound producer Michael Bakewell as his deputy, "radio drama took a big leap" at the Third Programme.⁵⁸ Apart from drawing new and young talent to the medium, Esslin was also "able to build on the work that had been done by McWhinnie and Bakewell, to which Gielgud hadn't been particularly sympathetic."⁵⁹ Beckett received the news with enthusiasm in a letter to Bray: "Glad to hear about Esslin, shall congratulate some time I suppose. Had a card signed by him, Michael & Newby."⁶⁰ This triumvirate had now become the driving force behind Beckett's work at the BBC, but Barbara Bray continued to play a crucial role as freelance outsider.

Words and Music

Even though Beckett did not expect Bray to do any more hard work for the Third, as he told her on 14 December 1960,⁶¹ she managed to recruit him for a new radio script. "In principle, yes, for something with John," he assured her on 12 November 1960, "if he is interested."⁶² Another condition that Beckett stipulated in this letter, was that the BBC should stop pushing him and not expect anything until the next year.⁶³ When he temporarily abandoned radio and theater in December 1958, to start working on *Comment c'est*, he hoped to "get back to that society game in about a year," as he wrote to Alan Schneider on 6 September 1959.⁶⁴ This estimate turned out to be accurate for his stage work, with *Happy Days* taking shape over the course of 1960, yet Beckett did not return to radio with quite the same eagerness. He was persuaded rather than drawn back to the medium. Throughout the 1950s, writing had been difficult, so that in the early 1960s he would much rather develop new ideas he was starting to get for plays like *Happy Days* or *Play*, as well as focus on translating *Comment c'est* into English. By agreeing to write for radio again, it seems that he was mostly indulging family and friends whose work he admired and wanted to support.

It is unclear whether it was Bray or Newby who revived the idea, but the BBC had not forgotten Beckett's promise to collaborate with his cousin on a new radio play for words and music in late 1956. Even though he had discussed the project with John, Beckett had at that time offered fragments of prose instead. But four years later, on 17 November 1960, he suggested to Bray that perhaps their original plans might be revived.[65] The letter does not specify any further details, but on 28 November 1960 Beckett told Robert Pinget that John had intended to build up the piece around a man and woman coughing. It came to nothing because the transition from words to music was difficult to imagine.[66] While Beckett still had "[n]o ideas" in early December,[67] having met Esslin in Paris the next month, he found a way to solve the problem with the original concept. As he explained to Pinget, two tyrants would command Words and Music to speak and hush, so that the passage from one to the other would not be arbitrary.[68] He began a difficult letter about the subject to John Beckett on 12 February 1961, but he did not finish it.[69] Instead, it was easier to just start drafting the script.[70] This early fragment is dated 15 February 1961 and it consists of only two folios removed from an exercise book. An Usher talks to Words and Music, announcing the arrival of their Master, but the draft breaks off before he arrives.[71] At this point, Beckett got no further than two brief notes in the "Eté 56" notebook, entered on 16 February 1961, under the working title "Words Music."[72]

Despite this failure, Beckett finished the letter to his cousin and told him he could go and have them "commissioned" by the BBC if John wished to.[73] One reason why he allowed himself to be engaged in such an official sense might be that the collaboration was intended to further John Beckett's musical career, rather than satisfy a creative need of his own. And because in early March "John, driving back home in a Mini from an evening playing Haydn string quartets with friends, had hit a wall about 4 a.m. in Little Bray breaking his arms and badly damaging his hip and his ankle,"[74] he could use all the extra support to get back on his feet creatively. After five months of convalescence, John wrote about the projected date for the completion of the program to Martin Esslin, who answered on 14 August 1961: "There certainly is no urgency in the sense that we don't want to hurry you unduly. On the other hand we are so eager and anxious to broadcast this work that we would, of course, be glad to have it as soon as it is at all possible."[75] This revived the project, and by 27 November Beckett had finished a first complete draft. Two days later, he showed the typescript to Bray, dispatching a copy to his cousin soon afterward.[76] John confirmed on 9 December 1961 that he would like to take it on, and Beckett officially "submitted" the script to Esslin, hoping it might be "acceptable" to the Corporation as well.[77]

There being an almost entirely new team at the Third Programme also explains why the relationship lost a personal touch and briefly slipped back into formality at this point. As the "new Beckett" did the rounds among staff, Michael Bakewell found it "delightful," Val Gielgud raised "no objection" and Esslin wrote "Agreed" at the bottom of the memo, when he returned to the office on "21/12."[78] The next day, he informed Beckett that the radio play "has now been accepted by all concerned,"[79] after which he instructed copyright department to "commission both Samuel Beckett and John Beckett officially."[80] However, it should also be noted that Esslin took immediate care to drop the officialdom: "Having got the official part off my chest, may I thank you for the wonderful lunch last Sunday and may I wish you and your wife a very Happy New Year."[81] He also championed Beckett internally with the same intensity and dedication as Bray and McWhinnie had before him, for example, when budgetary concerns were raised. By the end of February 1962, John Beckett had finished his music so that production plans could be made. "The number of instrumentalists we would use would be twelve" for "approximately thirteen minutes' worth of music," Michael Bakewell wrote in his memo of 19 June 1962, appending a "list of projected costs."[82] When Geoffrey Manuel, an Organizer of Production Facilities, remarked that "studio time + XP requirements do appear rather disproportionate," for a "final product that is 15" duration,"[83] Esslin stressed not only the script's literary and technical, but also its institutional importance:

> This is an extremely difficult operation, as the play (which is not 15′ but 30′ duration) is one of the most intricate merges of sound and music we have ever undertaken. Moreover this is supposed to be our prestige production in the Fortieth Anniversary Week, and in view of these circumstances, I think the booking is fully justified.[84]

Even though Beckett had found new support at the BBC, and his work was accorded prime importance again, he would never labor as closely on his scripts with Esslin as with McWhinnie. In fact, he left the production of *Words and Music* almost entirely in the hands of his cousin. John wrote his music independently of Beckett, who did not see the score until early October, when it had already been recorded together with Patrick Magee's parts.[85] John supervised the entire proceedings and he even let Magee re-record the songs because he had supposedly "sung too well."[86] It was not before 18 October 1962 that Beckett heard a first playback of the production in London, telling Bray it needed more editing.[87] After conferring with John, Esslin and producer Michael Bakewell, he approved a playback of the final cut on 30 October 1962, again informing Bray.[88] The adjustments Beckett made were minor, just two weeks before the broadcasting premiere on 13 November 1962. Bray was therefore right to complain in *The Critics* broadcast review of *Words and Music* on 9 December 1962: "it's rather ... a pity that the author himself couldn't have been ... more involved in the actual production."[89] He had written four days prior to the talk, merely wishing Bray good luck.[90]

Cascando

Like *Words and Music*, Beckett would refer to *Cascando* in his letters as a "commission," yet not one proposed by the BBC. He wrote the piece mostly to "please Chip,"[91] the nickname of Romanian-French composer Marcel Mihalovici, who had been asked by French RTF radio in late 1961 for a music-based radio script. Given the success of their recent collaboration on the *Krapp* opera,[92] he chose Beckett to write the text. He had completed his part by the end of January 1962 and posted the final typescript to *Minuit*.[93]

Remarkably, Beckett also forwarded a copy of the French text to P. H. Newby and his colleagues at the BBC on 1 June 1962.[94] Because the original letter bears the date "1.6.52," Esslin makes a strange assumption in his 1980 survey: "Clearly this was not the radio play of that title, but the poem. Mr. Newby assumes that he had heard about Beckett's poetry from someone familiar with the Paris scene. Nothing seems to have come of this first contact."[95] However, John Jordan, the WAC assistant who cataloged these BBC files in 1987, noticed it was an error and added a separate note. According to him, "it seems likely, from the content of both this letter & the rest of the file, that the correct date is 1.6.62."[96] Since the file also includes a French script of the radio play *Cascando*, and an anonymous note at the bottom of the memo states that a copy of the letter was forwarded "with text," there seems to be little doubt that it was indeed a case of misdating.

Esslin was positive about the script in his memo to Bakewell of 3 July 1962: "Vintage Beckett, but very difficult to understand for those who are unfamiliar with the basic Beckett situation. Yet, if at all feasible with the music, we ought to do it!"[97] For the time being, they were preoccupied with the recording of *Words and Music*, and Mihalovici would not finish his score until late in December. Also, Beckett had not yet translated *Cascando* into English, which took him almost a year and no less than five typescript versions. He sent the final text to Faber on 11 July 1963,[98] and a week later his London agent Rosica Colin approached the BBC about production details—Beckett having advised her the radio play had already been recorded.[99] When she learned that the BBC did not even have an English copy of the script, Colin attached a photostat to her letter of 22 July 1963.[100] The BBC also lacked Mihalovici's score, so a projected timing of "30' min approx" is all Bakewell could supply when he asked Peggy Wells to clear copyright for *Cascando* with Curtis Brown.[101]

Beckett had closely supervised the RTF recording of *Cascando* in Paris, but because it had been "[d]isastrous"[102] he urged the BBC to model their production on the German SDR version instead. A tape of the recording was dispatched from Stuttgart to London and Beckett listened to it at the BBC studios on 25 January 1964, along with Esslin and Bakewell, liking it "much better than French."[103] Esslin told Beckett that he had "invited Donald to produce Cascando and that he will—with inevitable Jack and Pat"[104]—who Beckett himself suggested for the roles of Opener and Voice, but the plans were changed when it was too late for him to do anything about it. On 30 September 1964, Esslin wrote:

> As it turned out Jack MacGowran was not available so Denys Hawthorne did the Opener, I think very well indeed. I listened to the recording yesterday and I found it very moving indeed. Donald has done an excellent job. It is much more subdued, less theatrical, than the German production, but the two voices are much more clearly differentiated. Pat Magee's performance, as always, was very good indeed.[105]

The comment suggests that Beckett had given a few pointers when he listened to the German version at the BBC studios but, as opposed to the RTF production, he was not present during rehearsals or recording sessions, and his opinion of the British version is not known either—if he ever heard it.

In his letter to Bray of 2 October 1964, Beckett seems to be considering another BBC commission, this time for a collaboration with both his cousins, John and Edward—a flute player—but he changed his mind, thinking it might be too soon for the youngest.[106] Instead, Beckett turned his attention to drama and prose in the following years, shifting his interest in broadcasting away from radio to television with *Eh Joe* (1965).

THE 1970s

Even though Beckett would not write any more radio plays in the 1960s, he did allow some of his other works to be broadcast by the BBC. The 1966 production of *Play* is an example,[107] but also the prose experiment *Lessness* in 1971—which Paul Stewart studies at length in this volume. That Beckett was involved in the adaptation process of both texts shows that he had not entirely lost interest in radio at this time. Two years later, the BBC could even persuade him to finish an older abandoned script for the medium.

"ALL BUT I"

During the 1970s, Beckett gave Jérôme Lindon two unpublished radio scripts for inclusion in his journal *Minuit*. The first to appear was *Esquisse radiophonique*, in issue five (September 1973). As the title indicates, it was an incomplete sketch, in fact a preliminary of *Cascando*, missing all the speech parts for the character called Voix. It was never recorded in Beckett's lifetime, but according to Esslin there were plans to do so at one point:

> When the play was first published, the composer Humphrey Searle, who was eager to write the musical part, suggested to the BBC that we should ask Beckett to translate it into English and to complete it. At first Beckett agreed as he was interested in collaborating with Searle; but after some months he informed me that he felt unable to proceed.[108]

The WAC does not hold a single document about these plans, but the surviving draft material at Boston College reveals just how seriously Beckett took the suggestion. The Burns Library holds six versions of the script—a manuscript and a typescript of the translated framework; two manuscripts and two typescripts of the English speech parts meant to fill it in.[109] Only the manuscripts of the speech parts are dated: 31 August and 1 September 1973. The fact that one of them precedes the first publication of the script in Lindon's journal casts doubt on Esslin's reconstruction of events.

A corrected set of *Minuit* proofs for *Esquisse radiophonique* in the papers of Barbara Bray suggests that she provided the BBC with an advance copy of the radio play.[110] Bray had brought Searle and Beckett together before, when Michael Bakewell tried to interest them in collaborating on a television opera in 1965. The composer refers to the meeting in *Quadrille with a Raven* (1982), his unpublished memoirs:

> She sent me a message that he would like to meet me and he came round to our hotel, which was not far from his own apartment in Montparnasse. Both he and I are rather shy and it was left to Fiona to carry on an animated monologue; in the end Beckett asked us both to have dinner with him at his favourite restaurant in the area, and we had a most amusing evening. It turned out that he had no ideas for further theatrical work.[111]

In his letter of 19 September 1965 to Patrick Magee, Beckett also mentioned his "dinner last night with the Searles," calling the evening "[v]ery enjoyable."[112] Bray may have sensed a second chance at collaboration when *Esquisse radiophonique* appeared in 1973, as well as a good opportunity to ask Beckett for a "new" radio play.

He had even thought of a new title for the expanded script. It is referred to as "all but I" and "all but one" in letters to Bray from Morocco dated 12 and 30 September 1973.[113] These variant wordings are interesting because they emphasize the central idea of the speech parts. The voice is able to remember all the family and friends it once knew, even house personnel like the maid or the gardener, as if moving through a mental portrait gallery. It can recall the marble white faces of the mother and the grandmother in detail, but one by one they start to disappear, leaving blank spaces behind. One face resists retrieval, and the voice cannot be free until it is conjured up. As the variants "I" and "one" in the title indicate, it is the absent face of the voice itself—that is, the I—which makes self-recollection impossible, even though it is the same self that enables remembrance of all the others.

In fact, all Beckett needed to do at this point was merge the last typescript of the framework with the last typescript of the speech parts into one composite document—but he never did so. Instead, he had a slightly revised translation of the French version appear in *Ends and Odds* (1976/1977), thus maintaining the illusion that the radio sketch had always remained unfinished. Esslin suggested "the play might nevertheless be produced without a text for the voice because it might be possible to treat it as no more than a faint mumbled murmur. But Beckett did not find this suggestion acceptable,"[114] and he also declined later requests.

ROUGH FOR RADIO

Yet the BBC did not relent. In addition to the thirtieth anniversary of the Third Programme—rechristened Radio 3 in 1970—the year 1976 also marked Beckett's seventieth birthday, and Esslin planned repeats of *Embers* and Jack MacGowran reading selected poems to honor both occasions together. When he heard that Beckett had just translated a second unknown radio script for Faber, published for the first time in *Minuit* 16 (November 1975) as *Pochade radiophonique*, he seized the opportunity to cap the celebratory broadcasts with a new piece. The sketch was dubbed *Radio II* in *Ends and Odds* but since "the BBC's four national radio networks are labelled Radios 1, 2, 3 and 4, it would clearly have been very confusing if Radio 3 ... had transmitted a play called *Radio II*."[115] As such, the title had to change and Beckett offered "Sketch for Radio" or "Rough for Radio" in his letter of 19 January 1976, with Esslin settling on the latter.[116]

Because the script was titled as a rough sketch, Esslin seized this opportunity to make a few suggestions for production. His first idea was to replace "Animator" with "Producer" to stress the radiophonic nature of the script, as he explains in his survey:

> In the *pochade* the Animator with his ruler and stenographer and additional acolyte reproduces the team of producer, secretary, and technician which Beckett must have encountered in his contacts with production teams at the BBC or the French radio. (In French *animateur* is a term used for a radio or television producer).[117]

Beckett was sorry to see "Animator" go, given his role in the team, and offered "Operator" as a compromise in his reply of 19 January 1976.[118] Esslin kept the original name but proposed more amendments in his letter of 9 February 1976. Wondering "what degree of reality to give to the action," he asked if Dick should make additional sounds, and whether the swish of the bull's pizzle should be stylized with a "shatter echo."

Also, "to give the piece an acoustic frame," Esslin suggested Fox be taken out of a metal cupboard prior to interrogation, and put back in afterward.[119] On 13 February, Beckett answered that Dick should only make sound when getting ready to strike, even if he need not. The shatter echo was unnecessary, but three different effects were required for the swish: no impact, on hard surface, and on flesh. He did not like the idea of the cupboard either, but suggested to have the party assemble before the animation chamber, followed by the sound of their entering, their settling down and Animator clearing his throat.[120] Encouraged by this suggestion, Esslin ventured to make a last enquiry on 17 February 1976: "Would this, for symmetry's sake, want a parallel movement of their leaving the room with the door closing?"[121] Beckett refused this sense of closure in his letter two days later, stating that the team should not leave.[122]

These wishes were largely respected, but Esslin added several other effects that were not discussed or pre-authorized, mostly to increase the "realism" of the script, like a popping sound when the plugs are removed from Fox's ears. Because of these liberties, and Beckett's remote involvement in the preparations, it was "with some trepidation" that Esslin sent him a tape of *Rough for Radio* on 3 March 1976—recorded in stereo to enhance the claustrophobic atmosphere.[123] Beckett's reaction of 15 March is missing from the WAC, but Esslin's reply of 18 March makes clear that he thought the result "did not come off,"[124] despite an all-star cast worthy of the occasion, with Harold Pinter (Animator), Billie Whitelaw (Stenographer) and Patrick Magee (Fox). According to Esslin's account, one crucial mistake was that "the production, which made the Animator and his team start briskly and become more weary and discouraged as time went on, should already have started at a high degree of weariness and despair."[125] This, however, is not clearly stated in the script and Beckett never brought it up in his letters either. Not only does it affirm the roughness of the radio play, but also Beckett's diminished interest in the medium at this late stage in his career. It seems that he was merely doing the BBC a polite favor with his pointers from a distance, as a gesture for their long-standing support of his work.

Rough for Radio, aired on Beckett's birthday (13 April), was an apt commemorative broadcast because, more than a "commissioner," the BBC had served as an "animator" for his writing over the previous 20 years, especially—but not exclusively, as some of the other chapters in this volume have shown – in radio. As with Fox, the pressure to be "inspired"[126] at times became too much for Beckett, especially as he got personally involved with the BBC toward the end of the 1950s, through his close friendship with McWhinnie and Bray. In fact, the original *Pochade radiophonique* may have been written in this period. While it is usually dated in the early 1960s, 1958 might perhaps be a more suitable context.[127]

In the year 1958, the strain of the commissioning process reached a peak for Beckett. Having been asked to write a half-hour libretto for Mihalovici, he complained to Thomas MacGreevy on 21 April that all commissions had a paralyzing effect on him.[128] Anxious for a new play, Rosset and Schneider were also conspiring to get Beckett to "write the next one in English," because "if the BBC can commission you, so can we," they said.[129] Beckett answered that he could not write to commission, had refused to do so for the BBC, and just promised to do his best. But he also admitted: "I feel the old tug to write in French again, where control is easier for me and probably excessive."[130] A few months earlier, Beckett had ascribed the failure of *Embers* to an infuriating "lack of brakes" in his English writing, as he told Barney Rosset on 26 December 1957.[131] Still being fascinated by the medium at the time, but unable to achieve a satisfactory result in his mother tongue, writing a radio play in French may have seemed like the only possible solution. The fact that Beckett let himself be coaxed by McWhinnie and Bray into allowing *Embers*—a script he dismissed as aborted and failed—to be broadcast nevertheless, may also explain why *Pochade radiophonique* is absent from Beckett's letters—even his personal correspondence with the two former BBC employees—except perhaps in the vaguest of terms. "A Personage for next time says nothing—just howls from time to time" he wrote to Bray on 17 November 1958, a month before starting on *Comment c'est*.[132] While this may be a sign that the prose text was already on his mind, it can also be read as a covert reference to *Pochade radiophonique*, with which Beckett could continue to explore the radio medium at ease, without the pressure of commitment—"promised" or "commissioned."

Therefore, the final conclusion of the BBC's role as commissioner of Beckett's radio plays, spanning a period of precisely 20 years, is quite remarkable. In 1976, after their failed attempt to "commission" Beckett one last time to complete a script he had discarded in 1961—yet allowed to be published unfinished in 1973—all he could provide was his only radio play never commissioned by anyone, originally written in French, but resulting directly from the BBC's request to write something radiophonic in 1956.

Notes

1. Martin Esslin, *Mediations: Essays on Brecht, Beckett and the Media* (London: Eyre Methuen, 1980), 125.
2. Ibid., 125.
3. S.E. Gontarski, "Greying the Canon: Beckett in Performance," in *Beckett after Beckett*, eds. S. E. Gontarski and Anthony Uhlmann (Gainesville: University Press of Florida, 2006), 143.
4. Letter from John Morris to the Head of Drama Val Gielgud, dated 18 Jul. 1956 in *SW 53-62*.
5. Memo by Donald McWhinnie, dated 15 May 1953 in *SW 53-62*.
6. Kate Whitehead, *The Third Programme: A Literary History* (Oxford: Clarendon, 1989), 86.
7. See *SW 53-62*.
8. Ibid.
9. Ibid.
10. Samuel Beckett in a letter to John Morris, dated 16 Nov. 1956. Quoted in Beckett, *Letters II*, 675.
11. For a detailed discussion of these broadcasts see Matthew Feldman, "Beckett's Trilogy on the Third Programme," in "Revisiting *Molloy, Malone meurt / Malone Dies* and *L'Innommable / The Unnamable*," *Samuel Beckett Today / Aujourd'hui* 26, eds. David Tucker et al. (Amsterdam: Brill, 2014), 41–62.
12. Memo by Donald McWhinnie, dated 21 Feb. 1957, in *SW 53-62*.
13. Clas Zilliacus, *Beckett and Broadcasting: A Study of the Works of Samuel Beckett for and in Radio and Television* (Åbo: Åbo Akademi, 1976), 149.
14. Quoted in Dirk Van Hulle, *The Making of Samuel Beckett's* Krapp's Last Tape / La Dernière Bande. (London and Brussels: Bloomsbury and University Press Antwerp, 2015), 138.
15. Dirk Van Hulle and Shane Weller, *The Making of Samuel Beckett's* L'Innommable / The Unnamable (London and Brussels: Bloomsbury and University Press Antwerp, 2014), 185.
16. Donald McWhinnie in a letter to Samuel Beckett, dated 31 Dec. 1957, in *SW 53-62*.
17. Beckett, *Letters III*, 98.
18. Quoted and translated in Van Hulle and Weller, *The Making of Beckett's* L'Innommable, 185.
19. Harvard University, Theatre Collection, mss Thr 70.3. For a brief discussion of this notebook see Garry Sandison, "Beckett's *Embers* and the Modernist Ovid: A Tiresian Poetic?" *Journal of Beckett Studies* 22.2 (2013), 180–200.

20. University of Texas at Austin, Harry Ransom Research Center, Samuel Beckett Collection, TXRC00-A1, box 3, folder 4.
21. Quoted in James Knowlson, *Damned to Fame: The Life of Samuel Beckett* (London: Bloomsbury, 1997), 790.
22. Memo by Leslie Stokes, dated 26 Feb. 1958, in *SW 53-62*.
23. Beckett, *Letters III*, 156.
24. Knowlson, *Damned to Fame*, 456–7.
25. 18 Nov. 1958, HRC, Abraham Leventhal Collection, box 1, folder 4.
26. Beckett, *Letters III*, 181.
27. Ibid., 184.
28. Trinity College, Dublin, Samuel Becket Collection (hereafter TCD) mss 4663 and University of Reading, Beckett International Foundation archives (hereafter UoR), mss 1396/4/6.
29. Beckett, *Letters III*, 208.
30. Beckett mentions the meeting in his letter to Barbara Bray of 18 Jun. 1959, see TCD 10948-1-036.
31. Samuel Beckett, *All That Fall and Other Plays for Radio and Screen*, ed. By Everett Frost (London: Faber and Faber, 2009), 47.
32. UoR mss 1396/4/6.
33. Letter of 6 Sep. 1959, quoted in Samuel Beckett, *No Author Better Served: The Correspondence of Samuel Beckett & Alan Schneider*, ed. by Maurice Harmon (Cambridge, MA: Harvard University Press, 1998), 56.
34. Beckett, *Letters III*, 184.
35. Samuel Beckett in a letter to Barbara Bray, dated 1 Jan. 1959, see TCD 10948-1-015.
36. Memo from Script Editor Barbara Bray to Miss H. Dean in *SW 53-62*.
37. Whitehead, *The Third Programme*, 140.
38. For more information about the censorship of *Embers* on the BBC Third Programme, see S. E. Gontarski, "Bowdlerizing Beckett: The BBC *Embers*," *Journal of Beckett Studies* 9.1 (1999), 127–31.
39. Zilliacus, *Beckett and Broadcasting*, 97; he was first to correct this misconception.
40. Donald McWhinnie in a letter to Samuel Beckett, dated 23 Apr. 1957 in *SW 53-62*.
41. Whitehead, *The Third Programme*, 209.
42. TCD 10948-1-001.
43. Undated and anonymous memo in *SW 53–62*.
44. Humphrey Carpenter, *The Envy of the World: Fifty Years of the BBC Third Programme and Radio 3, 1946–1996* (London: Phoenix Giant, 1997), 208.
45. Ibid., 211.

46. Whitehead, *The Third Programme*, 30.
47. Carpenter, *The Envy of the World*, 210–211.
48. Ibid., 211–2.
49. Beckett, *Letters III*, 366.
50. Whitehead, *The Third Programme*, 80.
51. *SW 53-62*.
52. Robert Pinget's papers are kept at the Bibliothèque littéraire Jacques Doucet in Paris. "Notre ami Sam" is cataloged as PNG 354-4, and the reference occurs on 61r-62r.
53. Carpenter, *The Envy of the World*, 191.
54. Ibid., 192.
55. Samuel Beckett in a letter to Barbara Bray, dated 11 Mar. 1959. Quoted in Beckett, *Letters III*, 211–2.
56. TCD 10948-1-082.
57. Samuel Beckett in a letter to Barbara Bray, dated 21 Dec. 1960, see TCD 10948-1-127.
58. Carpenter, *The Envy of the World*, 239.
59. Ibid., 239–40.
60. Letter of 29 Dec. 1962, quoted in Beckett, *Letters III*, 520.
61. TCD 10948-1-126.
62. Beckett, *Letters III*, 375.
63. TCD 10948-1-120.
64. Beckett, *No Author Better Served*, 56.
65. TCD 10948-1-121.
66. Pinget again recorded the remark in "Notre Ami Sam." PNG 354-4, 56r.
67. Beckett, *Letters III*, 378.
68. Pinget, "Notre Ami Sam," PNG 354-4, 62r.
69. Samuel Beckett in a letter to Barbara Bray, see TCD 10948-1-137.
70. This manuscript, long thought lost, was actually in the private possession of Irish book dealer Alan Clodd. After he passed away, his complete Beckett collection was sold to the National Library of Ireland in 2006, by Mags Bros. Ltd., except for the manuscripts. These were sold separately, and the *Words and Music* draft was acquired in 2013 by Princeton University (Leonard L. Milberg Collection, box 1, folder 2).
71. For a brief discussion of this draft see David Tucker, "'Oh Lovely Art': Beckett and Music," in S. E. Gontarski, ed. *The Edinburgh Companion to Samuel Beckett and the Arts* (Edinburgh: Edinburgh University Press, 2014), 373–85.
72. UoR mss 1227-7-7-1, 45r.
73. Samuel Beckett in a letter to Barbara Bray, dated 17 Feb. 1961, quoted in Beckett, *Letters III*, 399.
74. Knowlson, *Damned to Fame*, 483.

75. *SW 53-62*.
76. Samuel Beckett in a letter to Barbara Bray, dated 29 Nov. 1961, see TCD 10948-1-167.
77. *SW 53-62*.
78. Memo dated 20 December 1961, in *SW 53-62*.
79. *SW 53-62*.
80. Ibid.
81. Martin Esslin in a letter to Samuel Beckett, dated 22 December 1961 in *SW 53-62*.
82. *SW 53-62*.
83. Memo to Martin Esslin, dated 22 Aug. 1962 in *SW 53-62*.
84. Memo to Geoffrey Manuel, dated 4 Sep. 1962 in *SW 53-62*.
85. Samuel Beckett in a letter to Barbara Bray, dated 11 Oct. 1962. Quoted in Beckett, *Letters III*, 507–8.
86. Samuel Beckett in a letter to Barbara Bray, dated 17 Sep. 1962. Quoted in Beckett, *Letters III*, 501.
87. TCD 10948-1-205.
88. TCD 10948-1-208.
89. I am very grateful to Samantha Blake, BBC WAC Archives Researcher, for sending me a copy of this transcript on 30 Apr. 2014. Bray's comment can be found on p. 8.
90. See TCD 10948-1-212.
91. Samuel Beckett in a letter to Thomas MacGreevy, dated 4 Dec. 1961. Quoted in Beckett, *Letters III*, 444.
92. See Knowlson, *Damned to Fame*, 466–8.
93. John Pilling, *A Samuel Beckett Chronology* (Houndmills: Palgrave Macmillan, 2006), 158.
94. Letter from Samuel Beckett to P. H. Newby in *SW 53-62*.
95. Esslin, *Mediations*, 126.
96. Note by John Jordan, dated 21 May 1987 in *SW 53-62*.
97. *SW 53-62*.
98. Pilling, *A Beckett Chronology*, 163.
99. Letter from Rosica Colin to Michael Bakewell, dated 17 July 1963 in *SW 53-62*.
100. *SW 63-76*.
101. Ibid.
102. Knowlson, *Damned to Fame*, 507.
103. Samuel Beckett in a letter to Barbara Bray, dated 28 January 1964, quoted in Beckett, *Letters III*, 592–3.
104. Samuel Beckett in a letter to Barbara Bray, dated 29 August 1964, quoted in Beckett, *Letters III*, 619.
105. *SW 63-76*.

106. TCD 10948-1-306.
107. Zilliacus, *Beckett and Broadcasting*, 151–2.
108. Esslin, *Mediations*, 143–4.
109. MS 1991-01, box 11, folder 7.
110. TCD 10948-2-54.
111. Humphrey Searle, *Quadrille with a Raven*, 1982. Accessed 11 November 2015. http://www.musicweb-international.com/searle/titlepg.htm (Chap. 17, "Labyrinth").
112. Beckett, *Letters III*, 674.
113. See TCD 10948-1-540; and TCD 10948-1-544.
114. Esslin, *Mediations*, 144.
115. Ibid., 144.
116. *SW 73-87*.
117. Esslin, *Mediations*, 146.
118. *SW 73-87*.
119. Ibid.
120. Ibid.
121. Ibid.
122. Ibid.
123. Ibid.
124. Ibid.
125. Esslin, *Mediations*, 149.
126. Beckett, *All That Fall and Other Plays*, 60.
127. For a more detailed account of this alternative dating for *Pochade* see Pim Verhulst, "'Just Howls from Time to Time': Dating *Pochade radiophonique*," in "'Beginning of the murmur': Archival Pre-Texts and Other Sources," *Samuel Beckett Today/Aujourd'hui* 27, eds. Conor Carville and Mark Nixon (Amsterdam: Brill/Rodopi, 2015), 147–62.
128. See TCD 10402-218.
129. Beckett, *No Author Better Served*, 36.
130. Ibid., 37.
131. Quoted in Zilliacus, *Beckett and Broadcasting*, 149.
132. Beckett, *Letters III*, 174.

Imagining Radio Sound: Interference and Collaboration in the BBC Radio Production of Beckett's *All That Fall*

Catherine Laws

In the later work of Samuel Beckett there emerges a particular focus on the act of listening. The image of the listener, usually with head in hand, is often the focus of attention in his plays, poetry and prose. Sometimes, as in the television play *Ghost Trio*, Beckett dramatizes the act of listening to music. Elsewhere it is a voice that is the focus of attention: the voice of a reader, as in *Ohio Impromptu*, or the protagonist's own recorded voice, as in *Krapp's Last Tape*. Often the source of the voice is ambiguous, emerging from the darkness without clear origin or identity: is it real, imaginary or remembered? Or even one's own: the unstoppable, buzzing, "dull roar in the skull,"[1] such as the one that Mouth in *Not I* cannot escape.

An attentiveness to sound is certainly present in Beckett's earlier work. More specifically, his thinking about music—about philosophical, formal and expressive considerations, and about the activity of listening—permeates his writing, evident already in his monograph on Proust and the early novel *Dream of Fair to Middling Women*.[2] In particular, the idea of tuning recurs in different forms. Snippets of musical theories of tuning, melody and harmony are employed as part of his explicit and self-conscious grappling with the direction his writing should take and, more boldly, the possibilities for

C. Laws (✉)
Department of Music, University of York, York, UK

literature in the twentieth century. Metaphors of intonation and the vibration of overtones are used to contrast order and ratiocination with chaos and flux, exploring how writing might somehow "accommodate the mess" (as Beckett put it to Tom Driver).[3] Additionally, though, the difficulty of hearing clearly and as a result finding some kind of meaning in the world—the tension between attunement and interference in the process of listening, but also in more generally trying to make sense of things—forms a persistent thread in Beckett's writing. The incessant noise of the mind is already evident in Murphy's struggle through what Neary calls, echoing William James, "the big blooming buzzing confusion,"[4] and the protagonists of subsequent novels often find their heads to be, like Watt's, full of "voices, singing, crying, stating, murmuring, things unintelligible, in his ear."[5]

This focus on the significance of sound, music and listening really came to the fore in Beckett's radio work of the 1950s and 1960s. Music plays a significant dramatic role in *Words and Music* and *Cascando* (with certain similar concerns also apparent in the brief *Esquisse*, written between these two), pitted against words in a dramatic testing of their relative artistic powers. Moreover, radio, and later television, involves turning sound on and off, and Beckett directs attention to these functions, most explicitly in the operational "I open" and "I close" of *Cascando*,[6] the clicking and turning of knobs to try to hear the voices in *Esquisse radiophonique*, in the introductory lines of *Ghost Trio*—"Mine is a faint voice. Kindly tune accordingly"[7]—and "I switch on," "I switch off" in *What Where*.[8] However, as Brynhildur Boyce notes with respect to *Words and Music*, this also provides a concrete metaphorical context for "the activity of comprehension within the process of communication."[9] I would go further, arguing that the notions of tuning in and tuning up, whether in music, radio or television, offer a context for Beckett's persistent struggle with clarity of meaning and communication. Likewise, the failure to tune in, due to the hiss and fuzz of interference, real or metaphorical, can signify the problematics of expression: "headaches among the overtones"[10] indeed. Overall, radio, and particularly the different modalities of recorded sound, offered Beckett a specific focus for his concerns with questions of presence and absence, self and other, mind and body, the imagination and the real.

Beckett's radio plays were, until recently, relatively neglected in the otherwise extensive critical literature on the author. However, the work of Rosemary Pountney and radio director Everett Frost, along with more recent contributions by Julie Campbell, Ulrika Maude and others, has spurred more detailed consideration of this body of work. The prevalent view is of Beckett as a sophisticated composer of radiophonic soundscapes and word-music interactions. I by no means wish to undermine this view: Beckett's multilayered use of sound and music, conceptually, thematically and materially, is striking and powerfully effective. Nevertheless, some of the documents in the BBC's Written Archive Centre (WAC) at Caversham expose something less often considered: the limitations of Beckett's role with respect to the realization of his ideas for sound and music in this medium at this time. Beckett's scripts certainly do reveal a concern with the specifics of radio, but the gap between this conceptual starting point and the actual process of sound production is considerable, due to issues of technical know-how and Beckett's distance from the hands-on experimentation that took place in the recording studio. In an age of instant audio file sharing, it is easy to forget the separation of writing and production inherent to much radio drama in the 1950s and 1960s, and the fact that Beckett was located in France made things even more difficult. Beckett did not experience the production work in progress, struggled to hear the broadcasts due to reception problems, and then was generally refused recordings that would allow for repeated listening and detailed reflection and evaluation: all of this emerges more clearly from the WAC communications.

This chapter will explore these issues with specific respect to *All That Fall*, considering their broader significance for Beckett's work and within the culture of British broadcasting at the time. I am particularly concerned with matters of authority and control in the creative process. Beckett's radio work was necessarily collaborative, even co-creative: perhaps more so than has widely been acknowledged, since the overlap between technical realization and artistic insight was considerable. As Emilie Morin has recently noted, to date there has been little attempt to understand Beckett's radio drama "as the result of specific collaborations, affinities and legacies."[11] Given this, it is perhaps no surprise to find Beckett more open to the ideas and experimentation of others in radio than (usually) elsewhere: far from observing his own mantra of keeping "genres more or less distinct,"[12] his cooperative spirit here seems to extend to an openness to reworking and adaptation. The roles of collaborators such as Donald McWhinnie and Beckett's cousin, the composer John Beckett, are clearly significant in this respect: it seems, from the WAC materials, that the incorporation of particular radiophonic effects or newly composed music by trusted collaborators was an important factor in Beckett's willingness to respond to a wide range of commissions, from new plays through to adaptations of novels.

All That Fall and the Radio Soundscape

The writing of *All That Fall*, in 1956, involved a shift back to English for Beckett, after a decade of French texts that included the trilogy of novels *Molloy, Malone meurt,* and *L'Innommable,* along with numerous shorter pieces and the plays *En attendent Godot* and *Fin de partie.* Written for the BBC and first broadcast in January 1957, it was his first radio play, temporarily drawing his attention away from writing for theater, into the purely aural domain. The play introduces Beckett's first female protagonist, Maddy Rooney. The scene is rural; we follow Maddy's slow and laborious journey along a country road to Boghill railway station to meet her blind husband, Dan, and their equally protracted walk home. Along the way, Maddy encounters various characters—this is a relatively crowded play, by Beckett's standards—and near the end we learn the reason for Dan's reluctance to explain to Maddy why his train was delayed: a child had fallen onto the track.

As commentators have repeatedly pointed out, the viewpoint of *All That Fall* is Maddy's[13]; Everett Frost notes that the emphasis is on her *perception* of the journey.[14] On one level the scene appears realistic, even biographical; Beckett commented that he was drawing on his "boyhood memories,"[15] and James Knowlson shows how Beckett incorporated the names of local people from his hometown.[16] We follow the journey as if in real time, but the use of language, sound and music undermine the verisimilitude. As Anna McMullan observes, Beckett here "uses the radio medium to create a world that is simultaneously culturally and historically specific (post-independence middle-class south Dublin, circa the 1930s), and has the vast temporal and imaginative perspective of the fable."[17] The work is at once concrete and abstracted, estranged, and this is manifested in both the script and its production in sound.

Importantly, Beckett's inspiration was impressionistic and primarily aural; in a letter to Nancy Cunard (4 July 1956), he wrote: "Never thought about Radio play technique but in the dead of t'other night got a gruesome idea full of cartwheels and dragging of feet and puffing and panting which may or may not lead to something."[18] Not surprisingly, then, he gives numerous instructions for sound effects—sounds emanating from the landscape, and the sounds of Maddy moving through it. Additionally, much of Beckett's own correspondence with the BBC over the production of the play was concerned with the sound.[19] This first production created a deliberately unrealistic soundscape. The specifics of this are considered in more detail below, but overall the effect of the production decisions is to undermine naturalism and enhance the more self-conscious and ambiguous aspects of the script, emphasizing its strangeness. The animal noises that introduce the play were produced by human impersonators, footsteps were formed from artificially percussive timbres and unnaturally even rhythms, and the careful use of the proximity of voices to microphones subtly underlines the mediated quality of the voices, destabilizing the surface realism.

These sonic acknowledgements of the unreality of the events complement those spoken lines that point to the play's ephemeral, unstable status in the radio ether. As Clas Zilliacus notes, the lack of visual grounding allows for a freer leaping back and forth over the surface of language, encouraging playful linguistic associations.[20] When Maddy says "Do not imagine, because I am silent, that I am not present, and alive, to all that is going on,"[21] it is as much an acknowledgement of the ambiguous conditions of radiophonic presence as an indignant attempt to make her companions pay her more attention. Likewise, Maddy is both sonically embodied[22]—comically so, when we hear her trying to squeeze herself into a car—and yet not quite there. The implication is not simply that we are in Maddy's world, guided by her subjective perspective and experience (as argued by Kalb and others); rather, the self-consciously mediated character of the production as a whole suggests a more ambiguous "composedness" to the world: composed by Maddy herself, as her words and sounds guide us, but the radiophonic mediation points beyond this, reflexively, to other agencies: the author, a production team…and ultimately ourselves, as we piece together the ambiguous soundscape.

Even in a more naturalistic rendering, the radio medium inevitably sets us at a distance from the physical origin of sound. On the one hand, sound has an enveloping quality that draws us in; the concentration of sensual experience in the aural domain, detached from visual or other grounding, can produce a particularly intense and subjective experience. Radio drama often exploits this. Less often noted, though, especially in relation to Beckett, is the distancing effect of radio mediation. Recording and production processes always leave traces that undermine intimacy and immediacy: this remoteness is couched in the very action of tuning in, to find something "out there," and in the particular quality of radio sounds and voices, so carefully produced but still ultimately determined by broadcast conditions and the nature of our individual sound systems and listening environments. In particular, a recorded voice will always differ in quality of sound from its manifestation in the local acoustic environment, whether obviously or more subtly. In the original BBC production, Maddy's voice is recorded slightly closer to the microphone than others, subtly emphasizing the primacy of her subject position, but also, again, undermining the surface realism. Whatever the quality of the sound production and relay, an act of will—or of willed submission—is required to experience the sound as if direct and unmediated. As in his other radio and television plays, where the mediating powers of technology are often more explicitly invoked (in *Ghost Trio*, for example), Beckett is fully aware of this.[23] As Thomas van Laan comments, the play's condition as a radio text is "essential to its nature and meaning."[24] More particularly, we might see Beckett's exploration of this strange radiophonic condition of absent presence—what Julie Campbell calls "the ghostliness inherent in radio plays"[25]—as an instance of a wider modernist preoccupation with radio as, literally or metaphorically, "a 'medium' for spirits moving through the 'ether'"[26]; this underpins Emilie Morin's fascinating study of Beckett's radio plays as situated in the "peculiar confluences between modernism, occultism and technology."[27]

"[A] SPECIAL QUALITY OF BRUITAGE": IMAGINING SOUND

There are, therefore, aspects of the text of *All That Fall* that suggest a keen sense of the specifics of the radio medium. This is, to an extent, confirmed by Beckett's communications about the play. Even on sending the script to John Morris, the Controller of the BBC's Third Programme, Beckett noted that the play called for "a rather special quality of bruitage" and offered to "let you have a note on this if you are interested in the script for the Third Programme."[28] In the critical literature on the play, much has been made of Beckett's radiophonic prescience in this respect: recent critics, as evidenced in some of the above quotations, have paid considerable attention to the approach to sound in *All That Fall*, and its particular phenomenological impact. Certainly, Beckett was interested in the specificity of the medium. Gaby Hartel notes that as early as 1936 Beckett had read the English translation of Rudolf Arnheim's treatise *Film*,[29] which included a section specifically on the aesthetics of radio drama (though he does not seem to have read the later book, *Radio*). Beckett certainly seems to have absorbed some of the key tenets of the book, including the need to consider the specifics of radio writing in contrast to stage plays, the effects of collapsing of the unity of time and space in an acoustic context, and perhaps most of all the need to "allow the action to grow piecemeal from nothingness" in a manner "very reminiscent of a certain style of novel writing," since "at the beginning of a scene the listener-in has no idea as to who is speaking, or to whom, nor as to where the action is taking place."[30] Moreover, beyond the significance to the thematics and impact of *All That Fall* itself, the technical innovations in the use of sound for this production are regarded as seminal in the development of radio drama in the UK, leading directly to the founding of the BBC's innovative and hugely influential Radiophonic Workshop in 1958.[31]

Nevertheless, consideration of documents in the BBC's WAC reveals the limitations of Beckett's role in the production and the full nature of the collaboration with the BBC. Beckett clearly recognized that the play called for something quite special in terms of sound production. When John Morris followed up on the script, on 5 October 1956, he echoed Beckett's sense that a "special quality of 'bruitage'" would be necessary, but noted that its nature was "not quite clear from the text" and asked for "a note of your ideas on this,"[32] Beckett replied with a certain reticence and uncertainty: "I find it difficult to put down my thoughts about the bruitage. And I am not sure that what I want to say is worth saying. I feel it may be no more than an amateur's statement of what is common radio practice. For the moment I think I had better hold my peace. By the far the best would be for us to meet, or for me to meet the bruiteur, before production, and talk it over."[33]

Morris immediately offered a meeting with the producer, the Third Programme's Assistant Head of Drama, Donald McWhinnie, who was due to be in Paris later that month.[34] It seems that this was successful. From subsequent letters and memos it is clear that the two men got along very well,[35] and one meeting led to another: this was the start of a significant working relationship on both an individual and an institutional level, cemented by an immediate personal sympathy.

Subsequent to this, however, the realization of the play took place without Beckett's input. At the end of November, McWhinnie invited Beckett to London for the period of rehearsal and recording in early January 1957.[36] Beckett sent his apologies, explaining that the production of *Fin de Partie* was due to open at the Théâtre de l'Oeuvre on January 15.[37] Given his involvement in the rehearsal process for the stage play, this preference for staying in Paris seems understandable. However, in mid-December the opening of *Fin de Partie* was postponed by over a month, to February 20 (and later canceled altogether in that location), but Beckett wrote to

McWhinnie that he, even so, would not attend rehearsals: "I have finally decided that I should be very definitely less a help than a hindrance .... I'd only bother and upset you all."[38]

This seems reasonable, perhaps even admirably restrained and respectful of roles. Considered in context, however, it is more than a little surprising. In preceding years, with his first direct encounters with the theater, Beckett had shifted from claiming, in 1952, to "have no ideas about theatre"[39] to, by November 1955, having to be restrained by theater director Alan Schneider from giving extensive notes to the actors in Peter Hall's production of *Waiting for Godot* in London.[40] Additionally, through his developing working relationships with Schneider, Roger Blin and others, and with the start of the Paris rehearsals of *Fin de Partie*, Beckett was growing more directly involved in the realization of his plays. This process continued: overall, the six-year period of Beckett's radio writing was one in which he took an increasingly active role in the rehearsal of his stage plays, honing his practical sense of how to achieve the effects he had imagined.

Given this, the evidence of Beckett's sense of the possibilities of radio as an art form and the fact that was his first encounter with radio production, one might expect him to have been keen to get involved. On the contrary, in this instance, Beckett *preferred* to keep his distance; the situation was not simply dictated by practical circumstances. Clearly, he felt very supported by the BBC: as is discussed by Julie Campbell, as well as Dirk van Hulle ("The BBC and Beckett's Non-radiogenic Plays in the 1950s"), Pim Verhulst ("The BBC as "Commissioner" of Beckett's Radio Plays") and Erik Tonning ("Mediating Modernism: The Third Programme, Samuel Beckett, and Mass Communication") in this volume, the BBC had carefully prepared the ground, wooing him initially through Cecilia Reeves in the Paris office of the BBC, and Beckett must have been pleased that it was the Controller of the Third Programme himself, John Morris, who took such pains to write regularly to encourage and thank him. Even before *All That Fall* had been produced, Morris expressed his keen interest in further commissions: "I need hardly tell you that I shall be delighted if you will do some more for us, and I hope you will let me know as soon as you have an idea for a another piece for the Third Programme."[41]

Beckett also felt in safe hands, telling McWhinnie: "I'm not worrying, having talked with you here and felt your feeling for the thing, its ruinedness and stifledness and impudicity."[42] Nevertheless, Beckett had no experience of the actors cast for the play, and elsewhere in the same letter he challenges McWhinnie's ideas for the realization of the animal sounds in the opening:[43] again, his willingness to "let go" seems at odds with his broader attitude to his work at this time. This apparent preference for remoteness from the realization of the play (and subsequent BBC productions[44]) needs further probing.

Before attempting this, other aspects of Beckett's distance from the production preparations, recording and broadcast need to be considered. Beckett was kept informed by McWhinnie of the BBC's work on the play throughout mid to late December 1956 and January 1957. This was, though, in somewhat general terms. On December 13th McWhinnie reported that the team was "experimenting furiously with the various sound complications,"[45] and a letter dated New Year's Day 1957—a few days before the rehearsals and recording—noted that they have undertaken "a lot of experimentation with sound effects."[46] Quite what this means, though, is not explained to Beckett.

The only relatively detailed discussion concerns the disagreement between McWhinnie and Beckett about the animal noises. One of the most striking aspects of the production was the decision to use human voices to imitate the cow, sheep, dog and cockerel sounds, and this came from McWhinnie, not Beckett. Beckett was unhappy with the idea from the start, responding in a letter: "I do not see why the animal utterances by mere humans. I do not think this point arose when we met."[47] Beckett's next lines are telling, reinforcing the idea that, conceptually and aesthetically at least, the writer and producer had developed in their discussions a clear and shared sense of the status of sound in the work as recognizably concrete in origin but somewhat denatured and abstracted in its sonic materiality: "Perhaps your idea is to give them the unreal quality of the other sounds. But this, we agreed, should develop from a realistic nucleus."[48]

Beckett clearly is not expecting standard animal sound effects: he asks whether the BBC for some reason does not have recordings of the right animals, not for simple playback but in order that they might be "distorted by some technical means."[49] McWhinnie replies, noting the difficulty of achieving appropriate timing and balance of sounds with realistic effects. He also points out the familiarity of Third Programme listeners with these standard sounds, explaining that his preference is to "get away from standard realism" and to "get real style and shape into the thing."[50] This much is published in the third volume of Beckett's letters, but not the whole letter: McWhinnie concludes by asserting his expectation that this will work out well, but conceding that if the sounds are not effective when put into context, in rehearsal, he will of course think again.[51] He did not; the reasons for this are considered below. The production continued with human voices for animals, but Beckett remained unpersuaded: "I didn't think the animals were right."[52] For the later American realization, first broadcast in 1986, he asked the producer, Everett Frost, to abandon human imitators in favor of naturalistic animal recordings but to keep the general impressionistic approach to sound effects.[53]

"[D]ISTORTION AND FADING AND ENCROACHMENTS": TRYING TO LISTEN TO ALL THAT FALL

Once the production was broadcast, it was some time before Beckett could hear it properly. He listened to the first broadcast and wrote to congratulate McWhinnie, but noted that "reception on Sunday was very poor." His claim that "I heard well enough to realise what a good job" is a little undermined by the next line: "I did not agree with it all, who ever does, and perhaps I should have if I had lost less of the detail."[54] The repeat broadcasts were no easier to hear, and the problems with poor radio reception are noted frequently in Beckett's letters, especially in this period. In April 1957, he wrote to his friend A. J. ("Con") Leventhal, who was due to give a talk on Beckett's work on the Third Programme, that he would try to listen in, but "sometimes we can just hear."[55] The next month he wrote to McWhinnie that he was unable to hear the broadcast of *Fin de Partie*,[56] and at the end of the year he comments on trying to hear the BBC broadcast of *Molloy* while in Paris: "Reception execrable needless to say."[57] A rebroadcast of *Molloy*, along with *From an Abandoned Work*, listened to at his house in Ussy, is "Alas no clearer here than in Paris. More volume, but more interference. So I really can't comment relevantly."[58] Even some years later, the reception problems were still regarded as significant inhibiting factors in the ability to perceive the work in full and judge its success. In response to Beckett's somewhat negative response to *Rough for Radio 2*, broadcast in 1976, Martin Esslin (the producer, and by then Head of Radio Drama) wrote "Perhaps in better listening conditions it might sound better even to you."[59] While the considerable hiss and buzz of interference was a regular part of the radio listening experience of the time, this was even more so for Beckett, due to his location.

Of course, the BBC held recordings of the broadcasts, but they preferred not to send these out, even to writers; presumably the reasons were partly the time and expense of producing extra recordings, but also concerns about the impact of recording on the popularity and status of broadcasting. At Beckett's request, toward the end of January 1957 Cecilia Reeves arranged for him to listen to a repeat broadcast of *All That Fall* in the BBC's Paris office, "fed down" from French national radio, RTF (Radiodiffusion-Télévision-Française).[60] Even there, reception was variable: in this instance the sound was, as Beckett complained to McWhinnie, "clear for five minutes or so, then got worse and worse and was soon practically inaudible. Exasperating experience."[61] Beckett notes, in this letter, his hope that he might get to hear a recording. At this time, though, this was not at all straightforward. Copies were not routinely produced, so McWhinnie had to request one specially to take to the Paris Office for Beckett to hear: letters and memos show his requests for the recording and for permission to travel to Paris, so as to be able to listen to the recording with Beckett. This finally happened in mid-February, but listening on a single occasion was not likely to be satisfactory: it is easy to forget, in an age in which copying audio files is quick and listening portable, not only the difficulties of hearing material in the first place, but also the fact that listening was often a once-only occurrence. For an artist wishing to absorb, consider and reconsider the nature and effectiveness of the details of a production, this was extremely challenging.

The obvious solution was for Beckett to receive his own recordings, but this was a matter not simply of logistics but politics. Over a period of roughly a year, Cecilia Reeves and Donald McWhinnie lobbied for Beckett to receive copies of BBC productions: first *All That Fall* and then the subsequent adaptations of *Molloy* and *From An Abandoned Work*. Reeves and McWhinnie clearly expected their requests to face opposition, making strategic arguments designed to exploit the desire of those higher up in the Third Programme to continue the association with writers of such cultural status as Beckett. Arguing for a recording of *All That Fall*, McWhinnie not only stresses the significance of the play and the desire to maintain goodwill, but also suggests that competitors might move in if the BBC is not careful: "As you know, it is extremely rare for a writer of universal reputation to write specially for us .... My own feeling is that it would be only fitting to pay at least a modest tribute to a writer who has given us such a radio 'occasion' .... I know he would appreciate the gesture, which incidentally is almost certain to be made by other European radio organisations in due course."[62] McWhinnie was successful in this instance, confirming to Beckett in mid-April that a recording had been promised (though it took months before Beckett finally received the disc).[63]

Later appeals for recordings, though, were rejected. McWhinnie had, understandably, stressed that the request for the *All That Fall* disc was exceptional, aware that his BBC superiors would see it as a dangerous precedent.[64] To ask again, therefore, was problematic. Reeves did her best, noting that the provision of a recording "is a service which would be of great value for him in future writing for radio," and that it would be "exclusively for his own private listening,"[65] but the answer was a firm "no." A handwritten comment by the Third Programme's Head of Drama, Val Gielgud, on McWhinnie's typed memo, states: "There's an immense potential involvement if we present recordings to successful authors in this way for where do we stop? Discrimination is often exceedingly invidious, especially if Mr. A knows that Mr. B was given a copy!"[66]

Beckett's primary experience of hearing radio productions of his own work, then, continued to be one of hiss, fizz and buzz (or "distortion and fading and encroachments," [67] as Beckett put it): the comments on poor reception persist over the years. Occasionally he managed to obtain a recording: a letter from 1959 refers to hearing the BBC adaptation of *The Unnamable*, read by Patrick Magee: "I actually have the tape, but I'm not supposed to have it."[68] Mostly, though, he was only ever able to hear the broadcasts clearly by visiting the BBC's Paris Office when recordings were sent over, weeks if not months after they were first put out.

These details of production and reception confirm three things: firstly, that despite Beckett's keen sense of the specificity of the radio medium and desire to exploit its character, this remained somewhat conceptual and vague; secondly, that the opportunity to gain a more detailed understanding of the medium and its processes was available, but Beckett chose to remain at a distance from the sonic realization of his script; thirdly, that despite the discussions between McWhinnie and Beckett about the approach to sound, and despite the critical focus upon the phenomenology of Beckett's radio work, for the author, hearing these things clearly—receiving the piece as conceptualized and realized by its producers—was rarely possible, even some time after the event of broadcast. Overall, the process, from Beckett's perspective, was characterized by distance and interference. This is not, however, entirely negative: I will argue below that this very remoteness—the estrangedness of the situation of reception for Beckett—was not only conducive to the development of the particular production quality of this play, but also strongly tied in to certain of Beckett's ongoing concerns. Nevertheless, this point of view is somewhat different from the critical approaches to the play to date. Moreover, it calls into question the tendency, apparent even in recent considerations of the sonic materiality of the work, to cast Beckett as the primary creative authority, with McWhinnie and his team in minor supporting roles. Beckett may have had "a very sound idea of the problems of writing for radio," as John Morris noted in a memo after their first meeting in Paris in July 1956,[69] but he did not have the specific notions of sound developed by the production team.

The BBC Context

To fully comprehend this, we need to consider the other side of the production context, in London, rather than Paris: the ideals and politics of those working for the BBC Third Programme at the time, and technical and aesthetic developments in the possibilities for radiophonic sound in general and radio drama in particular.

As Julie Campbell has noted, the launch of the BBC's Third Programme in 1946 was an explicit move to provide a dedicated home for "serious art" with the aim of developing an audience willing to listen attentively to challenging artistic output.[70] As the output developed in the 1950s, there were concerns to reduce the perceived stuffiness of the presenting. The appointment of Morris, Controller from 1953 to 1958, reportedly met with considerable concern, his age (57) and explicit determination to "kill the lecture and introduce talk" leading to rumors that he had been put in place to oversee the dismantling of the network.[71] Even Morris, however, emphasized that the Third Programme "should not compromise: it should make no concessions to popular taste,"[72] and of course his instrumental role in bringing Beckett to the BBC hardly supports the idea of Morris as wanting to lighten the output.

Beckett's *All that Fall* was produced at a significant point in the development of the Third Programme. The techniques used for the recording were—as discussed below—not only innovative in themselves but indicative of an underlying concern with the nature and possibilities of radio drama. As a result, the production is considered hugely significant: in a book co-edited by Desmond Briscoe, a key member of the production team for *All That Fall*, the work is described as the "first collaboration of consequence for the new experimenters"[73] and "the first programme to contain what later came to be known as 'radiophonic' sound."[74] However, in order to understand the circumstances of *All That Fall*, its significance, and the relationship between Beckett as writer and the team that produced the piece, it is important to understand the situation for radio drama at the BBC in the mid-1950s, and specifically the relationship between drama, features and music in the Third Programme.

As Kate Whitehead notes, up until the end of the war, prior to the founding of the Third Programme, the BBC's radio Features and Drama Units formed a single department under the control of Val Gielgud.[75] However, the Features Unit had developed out of the Research Unit, "a group of four producers charged with the task of experimenting with radio's potential as an artistic medium in its own right."[76] This group, influential in years to come, included Lance Sieveking who was already interested in technical innovations in sound recording, manipulation and broadcast, and in theories of the new media of the time: as well as producing his own innovative features both before and after the War, including numerous adaptations of novels, Sieveking worked on the translation of Rudolf Arnheim's *Film* (first published in German, in 1932 as *Film als Kunst*).

During the war, the feature, as something of a hybrid of documentary and drama, had primarily been used for conveying news information in a more entertaining, "even emotive"[77] way: a form of propaganda designed to boost the morale of listeners. Subsequently, though, after the War, the Features Unit was again set free from this role and was able to continue to use the same innovative radiogenic techniques for a wider range of creative projects. As Whitehead puts it, features "became associated with quality and innovation, attracting the most talented producers and writers."[78] In contrast, drama was primarily focused on entertainment, producing adaptations of mainstream stage plays with little in the way of dramatic or technical innovation. Asa Briggs, in his history of broadcasting in the UK, acknowledges this: "The history of radio drama during the ten years from 1945 to 1955 may seem unadventurous in retrospect."[79]

Gielgud, who in the 1950s and 1960s was less than enthusiastic about Beckett's work for the BBC,[80] was unhappy with the role of Features within his department. Even in the 1920s and 1930s, Gielgud railed against the more experimental work of producers such as Sieveking,[81] and in 1945 he tried to have the unit disbanded and absorbed into the News Division.[82] This suggestion was predicated upon a clear distinction between documentary and news on the one hand, and literary and dramatic output on the other; a distinction that features producers simply did not recognize.

Instead, the department was split into two separate units, with Gielgud remaining in charge of Drama. Laurence Gilliam, who led the Features Unit when it was part of Gielgud's department, and then the Features Department when it gained autonomy, expressed his sense of the difference between a radio feature and a documentary or news program: features programs were designed to "make the listener feel as well as think, to entertain as well as to inform."[83] However, there was an underpinning aesthetic at work here: the ability to inhabit this ambiguous landscape grew out of a willingness to think beyond conventional forms and techniques, to "slowly, obstinately and with growing success" explore "the possibilities of the radio medium itself."[84] Soon afterwards, in 1951, an article in the *BBC Quarterly* positioned the radio feature similarly as *the* truly radiogenic art form: "Here the sound medium is used in an original, positive, even creative way. The feature *is* the radio art-form. The very limitations of the medium are transformed into advantages to create something new which can be expressed no other way."[85]

The constituting of the Features and Drama Departments as separate entities took place in the same period as the planning of the new Third Programme. Overall, this atmosphere of relative autonomy, combined with the excitement generated by the emergence of the new network, seems to have given features producers, in particular, a strong sense of creative possibility.[86] Whitehead notes that whereas in 1948 a BBC list of "Plays Performed During the First Two Years of the Third Programme" contained only items attributed to the Drama Department, a 1956 list of plays for the network's first ten years had roughly as many items from Features as Drama, divided into three categories "Original Pieces for Radio," "Adaptations" and "Stage Plays," with Features providing most of the former.[87]

There was some dissatisfaction with this situation. In 1954, John Morris complained to Gielgud that the drama output was inadequate and that he wanted more new productions. In a strongly worded memo he stated that if couldn't get what he wanted from Drama, he would fill drama space with features.[88] However, the appointment of Donald McWhinnie changed all this. McWhinnie arrived in 1953, as Gielgud's Assistant Head of Drama, and immediately began to encourage more young writers to write for radio, but also to instill a "growing enthusiasm within Drama Department for experimenting with radio as a dramatic medium in its own right."[89] Briggs refers to "McWhinnie's concentration in the Light Programme's *Radio Theatre* series in 1954–5 on plays especially, written for radio."[90] McWhinnie was evolving his own ideas about the possibilities for radio, influenced by the productions of Sieveking and other innovators, and also by Arnheim (especially in terms of the use of voices[91]): this culminated in his own book, *The Art of Radio* (1959), which combines theoretical reflection with detailed accounts of specific productions.

McWhinnie's championing of the avant-garde was by no means accepted within the Drama Department: his relationship with Gielgud was always difficult, with many proposals rejected (including Harold Pinter's first script for radio), and even after the success of *All That Fall* McWhinnie had difficulty persuading Gielgud to accept Beckett's next radio play, *Embers*.[92] Nevertheless, with McWhinnie's success in enticing more young writers, and his interest in new sound techniques for radio, there was less of a distinction between Drama and Features. The production of *All That Fall* was, as explained below, crucial in this respect. By 1959 the number of Features Department staff had been significantly reduced, leading to the gradual demise of the department: McWhinnie's approach broke down the previous BBC distinctions between Drama and Features, with many Features producers then starting to work more consistently within Drama.

This sets the scene for the BBC's courting and encouragement of Beckett: his status as an exciting and innovative writer was attractive to McWhinnie and Morris. As Jeff Porter notes, "What Beckett achieved in *All That Fall* was made possible in large part by the aims of the BBC's Third Programme, which commissioned from him an original play that it hoped would showcase radio as an unique medium."[93] I would go further: the potential of the technical developments and creative tensions within the BBC in the late 1940s and 1950s were understood by McWhinnie as offering a unique possibility, if fused with innovative script writing. *All That Fall* was, of course, one of many plays that attempted to exploit the specifics of the medium but, as explained below, the coincidence of its production with the fruition of certain aesthetic and technical developments meant that it was something of a turning point for radio drama in this country. Meeting Beckett, discovering him "to be enthusiastic about experimentation in sound,"[94] and encountering a script grounded in a sense of the characteristics of the radiophonic soundscape but lacking any specifics of realization: all this must have been hugely exciting.

SOUND, SOUND EFFECTS; MUSIC, MUSIQUE CONCRÈTE: NEGOTIATING RADIOPHONICS

The politics of Drama versus Features within the Third Programme forms only one part of the story. While the relationships developed between the Features Department and writers consolidated the position of the Third Programme in terms of literary and dramatic innovation, experimentation with sound was of course related to developments in new music, and was therefore of concern to the Music Department. Theories such as Arnheim's were influential for those, like Sieveking and McWhinnie, who wanted to consider the specific dramatic qualities of radio in relation, or contrast, to the stage, and to newly developing film techniques. However, it was in music, especially in France and Germany, that innovative techniques in the recording and manipulating of sound were fast developing. Moreover, the theoretical concerns here were primarily articulated in relation to musical, rather than literary or theatrical, aesthetics.

In the mid-1950s, a number of those working in radio drama and features at the BBC had become interested in the developments in *musique concrète* (especially the work of Pierre Schaeffer and Pierre Henri) at the Club d'Essai and the *Groupe de Recherche de Musique Concrète* based at RTF in Paris, and the techniques of electronic music pioneered by Herbert Eimert and Karlheinz Stockhausen in the studio at Westdeutsche Rundfunk (WDR) in Cologne.[95] It was the French developments that were of most interest, perhaps in part due to the closer proximity and stronger relationship between the BBC and RTF, but from the comments of McWhinnie and others it is clear that this interest was also aesthetic.[96] McWhinnie, composer-producer Douglas Cleverdon and others were particularly interested in the French focus on the electronic manipulation of concrete sound; that is, the electronic treatment of recordings of non-musical sound, as opposed to the primary focus upon the development from scratch of new electronic sound that formed the basis of German developments in *Elektronische Musik*.

In fact, the French and German approaches were more similar than is often recognized. Stockhausen studied *musique concrète* techniques in Paris with the Club d'Essai composers, and works such as his *Gesang der Jünglinge* and Pierre Henry's *Haut voltage*, both from 1956, combine techniques developed in both the French and German studios. There were disagreements: some of the German electronic composers believed the predication of the French approach on concrete sounds to be problematic, since, they felt, the resultant music was bound to retain traces of the originating context. Deriving sounds in this way would, the Germans argued, inevitably lead audiences toward an associative listening process, in which they would be more likely to make imaginative connections to the sounds of the world beyond the piece. Such processes would undermine the aesthetic of absolute musical, entirely abstracted and free from references external to the music itself, upon which the Germans predicated their own compositions. Herbert Eimert, in particular, asserted his opposition "to all metaphorical synaesthetic interpretation, that is ... to the idea of composition and interpretation by association and reference."[97] Likewise, in an early article in *Die Reihe*, founded and edited by Eimert and Stockhausen, music theorist Hans Heinz Stuckenschmidt asserted the superiority of the German approach due to its focus upon creating new sounds from scratch, rather than manipulating recorded materials. This, he felt, formed a continuity with established idealist aesthetics of music: "the construction from nothing is the true and most important process in the creation of music from sound material."[98]

Nevertheless, the French composers working in this field were, like the Germans, keen to promote the purely musical qualities of their work above the obvious potential for the use of electronic techniques in radio, film and television. Pierre Schaeffer had adopted the term "acousmatic" from Pythagoras, who applied it to his practice of teaching from behind a curtain, denying his students a visual source for his words and thereby, in theory at least, focusing their attention entirely on what he had to say.[99] For Schaeffer, the repetition made possible by recording facilitated the divorcing of sound from its originating context, affording the listener an entirely phenomenological experience: the subjective perception of purely "sonorous objects."[100] Schaeffer contrasted this with "the curiosity put into play" with acoustic sound, where the interpretative relationship between objective sound source (whether a voice, musical instrument, radio, or whatever) and the subjectively perceived sound is of prime importance in determining the significance of what is heard. Acousmatics, instead, "marks the perceptive reality of sound as such, as distinguished from the modes of its production and transmission."[101] Acousmatic listening should, then, focus on the sound "itself" independent of a relationship to its source: "by exhausting this curiosity, it [the repetition of the physical signal] gradually brings the sonorous object to the fore as a perception worthy of being observed for itself."[102] The prime danger, the French and German electronic composers agreed, was that electronic music would be regarded as interesting only subordinately, for dramatic effect. In this way, both groups equally keen to frame their work as extending the lineage of absolute music: as Niebur notes, "the musical culture out of which *musique concrète* and *Elektronische Musik* grew was inextricably bound up in nineteenth-century Romantic notions of musical autonomy and the idea that each composition should be functional—that is, oriented toward an internal integrity."[103]

Of course, McWhinnie's own interest was in exploiting exactly the curiosity that Schaeffer wished to circumvent: the dramatic tension between the concrete origin of the sounds and the abstractedness of the manipulated result. Indeed, his comments to Beckett on his decisions about the animal sounds in *All That Fall* reflect exactly this. He wanted to gain a better understanding of the technical processes of *musique concrète*, and his trip to Paris in late 1956, when he first met Beckett, was in fact organized primarily around a visit to members of the Club d'Essai at RTF. By this time there were considerable differences of opinion between the key members of the group, but McWhinnie was nevertheless able to gain a substantial understanding of their approaches. He reported back to colleagues, apparently less than impressed either by the radio scripts that he saw in France, or what he saw as the French composers' "preoccupation with 'noises,'" noting, more importantly, that "in their handling of sound they are miles ahead."[104] McWhinnie proposed that those involved in BBC productions should listen to French recordings, and that the institution should develop its own dedicated facilities for experimentation. Certainly, by late 1956 the BBC Drama Department had acquired some such recordings: a letter from Barbara Bray, by then a commissioning editor for the Drama Department, to the writer Giles Cooper, notes: "We have here an album of RTF recordings which involve *musique concrète* and allied effects, which I and many others found very exciting and indeed inspiring."[105] As a result of McWhinnie's efforts, in April 1956, a meeting of the Entertainment Division considered a proposal to set up a small laboratory for experimentation with recorded sound,[106] and by the end of the year an Electrophonic Effects Committee, soon renamed the Radiophonic Effects Committee, had been set up to consider the facilities required and to direct the development of what became the Radiophonic Workshop.[107]

However, none of this was straightforward, especially politically within the BBC. The Third Programme had, from the early 1950s, occasionally broadcast *musique concrète*, including Schaeffer and Henry's seminal *Symphonie pour un homme seul* (1950). In mid-1955, Cleverdon started campaigning for more regular broadcasts,[108] and that year saw the BBC put out the first electronic music written for an English feature: Tristram Cary's *Japanese Fishermen*.[109] However, Cleverdon, despite being a composer as well as a producer, was housed within Features not Music, and this was significant: at this time, many in the Music Department were hostile to European avant-garde composition,[110] not least when it involved electronic sound.

Louis Niebur has traced this antagonism, noting a reluctance from the Music Department to consider the early pioneers of electronic sound to be composers of music at all.[111] The references to "effects" instead of "music" abound, suggesting not only a simplistic differentiation of electronically and acoustically produced music, but also a failure to recognize the distinctions between naturalistic sound effects and electronically manipulated sound that were crucial to the thinking of drama and features producers: McWhinnie's *The Art of Radio* discusses in some detail what he sees as the problems of "natural sounds" in radio drama.[112] Such prejudices were enforced operationally: in these years, during the process of negotiating the development of the Radiophonic Workshop, the Music Department asserted its determination to remain concerned only with sounds "produced on instruments played by musicians ... expressed in existing forms of notation," preferring that the Entertainment Division (Drama and Features) should deal with those sounds "produced by technical methods, embracing the techniques already developed in other countries ... and music concrete [*sic*] based on natural sounds."[113]

McWhinnie therefore had to tread carefully. His innovative approach in the mid-1950s effectively integrated many of the strengths of Drama and Features at the BBC, previously operating so separately, but the impact upon relations with Music was less positive. Aesthetically, his interest was in the territory between the conventional radio play and music: in using recorded and electronically produced sound to enhance the potential of radio, operating in a dramatic field in which the concrete origin of sound *is* significant, allusive and referential, but does not simply substitute for the lack of visual signs. This required a manipulation and exploitation of the very concreteness which many electronic music pioneers in Europe were keen to erase, but with an underlying sense of the ways in which the relationships between sounds in time take on meaning: a musical sense of form tied into the images and associations generated by the text and the concrete origins of the soundscape.

Given the tensions at the BBC, it is not surprising, then, that in his introduction for a press listening session to what McWhinnie considered the first BBC "radiophonic poem," *Private Dreams and Public Nightmares*, broadcast in October 1957, with a script by Fredrick Bradnum, he was at pains to assert its status as something other than music: "By radiophonic effects, we mean something very near to what the French have labelled *musique concrète*—concrete music. Not music at all really. It doesn't necessarily come out of musical instruments and it can't be written down. It's simply sounds, or patterns of sound, which are manufactured by technical processes."[114] The reference to "effects" and "not music" may have been designed to placate both those in the Music Department and any listeners who might accept these sounds in dramatic contexts but not recognize them as musical in themselves.

There is a danger, in sketching the "high art" context for *All That Fall* in relation to *musique concrète* and to BBC radio drama and features, of failing to note that important technical developments also came from the use of sound effects in radio comedy and science fiction.[115] *The Goon Show*, in particular, from the early 1950s, exploited the manipulation of sound effects, including virtuoso combinations of sounds on "grams" as well as distortions and mixes designed for comic impact.[116] Footsteps, stylized in sound or played back either very slowly, for comic delay, ridiculously fast, were a common feature: no doubt the experience here fed, on some level, into the creation of the footstep sounds for *All That Fall*. Of course, McWhinnie's aim was primarily aesthetic: to incorporate radiophonic sound as integral to dramatic forms. His production of Giles Cooper's *Mathry Beacon* in 1956, before *All That Fall*, had moved in this direction in the use of sound effects,[117] but the lack of technical knowledge at the BBC meant he had been unable to take this further. The developments toward *All That Fall* were taking place at exactly the same time as McWhinnie and colleagues were sharing recordings from France and trying to find ways to imitate the effects, but with a purpose defined precisely in contrast to the aims of the pioneers of *musique concrète*. Whether this aesthetic was already in place before encountering either *musique concrète* itself and the antipathy toward it in some quarters, or influenced by the need to allay the fears of the Music Department and other skeptics in authority within the Third Programme is hard to determine. What is interesting is McWhinnie's perception that, however defined in relation to musical or dramatic aesthetics, the development of radiophonic sound was essential to a conception of radio drama in which the integration of all aspects of the soundscape—words, naturalistic effects and electronic sounds of all kinds—was, overall, fundamentally musical: where the connectivity between sound events might lie in the rhythmic, melodic or timbral patterning as much as in connections between events or ideas.

Overall, then, *All That Fall* came at a significant time at the BBC in terms of *both* the internal relationship between radio writing for Drama and the production values of features, and the external impact of European developments in electronic music. Given the evidence of the WAC and other materials, it is hardly surprising that the idea of Beckett writing for radio should be so encouraged and supported by many of those at the Third Programme, and that his willingness to consider the specifics of the medium was a bonus. Moreover, rather than Beckett's play demanding specific techniques for realization by the production team, the script appeared at exactly the time when a process of research, listening and practical experimentation, led by McWhinnie, was in need of suitable cases for application. That Beckett's script arrived at the Third Programme just as McWhinnie and others (including Barbara Bray, soon to become Beckett's lover) were listening to *musique concrète*, gradually determining how such sounds could be produced, and thinking about their most appropriate use, was opportune; that McWhinnie could visit Beckett while in Paris to visit RTF, and that their conversations would therefore turn around not just Beckett's script but the particularities of sound in radio was ideal; that Beckett then stayed away and let them get on with it led to certain approaches that may not otherwise have materialized.

Producing Sound: Experimentation, Performance and Collaboration

The concerns of McWhinnie and his team, throughout the process, were both practical and aesthetic, focused on finding the most appropriate sonic manifestation of Beckett's world, and more fundamentally with exploiting the dramatic tensions of manipulated concrete sound within a more abstractly conceived formal, musical structure. This is apparent in the approach to *All That Fall*: McWhinnie's determination to hold on to the imitation animal sounds is one manifestation of this, but the decision was not just tied to his sense of the right sounds for that dramatic moment. Rather, it was one element in an underlying formal conception of the relationships between sounds across the whole play. Beyond the animal noises, there was a more general shift away from the use of "natural" sound effects, whether recorded or produced live in the studio, in favor of simulation. Imitation footsteps were produced by experimenting with different kinds of drum sounds, then blended with actual footstep sounds in different ways, so as to produce a variety of footstep-like sounds with different degrees of naturalism.[118] Likewise, the recorded sound of "an actor's tongue playing tunes on the roof of his mouth" contributed to the sounds of the donkey-and-cart,[119] and flutter echo effects, derived from listening to recordings of *musique concrète,* were used for the first time in any BBC radio drama, notably for the sounds of the Up-Mail train passing through the station: "when we faded up the replay knob of the recording machine while it was still recording, we produced tape feed-back."[120] Technically, all of this was tricky to realize at this time: Briscoe confirms that the mixing took place live in the studio, and that after the period of experimentation he had to teach the studio manager quite how everything would work.[121]

In *The Art of Radio*, published two years after *All That Fall* was first broadcast, McWhinnie reiterated his sense, expressed in the earlier quoted letter to Beckett, that for this play, "strict realism would have been too crude, complete stylization pretentious."[122] However, while all these sounds lay somewhere between realistic effects and purely musical abstraction, the degree of concreteness varied according to whether they should be received by the listener as perceptual—coming to us via Maddy's consciousness—or "real": as signifiers of activity in the environment. McWhinnie's idea was that the former "must begin as fantasy and resolve into some form of perceptible reality; thus the donkey-and-cart, the bicycle, the car, which approached her [Maddy] on the road, were initially distorted and only gradually emerged into a recognizable sound. On the other hand, the footsteps of Mr. and Mrs. Rooney, their real journey, must gradually attract poetic and symbolic overtones, so that eventually even the wind and rain which beat against them are almost musical in conception."[123] In this sense, the extent of the sonic concreteness or abstraction was composed across the whole play according to these core principles; the degree of naturalism or distortion in any one sound was determined by the status the production team accorded the sound-generating actions within the imagined perceptions of Maddy or the listener.

Beyond the attention to qualities of sound lay an underlying conception of rhythmic unity. This was founded on the decision to set the sounds of Maddy's footsteps, first heard straight after the silence that follows the introductory animal noises, in a strict four-beat meter, forming a sonic relationship with the pattern of four animal sounds: "our concern is to consolidate the underlying rhythm, and to merge, imperceptibly, the musical and realistic elements of the play."[124] The four-beat pattern persists in varied manifestations, realized as animal sounds, in more and less realistic footsteps, and at times even vocally. When Maddy leaves Christy, drum brushstrokes replace the sound of her footsteps in a strict, formal manner, setting up a pattern that, McWhinnie decided, should determine the delivery of the next speech: "four pairs of footsteps followed by four pairs of drumstroke, then Mrs Rooney soliloquizes in the same rhythm."[125] Toward the end of the play, as Maddy and Dan return home, we again hear the same patterns, but here there is quite a jump from the more realistic footstep sounds to an entirely percussive effect in an artificially regular rhythm. McWhinnie notes: "From this point on we use the symbolic footsteps as a purely musical device, and sometimes simply for the sake of their own musical effect."[126]

The production concept was, then, on the one hand rooted in an ambiguous sonic state, never entirely concrete nor wholly abstracted; if all radio sound is acousmatic in the literal sense, since the sounds emanate from an unseen source, the sound of this play is never truly acousmatic in Schaeffer's terms: the sounds are never sonorous objects of pure perception, transcending the context of origination. On the other hand, the conception was fundamentally musical in the attention to the qualities, structures and relationships of sound: this is apparent in McWhinnie's lengthy commentary in *The Art of Radio*, characterized by references to the rhythmic relationships and contrasts, and the tonal effects of voices.[127] Finally, having worked his way through the key moments of the play, McWhinnie comes to the sequences of sounds heard as Maddy and Dan walk home: the strict patterning of dragging feet, wind and rain sounds, and the silences that occur as the couple halt momentarily. Here, he sums things up: "If this is not music, what is it?"[128]

From all this, it becomes easier to understand why McWhinnie was so reluctant to change his ideas about the animal sounds in response to Beckett's comments. For McWhinnie and his team, the phenomenological and emotional impact of the play was predicated on a relational sense of the qualities of sound and their patterning. To change one aspect of this, especially the first set of sounds in the whole play, was to undermine the entire conceptual basis of the soundscape. Indeed, the more we understand about the detail of this production and the behind-the-scenes communications and processes, the less likely it seems that Beckett had a clear understanding of McWhinnie's exact approach. It may be that this integrated, musical conception of the play was discussed when the author and producer met. However, the written communications do not give this impression. In arguing for the simulated animal sounds (in the letter quoted above), McWhinnie reiterates the general desire for stylization, but his answer includes none of the specifics one might expect if this exchange was following from more detailed discussion of the sound production. Likewise, McWhinnie does not comment on the implications of a change in approach for the overall sound design, suggesting that this simply had not been shared.

McWhinnie also notes to Beckett that using existing recordings of animals was difficult because "it is almost impossible to obtain the right sort of timing and balance with the realistic effects."[129] This was generally true. The post-war development of the use of magnetic tape offered producers more possibilities for editing and shaping sound materials, but this was still quite new at the BBC: tape machines were increasingly used for some techniques, but sound effects continued to be worked on "grams" in a more traditional manner, using discs from the BBC's large Sound Effects Library and mixing the sounds into the production.[130] This was a skilful business, especially since some of the BBC's discs played from the middle outwards (rather than the pick-up working inwards from the edge of the disc): Briscoe writes about learning to create a complex sound picture by operating six or eight turntables at once, some spiraling inwards and some outwards.[131] This was not feasible for McWhinnie's and Briscoe's ideas for *All That Fall*, though. What McWhinnie does not seem to have explained to Beckett is that it was really the decision that the sounds should appear in a strict rhythm that could then be picked up for other sound sequences that made Beckett's idea of working from existing sound effects entirely unworkable; as McWhinnie notes in his book, "the actual sound of a cow mooing, a cock crowing … are complex structures, varying in duration and melodic shape,"[132] so catching exactly a very short burst of sound that contained enough of the key elements for the sound to have the right, recognizable quality was hard enough, but doing so in a strict rhythmic sequence, and then gradually slowing "into inarticulate, choked-off silence"[133] was impossible.

This was, then, a matter of *performance*, not just technical expertise: an ensemble of actors and sound producers could manage it, using a combination of voices, instruments and manipulations of recorded sound.

Again, this aspect of the production history is somewhat neglected in most critical accounts (except for McWhinnie's own, but his book is now out of print). It is also quite particular to this period of radio drama (and contrasts with the practicalities of *musique concrète* and most other electronic music at the time), since the shift toward recording on, and then cutting and splicing, magnetic tape meant that the timing and blending of sound became matters of editing and production. In *The Art of Radio*, McWhinnie not only stresses the significance of both actors and other sound producers as performers—literally, in their performance of the piece in the studio in real time for recording—but also seems to equate the very act of realizing a script in sound as performative: "the heart of any play is laid bare only in performance" and, more fundamentally, "interpretation is performance."[134] Again, this emphasizes the significance of the materiality of sound production to the subsequent sense of what this play "is": matters of interpretation, performance and production, inspired by Beckett's text but developed away from him and in material forms he could not have suggested or described, have subsequently come to be understood as fundamental to the play: how it takes effect and what it means. This is reinforced by the importance attributed to the sound (and silences) of the play in reviews of the first broadcasts ("fullest of full marks to the 'effects' man"),[135] and by the attention to the phenomenological impact of the production choices—the qualities of sound and their patterning—in recent critical literature.

Here, and elsewhere, McWhinnie points to the substantial and truly significant role of his team at the BBC. Sound production was a deeply collaborative business, and an internal memo shows that McWhinnie had a very clear idea of who he wanted on his team for *All That Fall*.[136] The work involved the whole team not just in exploring possible new sounds, but in considering their impact within the piece as a whole. McWhinnie's congratulatory message to the team after the recording, copied to the Head of Drama, is revealing in this respect: he stresses the technical achievements of the individual members of the team—Briscoe's handling of the "complex in the extreme" work on the panel, Norman "Baines's"[*sic* for Bain] "first-rate" timing and mixing on "grams," and the "intelligence and alertness" of Angela Palin on "spot"—but he also signals that parts of the process were creative, not just technical, due to the need to "create a style" for the play, confronting artistic problems that could "not be solved by any conventional or routine means."[137] Overall, the WAC files contain a number of letters and memos from those high up in the Third

Programme, including Morris, Gielgud and Joyce Rowe of the Sound Publicity Office, congratulating Beckett, McWhinnie, but also the production team as a whole on "a tremendously difficult production job."[138] Whitehead notes that this kind of co-creativity had emerged in the earlier work of the Features Unit where, "in contrast to drama, production methods were more fluid and impromptu"; this was consolidated with technical developments in the mid-1950s, the use of magnetic tape allowing for a more integrated approach to sound, somewhat equalizing the status of text and other elements of the soundscape—of writer and producer—and thereby, as Whitehead says, altering "the very nature of authorship."[140]

Douglas Cleverdon commented that in the early stages of the radiophonic work at the BBC there was a realization that "[t]hough the finest radio comes from poet's words...there are certain occasions when you wish to widen the impact of the words with something else."[141] It is hard, then, to agree with Jeff Porter, that while McWhinnie's and Briscoe's ideas for *All That Fall* were "smart and resourceful," ultimately they took "most of their cues from the playwright."[142] Likewise, if it is, as Katarzyna Ojrzyńska suggests, possible to link the four-square organization of *Quad* or the steps of *Footfalls* to the specific four-beat patterning of the BBC production of *All That Fall*,[143] then this is Beckett's response to the input of the production team. However, McWhinnie himself continued to stress that "[t]he writer is the key figure in imaginative radio," criticizing those producers who "have found an outlet for their own egotism in reconceiving what he writer has written."[144] He seems to have agreed with Desmond Briscoe that "Beckett's script was remarkable, really remarkable."[145] Clearly, though, what was so exciting was a combination of specificity about the concern for special qualities of sound and a vagueness about what they would be. Briscoe continues: "He wrote 'silence' and 'pause,' quite obviously differentiating between the two. When he demanded sounds, he didn't say they had to be made in any particular way, but the whole nature of the script led to experimentation."[146]

Perhaps there is nothing surprising here: it is, after all, the script that was the starting point for the work, and McWhinnie notes that "The creative purpose of any production is to evolve from the author's blueprint an aural style which is completely appropriate and special."[147] Nevertheless, there is a danger of underplaying the truly significant artistic contribution of the production team for *All That Fall*. It is perhaps important, also, to note firstly that Beckett's lack of involvement was not wholly typical of BBC practices at that time—some authors involved themselves more directly in matters of sound production—and also that not all radio scripts of the period were presented, like Beckett's, no differently to a stage script. For example, Bradnum's *Private Dreams and Public Nightmares*, produced shortly after *All That Fall*, places the spoken words on the right hand side of the page, with sounds described on the left, in parallel.[148] Bradnum still gives no specific instructions for production, but nevertheless takes a step toward representing sound on the page in relation to, and of equal significance to, words.

Estrangement and Interference

We might, then, conclude that *All That Fall* is characterized by two forms of interference. As noted earlier, radio gave Beckett a renewed focus for exploring ideas of tuning as a metaphor for failed communication and misunderstanding: as Steven Connor says, "[i]nterference, scrambling, fading of signal, detuning, all the vicissitudes that beset the listener are made part of Beckett's writing for the medium."[149] Moreover, Beckett's own listening to this and other productions was impeded by exactly these problems of reception. However, the realization of the play was also defined by the "interference" of the BBC production team. The use of this term might seem surprising, implying unwanted meddling or intervention, in contrast to the more positive notion of collaboration. Certainly, if collaboration is the willingness to subject one's work to interference, with the aim of achieving something beyond the capabilities of an individual, then *All That Fall* was collaborative. Nevertheless, rather than collaboration as teamwork and active partnership, in this case Beckett chose to keep out of the process, ensuring a degree of creative autonomy for the production team.[150] As a result it was inevitable that the realization in sound of a text on paper would take the piece in directions unforeseen by the author. The starting point was collaborative, for sure, and a sense of common understanding pervaded the project, providing a *spirit* of collaboration that was not manifested in practice: a positive form of interference was, in this sense, facilitated by Beckett's distancing of himself.

In *All That Fall*, with Beckett's return to English, the setting and the interactions between characters project a superficial naturalism, but the self-conscious use of language manifests exactly a sense of estrangement: this is especially so with Maddy, who explicitly asks, "Do you find anything ... bizarre about my way of speaking?"[151] Beyond this, though, Beckett's very sense of the medium, as I have discussed, heightens this quality of betweenness, of things not quite being as we might expect, of ambiguity and uncertainty with regard to the status of characters and events. As John Pilling has argued, the need for strangeness became increasingly embedded in Beckett's creative decisions, in the choice of language and medium: "whichever medium he adopted, its strangeness could at last be felt as intrinsic to it, rather than just an involuntary by-product of an idiosyncratic aesthetic position."[152] What McWhinnie and his team produced, through their combining of aesthetic and technical developments from both BBC Features and European electronic music, was a radiophonic manifestation of this same in-betweenness, this same connection to, yet estrangement from, the world: something that radio, at that time, was ideally placed to explore and exploit. Beckett could not do this himself; he knew this, and perhaps even suspected that his own direct involvement might compromise the experimental process. In this sense, his distance from the working process facilitated the estrangement he sought in the realization of the work: radio interference would mark a listener's reception of the piece, but interference in the creative process was necessary to embed the thematic estrangement in the very fabric of the sonic landscape.

NOTES

1. Samuel Beckett, *Collected Shorter Plays of Samuel Beckett* (London: Faber and Faber, 1984), 218.
2. This is discussed in detail in Catherine Laws, *"Headaches Among the Overtones": Music in Beckett / Beckett in Music* (Amsterdam: Rodopi, 2013).
3. Tom Driver, "Beckett by the Madeleine," *Columbia University Forum* 4.3 (1961), 24.
4. Samuel Beckett, *Murphy* (London: Picador, 1973), 6.
5. Samuel Beckett, *Watt* (London: Calder, 1976), 27.
6. Beckett, *Collected Shorter Plays*, 137.
7. Ibid., 248.
8. Ibid., 311.
9. Brynhildur Boyce, "Tuning In/Tuning Up: The Communicative Efforts of Words and Music in Samuel Beckett's *Words and Music*," in *Beckett and Musicality*. eds. Sara Jane Bailes and Nicholas Till (Farnham: Ashgate, 2014), 63. Steven Connor, too, draws attention to the ways in which radio offers Beckett a literal context for the metaphorical on-off "switches and switchings," "alternation and oscillation" that pervades Beckett's work: Steven Connor, "I Switch Off: Beckett and the Ordeals of Radio,"

in *Broadcasting Modernism*, eds. Debra Rae Cohen, Michael Coyle and Jane Lewty (Gainesville: University of Florida Press, 2009), 285.
10. Late in 1957 Samuel Beckett wrote to Alan Schneider, "My work is a matter of fundamental sounds .... If people want to have headaches among the overtones, let them."(*Letters III*, 82 [29 December 1957]): another example of Beckett using metaphors of tuning, this time from the period of the radio plays.
11. Emilie Morin, "Beckett's Speaking Machines: Sound, Radiophonics and Acousmatics," *Modernism/Modernity* 21.1 (2014), 1.
12. *Letters III*, 63–4 (6 April 1957).
13. See, for example, Clas Zilliacus, *Beckett and Broadcasting* (Åbo: Åbo Akademie, 1976), 46; Ruby Cohn, *A Beckett Canon* (Ann Arbor: University of Michigan Press, 2001), 233; Linda Ben-Zvi, "Samuel Beckett's Media Plays," *Modern Drama* 28.1 (1985), 27.
14. Everett Frost, "Fundamental Sounds: Recording Samuel Beckett's Radio Plays," *Theatre Journal* 43.3 (1991), 367.
15. *Letters II*, 633.
16. James Knowlson, *Damned to Fame* (London: Bloomsbury, 1996), 428–29.
17. Anna McMullan, *Performing Embodiment in Samuel Beckett's Drama* (Abingdon: Routledge, 2010), 73. My summary here is supported by Rosemary Pountney's work, which shows that Beckett often moved through a process of "vaguening" successive drafts of his plays, removing certain of the more concrete references so as to enhance the ambiguity. *All That Fall* was written quite quickly, with few drafts, but there is still evidence of this method. In particular, Beckett removed details about the situation leading to the child's death (Rosemary Pountney, *Theatre of Shadows: Samuel Beckett's Drama 1956–76* [Gerrards Cross: Colin Smythe, 1988], 103–5).
18. *Letters II*, 631.
19. See Zilliacus, *Beckett and Broadcasting*, 69.
20. Clas Zilliacus, "*All That Fall* and Radio Language," in *Samuel Beckett and the Arts: Music, Visual Arts, and Non-Print Media*, ed. Lois Oppenheim (New York: Garland, 1999), 302.
21. Beckett, *Collected Shorter Plays*, 25.
22. Ulrike Maude discusses this in detail in *Beckett, Technology and the Body* (Cambridge: Cambridge University Press, 2009).
23. I do not, though, agree with Kevin Branigan (*Radio Beckett: Musicality in the Radio Plays of Samuel Beckett* [Oxford: Peter Lang, 2008], 14, 31, 51) that this reflexivity is part of an overall disintegration of language and representation toward a state of "pure" music. This idealized notion of music is sometimes present in Beckett, especially in his early writing, but

the overall picture is much more complex. The use of music in Beckett's work is always linked to an exploration of its very impurity in action—its distortion at the point of reception and in the memory, for good and bad—and the musical effects of the work are closely bound to the very tensions between music and language.

24. Thomas van Laan, "*All That Fall* as 'a Play for Radio'," *Modern Drama* 28.1 (1985), 39.
25. Julie Campbell, "'A Voice Comes to One in the Dark. Imagine': Radio, the Listener, and the Dark Comedy of *All That Fall*," in *Beckett and Death*, eds. Steven Barfield, Philip Tew, and Matthew Feldman (London: Continuum, 2009), 147.
26. Matthew Feldman, Erik Tonning and Henry Mead, "Introduction," to *Broadcasting in the Modernist Era* (London: Bloomsbury, 2014), 2.
27. Emilie Morin, "Beckett's Speaking Machines: Sound, Radiophonics and Acousmatics," 5.
28. *Letters II*, 656.
29. Gaby Hartel, "Emerging Out of a Silent Void: Some Reverberations of Rudolf Arnheim's Radio Theory in Beckett's Radio Pieces," *Journal of Beckett Studies* 19.2 (2010), 220, 222.
30. Rudolf Arnheim, *Film*, trans. L. M. Sieveking and Ian F. D. Morrow (London: Faber and Faber, 1933), 214, 222, 215.
31. Martin Esslin, *Meditations: Essays on Brecht, Beckett, and the Media* (London: Sphere Books, 1983), 129.
32. Cited in *SW 53-62*.
33. *Letters II*, p. 656, n.3. The full letter is reproduced in *SW 53-62*.
34. See Donald MacWhinnie's letter of 16 November 1956 in *SW 53-62*. The chronology for 1957 in the third volume of Beckett's published letters states that Beckett first met McWhinnie on 19 February 1957 (*Letters III*, 3). From the letters themselves, this cannot be correct: they met toward the end of October 1956.
35. See, for example, correspondence from late 1956 in *SW 53-62*, and *Letters, II*, 675ff.
36. McWhinnie to Beckett on 28 Nov. 1956, in *SW 53-62*.
37. Beckett to MacWhinnie on 5 Dec. 1956, in *SW 53-62*.
38. See *Letters II*, 688, corresponding to *SW 53-62*.
39. *Letters II*, 316.
40. *Letters II*, 579 n1.
41. John Morris to Beckett on 16 Nov. 1956, in *SW 53-62*.
42. Beckett to McWhinnie on 18 Dec. 1956, in *Letters II*, 688, corresponding to *SW 53-62*.
43. *SW 53-62*.; see also *Letters II*, 687.

44. Beckett was not involved in the rehearsal or recording of any of his BBC radio plays. In 1963 he agreed to assist with the RTF production of *Cascando*, but this was a very bad experience: "*Cascando* was recorded before I left in the crazy RTF studios. Different studio every time (in a different recording ambience) & different technicians. A 4 hour session boiled down to 2 hours work, the other two devoted to finding tape, unwinding it, repairing apparatus, answering phone, etc. Disastrous." (*Letters III*, 548, n7).
45. *SW 53-62*.
46. Ibid.
47. *Letters II*, 687.
48. *Letters II*, 688.
49. Ibid.
50. *Letters III*, 688–89, 1.1.57. McWhinnie also set out the thinking behind this approach in his book *The Art of Radio* (London: Faber and Faber, 1959), 133–4.
51. See McWhinnie to Beckett, in *SW 53-62*.
52. *Letters III*, 12.
53. Frost, "Fundamental Sounds," 365. The American production was part of the Beckett Festival of Radio Plays (American premiere productions), coproduced by Soundscape Inc. and the West German radio station RIAS. It was first broadcast on Beckett's eightieth birthday. For a full account of the American production, see Frost's article.
54. *Letters III*, 12–13, corresponding to *SW 53-62*.
55. *Letters III*, 45.
56. *Letters III*, 47.
57. *Letters III*, 77.
58. *Letters III*, 78.
59. See *SW 73-82*.
60. Cecilia Reeves to John Morris on 22 Jan. 1957, in *SW 53-62*.
61. Beckett to McWhinnie on 29 Jan. 1957, in ibid.
62. See Donald McWhinnie's memo of 1 Apr. 1957, in ibid.
63. See memo of 8 Sep. 1957 in *ibid*.
64. Donald McWhinnie's memo of 1 Apr. 1957, in ibid.
65. See Cecilia Reeves memo of 4 Feb. 1958, in ibid.
66. See Val Gielgud to McWhinnie on 7 Feb. 1958, in ibid.
67. *Letters III*, 78, 23 Dec. 1957.
68. *Letters III*, 214, 20 Mar. 1959.
69. John Morris memorandum of 18 Jul. 1956, in *SW 53-62*.
70. Julie Campbell, "Beckett and the Third Programme," in *Beckett in the Cultural Field / Beckett dans le champ culturel, Samuel Beckett Today/*

Aujourd'hui 25, eds. Jürgen Siess, Matthijs Engelberts and Angela Moorjani (Amsterdam: Rodopi, 2013), 110–1.
71. Kate Whitehead, *The Third Programme: A Literary History*, (Oxford: Clarendon, 1989), 28–9.
72. In Campbell, "Beckett and the Third Programme", 111.
73. Desmond Briscoe and Ray Curtis-Bramwell, *The BBC Radiophonic Workshop: The First 25 Years* (London: BBC, 1983), 13.
74. Ibid., 14.
75. Whitehead, *The Third Programme*, 110.
76. Ibid.
77. Ibid.
78. Ibid., 111.
79. Asa Briggs, *The History of Broadcasting in the United Kingdom*, vol. IV (Oxford: Oxford University Press, 1979), 691.
80. Even after the success of *All That Fall*, Gielgud was not keen to accept Beckett's next radio play, *Embers*: see Whitehead, *The Third Programme*, 140.
81. Louis Niebur, *Special Sound: The Creation and Legacy of the BBC Radiophonic Workshop* (Oxford: Oxford University Press, 2010), 8.
82. Whitehead, *The Third Programme*, 112.
83. Laurence Gilliam, *BBC Features* (London: Evans, 1950), 10.
84. Ibid., 9.
85. Quoted in Whitehead, *The Third Programme*, 113.
86. Ibid., 114.
87. Ibid., 142.
88. Ibid., 141.
89. Ibid., 144.
90. Briggs, *Broadcasting in the United Kingdom*, IV, 694.
91. McWhinnie, *The Art of Radio*, 105–6.
92. Whitehead, *The Third Programme*, 140.
93. Jeff Porter, "Samuel Beckett and the Radiophonic Body: Beckett and the BBC," *Modern Drama* 53.4 (2010), 432.
94. Briscoe and Curtis-Bramwell, *The BBC Radiophonic Workshop*, 14.
95. There were, of course, significant developments elsewhere, especially in Milan (with the work of Luciano Berio and Bruno Maderna at the Studio di fonologia musicale) and in the USA (especially Columbia-Princeton). However, these were founded a little later than those in Paris and Cologne, in 1954 and 1955.
96. McWhinnie, *The Art of Radio*, 85–8; Briscoe and Curtis-Bramwell, *The BBC Radiophonic Workshop*, 27–8.

97. Hans Heinz Stuckenschmidt, "The Third Stage: Some Observations on the Aesthetics of Electronic Music," trans. Hans G. Helm, *Die Reihe* 1 (1958 [1955]), 11.
98. Ibid.
99. Emilie Morin has noted the significance of *musique concrète*, and especially Schaeffer's notion of acousmatics, for the context in which *All That Fall* was written and produced. Where Morin maps a direct connection between Beckett's use of radio sound and acousmatics, I argue that it was McWhinnie who formed the significant link, grappling with both the aesthetics and the technicalities of the French developments. Beckett must have been aware of some this context, but it was primarily mediated by his producer. Moreover, the differences between Schaeffer's acousmatics and the approach to sound in *All That Fall* are important, as I explain later in this paper. Schaeffer sought to exhaust the aural curiosity that arises from the divorcing of sound from its visual referent, so as to allow the listener to focus on sonic objects in themselves, whereas McWhinnie's radiophonics exploit the drama of that curiosity, amplifying the tension between naturalism and ambiguity in Beckett's text. Morin's paper has wider concerns, however: importantly, she situates Beckett's work in the broader modernist context of developing technologies for sound transmission. See Morin, "Beckett's Speaking Machines: Sound, Radiophonics and Acousmatics," 1–10.
100. Pierre Schaeffer, "Acousmatics," trans. Daniel W. Smith, in *Audio Culture: Readings in Modern Music*, eds. Christoph Cox and Daniel Warner (New York and London: Continuum, 2004), 77–8.
101. Ibid., 77.
102. Ibid., 78.
103. Niebur, *Special Sound*, 5.
104. Briscoe and Curtis-Bramwell, *The BBC Radiophonic Workshop*, 27.
105. Niebur, *Special Sound*, 27.
106. Ibid., 35.
107. Briscoe and Curtis-Bramwell, *The BBC Radiophonic Workshop*, 28.
108. Niebur, *Special Sound*, 16–7.
109. Ibid., 16.
110. Ibid., 17–9. This situation changed dramatically in 1959, with the appointment of William Glock as controller of Music.
111. Niebur, *Special Sound*, 40–5.
112. McWhinnie, *The Art of Radio*, 77–85.
113. In Niebur, *Special Sound*, 40.
114. In Briscoe and Curtis-Bramwell, *The BBC Radiophonic Workshop*, 22.

115. Niebur explores the significance of radio comedy and science fiction in the development of the BBC Radiophonic Workshop: see 9–14, especially.
116. The extent of the Goons' reliance on sound effects is revealed by a letter to the *Listener*, from Spike Milligan, blaming the newly formed Radiophonic Workshop for the demise of the show in 1960. Milligan claimed that the Workshop was unwilling to help the Goons develop new electronic sounds once they had exhausted the available possibilities (in Briscoe and Curtis-Bramwell, *The BBC Radiophonic Workshop*, 38).
117. McWhinnie, *The Art of Radio*, 82–3.
118. Briscoe and Curtis-Bramwell, *The BBC Radiophonic Workshop*, 18.
119. McWhinnie, *The Art of Radio*, 136.
120. In Briscoe and Curtis-Bramwell, *The BBC Radiophonic Workshop*, 18.
121. Ibid.
122. McWhinnie, *The Art of Radio*, 85.
123. Ibid.
124. Ibid., 134.
125. Ibid., 138.
126. Ibid., 148.
127. Everett Frost suggests that McWhinnie's fundamentally musical understanding of radio carries traces of Schopenhauer's philosophy of music, via Arnheim's theory of radio ("The Sound Is Enough: Beckett's Radio Plays," in *The Edinburgh Companion to Samuel Beckett and the Arts*, ed. S. E. Gontarski (Edinburgh: Edinburgh University Press, 2014), 252–4). This provides a fascinating parallel to Beckett's own recourse to Schopenhauer, evident from 1930 onwards. Nevertheless, it is important to note McWhinnie's retention of referential qualities of sound within an overall design that was, in certain respects, musically conceived: despite its musicality, McWhinnie's approach to sound never quite "transcended referentiality" (Frost, "The Sound Is Enough," 253), hence his desire to distinguish his approach from that of *musique concrete*, as discussed here.
128. McWhinnie, *The Art of Radio*, 148.
129. *Letters II*, 688, and *SW 53-62*.
130. Briscoe and Curtis-Bramwell, *The BBC Radiophonic Workshop*, 16.
131. Ibid., 16–7.
132. McWhinnie, *The Art of Radio*, 133.
133. Ibid., 134.
134. Ibid., 151.
135. This comment is in the review in *The Irish Press*. However, comments on sound abound: see, especially, *SW 53-62*.
136. Cited in *SW 53-62*.
137. Cited in ibid.

138. See for example, correspondence dated 14 Jan. 1957, in ibid.
139. Whitehead, *The Third Programme*, 117.
140. Ibid., 116.
141. In Briscoe and Curtis-Bramwell, *The BBC Radiophonic Workshop*, 28.
142. Porter, "Samuel Beckett and the Radiophonic Body," 442.
143. Katarzyna Ojrzyńska, "Music and Metamusic in Beckett's Early Plays for Radio," in *Beckett and Musicality*, ed. Sara Jane Bailes and Nicholas Till (Farnham: Ashgate, 2014), 53.
144. McWhinnie, *The Art of Radio*, 103.
145. Briscoe and Curtis-Bramwell, *The BBC Radiophonic Workshop*, 18.
146. Ibid.
147. McWhinnie, *The Art of Radio*, 128.
148. Ibid., 87.
149. Connor, "I Switch Off," 289.
150. A full discussion of different modes of collaboration in the arts is unnecessary here, but we might note Vera John-Steiner's distinction between collaborative and cooperative practices. Drawing upon psychological studies by Damon and Phelps, John-Steiner's notion of cooperation is perhaps a more appropriate term for the process of *All That Fall* than collaboration: "The participants in cooperative endeavors each make specific contributions to a shared task. However, their level of involvement may differ, as well as their sense of intellectual ownership of the resulting product" (John-Steiner, *Creative Collaboration* [Oxford: Oxford University Press, 2000], 12).
151. Beckett, *Collected Shorter Plays*, 13.
152. John Pilling, "The Predator and his Prey: Strategies and Strangeness in Beckett's Early Poems" *Journal of Beckett Studies* 24.1 (2015), 28.

Author, Work and Trade: The Sociology of Samuel Beckett's Texts in the Years of the Broadcasts for BBC Radio (1957–89). Copyright and Moral Rights

Stefano Rosignoli

> I have lived on it…till I'm old.
> Old enough.
>
> Samuel Beckett, *Cascando*

At the early stages of the supply chain in publishing is its most delicate point, when an author, as first owner of the intellectual property in a given "work of the mind," *transfers* or *trades* that copyright to a publisher. Whether it is one or the other depends on national legal systems: whereas civil law considers copyright as a *human* right, dwelling on the range and limits of a capacity of control that can be ceased by, but not alienated to the author, common law on the other hand regards copyright as a *property* right, so that it can be "sold, assigned, licensed, given away or bequeathed."[1] The difference is played out in terms of the moral rights of the creator, traditionally an integral part of copyright legislation in continental Europe, but separately introduced in their entirety in the UK only in 1988. If the author decides to retain copyright, as is usually the case in literary

---

S. Rosignoli (✉)
School of English, Trinity College Dublin, The University of Dublin, Dublin, Ireland

publishing, he himself or his representatives handle rights directly, or provide licenses concerning *volume* rights, listed in the package granted to the first publisher, and possibly an additional set of *subsidiary* rights, renegotiated at each new dealing.[2] The increasing industrialization of publishing has enhanced the representative role of literary agents in the first-hand management of copyright and in the negotiation of licenses to second parties, so that agents not only have become the main interlocutors for both authors and publishers, but also advocate authorial interests.[3] Licensing copyright nowadays may also involve literary scouts, who liaise with publishers and agents in a given territory, with the purpose of keeping their foreign clients updated on that specific market and pitching texts suitable to their editorial profiles. Other parties might take part in the licensing of copyright as independent consultants, but companies tend to slim down the system to reduce the risks by way of consolidating professional relationships based on experience and trust. Agents, scouts and consultants all work as mediators between authors and licensees. Their influence has strengthened steadily during the twentieth century, broadening the range of contractual options at the author's disposal, nowadays wider than ever,[4] and fostering the circulation of texts prior to their acquisition.

Even if literary agenting practice was already established when Beckett was still struggling to have his early works in English published,[5] the professional profile of intermediators at the time was much more blurred than at present, and agreements were frequently stipulated on the basis of face-to-face dealings between authors and publishers. The post-war transformation of publishing and the media into a widespread web of trading exchanges exposed Beckett to cultural commerce, but did not erase his personal bond with publishers or the importance he assigned to his main activity as an artist, which Beckett preserved by consolidating working relationships and stepping back from the business aspects of publication:

> As you know I am incapable of understanding contracts. My "method" consists, when they are drawn up by those in whom I have confidence, in signing them without reading them. Any contract drawn up by you, and involving me alone, I shall sign in this fashion. Those involving Lindon and me I submit to him and sign when he tells me to. To the former category belongs my translator's contracts with Grove and I leave it entirely to you

to formulate them as you think fit. I know your friendship for me, and your probity, and the possibility of your deriving from them excessive benefits does not at any time cross my mind.[6]

Instances of *trust* and *detachment* resurface in Beckett's business letters to the most intimate among his contacts, in France, England and the USA, in the years of Beckett's works for BBC Radio. These features can be traced, for example, in Beckett's effort to rekindle the dialogue with Girodias aimed at settling contracts between Olympia Press and Minuit: "Comme je vous l'ai déjà dit à plusieurs reprises, je suis incapable de m'occuper de l'aspect commercial de mon activité et j'y ai renoncé une fois pour toutes. Pour tout ce qui s'y rapporte je m'en remets entièrement à Monsieur Lindon" (As I have said several times, I am not able to look after the commercial side of my activity, and I have abandoned that once and for all. In anything to do with it I rely entirely on Monsieur Lindon.)[7] Or again, in an enquiry sent by Beckett to Rosset concerning the assignment of Canadian rights, which anticipated: "I shall abide by whatever you say."[8] All these scattered but recurrent comments draw attention to Beckett's distinction between the creative and the managerial side of literary activity, and to his decision to avoid involvement with the latter as much as possible.

Regardless of the size, the reputation, the political leanings of Beckett's business partners, or simply their *positioning* in the market, none of them could avoid the commerce of copyright and consequently begin a process of cultural commodification. With the increasing international trade of intellectual property, authors (or their representatives) now allocate licenses according to contractual details and the profiles of the licensees—essentially their financial clout and their ability to manage rights across different countries and markets.[9] It cannot be denied that the publishing environment was, and still is, characterized by a set of standard operations implying commodification. But it also brings with it the opportunity for literary authors to outsource duties that they may feel as extrinsic to artistic creativity, or for which they feel completely unfit. And although Beckett was not indifferent to financial matters,[10] there is indeed consistent evidence of his feeling of inadequacy with regard to mere business, and of his preference for concentrating on the creative side of his involvement, to the extent that the subdivision of duties between him and his partners is much more sharply defined than with most literary authors.

An enquiry into the exceptions to Beckett's standard policy, that is to say an analysis of the reasons for and range of Beckett's participation in copyright deals in the years of the BBC broadcasts, is, therefore, of great relevance to a general discussion of the sociology of Beckett's texts.

Despite the many alliances secured during Beckett's swift resurgence in the literary environment, it would be inaccurate to consider the management of his intellectual property since 1950 as stable. It was in fact affected by inner turmoils that led to frequent readjustments. The rising fame and diverse artistic directions of Beckett's work caused headaches for those looking after his interests, as confessed by Margaret McLaren when experiencing complications over territorial restrictions: "Samuel Beckett, by the way, has agents, publishers, stage managements etc. throughout the world and it is frightfully difficult trying to keep his affairs in order."[11] Beckett sometimes needed to arbitrate to solve a stalemate that opposed publishers in a single territory. For instance, in the early Sixties, Beckett was drawn into the disagreements between Fischer and Suhrkamp on German rights,[12] and between Olympia and Calder on English rights,[13] in the course of a reassessment of his affairs that prized publishers for their loyalty. Earlier on, the representation of Beckett's interests in the UK and Commonwealth was split between Rosica Colin and Curtis Brown, due to lack of communication between Beckett and Lindon over *All That Fall*, sent by the author to Curtis Brown "with instructions to them to handle all rights" as the play was written in English and so not controlled by the French publisher.[14] The administration of publication and theatrical rights was split between the two agencies, with consequences up to the present day.[15] However, this did not prevent a dispute being raised about the administration of broadcasting rights in the works not written for radio, particularly when the genre of the work was still under discussion. The initial contract for a broadcast of *Lessness* (signed with Curtis Brown after weeks of discussion)[16] was questioned by John Calder, who claimed to be the owner of the copyright (*Lessness* being a prose work and not a play) and to have made the first offer of a radio production to Martin Esslin at the BBC.[17] Penelope Sinclair replied reporting Beckett's hesitant impression that publication rights only had been licensed to Calder and that the contract for a radio broadcast should be dealt with Curtis Brown.[18] The matter was eventually settled in favor of the publisher, following the intervention of Richard Odgers in the discussion.[19] Mindful of the disagreement, and aware of the importance of the precedent, Calder reiterated his role when he authorized a reading of *The Lost Ones*.[20] On all these occasions, Beckett appears to have intervened simply because he could not do otherwise, hence his reluctance, expressed most concisely to Stefani Hunzinger in November 1962: "Il n'est pas dans mes habitudes de m'occuper de ces questions. Elles ne m'intéressent pas et j'ai autre chose à faire" (It is not my habit to concern myself with these matters. They do not interest me, and I have other things to do).[21]

A far more urgent incentive for Beckett to intervene in the licensing of copyright was the prevention of improper usage of his work, reaffirming what continental law, and nowadays even UK law, deems a primary *moral right* of the creator. Under this designation, British law has come to gather chiefly the right of *paternity* ("the right to be identified as the author") and of *integrity* ("the right to object to derogatory treatment of the work"). Following the preliminary provisions of the "Copyright Act" 1956, moral rights were fully introduced in the UK, on the example of continental *droit moral*, with the "Copyright, Designs and Patents Act" 1988 (effective since 1 August 1989), so that by an incredible coincidence the collaboration between Beckett and the BBC tallies with the essential reform of UK law that curbed the trading—and consequently the commodification—of intellectual property.[22] More specifically, the UK "Copyright Act" 1956 introduced rights regarding false attribution of work and the privacy of certain photographs and films, restated in 1988 but with significant changes to the latter, as the ownership of photographs and films was reassigned to the maker rather than the commissioner, so that a new discussion was opened on the balance between freedom of expression and right to privacy.[23] Sections 77 and 80 respectively of the "Copyright, Designs and Patents Act" 1988 introduced the two primary moral rights of paternity and integrity, as outlined above.[24] On 1 August 1989, moral rights became effective and were treated as a separate set of rights, so that authors and heirs of an estate could trade copyright but retain moral rights on a given work. However, the Act stated that UK moral rights lasted as long as the work was under copyright, that they were subject to consent and waiver, and that paternity had to be asserted in writing, as opposed to a continental tradition that sees *droit moral* as perennial and inalienable, and does not force the formal assertion of paternity.[25] It should also be recalled that "The practical upshot of the transitional provisions [i.e. Schedule 1 to the 1988 Act] is that, in respect of works contracted for and completed before 1 August 1989, moral rights will not apply," and that even nowadays "moral rights in the UK do not apply to every case, and are subject to numerous exceptions under UK law."[26]

Following the example of James Joyce, Beckett reaffirmed the integrity of his work against any distortion affecting it. Joyce campaigned for this authorial prerogative, together with the right of paternity, in his "Statement regarding the piracy of *Ulysses*," delivered to the press in 1927,[27] and in his short address to the 15th International PEN Congress (Paris, 20–27 June 1937) on the "Droit Moral des Écrivains."[28] Both times, he stood up against Samuel Roth's piracy of *Ulysses* in the USA. Even if in 1937, to Joyce's great annoyance, the PEN Club eventually contradicted its own charter, giving priority to urgent political matters,[29] he was nonetheless able to draw a conclusion from the injunction issued by the New York Supreme Court against Roth in December 1928. Joyce perceived this as an acknowledgment by the US common law system that "defending the integrity and dissemination of one's work was analogous to defending the integrity of one's name":[30]

> Il est, je crois, possible de tirer une conclusion juridique de cet arrêt dans le sens que, sans être protégée par la loi écrite du copyright et même si elle est interdite, une oeuvre appartient à son auteur en vertu d'un droit naturel et qu'ainsi les tribunaux peuvent protéger un auteur contre la mutilation et la publication de son ouvrage comme il est protégé contre le mauvais usage qu'on pourrait faire de son nom.[31]
>
> (It is, I think, possible to draw a juridical conclusion out of this ruling in the sense that, without being specifically protected by written copyright law even when it is forbidden, a work belongs to an author by right of natural law and therefore the bench can protect an author against the mutilation and the publication of his work just as he is protected against the wrong use of his name.)[32]

One of Joyce's great bequests to Beckett was precisely this deep commitment to aesthetic autonomy in safeguarding the integrity of the work of art, as expressed in Joyce's rare public stance in 1937. Moral rights exist specifically to support authorial efforts in that sense. However, it is not simply the late reception of this set of rights by the UK common law system, but also the costs and exceptions to defend them even nowadays,[33] that encourage authors, and Beckett as well at the time of the broadcasts for BBC Radio, to preserve texts by simply imposing restrictions or turning down licenses. Beckett's resistance toward the attempts, from the BBC in particular, to integrate his work into Christian morality offers perhaps the most unmistakable examples:

Request for permission to include Lucky's meditation in a programme of excerpts from various writers entitled FOR CRYING OUT LOUD to be performed by Sylvia Read and William Fry in churches at the Edinburgh Festival and subsequently all over the islands. "A Kaleidoscope of Christian Witness. Equally Suitable for Church or Stage performance." You'll never guess what I said.[34]

The range of Beckett's involvement in copyright management to safeguard his work expanded significantly, as even when their integrity was not at stake, Beckett blocked the reading of texts that he no longer felt comfortable with, or rediscussed productions that were thought to deserve more careful treatment. The simultaneous copyright vicissitudes of *Three Dialogues* and *Play* illustrate the former and the latter instance respectively, while also contradicting the outcome that we might have expected from both ventures. This underlines how unpredictable Beckett's decisions could be at times.

Beckett's contacts at the BBC were taken aback when he refused to clear copyright on *Three Dialogues*. The request had been expected to be mere routine, as Martin Esslin, who would have produced the reading (Third Programme, first quarter of 1966, estimated length 25'),[35] had already received the go-ahead to reprint the text in English in his forthcoming collection *Samuel Beckett*.[36] John Calder also issued it together with *Proust* in 1965 and had organized a public reading earlier, at the Traverse Theatre in Edinburgh, where Esslin had first listened to extracts from the text, judging it "excellent radio and an important statement about modern art."[37] Despite these provisos, in reply to an enquiry sent to Margaret McLaren, which proposed for Beckett and Duthuit a joint fee of £50 per broadcast in the BBC UK Services,[38] the agent regretfully informed Jack Beale that "Mr. Beckett doesn't wish this reading to be given."[39] A few days later, the author replied adamantly to Esslin's praises: "Rightly or wrongly I regret the Duthuit Dialogues and prefer not to have them broadcast."[40] The reason for Beckett's response might be traced not least to the peculiar bond he had with *Three Dialogues*. Since its conception, and particularly of the last segment on Bram van Velde, Beckett's correspondence gave voice to his indolence while at the same time confessing the intimate nature of his piece, more concerned with Beckett's growing poetics rather than with his chosen subject. In March 1949, he perceived his "kind of joint study" as "dragged out of me," trusting that Duthuit could "mollify my generalisation," which was felt to harm the painter's work.⁴¹ But as early as the end of June 1949, Beckett harshly assessed the text as "de la folie furieuse où personne n'a le droit d'entraîner un autre" (a kind of madness into which no one has the right to drag anyone else), feeling incapable of reconstructing Duthuit's voice, "celle qui me rappelle qu'il ne s'agit pas que de moi" (the voice that reminds me that it's not all about me).⁴² Beckett appears here to have grown disaffected with his speculations, and haunted by the sense of guilt at using Bram van Velde as a proxy. In May 1949 he considered the thoughts gathered with Duthuit as plain "sens commun, bon et rond comme le dos de d'Alembert" (common sense, good and round, like d'Alembert's back), growing out of "la vieille phrase de Geulincx citée dans Murphy, un peu à l'aveuglette il est vrai" (the old sentence from Geulincx quoted in Murphy, admittedly a little hastily) *Ubi nihil vales, ibi nihil velis*.⁴³ In February 1957, on the contrary, he labeled his own theorizing as "de l'algèbre de cirque" (convoluted nonsense), which could only provide "le pire des services" (the worst of turns) to Duthuit.⁴⁴ Asked to deliver a French translation of *Three Dialogues* for the catalogue that Jacques Putman was preparing for an exhibition on Bram van Velde at the Galerie Michel Warren in Paris, Beckett eventually delivered only the third segment of the text.⁴⁵ By 1957, the intimate friendship between Beckett and Duthuit had also long faded away,⁴⁶ so that the proposal for a radio broadcast of *Three Dialogues* in the early 1966 had even less chance of meeting Beckett's approval.

The request to clear copyright for a broadcast of *Play* had initially a negative outcome: quite unsurprisingly, as the project involved adaptation. In Martin Esslin's version of the events, while plans were being made for a rebroadcast of *All That Fall* and a reading of Beckett's poetry in the first quarter of 1966, the wish to add a third broadcast, never aired before, persuaded P.H. Newby to develop the experiments attempted off-the-record by the Rothwell Group, scheduling an official production of *Play* for the Third Programme.⁴⁷ Beckett's initial opposition was reported by Margaret McLaren during a phone call with Jack Beale, who transmitted the author's unequivocal point of view: "I understand he does not wish his stage works to be performed in any other medium."⁴⁸ On the same day, Esslin turned discreetly to Beckett and clarified his own initial skepticism about adaptation.⁴⁹ Esslin's enquiry and the amount of energy he invested in the project, even at an early stage, might, however, leave room to speculate on the part he played along the way toward broadcast. Beckett asked to hear the Rothwell Group recording during his next trip to London, displaying a certain degree of flexibility: "If I find it possible I'll withdraw my opposition."[50] He was in London between 25 January and 7 February 1966, when among other commitments he took part in the recording of *MacGowran Speaking Beckett* at Pye Studios.[51] As could happen when Beckett's closest collaborators dealt with him directly rather than through his representatives, Beckett approved the project verbally despite his skepticism,[52] and the agent was informed by Jack Beale only weeks afterwards: "Now it seems someone has been at work, and managed to persuade Mr. Beckett to change his mind, at any rate to the extent of giving us permission in principle to broadcast PLAY at an approximate length of thirty minutes."[53] Nevertheless, it is revealing of Beckett's unease with the entire project that he decided to retain rights with the BBC External Services when he signed the original contract.[54] And despite the guidance provided during production, he must have experienced dissatisfaction even later, as he reluctantly renewed the license for one single broadcast with the BBC domestic services,[55] and only very cautiously allowed limited copyright clearance in foreign countries on a case-by-case basis.[56]

The need to reaffirm authorial prerogatives in copyright resurfaced on a number of other occasions, so that Beckett could rebuke his British publisher: "Please go easy with these readings. Imagination.. should not be read now. Why that passage from Molloy? I don't want to interfere with anything under way, but please no more without my knowing what extracts and read how & by whom. Forgive if I sound cantankerous."[57] Yet Beckett was no stranger to irony: "Piles of letters. All no. Refused Stuttgart fee. Refused Duthuit dialogues BBC. Wrote crankily to Calder about his readings. Time they buried me."[58] In all cases, there is little doubt that Beckett's stewardship of his work was imbued by a *continental* perception of authorship, expressed by the law in a wide array of moral rights exceeding those introduced in the UK in 1988 (and including, for instance, the right "to withdraw a work from circulation on the ground that the author is no longer happy with it").[59]

Appendix

The Agreements with BBC Radio

This appendix is meant to integrate critical discourse with supporting data. The table presented here gathers a large body of information up to the year

1985, available at the time of writing this chapter (2015) in a series of files "vetted and declared open for research," as stated in writing by the BBC upon releasing each file. The table supplies contractual and financial details exclusively on first broadcasts and first clearance of copyright for the BBC original radio plays, dramatized readings and non-dramatized (or "single-voice") readings in their integral versions.[60] Therefore, it does not intend to give account of extensions or renewals of the licenses, which could cover for instance: many uncut rebroadcasts of the original recordings (e.g. a rebroadcast of *All That Fall* to mark the award of the Nobel Prize for Literature to Beckett);[61] many uncut first broadcasts of the original recordings in the BBC's External Services (e.g. broadcasts of *Embers* and *The Old Tune* in Germany proposed in July 1966);[62] all the first broadcasts of excerpts as part of other BBC Radio or TV programs (e.g. an extract from *All That Fall* included in the celebratory episode *Mary O'Farrell*).[63] When not covered by the original contracts, these and other broadcasts were subject to separate conditions and to the payment of separate fees. Needless to say, non-UK productions and non-BBC UK productions are excluded as not pertinent to the present research. A few of the productions proposed by the BBC but later turned down have been discussed during the course of this chapter. Copyright matters related to the broadcasts for BBC Television were the subject of a parallel research.[64] To track down all the agreements for BBC Radio appears not only difficult, but well-nigh impossible due to the merely partial availability of the documents, so that at present even a deeper enquiry would eventually prove incomplete. It should also be clear by now that the purpose of my research was not to give an account of all transactions and thereby assess Beckett's overall income, but rather to describe the typical modes of a series of commercial exchanges.

The main sources for the data gathered in the table are the contracts between licensor (i.e. Beckett's publisher or Beckett's agent, varying by the type of broadcast and allocation of broadcasting rights at the time of signature) and licensee (i.e. the British Broadcasting Corporation), integrated by a vast and valuable correspondence among all the parties involved in the agreement. Although the contracts sent out by the BBC Copyright Department for signature are not always available nowadays, the enclosed top-page forms returned to the BBC are open for consultation. These forms are of great relevance for research on Beckett's readings, for two primary reasons. Firstly, because they provide concisely on the recto side of the pages the terms of the attached contracts, and specifically: agreeing parties, fees agreed, terms of payment, title of the work, hosting program (if any), broadcasting service, date of first broadcast (frequently an estimate), languages and territories, and duration of the agreement. Secondly, because the forms state on the verso the standard scale of payments, based on collective licenses stipulated periodically between the Publishers' Association (or the Publishers Licensing Society), the Society of Authors (or the League of Dramatists) and the BBC itself.[65] The practice of collective licensing traditionally observed by the BBC for dramatized and non-dramatized readings, which is intrinsic to the history of the Third Programme,[66] represents nowadays a significant exception to the rationale followed by commercial companies, which typically negotiate fees on a case-by-case basis.[67] Thus it is possible both to compare fees in commercial and public service broadcasting, and the conditions granted by the BBC to Beckett against those accorded to authors in general.

The contracts for the radio plays were signed directly with Beckett's agents at Curtis Brown, who managed his theatrical rights internationally. Nonetheless, reaching a deal was not as straightforward as it might have been, due to territorial restrictions on transcription broadcast distribution. At the end of 1962, for instance, a contract for permanent non-exclusive transcription rights in *Words and Music* had to be canceled,[68] due to a request from the agent (on behalf of Beckett) to omit North America, which was not among the territories managed by Curtis Brown.[69] It proved harder, on the other hand, to settle the administration of broadcasting rights in the readings. Early agreements were made with Curtis Brown for readings based also on prose works, such as *Molloy*, *Malone Dies*, *The Unnamable* and *From an Abandoned Work*. However, the poetry readings were dealt with by Calder & Boyars, and, as previously mentioned, Calder successfully contested the administration of broadcasting rights on *Lessness*, gaining the opportunity to make a precedent of this. Beckett showed a degree of generosity in assigning broadcasting rights on the prose to Calder, as previously made in 1957 when assigning performance rights in the USA to Barney Rosset for *Endgame* (in spite of the fear of receiving "thunderbolts upon my head" from Curtis Brown).[70] On both occasions, Beckett's resolution was at odds with an agenting practice that, in more recent years, has favored fixed-term licenses and the retention of entire categories of rights (originally subsidiary rights), providing authors greater room for maneuvre and frequently higher revenues.[71]

In considering the matter of Beckett's revenues, it is important to make brief reference to a more general point. Among the early, laudatory reviews of *All That Fall*, we find a clever piece by Roy Walker for *Tribune*, which, in drawing a parallel with *Under Milk Wood* by Dylan Thomas (1954), offered a blunt assessment of the radio broadcasting market and interpreted the difficulties of encouraging established contemporary authors to focus on radio:

> Nationalities apart, why are these good things so few and far between?
> The secondary reason is mainly economic. About £ 400 is spent on producing a radio play. The writer's cut cannot compare with the royalties from a stage play, although national publicity is an incentive to new or unknown authors.
> The B.B.C.'s attempts to rope in the big names with fancy fees often produced merely early, rejected or otherwise discarded work, vamped up for the occasion.
> Even if the money is there, the West End is the better bet. You can get your broadcasts later. When a successful stage play dies it goes, after a few years in limbo, to Broadcasting House for a brief disembodied life on the air.[72]

These difficulties were confirmed just a few months later in a memo by McWhinnie, avowing that "it is extremely rare for a writer of universal reputation to write specially for us, and when the result is a major dramatic work bringing us a vast amount of prestige we may consider ourselves fortunate."[73] In the same message, highlighting not least McWhinnie's wish to focus more on the contemporary,[74] he also mentioned the "somewhat inadequate rates he [i.e. Beckett] was paid for 'All That Fall'"—confirming that Barbara Bray's plead to correspond a fee "as generous as the regulations permit" had been unsuccessful—[75]and the "most modest rates" for *Fin de partie*, for which a contract had just been signed.[76] Prominent contemporary authors were encouraged to use radio as a medium for theatrical revivals, therefore, whereas Robert Pinget, for instance, must certainly have benefited from the Third Programme at the time of his collaboration, chiefly in terms of audience. Furthermore, as McWhinnie's allusion to the broadcast of *Endgame* in French suggests, even the fees on non-original works could appear inadequate, and the mark-up of one-sixth or 25 per cent to the standard scale of payment—granted to Beckett since 1961[77] and 1962[78] respectively, with occasional variations from one to the other—did not fully include him in the "established" or "eminent" categories of authors working for the BBC.[79] The slow updating of collective licenses certainly did not favor him financially either, as repeatedly pointed out by John Calder in his correspondence with the BBC.[80]

	Licensor (UK representative or rights holder)	Licensee (with responsible for copyright clearance)	Signature of the agreement	Main services and territories (summary)	Fees paid (with invoice details)	Notes on the agreement
All That Fall (monophonic)	Curtis Brown Ltd.	Heather Dean/BBC, Copyright Department	Lawrence Hammond/Curtis Brown, 22 January 1957 (final agreement)	Broadcast performances in English in the BBC Overseas Service; broadcast performances in foreign languages in the BBC Overseas Service; repeat performances in the BBC Service for the United Kingdom	130 guineas (£136.10s.0d) totally, payable on acceptance of the manuscript (contract ref. 01/CT/HD, note of payment A 1220 HD.202 [repeat]; CRCB)	The first agreement was canceled and a second one was signed, to adjust timing and fee to the author: originally 60 guineas (£63.0s.0d) for 45'
Fin de partie	Curtis Brown Ltd.	Heather Dean/BBC, Copyright Department	Lawrence Hammond/Curtis Brown, 21 March 1957	Broadcast performances in the BBC's Services for the United Kingdom; broadcast performances in English in the BBC's Overseas Services; broadcast performances in foreign languages in the BBC's Overseas Services	£73.0s.0d totally, payable on broadcasting, standard scale without increase (contract form ref. 01/CT/HD, notes of payment 1220 HD.556; CRCB)	
Malloy	Curtis Brown Ltd.	Heather Dean/BBC, Copyright Department	Prudence Hopkins/Curtis Brown, 23 July 1957	Broadcast performances in the BBC's Services for the United Kingdom; broadcast performances in English in the BBC's Overseas Services; broadcast performances in foreign languages in the BBC's Overseas Services	£40.13s.4d totally (contract form ref. 01/CT/HD, note of payment not traced; CRCB)	

(continued)

(continued)

	Licensor (UK representative or rights holder)	Licensee (with responsible for copyright clearance)	Signature of the agreement	Main services and territories (summary)	Fees paid (with invoice details)	Notes on the agreement
From an Abandoned Work	Curtis Brown Ltd.	Heather Dean/BBC, Copyright Department	Lawrence Hammond/Curtis Brown, 25 November 1957	Broadcast performances in English in the BBC Overseas Service; broadcast performances in foreign languages in the BBC Overseas Service; repeat performances in the BBC Service for the United Kingdom	20 guineas (£21.0s.0d) totally, payable on acceptance of the material, standard scale without increase (£21.0s.0d) (contract ref. 01/CT/HD, note of payment not traced; *CRCB*)	
Malone Dies	Curtis Brown Ltd.	Heather Dean/BBC, Copyright Department	Margaret McLaren/Curtis Brown, 28 February 1958	Broadcast performances in the BBC's Services for the United Kingdom; broadcast performances in English in the BBC's Overseas Services; broadcast performances in foreign languages in the BBC's Overseas Services	£73.0s.0d totally, payable on broadcasting, standard scale without increase (contract ref. 01/CT/HD, note of payment A 1220 HD 1023 [repeat]; *CRCB*)	
The Unnamable	Curtis Brown Ltd.	Heather Dean/BBC, Copyright Department	Margaret McLaren/Curtis Brown, 26 November 1958	Broadcast performances in the BBC's Services for the United Kingdom; broadcast performances in English in the BBC's Overseas Services; broadcast performances in foreign languages in the BBC's Overseas Services	£62.0s.0d totally, payable on broadcasting, standard scale without increase (contract ref. 01/CT/HD, note of payment A 1220 HD 155 [repeat]; *CRCB*)	

Embers	Curtis Brown Ltd.	Heather Dean/BBC, Copyright Department	Margaret McLaren/Curtis Brown, 23 February 1959	Broadcast performances in English in the BBC Overseas Service; broadcast performances in foreign languages in the BBC Overseas Service; repeat performances in the BBC Service for the United Kingdom	90 guineas (£94.10s.0d) totally, payable on acceptance of the manuscript (contract ref. 01/CT/HD, note of payment A 1220 HD 712 [repeat]; *CRCB*)
Waiting for Godot (BBC Radio version)	Curtis Brown Ltd.	Heather Dean/BBC, Copyright Department	Margaret McLaren/Curtis Brown, 30 October 1959	Broadcast performances in the BBC's Services for the United Kingdom; broadcast performances in English in the BBC's Overseas Services; broadcast performances in foreign languages in the BBC's Overseas Services	£90.0s.0d totally, payable on broadcasting, usual scale without increase (contract ref. 01/CT/HD, note of payment A 1220 HD 417 [repeat]; *CRCB*)
The Old Tune	Curtis Brown Ltd.	Heather Dean/BBC, Copyright Department	Margaret McLaren/Curtis Brown, 15 December 1959	Broadcast performances in English in the BBC Overseas Service; repeat performances in the BBC Service for the United Kingdom	30 guineas (£31.10s.0d) totally, payable on signature of the agreement (contract ref. 01/CT/HD, note of payment not traced; *CRCB*)

(*continued*)

(continued)

	Licensor (UK representative or rights holder)	Licensee (with responsible for copyright clearance)	Signature of the agreement	Main services and territories (summary)	Fees paid (with invoice details)	Notes on the agreement
From the Fifties: Waiting for Godot	Curtis Brown Ltd.	Heather Dean/BBC, Copyright Department	Margaret McLaren/Curtis Brown, 23 May 1961	Broadcast performances in the BBC's Services for the United Kingdom; broadcast performances in English in the BBC's Overseas Services; broadcast performances in foreign languages in the BBC's Overseas Services	£92.15s.0d totally, payable on broadcasting, standard scale increased by one sixth (contract form ref. 01/CT/HD, note of payment HD 188; *CRCB*)	
Endgame	Curtis Brown Ltd.	Heather Dean/BBC, Copyright Department	Margaret McLaren/Curtis Brown, 29 January 1962	Broadcast performances in the BBC's Services for the United Kingdom; broadcast performances in English in the BBC's Overseas Services; broadcast performances in foreign languages in the BBC's Overseas Services	£118.8s.4d totally, payable on broadcasting, standard scale increased by one sixth (contract form ref. 01/CT/HD, notes of payment A 1220 HD 605; *CRCB*)	
Words and Music	Curtis Brown Ltd.	Heather Dean/BBC, Copyright Department	Margaret McLaren/Curtis Brown, 27 February 1962	Broadcast performances in English in the BBC Overseas Service; broadcast performances in foreign languages in the BBC Overseas Service; repeat performances in the BBC Service for the United Kingdom	75 guineas (£78.15s.0d) totally, payable on broadcasting (contract form ref. 01/CT/HD, note of payment A 1220 HD 1282 [repeat]; *CRCB*)	

Wrth aros Godot (*Waiting for Godot*, Welsh version)	Curtis Brown Ltd.	D.L. Ross/BBC, Copyright Department	Margaret McLaren/Curtis Brown, 17 July 1962	Broadcast performances in the BBC's Services for the United Kingdom; broadcast performances in English in the BBC's External Services; broadcast performances in foreign languages in the BBC's External Services	£81.13s.4d totally, payable on broadcasting, standard scale increased by 25% (contract form ref. 01/CT/DLR, note of payment A 1220 DLR 2339; *CRCB*)	Proposed together with a production of *Endgame* in Welsh, soon discarded (*CRCB*)
Cascando	Curtis Brown Ltd.	Elsie Wakeham/BBC, Copyright Department	Margaret McLaren/Curtis Brown, 19 March 1964	Broadcast performances in English in the BBC Overseas Service; broadcast performances in foreign languages in the BBC Overseas Service; repeat performances in the BBC Service for the United Kingdom	100 guineas (£105.0s.0d) totally, payable on broadcasting (contract form ref. 01/CT/EHW, note of payment EW 2270 A.1220; *CRCB*)	

(*continued*)

(continued)

	Licensor (UK representative or rights holder)	Licensee (with responsible for copyright clearance)	Signature of the agreement	Main services and territories (summary)	Fees paid (with invoice details)	Notes on the agreement
Poems by Samuel Beckett	Calder & Boyars Ltd.	Jack Beale/BBC, Copyright Department	John Calder/Calder & Boyars, 2 October 1965	Broadcast performances in the BBC's Services for the United Kingdom; broadcast performances in English in the BBC's External Services; broadcast performances in foreign languages in the BBC's External Services	"Whoroscope" (97 lines: £15.6s.3d), "Enueg I" (76 lines: £12.17s.3d), "Serena II" (53 lines: £10.8s.3d), "Malacoda" (29 lines: £6.14s.9d), "Alba" (17 lines: £5.10s.3d), "Cascando" (37 lines: £7.19s.3d), "Saint-Lô" (4 lines: £1.16s.9d), "my way is in the sand flowing" (9 lines: £3.13s.6d), "what would I do without this world faceless incurious" (15 lines: £3.13s.6d), "I would like my love to die" (4 lines: £1.16s.9d): £69.16s.6d totally, payable on broadcasting, standard scale increased by one sixth (contract form ref. 01/CT/JB, note of payment JB 4621; CR 65–69)	
Play	Curtis Brown Ltd.	Jack Beale/BBC, Copyright Department	Margaret McLaren/Curtis Brown, 8 March 1966	Broadcast performances in the BBC's Services for the United Kingdom	£39.7s.6d, payable on broadcasting, standard scale increased by 25% (contract form ref. 01/CT/JB, note of payment JB 5233; CR 65–69)	The initial fee to the author was £62.10s.0d, based on a provisional length of 30' (Jack Beale to Margaret McLaren, 28 February 1966; CR 65–69)

More Poems by Samuel Beckett	Calder & Boyars Ltd. and Curtis Brown Ltd.	Jack Beale/BBC, Copyright Department	With Curtis Brown: Margaret McLaren, 8 March 1966 ("Unpublished"/"Span [*sic*] the years of learning" [i.e. "Gnome": see Samuel Beckett, *The Collected Poems of Samuel Beckett*, a critical edition edited by Seán Lawlor and John Pilling (London: Faber & Faber, 2012), 349]) and 18 May 1966 ("Age is when to a man", from *Words and Music*); with Calder & Boyars: John Calder, 5 April 1966	Broadcast performances in the BBC's Services for the United Kingdom; broadcast performances in English in the BBC's External Services; broadcast performances in foreign languages in the BBC's External Services	From *Poems in English*: "The Vulture" (6 lines: £1.16s.9d), "Echo's Bones" (5 lines: £1.16s.9d), "Da Tagte Es" (4 lines: £1.16s.9d), "Serena I" (53 lines: £10.8s.3d), "Serena III" (27 lines: £6.14s.9d), "Sanies I" (52 lines: £10.8s.3d); from *Watt*: "who may tell the tale" (8 lines: £1.16s.9d), "Watt will not" (26 lines: £6.14s.9d); from *Words and Music*: beginning of "Age is when to a man" (9 lines: £3.13s.6d); "Unpublished Poem"/ "Span [*sic*] the years of learning" [i.e. "Gnome": see Beckett, *The Collected Poems of Samuel Beckett*, 349] (5 lines: £1.16s.9d): £41.13s.0d (Calder & Boyars Ltd.) + £5.10s.3d (Curtis Brown Ltd.), payable on broadcasting, standard scale increased by one sixth (contract forms ref. 01/CT/JB, notes of payment JB 5304 and JB 5305; *CR* 65–69)	Permissions were cleared by the agent rather than the original publisher for two of the poems read: the "Unpublished Poem"/ "Span [*sic*] the Years of Learning" [i.e. "Gnome": see Beckett, *The Collected Poems of Samuel Beckett*, 349], as it was thought to be still unpublished by Beckett himself (althought it had appeared on *Dublin Magazine*, IX, n.s., July-September 1934, 8) and so added by the author from memory in conversation with Calder; and "Age is when to a man", from *Words and Music*, as the BBC Copyright Department could not trace the licensor (Barney Rosset/Grove Press), even consulting Susan Goodridge/Faber and Faber (*CR* 65–69). A section from *Imagination Dead Imagine*, initially thought for inclusion, was later discarded (Marion Boyars to Jack Beale, 3 February 1966, with a note from 9 February 1966; *CR* 65–69)

(*continued*)

(continued)

	Licensor (UK representative or rights holder)	Licensee (with responsible for copyright clearance)	Signature of the agreement	Main services and territories (summary)	Fees paid (with invoice details)	Notes on the agreement
Imagination Dead Imagine	Calder & Boyars Ltd.	Rosemary Nibbs/BBC, Drama Department; Jack Beale/BBC, Copyright Department	Marion Boyars/Calder and Boyars, 24 November 1966	Broadcast performances in the BBC's Services for the United Kingdom; broadcast performances in English in the BBC's External Services; broadcast performances in foreign languages in the BBC's External Services	£14.15s.2d totally, payable on broadcasting, standard scale increased by one sixth (contract form ref. 01/CT/JB, note of payment JB 5793; *CR 65–69*)	Initially meant to be part of the second reading of SB's poems (Marion Boyars to Jack Beale, 3 February 1966, with a note from 9 February 1966; *CR 65–69*). The initial fee to the author was £26.16s.8d, based on a provisional length of 20' (Jack Beale to John Calder, 23 November 1966; *CR 65–69*)
Lessness	Curtis Brown Ltd. (first contract); new contract Calder & Boyars Ltd.	David Gower/BBC, Copyright Department	Penelope Sinclair/Curtis Brown, 15 July 1970 (first contract); new contract John Calder/Calder & Boyars, 3 September 1970	Broadcast performances in the BBC's Services for the British Isles; broadcast performances in English in the BBC's External Services; broadcast performances in foreign languages in the BBC's External Services	£42.29 totally, payable on broadcasting, standard scale increased by one sixth (contract form ref. 01/CT/DG, note of payment JMH 1278; *CR 70–74*)	The initial contract countersigned by Penelope Sinclair was cancelled when it was clarified that Beckett considered *Lessness* as prose work and not a play, and that not only publication but also broadcasting rights were controlled by Calder & Boyars Ltd. (Jack Beale to John Calder, 28 August 1970; *CR 70–74*). The initial fee to the author was £44.0s.8d, based on a provisional length of 35' (David Gower to Penny Sinclair, 12 June 1970; *CR 70–74*)

All That Fall (stereophonic)	Curtis Brown Ltd.	Joan Hedgecock/ BBC, Copyright Department	Not traced	Not traced	£250.0s.0d totally, payable on broadcasting (contract form ref. not traced, note of payment JMH 760; CR 70–74)
The Lost Ones	Calder & Boyars Ltd.	David Gower/BBC, Copyright Department	Marion Boyars/Calder & Boyars, 5 September 1972	Broadcast performances in the BBC's Services for the British Isles; broadcast performances in English in the BBC's External Services; broadcast performances in foreign languages in the BBC's External Services	£156.60 totally, payable on broadcasting, standard scale increased by 25% (contract form ref. 01/CT/DG, note of payment DG 93; CR 70–74)
First Love	Calder & Boyars Ltd.	Joan Hedgecock/ BBC, Copyright Department	Marion Boyars/Calder & Boyars, 12 April 1973	Broadcast performances in the BBC's Services for the British Isles; broadcast performances in English in the BBC's External Services; broadcast performances in foreign languages in the BBC's External Services	£153.90 totally, payable on broadcasting, standard scale increased by 25% (contract form ref. 01/CT/JMH, note of payment JMH 2600; CR 70–74)

(*continued*)

(continued)

Licensor (UK representative or rights holder)	Licensee (with responsible for copyright clearance)	Signature of the agreement	Main services and territories (summary)	Fees paid (with invoice details)	Notes on the agreement
Texts for Nothing (four readings)	Calder & Boyars Ltd.	Joan Hedgecock/BBC, Copyright Department	John Calder/Calder & Boyars, 11 August 1974	Broadcast performances in the BBC's Services for the British Isles; broadcast performances in English in the BBC's External Services; broadcast performances in foreign languages in the BBC's External Services	£387.15 totally for the four readings (£96.81 for the first reading, £96.78 for each of the remaining three readings), payable on broadcasting, standard scale increased by one sixth (contract form ref. 01/CT/JMH, note of payment JMH 514; CR 70–74 and CR 75–79)	
Rough for Radio [II] (*Pochade radiophonique*)	Spokesmen	Kathryn M. Pratt/BBC, Copyright Department; Lyn J. Fern/BBC, Copyright Department	Barry Marshall/Spokesmen, 19 February 1976	Broadcast performances in the BBC's Services for the British Isles; broadcast performances in English in the BBC's External Services; broadcast performances in foreign languages in the BBC's External Services	£62.0s.0d totally, payable on broadcasting, standard scale increased by 25% (contract form ref. 01/CT/KMP, note of payment not traced; CR 75–79)	
For to end yet again	John Calder (Publishers) Ltd.	Lyn J. Fern, David Gower and Mary Nielsen/BBC, Copyright Department	Irene Staunton/John Calder (Publishers), 4 August 1976	Broadcast performances in the BBC's Services for the British Isles; broadcast performances in English in the BBC's External Services; broadcast performances in foreign languages in the BBC's External Services	£39.20 totally, payable on broadcasting, standard scale increased by one sixth (contract form ref. 01/CT/DG/R, note of payment DG/R 891; CR 75–79)	

The Drunken Boat	John Calder (Publishers) Ltd.	Lyn J. Fern/BBC, Copyright Department; David Gower/BBC, Copyright Department;	Irene Staunton/John Calder (Publishers), 19 January 1977	Broadcast performances in the BBC's Services for the British Isles; broadcast performances in English in the BBC's External Services; broadcast performances in foreign languages in the BBC's External Services	£23.10 totally, payable on broadcasting, standard scale increased by one sixth (contract form ref. 01/CT/DG/R, note of payment DG/R 411; *CR 75–79*)
From an Abandoned Work	Rosica Colin Ltd.	Kathryn Turner/BBC, Copyright Department	Samuel Beckett, 12 September 1979	Broadcast performances in the BBC's Services for the British Isles; broadcast performances in English in the BBC's External Services; broadcast performances in foreign languages in the BBC's External Services	£89.84 totally, payable on broadcasting, standard scale increased by one sixth (contract form ref. 01/CT/KMT, note of payment KMT 7086; *CR 75–79*)
Company	John Calder (Publishers) Ltd.	Marian E. Tregear/BBC, Copyright Department	Alice Watson/John Calder (Publishers), 6 June 1980	Broadcast performances in the BBC's Services for the British Isles; broadcast performances in English in the BBC's External Services; broadcast performances in foreign languages in the BBC's External Services	£385.18 totally, payable on broadcasting, standard scale increased by one sixth (contract form ref. 01/CT/MET, note of payment MET 982; *CR 80–84*)
Ill Seen Ill Said	John Calder (Publishers) Ltd.	Kathryn Turner/BBC, Copyright Department	Anthony Eyre/John Calder (Publishers), 23 November 1981	1. Services for the British Isles; 2. External Services: (a) English Language Services; (b) Foreign Language Services	£476.30 totally, payable on broadcasting, standard scale increased by one sixth (contract form ref. 01/CT/KMT, note of payment KMT 1269; *CR 80–84*)

(continued)

(continued)

	Licensor (UK representative or rights holder)	Licensee (with responsible for copyright clearance)	Signature of the agreement	Main services and territories (summary)	Fees paid (with invoice details)	Notes on the agreement
Worstward Ho	John Calder (Publishers) Ltd.	Kathryn Turner/BBC, Copyright Department	Nancy Webber/John Calder (Publishers), 21 January 1983	BBC Radio Services for the British Isles, External Services in English and in foreign languages	£306.13 totally, payable on broadcasting, standard scale increased by one sixth (contract form ref. 01/CT/KMT, note of payment KMT 2292; CR 80–84)	
A Piece of Monologue	n/a	n/a	n/a	n/a	n/a	
Stirrings Still	n/a	n/a	n/a	n/a	n/a	

Acknowledgments

I thank Matthew Feldman (Teesside University) for involving me in this project on Beckett and BBC Radio; Mark Nixon (University of Reading) for his observations based on his research on Beckett and publishing; Lois More Overbeck (Emory University) for her interest in my project and availability to discuss it in London and Reading. An extract from the chapter was delivered during the annual Beckett International Foundation Seminar, on 30 October 2015 (Conference Room, Special Collections, The University of Reading), and I am grateful for any expression of interest received on that occasion, particularly to James Knowlson and John Pilling. I am also very grateful to Louise North (Archives Researcher) and Matthew Chipping (Archives Researcher) of the BBC Written Archives Centre (BBC WAC) in Caversham; Steven Dryden (Sound Archive & Humanities Reference Specialist) of the British Library in London; and Guy Leonard Baxter (University Archivist) of the University of Reading, Special Collections.

Abbreviations

A.H.D.(S.) Assistant Head of Drama (Sound)
C.T.P.   Controller, Third Programme
H.D.(S.)   Head of Drama (Sound)
S.E.D.(S.) Script Editor, Drama (Sound)

Notes

1. Lynette Owen, *Selling Rights*, 7th ed. (London: Routledge, 2014), 3.
2. Ibid., 60–1.
3. John B. Thompson, *Merchants of Culture: The Publishing Business in the Twenty-First Century*, 2nd ed. (Cambridge: Polity Press, 2012), 62–3.
4. Owen, *Selling Rights*, 5.
5. Thompson, *Merchants of Culture*, 59–61.
6. SB to Barney Rosset, 6 April 1957; in *Letters III*, 38.
7. SB to Maurice Girodias, 7 January 1958; in *Letters III*, 91–2.
8. SB to Barney Rosset, 5 May 1959; in *Letters III*, 229.
9. Owen, *Selling Rights*, 47.
10. Beckett's awareness of the writer's financial needs seems to be implied in a passage of *Cascando* quoted in my exergum: "I have lived on it…till I'm old. Old enough"; Samuel Beckett, *The Complete Dramatic Works* (London: Faber and Faber, 2006), 300.

11. Margaret McLaren, Curtis Brown, to Edward Caffery, BBC Copyright Department, 31 August 1965; in *CR 65–69*.
12. Gaby Hartel, "'Cher ami'—'Lieber Samuel Beckett': Beckett and his German Publisher Suhrkamp Verlag," in Mark Nixon, ed., *Publishing Samuel Beckett* (London: The British Library, 2011), 134–5.
13. Justin Beplate, "Samuel Beckett, Olympia Press and the Merlin Juveniles," in Nixon, ed., *Publishing Samuel Beckett*, 107–8.
14. SB to Rosica Colin, n.d. [after 18 January 1957]; in *Letters III*, 16–7.
15. Mark Nixon, "Introduction: 'Silly Business'—Beckett and the World of Publishing," in Nixon, ed., *Publishing Samuel Beckett*, 5.
16. Penelope Sinclair, Curtis Brown, to David Gower, BBC Copyright Department, 15 July 1970 (and message by Frederica F. Dennis, Curtis Brown, 16 July 1970; with attached contract form); in *CR 70–74*.
17. John Calder, Calder & Boyars, to David Gower, BBC Copyright Department, 7 August 1970; in *CR 70–74*.
18. Penelope Sinclair, Curtis Brown, to David Gower, BBC Copyright Department, 13 August 1970; in *CR 70–74*.
19. Richard Odgers, Curtis Brown, to R. [Donald?] Walford, BBC [Copyright Department?], 27 August 1970; in *CR 70–74*.
20. John Calder, Calder & Boyars, to the BBC Copyright Department, 11 August 1972; in *CR 70–74*.
21. SB to Stefani Hunzinger, S. Fischer Verlag, 18 November 1962; in *Letters III*, 516–7.
22. "The introduction of moral rights to the copyright countries has been challenged to different degrees …. In fact moral rights, like all individual rights, are apt to frustrate powerful interests. If they cannot do so, they cannot fulfil their purposes." Elizabeth Adeney, *The Moral Rights of Authors and Performers: An International and Comparative Analysis* (Oxford: Oxford University Press, 2006), ln. 08. Adeney stresses in particular the difficulty of introducing moral rights in the United States.
23. *Clark's Publishing Agreements: A Book of Precedents*, ed. Lynette Owen, 9th ed. (Haywards Heath: Bloomsbury Professional, 2013), 717–8.
24. Ibid., 715–6.
25. Owen, *Selling Rights*, 20–1; 58.
26. *Clark's Publishing Agreements*, 718–9.
27. James Joyce, *Letters of James Joyce*, eds. Stuart Gilbert and Richard Ellmann (New York: The Viking Press, 1966), vol. 3, 151–3.
28. James Joyce, "Communication de M. James Joyce sur le Droit Moral des Écrivains," in *XVe Congrès International de la Fédération P.E.N.* (Paris: P.E.N., 1937), 24.
29. Richard Ellmann, *James Joyce*, new and revised edition (New York: Oxford University Press, 1982), 703–4.

30. Carol Loeb Shloss, "Privacy and Piracy in the Joyce Trade: James Joyce and *Le Droit Moral*," *James Joyce Quarterly* 37.3–4 (Spring-Summer 2000), 451.
31. James Joyce, *The Critical Writings of James Joyce*, eds. Ellsworth Mason and Richard Ellmann (New York: The Viking Press, 1959), 274–5.
32. Shloss, "Privacy and Piracy in the Joyce Trade," 449.
33. Owen, *Selling Rights*, 21.
34. SB to Barbara Bray, 4 August 1962; in *Letters III*, 490–1. Beckett's earlier reply to Curtis Brown was even more direct: "I don't want Lucky in churches in Edinburgh or anywhere else and should be obliged if you would refuse permission for this" (SB to John Barber, Curtis Brown, 3 August 1962; in *Letters III*, 491 n. 4).
35. Martin Esslin, H.D.(S.), to Rosemary Nibbs, BBC Drama Department, 5 October 1965; in *SW 63–67*.
36. Martin Esslin, H.D.(S.), to SB, 30 September 1964; in *SW 63–67*. See Martin Esslin, ed., *Samuel Beckett: A Collection of Critical Essays* (Englewood Cliffs, NJ: Prentice Hall, 1965); 16–22.
37. Martin Esslin, H.D.(S.), to SB, 3 November 1965; in *SW 63–67*. See *Letters III*, 678 n. 2.
38. Jack Beale, BBC Copyright Department, to Margaret McLaren, Curtis Brown, 15 October 1965; in *CR 65–69*.
39. Margaret McLaren, Curtis Brown, to Jack Beale, BBC Copyright Department, 27 October 1965; in *CR 65–69*.
40. SB to Martin Esslin, H.D.(S.), 9 November 1965; in *Letters III*, 678.
41. SB to Thomas MacGreevy, 27 March 1949; in *Letters II*, 146.
42. SB to Georges Duthuit, n.d. [28 June 1949?]; in *Letters II*, 168–9.
43. SB to Georges Duthuit, n.d. [on or after 30 April, before 26 May 1949]; in *Letters II*, 148–50. See Samuel Beckett, *Murphy*, ed. J.C.C. Mays (London: Faber & Faber, 2009), 112.
44. SB to Jacques Putman, 5 February 1957; in *Letters III*, 17–8.
45. See SB to Jacques Putman, n.d. [before 13 March 1957] and 13 March 1957; in *Letters III*, 27–8 and 28–30.
46. *Letters III*, 29–30 n. 2.
47. Martin Esslin, H.D.(S.), to SB, 3 November 1965; in *SW 63–67*.
48. Jack Beale, BBC Copyright Department, to Rosemary Nibbs, BBC Drama Department, 3 November 1965; in *SW 63–67*. Pen note by Rosemary Nibbs, BBC Drama Department, 3 November 1965; in *CR 65–69*.
49. Martin Esslin, H.D.(S.), to SB, 3 November 1965; in *SW 63–67*.
50. SB to Martin Esslin, H.D.(S.), 9 November 1965; in *Letters III*, 677.
51. John Pilling, *A Samuel Beckett Chronology* (Basingstoke: Palgrave Macmillan, 2006), 171.

52. N.n., S.E.D.(S.), to Rosemary Nibbs, BBC Copyright Department, 7 February 1966; in *SW 63–67*.
53. Jack Beale, BBC Copyright Department, to Margaret McLaren, Curtis Brown, 28 February 1966; in *CR 65–69*.
54. Judith Leonard, Curtis Brown, to Jack Beale, 8 March 1966, with attached contract form; in *CR 65–69*.
55. Margaret McLaren, Curtis Brown, to Jack Beale, BBC Copyright Department, 30 May 1967, with attached contract form; in *CR 65–69*.
56. By way of example, a request to grant limited rights to the BBC Transcription Service was turned down by Beckett's agent (Judith Leonard, Curtis Brown, to Olive Howell, BBC Copyright Department, 3 October 1967; in *CR 65–69*), but limited rights in Sweden were granted with the proviso that each case be considered individually in future (Judith Leonard, Curtis Brown, to Olive Howell, BBC Copyright Department, 21 February 1968; in *CR 65–69*).
57. SB to John Calder, 23 October 1965; in *Letters III*, 677 n. 4.
58. SB to Barbara Bray, n.d. [23 October 1965?]; in *Letters III*, 677.
59. Lionel Bently and Brad Sherman, *Intellectual Property Law*, 4th ed. (Oxford: Oxford University Press, 2014), 272.
60. See Owen, *Selling Rights*, 282–4; 296–7.
61. *All That Fall*, a special rebroadcast of his play for radio to mark the award to Samuel Beckett of the Nobel Prize for Literature, produced by Donald McWhinnie, BBC Radio 3, 1 January 1970; *Radio Times* 185.2406/7 (18–25 December 1969), 87.
62. Olive Howell, BBC Copyright Department, to Margaret McLaren, Curtis Brown, 5 July 1966; in *CR 65–69*.
63. *Mary O'Farrell*, a recollection by Henry Reed, with some recordings of her radio performances, produced by Douglas Cleverdon, BBC Radio 3, 4 January 1969; *Radio Times* 182.2356 (2 January 1969), 9. Mary O'Farrell died in London on 10 February 1968.
64. Jonathan Bignell, "Performing Right: Legal Constraints and Beckett's Plays on BBC Television," in Conor Carville and Mark Nixon, eds., "'Beginning of the murmur': Archival Pre-texts and Other Sources," *Samuel Beckett Today/Aujourd'hui* 27 (Amsterdam: Rodopi, 2015), 129–42.
65. Owen, *Selling Rights*, 282.
66. Kate Whitehead, *The Third Programme: A Literary History* (Oxford: Clarendon Press, 1989), 92–105.
67. Owen, *Selling Rights*, 294.
68. Margaret McLaren, Curtis Brown, to Elsie Wakeham, BBC Copyright Department, 17 December 1962, with attached contract; in *CRCB*.
69. Elsie Wakeham, BBC Copyright Department, to Margaret McLaren, Curtis Brown, 28 December 1962; in *CRCB*.

70. SB to Barney Rosset, 6 April 1957; in *Letters III*, 39. Significantly, on that occasion the decision had been taken "de façon à éviter que la pièce soit montée dans de mauvaises conditions" [so as to avoid the play's being staged in unsatisfactory conditions], as Jérôme Lindon had suggested: the intention once again was to safeguard the integrity of the work during its performance (*Letters III*, 41 n. 4).
71. Owen, *Selling Rights*, 47; 61; 69; 74; 294.
72. Roy Walker, "It's Tragic, Mysterious and Wildly Funny," *Tribune*, 18 January 1957, 8: a typewritten copy of the review was included in the publicity dossier of *All That Fall*; in *SW 53–62*.
73. Donald McWhinnie, A.H.D.(S.), to n.n., C. Ent., 1 April 1957; in *SW 53–62*.
74. See Clas Zilliacus, *Beckett and Broadcasting: A Study of the Works of Samuel Beckett for and in Radio and Television*, Acta Academiae Aboensis, ser. a humaniora, humanistiska vetenskaper · socialvetenskaper och juridik · teologi 51.2 (Åbo: Åbo Akademy, 1976), 12–4.
75. Barbara Bray, S.E.D.(S.), to Heather Dean, BBC Copyright Department, 22 October 1956; in *CRCB*.
76. Lawrence Hammond, Curtis Brown, to Heather Dean, BBC Copyright Department, 21 March 1957, and attached contract; in *CRCB*.
77. Margaret McLaren, Curtis Brown, to Heather Dean, BBC Copyright Department, 23 May 1961; in *CRCB*.
78. D.L. Ross, BBC Copyright Department, to Margaret McLaren, Curtis Brown, 16 July 1962; in *CRCB*.
79. See Whitehead, *The Third Programme*, 103.
80. See for example John Calder, Calder & Boyars, to Heather Dean, BBC Copyright Department, 22 January 1969; in *CR 65–69*.

Changing My Tune: Beckett and the BBC Third Programme (1957–1960)

John Pilling

> *I have my faults, but changing my tune is not one of them.*
>
> Beckett, *The Unnamable*

The story of Beckett and broadcasting was so well told almost 40 years ago by the Finnish-Swedish scholar Clas Zilliacus[1] that virtually all subsequent commentary on the subject stands either explicitly or implicitly in Zilliacus's shadow. However, Zilliacus makes it plain from the outset that his concern is exclusively with "the writings of Samuel Beckett expressly conceived for presentation in radio and television"[2]; this naturally excludes the broadcast versions of the prose fiction and *The Old Tune*. Within Beckett's dramatic oeuvre, *The Old Tune* is a manifest anomaly, without predecessors or progeny, a "one-off" easily enough dismissed as an aberration. How could it be otherwise, given that it is a text Beckett extracted and adapted from the play *La Manivelle* by the Swiss writer Robert Pinget?[3] Almost the only comparable enterprise in which Beckett manipulates someone else's pre-existent material is *Long After Chamfort*, poems "re-cycling" the great eighteenth-century pessimists' prose aphorisms expressive at one remove of Beckett's own world view. But *Long After Chamfort* makes its old tunes

---

J. Pilling (✉)
Department of English Literature, University of Reading, Reading, UK

© The Author(s) 2017
D. Addyman et al. (eds.), *Samuel Beckett and BBC Radio*,
New Interpretations of Beckett in the 21st Century,
DOI 10.1057/978-1-137-54265-6_8

new, even when it passes them off as (in *Murphy*-speak) "nothing new." By contrast, it seems clear from private correspondence that Beckett acted on Pinget's behalf largely in the hope of getting his friend better known, and to put Pinget in a position to acquire more stimulating and lucrative commissions at a time when, after early success, Pinget was having difficulty in finding a publisher to support his experiments. This said, it is self-evident that the "translation" of *La Manivelle* is expertly done, however "impertinent" Beckett may have thought it,[4] even if it was primarily a gesture on behalf of a friend. Although Zilliacus quite naturally omitted *The Old Tune* from his concerns, along with the five adaptations Beckett made from his own prose fiction around this time, these "non-canonical" works all replay and reconfigure their points of origin in inventive and challenging ways. These adaptations—from *Molloy, From an Abandoned Work, Malone Dies, The Unnamable* and *How it is*—were created between 1957 and 1960 by the BBC producer Donald McWhinnie working in close collaboration with Beckett, usually by letter but also on the basis of many meetings, and on at least one occasion with Beckett actually present during the recording of the program. There were even, when Martin Esslin took over editorial control, attempts to interest Beckett in a radio broadcast of *Three Dialogues with Georges Duthuit*, an idea which Beckett was, predictably enough, very much against on the grounds—if not exactly firm grounds, as his own adaptations had demonstrated—that the medium for which he had written a given work was the only medium in which it could be presented.[5]

Much as with Beckett's unfinished Johnson fragment *Human Wishes* of 1940, where he had struggled 20 years earlier with his own version of Johnsonese, so here he was struggling with rendering Pinget's play into something not quite "real," and effectively a kind of dialect all on its own: what tends to get called "Stage Oirish," a marginal idiolect of perhaps wider distribution than Pinget's apparently Savoyard version of standard French. In a letter to Barbara Bray of 13 November 1959, Beckett told her that his "rough version" was "[a] bit too free and Irish," and then a few days later claimed that he had tried to keep down the Irishisms but had found that they kept breaking through.[6] A few days later still he was obliged to admit to her: "I can't do it … without the help of Irish rhythms and inversions,"[7] and it is precisely by way of its "Irish" verbal surface that it achieves its effect. Indeed, that effect is such as to call into question whether Beckett had really tried to keep down the Irishisms, or rather had exploited them for all they were worth. In a private communication my colleague Ronald Knowles has made the very good point that the set-up of

The Old Tune could almost be taken as a parody of those stories in Joyce's *Dubliners* which depend on chance meetings (e.g. "An Encounter"), and although Beckett's version of Pinget cannot usefully be seen as a parody,[8] it is clear that there is an element of pastiche at the heart of the enterprise, even with no critique of Pinget's original intended.

How much of an enterprise it was is difficult to reconstruct with any accuracy; but although a first draft of *The Old Tune* only took Beckett a little more than a week,[9] the amount of commitment to it, and effort expended on it, is not easy, I think, to reconcile with Beckett's adamant avowals (e.g. in a letter of 26 September 1986 to S.E. Gontarski) that it is "his [Pinget's] vision not mine." Shane Weller has gone so far as to say that Pinget's vision is "consumed" by Beckett's,[10] and the evidence for a similarly dogged commitment in 1950 to another enterprise which certainly was *not* Beckett's "vision"—the *Anthology of Mexican Poetry* under the editorial supervision of Octavio Paz—tells something of the same story. We could be forgiven for inferring that getting involved in *The Old Tune*, even with the treatment intended to be "on the light side as [Pinget] wants it,"[11] turned out to require a considerable investment of time and trouble, typical of all the "labours of poetical excavation"[12] which Beckett endured, even when he felt he was doing little more than telling himself the same old story. In November 1959 letters to Barbara Bray—also a friend of Pinget—Beckett spoke of the play as to all intents and purposes finished. A letter on 14 November 1959 to her records: "Finished *La Manivelle* earlier than I expected. Herewith. I hope I can improve it later, but for the moment can't do more. The names could be improved.... The doubtful passages are the military and legal."[13] Beckett went on: "If anything here too wrong or invraisemblable for English listeners please point out, though accuracy obviously secondary consideration."[14] Yet on 1 December 1959 Beckett wondered whether or not a better job could be done by "someone more in sympathy with English listeners and more alive to their needs than I am";[15] and on 12 February 1960 Beckett told Bray, who liked what he had done, that he felt he had not made the best of a good opportunity.[16] The pattern here—a pattern which is by no means unique to *The Old Tune*—is essentially something like: I know what I want but perhaps need some help—I'm not cut out for this—I haven't been successful, even though I may have been helped a little, but I did try, and anyway it's my fault and nobody else's—Oh well, never mind, no matter. But Beckett obviously did mind, and it did matter—he was still making changes to the text of

The Old Tune in early April 1960[17]—if just not quite so much as the kind of enterprise which he would have pursued even more vigorously had it been specifically and exclusively on his own behalf.[18]

As regards the names of the characters in *The Old Tune*,[19] Beckett can be seen trying out alternatives, and even some phrases, in the ETE 56 notebook at the Beckett International Foundation, University of Reading. He was obviously glad of any opportunity to "off-load" names that had intrigued or amused him over the years, or in one case at least—Cream saying "you're the lucky jim Gorman, you're the lucky jim"—to say "thank you" to Barbara Bray for a recent gift.[20] But it was the "doubtful" passages, rather than the names, which exercised minds other than Beckett's. Of the very few really trenchant comments on Beckett's version of Pinget's play, one of the more striking is to be found in an internal BBC memo of early 1960 (held in the BBC Written Archives Centre [WAC] at Caversham) which raises the perfectly fair question of whether or not the character Gorman is committing an anachronism by speaking of "The Foot," and whether Chatham (a naval base, not an artillery establishment) is an appropriate place for him to associate it with anyway. It was the writer and BBC producer P.H. Newby who made this comment,[21] with Newby applying precisely the attention to detail that we know Beckett himself typically prided himself on. But it raises the interesting question as to (a) whether Beckett had been cavalier, or simply at a loss, in dealing with local and/or distinctively English specifics[22]; or (b) whether Beckett had merely been (for once) inattentive; or (c) whether the names and places chosen were actually part of Beckett's "point," if only as names and places which took on a kind of substance for as long as they occupied a few moments in the total soundscape. The play as we have it perhaps implies that Beckett was mainly playing with names—whether of person or place—principally for their own sake. In treating names as if they were not of any real utility as badges of identity but rather entities possessing their own life, Beckett seems to be asking us to "look" at them as discrete objects situated at one remove, a tactic also employed at the level of ordinary idiomatic phrasing, with parts of the play sounding "distinctly outmoded, the relic of a past era, and even caricaturally so."[23]

Traces of Beckett's continuing attempts to hone *The Old Tune* are visible in other letters to Bray. On 20 November 1959 Beckett told her he had given Pinget *The Old Tune* the previous evening, adding that he thought perhaps a few words needed adding at the end, a subject to which he returned in a letter to Bray on 1 December 1959, which describes Pinget's people as "displaced persons."[24] Clearly what was also "displaced," or not yet in place, was what ought to be the final text. Beckett characteristically registered his own dissatisfaction with the result, expressing the hope that the text could be improved at proof stage. The dissatisfaction continued, and Beckett was still discussing changes with Barbara Bray several weeks later, in February and March 1960.[25] Similarly, having apparently decided early on that "The Bluebells of Scotland" would be perfect for the purpose of *which* old tune the barrel-organ should play,[26] an alternative possibility ("Roses are blooming in Picardy," as sung by the consumptive postman in *Watt*) suggested itself.[27] Scotland? Picardy? Why not "Danny Boy," we might want to ask, given the prevailing "Irishness" of Beckett's version? Presumably precisely to underwrite the displacement in time and space that Gorman and Mr Cream experience,[28] a move further consolidated by what sound like distinctively English elements in the play's place names. Where "Wougham" or "Cruddy"[29] might be is anyone's guess. The whole "point" of the tactic, insofar as it has one, is to mix in unlikely-sounding or deliberately invented place names to figure forth against a background comprising elements that any English-speaking audience could easily enough imagine for themselves, and to further imply that none of the names has a hidden significance anyway. In any event "The Bluebells of Scotland" qualifies for the title "old tune" without there having to be any further "meaning" attached to it, and the melody—which is only heard in snatches, and only heard five times[30]—would be instantly recognized (if not necessarily identified by name) by almost anyone. What no audience could possibly have known, however, was that Beckett had taken the title for his Pinget adaptation from an abandoned play of his own, of late 1956: *The Gloaming*, itself obviously a title with Hiberno-Scottish connotations,[31] even though the word "gloaming" is not exactly uncomfortable in certain local and demotic English contexts. There was more than one old tune, some of them very old chestnuts indeed,[32] in the making of this curious, but undoubtedly intriguing, exercise in sound, sense and sensibility. Also written in late 1956, and of course much better known than either *The Gloaming* or *The Old Tune*, was Beckett's only other explicitly "Oirish" play, *All That Fall*, one of the first plays to foreground highly stylized (and "unnatural") animal sounds,[33] and using for its music a few bars from a string quartet by Franz Schubert ("Death and the Maiden"). Irish voices, all right:[34] but the tunes are from somewhere else.

Far more compelling than *The Old Tune* are the five adaptations of Beckett's prose fictions which he made, with the help of producers and technicians, for broadcast by the BBC. All five of these adaptations featured the actor Patrick Magee (of whom more anon) in solo monologues on the Third

Programme, and they occupied mid-evening, mid-week slots in the broadcasting schedules. They were naturally in no way intended to supplant the works from which the extracts were to be taken, and although the texts used (other than *How it is*) can be accessed via the manuscript resources housed at the BBC WAC, apparently no copies of the actual broadcasts are held there.

In preparing these broadcasts, a number of practical matters, all of them allied with the issue of editing, had to be addressed:

(a) the choice of an interpreter
(b) an estimation of the special skills required of any performer if he was to be in a position to create any kind of impact with unconventional material by an author far from well known either to the general public or to the specialist few in a genre outside drama
(c) whether music would, or would not, be an added bonus (both Beckett and McWhinnie obviously thought it would be, and there was Beckett's cousin, the composer and harpsichord player John Beckett, ready and able to make an appropriate and sympathetic contribution).

For the first 20 years of Beckett's dealings with the BBC, more than two-thirds of the total time the relationship lasted, there was one constant among many variables. Beckett was happy to work on the production aspect first with Donald McWhinnie, and then later with Barbara Bray, Martin Esslin, and a number of other very gifted individuals. But the thread which bound all the various enterprises together was on the level of performance rather than production, and here the dominant figure was the Armagh-born actor Patrick Magee (1922–1982). In Beckett's ensemble pieces Magee played Mr Slocum in *All That Fall* (first broadcast 1957), the Music Master and the Riding Master in *Embers* (1959), Vladimir in *Waiting for Godot* (1960), Gorman in *The Old Tune* (1960), Words in *Words and Music* (1962); Voice in *Cascando* (1964); Fox in *Rough for Radio* ("Radio II"; 1976); and he was one of the six voices used in *Lessness* (1971).[35] But Magee came into his own, and in more than one sense of the phrase, in Beckett's monologues,[36] derived from his experiments in prose fiction: *Molloy* (1957); *From an Abandoned Work* (1957); *Malone Dies* (1958); *The Unnamable* (1959); *How It Is* (1960; broadcast 5 April 1960)[37]; *First Love* (1973; broadcast 7 July 1973) *Texts for Nothing* (1974); *Ill Seen Ill Said* (1982). Magee, who was later to feature in films like *Marat/Sade*, and in a whole host of other and much poorer films, was by no means well known in the mid- to late 1950s outside of theater circles. But with the obvious exception of *Waiting for Godot*, Beckett was also not nearly so well known at this time as he would later become, and his prose fiction was in any case not of a kind to ensure widespread popular acclaim. The Beckett-Magee tandem worked well because both men were free of the trappings of celebrity and could work together on their own, uncompromising terms. It was not until the difficulties caused by Magee's personal manner in the recording studio (or on the stage set) became too difficult to cope with that the relationship was in any way compromised, although Magee's increasing involvement in film work naturally meant that he might not be available for a given broadcasting project. The shift was further affected by the fact that Beckett was, at much the same time, thinking in terms of the roles which an actress might embody better and with more sustained commitment than a not particularly famous but famously difficult actor. When the going was good Magee was a natural choice for Beckett's stage works, for broadcasts, and for other ancillary projects,[38] and the sheer number of these various enterprises speaks volumes as to Beckett's increasing satisfaction with Magee's performances, and his growing conviction that he had indeed found his ideal interpreter. It is important to remember that, whether as a playwright or as a writer of prose fiction, Beckett had a perfectly natural concern about who was to be the figurehead in what was to be put in front of what was potentially the largest audience his work ever would or could address.[39]

But Beckett would not have been Beckett if he had not looked at every aspect of a given performance with a very keen eye, and indeed an eye almost certain to discover shortcomings the longer it looked. (This pattern is observable throughout Beckett's life in relation to a number of literary works begun with enthusiasm, but in due course faulted.[40]) Of course where BBC tapes were concerned, this vigilance could only be exercised within the more intimate and restricted ambit of what could be heard. In discussing Magee's first two broadcasts (of *Molloy* and *From an Abandoned Work*) Beckett told his American producer Alan Schneider: "I think Magee's performance is remarkable."[41] But in a letter to the producer of these two broadcasts Beckett raised the issue of whether Magee could perform equally well when it came to "the Sapo passages" ("I don't like them," Beckett added) in *Malone Dies*,[42] and thought he might be "less suited to them." McWhinnie disagreed, and Sapo survived.

In an earlier letter to McWhinnie Beckett had already registered his feeling that in the reading of *From an Abandoned Work* Magee might perhaps have been more "rushed and telescoped and slightly over-querulous" than had been the case with *Molloy*.[43] This did not, however, significantly affect Beckett's commitment to the actor who was conveying his vision to a mass audience, and it is clear that other practical matters, including many of which Beckett naturally had little knowledge or personal experience, quickly became uppermost in his dealings with the team that was necessary to make this happen. Each member of the team had a potential creative input to impart to a given project, and each of them was likely to possess either a greater technical skill or a more astute sense of what the public and their own paymasters would be prepared to accept.

In almost every case—although I shall only consider one here—Beckett's initial instinct was to shoulder arms, as it were, and to adopt an attitude of studied indifference to the whole business. In a letter to Barbara Bray on 17 November 1958 regarding what was to become the fourth broadcast of an adaptation based on his prose fiction (*The Unnamable*, which aired on 19 January 1959), Beckett wrote: "I have no ideas positive or negative on *The Unnamable* extracts and leave it entirely to you and Donald [McWhinnie]."[44] But Beckett could rarely maintain this *laissez-faire* front. Faced in the interim with the BBC proposals, Beckett wrote again to Bray registering concern at the extracts chosen:

> These will add up to something little intelligible and my feeling now is that we plump for the whole hog and give the bastards a single long unbroken extract ending at the end (say from "Help" p.157 to end or from "Yes, in my life" p.153 to end .... I think this would be much more effective than the dribs and drabs and would certainly give Magee a better chance to crown his readings with something really unbearable.[45]

In the event it was more a matter of "dribs and drabs" than Beckett left to his own devices would probably ever have countenanced. The BBC script (1959) comprises ten extracts, which make no pretense of preserving the continuity of the original.[46] Beckett seems to have found this remarkably radical compromise more tolerable than did the Third Programme audience, whose reaction was not sufficiently positive to support any moves toward repeats.[47] Yet we should not, I think, infer from this that Beckett's attitude to excerpts had altered very much; from the outset it must have been evident to Beckett that the publication of a book and a radio broadcast were two very different things, each of which was likely to become embroiled in all kinds of difficulties specific to each medium.

In a letter of 14 December 1953 Beckett had told the publisher Barney Rosset: "The excerpt is always unsatisfactory, but let it at least be continuous. I don't mind how short it is, or with how little beginning or end, but I refuse to be short-circuited like an ulcerous gut."[48] Yet he had been more than ready to sacrifice Sapo for the *Malone Dies* broadcast, even though McWhinnie had seen much less need for short-circuiting in that earlier case, and had given Sapo almost 50 % of the coverage in the script from which Magee recorded.[49] Perhaps the radio experience was proving less satisfying than Beckett had thought it might be. On 15 December 1958 Beckett wrote to Bray to agree to her suggestions as to which sections of *The Unnamable* should be chosen, citing in particular the good sense of including the opening paragraph(s). It seems somewhat ironic that, even though subsequent broadcasts invariably involved Beckett in some kind of advisory capacity, he was never again to be quite so adamant in protecting the integrity of the written word, other than when he could obviously exercise full *force majeure* by refusing point blank, or suitably diplomatically, requests for permissions to broadcast works which he decided he did not wish to underwrite in radio terms (notably *Three Dialogues with Georges Duthuit*).[50]

Of course, for Beckett to become a BBC icon a certain amount of compromise was simply unavoidable. But for Beckett to remain Beckett, a certain amount of truculence, intransigence, and commitment—combined with some shrugging of the shoulders—was to be expected. Whether enterprises of this kind were kept alive by Beckett's painstaking attention to detail or were threatened in their realization by it, his involvement remained an unavoidable fly, or rather swarm of flies, in the ointment, if there was ever to be something rather than nothing at the end of it all. But in due course, partly as Beckett's theatrical vision changed in character, and no doubt partly as a reflection of how the character of home entertainment altered massively as television began to dominate all other media, the details and the patterns had to take on different forms.

NOTES

1. Zilliacus, *Beckett and Broadcasting* (Abo: Abo Akademi, 1976).
2. Ibid., 9.
3. Two years before *Beckett and Broadcasting* appeared, Zilliacus had published in the Stockholm literary magazine *Moderna Språk* "Scoring Twice:

Pinget's *La Manivelle* and Beckett's *The Old Tune*," but this relatively brief essay in a relatively remote source proves in some ways more penetrating on Pinget than on Beckett. It remains one of the very few studies of *The Old Tune* available, but in this connection see Shane Weller, *On In Their Company: essays on Beckett, tributes and sketches* (2015); and Marie Smart, "New Novel, Old Tune" in *Modernism/modernity*.

4. Beckett, *Letters III*, 293. In his unfinished memoir "Notre ami Samuel Beckett" Robert Pinget speaks of *La Manivelle* as having been "transposé" by Beckett, and notes some "anomalies," which seem to have been of no great significance for so long as the two writers were close friends, but with which Pinget became increasingly uncomfortable as their relationship proved more difficult to sustain.

5. The letter of 5 October 1965 suggests a 25-minute presentation of *Three Dialogues* (BBC Written Archives, Caversham). An undated Esslin letter later than November 1965 has Esslin wondering why Beckett should be against this manner of dissemination, which he extends to *Play*. Beckett's strictness in these matters was only very rarely softened, which is why the Beckett Estate tends to veto "cross-over" enterprises. On 27 August 1957 Beckett wrote to Barney Rosset of Grove Press to say "frankly the thought of *All That Fall* on a stage, however discreetly, is intolerable to me." He had earlier emphasized, "It is no more theatre than *End-Game* [*sic*] is radio and to 'act' it is to kill it" (*Letters III*, 63–64). Rosset was obliged to change his plans, with Beckett "worried and perplexed," fearing that he might be too late to put a stop to the publisher's plans as announced in the *New York Times*. A (presumably unauthorized?) staged performance of *The Old Tune* was apparently played at the Royal Playhouse in New York City in late March 1961.

6. Earlier in the same month that the BBC broadcast Pinget's *La Manivelle* (July 1959) Beckett had made one of his relatively infrequent (since the death of his mother in 1950, and his brother Frank in 1954) returns to Ireland (to be awarded an Hon. D.Litt. at his *alma mater* TCD). But memories of Ireland and "heroic days" growing up there surface in a February 1959 letter to Barbara Bray (*Letters III*, 204), and Beckett's ear for Irish idioms, always acute, would not have needed very much further animation after hearing the audiotapes of the *All That Fall* broadcast.

7. Beckett to Bray, 1 December 1959; *Letters III*, 260.

8. Marie Smart claims it is "evident" that "Beckett saw his translation of *The Old Tune* as a form of self-parody," which prompts her to suggest that "*Happy Days* is a play that Beckett could not have written until he had realized that his own work had slipped into familiar cliché and convention," and that "*Waiting for Godot* had itself become, like the radio or an old-fashioned car, a contemporary relic" (Smart 2014, 537). These are

unhistorical views which anyone who listened to the radio in the 1950s, or for whom the prospect of one day driving even an old-fashioned car was a consummation devoutly to be wished, may find it hard to square with the idea that *The Old Tune* is "an instructive example of Beckett's historical specificity" and "a vaudeville radio routine…played out in the First World War" (ibid., 543). In 1930 (in "Le Concentrisme") Beckett described vaudeville as an inferior art form ("dégrader en vaudeville de Labiche cet art," *Disjecta*, 42), even if in *Proust* (1931), it becomes a more "complete" form than opera in the way it "inaugurates the comedy of an exhaustive enumeration" (1965 ed., 92). Smart, not unnaturally, chooses to leave unexamined how a medium like radio could in any really meaningful sense make common cause with a *staged* comic routine *performed* in front of an audience, and she implicitly attributes to Beckett (and by extension Pinget) the notion that the radio was "a symbol of the peculiarity of the postwar moment" (543).

9. *Letters III*, 254.
10. In one of the few sustained attempts in English to treat Pinget on his own terms, with Pinget and Beckett kept as separate as possible, Stephen Bann describes Beckett as "solipsistic" and credits Pinget with "a much fuller range…of human relationships" (24). Bann describes the novel *Clope au dossier* (1961) as "the work in which Pinget is most close to Beckett" (ibid., 25), but only refers to *La Manivelle* (in a footnote; ibid., 22) as deriving from *Clope*, making no mention of *The Old Tune*. In pursuing the conviction that the novel *L'Inquisitoire* (which contains a "rue Sam" and a "rue Suzanne") is "Pinget's most impassioned and profound statement of the artist's concern for the inclusiveness of truth" (ibid., 29), Bann makes no mention of *Comment c'est*, but is keen to stress that Pinget's is a "cumulative vision" which "may be said to demand a new type of attention from the reader" (ibid., 33).
11. *Letters III*, 250.
12. *Proust* and *Three Dialogues with Georges Duthuit* (London: John Calder, 1965), 29.
13. *Letters III*, 254–5.
14. It is not clear what Beckett means here by "accuracy," or why "accuracy" should be "secondary." *Embers* had, for all its shortcomings, been an opportunity for Beckett to explore whether or not the radio play and "realism" necessarily had anything to do with one another, an issue which had also been in his mind during the composition of *All That Fall*. In a letter to Barney Rosset of 23 November 1958, Beckett described the play later to be called *Embers* (sent to the BBC without a title; *Letters III*, 203) as "a kind of attempt to *write* for radio and not merely exploit its technical possibilities" (*Letters III*, 181). Pinget was working with Beckett on the translation

of *Embers* into French as *Cendres*. One of the shortcomings of *The Old Tune* both as a text and as a broadcast may, ironically, be that both come across as too much like unmediated *tranches de vie*, with few of the surprises experimented with in *Embers*. The concurrent difficulties that Beckett was experiencing with "Pim," the working title of the radically unconventional *Comment c'est*, may also have been a factor.

15. *Letters III*, 260.
16. 12 February 1960; not selected for *Letters III*.
17. Beckett to Robert Pinget 2 April 1960; *Letters III*, 324.
18. The whole issue of Beckett's input is, perhaps somewhat surprisingly, clarified by Megan M Quigley in her important essay on Beckett and Alfred Péron in *James Joyce Quarterly* 41:3 (2004). There, she demonstrates that "rather than literally translate *Finnegans Wake* into French, Beckett attempted to recreate [*Anna Livia Plurabelle*] in French," introducing his own "aura" (474, 480). The *non*-necessity of translating "Plurabelle" as "Pluratself" (for a translation into French) seems decisive in this connection.
19. The surnames Cream (always addressed as "*Mr* Cream") and Gorman (only twice addressed as "*Mr* Gorman," although Cream, the older of the two men, for the most part maintains the "right" balance between familiarity and formality) are taken over from the opening tableau of *Watt*, apparently set in the vicinity of Dublin's Harcourt Street Station near TCD. Shane Weller (35 fn7) estimates that there are more than thirty personal names in *La Manivelle* and *The Old Tune*. In the "Addenda" to *Watt* is the instruction: "Change all the names." For a "lost" personal name and a "lost" place name, see Samuel Beckett, *Molloy*, ed. Shane Weller (London: Faber, 2009), 83; yet Malone asks: "But of whom may it not be said, I know that man?" (Samuel Beckett, *Malone Dies*, ed. Peter Boxall [London: Faber, 2010], 102). "The Duck" is a name given to Miss Dew "to be going on with" (*Murphy*), but the phrase "whose name we shall never know" sticks, as it were, to the Student in *Dream of Fair to Middling Women* (and later in "A Wet Night" in *More Pricks Than Kicks*). Beckett never really resolved the tension between needing to name his "people," and not needing to.
20. Samuel Beckett, *Collected Shorter Plays* (London: Faber, 1984), 185. In late January 1960, Bray had sent Beckett a radio adaptation of Kingsley Amis's 1954 novel *Lucky Jim* (*Letters III*, 291 fn2).
21. *Letters III*, 255 fn1.
22. See Beckett's letter of 13 December 1959 to Pinget (*Letters III*, 264).
23. Weller, *On in their Company*, 30.
24. *Letters III*, 260. For the view that the voices of Cream and Gorman "seem to sound in a vacuum," and the (mistaken?) view that as characters they are seeking to "make a coherent and reliable whole of their lives," see Kevin

Branigan, *Radio Beckett: Musicality in the Radio Plays of Samuel Beckett* (Bern: Peter Lang, 2006), 29. The actor Pierre Chabert, in a solo performance, realized that "Certain words ha[d] to be disarticulated ... in order to achieve special attention" to reinforce the "decentralisation" which Beckett was looking for in assisting in the production of Pinget's stage play *L'Hypothèse* in October 1965 (in a gallery of the Musée de l'Art Moderne), and in March 1966 at the Théâtre de l'Odéon ("Rehearsing Pinget's *Hypothesis* with Beckett," in *As No Other Dare Fail* (London: John Calder, 1986), 130–31). Chabert reports that "Beckett, with Pinget's agreement, made substantial cuts in the text," ibid.), but relations between the two men had already by then been put under some strain. Pinget began to spend more time in the company of Beckett's mistress, the BBC producer Barbara Bray, but was never favored with as much public and critical acclaim as Beckett.

25. See *Letters III*, 288ff, 313.
26. Beckett to Barbara Bray, 14 November 1959; *Letters III*, 255.
27. Robert Pinget, "Notre ami Samuel Beckett" (a December 1960 entry in the unpublished typescript). Pinget apparently preferred "The Bluebells of Scotland," and was clearly beginning to have difficulties not only with *Comment c'est*, but also with Beckett himself, in a friendship that proved hard to sustain over the years, despite Beckett participating in the realization of *L'Hypothèse*. For emphasis on "the *sound itself* rather than upon the sound-producing *mechanism*," see Weller (29), who reinforces the point by reference to Régis Salgado's essay "Beckett et Pinget: l'échange des voix" in *Études Anglaises* 59 (2006), 31–46. Beckett remembered the barrel organs, and their organists of his early Dublin days, but, after exploring the repetitive potentialities of machine-produced sound in *Krapp's Last Tape*, must surely have relished the more limited repertoire of the barrel organ, especially if—as seems very likely—he wished to pay an oblique homage to the last lied ("Der Leiermann" [The Hurdy-Gurdy Man]) in Schubert's great *Winterreise* cycle. Ian Bostridge, in *Schubert's Winter Journey: Anatomy of an Obsession* (London: Faber, 2015), describes the hurdy-gurdy as "the perfect instrument for the expression of alienation" (469), and considers it "unsurprising that many have seen the hurdy-gurdy man as a figure of death, only encouraged in this by the strong sixteenth-century iconographic association between the two in the dance-of-death, or *Totentanz*, genre" (481).
28. Beckett's use of the word "chinoiseries" to describe what he thought of the issues which the BBC had raised (letter of 13 December 1959 to Robert Pinget, *Letters III*, 264; cf. the "anomalies" of a letter to Pinget of 30 November 1959; ibid., 256) makes a nice, and at the same time ironic, addition to the displacements.

29. Beckett, *Collected Shorter Plays*, 179.
30. The stage direction "(*Roar of engine*)" occurs some 15 times.
31. Cf. "The penny pleasure of homing in the gloaming" in an April 1933 letter to Thomas MacGreevy. (Harry Lauder's "Roamin' in the Gloamin" becomes "Ramble in the twilight" in the *More Pricks Than Kicks* version of the story "A Wet Night," taken over from *Dream of Fair to Middling Women* [202]).
32. The arse/moon association (*Collected Shorter Plays*, 186), revived for *Waiting For Godot*, is first found ("suitably" dignified as "cock") in line 7 of the 1933 poem "Serena III". The phrase "staring up at the lid" (*Collected Shorter Plays*, 187) is adapted from "grinning up ... " in *Dream of Fair to Middling Women* (1992, 146; and item (646) in the *"Dream" Notebook*), reprised in the 1933 story "Draff" (*More Pricks Than Kicks*, 175). Signs of creative fatigue perhaps, not that Beckett was ever averse to recycling material, irrespective of where he had acquired it.
33. Beckett famously describes the Irish as a "characteristic agricultural community" in his posthumously published essay "Censorship in the Saorstat" (Beckett, *Disjecta*, 87).
34. At one point in *The Old Tune* Gorman and Cream swap "all right"s (*Collected Shorter Plays*, 185), although beneath the bonhomie they are not much more at one with each other than they are with their surroundings.
35. Magee did not play Hamm in the Michael Bakewell production of *Endgame* broadcast on the BBC on 22 May 1962, but performed the role on stage at the Royal Court in 1964.
36. "Magee Monologue" was Beckett's working title for what became *Krapp's Last Tape*; he was prompted to write it (early in 1958), and to use audiotape as an element in a play intended for the stage, by hearing the Magee broadcasts of late 1957. A little-known illustration of how Magee became the first-choice figure in the BBC's eyes is the internal memo written by the producer R.D. Smith on 5 January 1967 suggesting that Magee would be ideal for *The Calmative*, an idea which was never realized.
37. No copy of the script used for this broadcast seems to have survived in the Written Archives at Caversham, and the broadcast is not mentioned by Zilliacus. But see *Letters III*, 306.
38. On TV Magee performed *Krapp's Last Tape* (first broadcast on BBC 2 on 29 November 1972). Two projects with Magee which failed to materialize were a second LP record of extracts for Claddagh in Dublin (the first had featured Jack McGowran) and a televized *Krapp's Last Tape* for RTE. A very rare tape of Magee reading some lines from a piece of Beckett juvenilia is in the audio and video section of the Knowlson collection at the Beckett International Foundation, University of Reading. A seven-inch single produced by John Calder for special distribution, featuring Magee giving a

public performance (of page 114 of the Calder 1964 *How it is*), probably dating from 1972, is also in the collection.
39. Zilliacus gives the positive, negative and middling responses in "Reaction profiles" from the BBC Listening Panel (*Beckett and Broadcasting*, 209). Federman and Fletcher list no reviews of the five broadcasts with which I am here concerned, and very few for any of the other BBC Beckett broadcasts.
40. An example typifying what happened on many other occasions would be Gottfried Keller's autobiographical novel *Der grüne Heinrich*, Beckett's reactions to which were entered in his German Diaries of 1936–1937.
41. Beckett to Schneider, 29 January 1958.
42. Beckett to McWhinnie, 26 February 1958; *Letters III*, 110.
43. Beckett to McWhinnie, 23 December 1957; *Letters III*, 78–79.
44. *Letters III*, 174.
45. Beckett to Bray, 29 November 1958; *Letters III*, 183.
46. The 24-page script at Caversham corresponds to pp. 1–5; 7–8; 14; 37–41; 62–63; 92–95; 114–17; 119–20; 123–24; and 132–34 of the current Faber text: less than one-quarter of the whole, and necessarily excluding any of the more extended *episodes* in a novel not quite so obliging in this respect as perhaps its author would have liked.
47. See Zilliacus, *Beckett and Broadcasting*, 209: 44 % of listeners graded the broadcast of *The Unnamable* below the median grade of "B," twice as many as did so in response to *Malone Dies*.
48. Beckett, *Letters II*, 432, regretting the omission of the first 13 pages from the *New World Writing* extract from *Molloy*.
49. Recording *Malone Dies* occupied two days early in June 1958 (for John Beckett's music) and two days a week or so later (for Magee's voice). Sapo material can be found on pp. 10–13, 14–19, and 22 of the 26 marked up pages of the BBC Caversham script. See also my essay on *Malone Dies* in *Samuel Beckett Today/Aujourd' hui* 26 (Amsterdam: Rodopi, 2015), esp.131, 133.
50. Beckett to Martin Esslin, 9 November 65; *Letters III*, 678.

"My God to Have to Murmur That": *Comment C'est/How It Is* and the Issue of Performance

Elsa Baroghel

From the mid-1950s, Beckett's newfound international recognition brought about a flurry of interest from radio stations all over the world in broadcasting old and new works by him. The controllers and producers of the BBC Third Programme were particularly active in promoting Beckett's works, commissioning pieces written especially for the radio and following his writing career closely. Despite claims denouncing the Third Programme as elitist, or "a ghetto for the intelligentsia,"[1] its prominent national status meant that the BBC was on the hunt for new literary material worthy of their broadcasts; as Marion Boyars (then UK editor of Beckett's works in partnership with John Calder) once said in a November 1966 letter to the BBC: "I know they are always shouting for stories."[2]

From December 1958 to August 1960, Beckett was painstakingly composing his first major prose work since *Textes pour Rien* (written in 1950–1951), the work published in French as *Comment c'est* in 1961, and then in Beckett's English translation, *How It Is*, in 1964. The language and typography used in *Comment c'est/How It Is* reflect a heightened attention to rhythm and sonority, conferring a phonogenic character to the text that,

---

E. Baroghel (✉)
Faculty of Medieval and Modern Languages, University of Oxford, Oxford, UK

on the face of it, would appear particularly suitable for the radio, perhaps even one of Beckett's most radiogenic prose works. The BBC Written Archive Centre (WAC), however, despite attesting to the BBC's lasting interest in lesser-known or early works, holds no records of *How It Is* ever being broadcast, or of any enquiries related to clearing radio rights for this work.

James Knowlson's 1984 article "The Works of Samuel Beckett: a Discography" in *Recorded Sound* reviews audio material held in the National Sound Archive, drawing attention to the ease with which some of Beckett's works not intended for the radio lend themselves to the recorded format: "[I]f [the] radio plays were written for aural reception, other works of Beckett were not. Yet they still come through extremely strongly in recorded sound."[3] The contents of the BBC WAC files illustrate such versatility. On 15 October 1958, Donald McWhinnie, Assistant Head of Radio Drama at the BBC, enquired with John Calder about doing a broadcast of *The Unnamable* (about to be published in England) as was done with recordings of *Malone Dies* and *From an Abandoned Work* a few months earlier. This was one of countless requests addressed to Beckett's publishers by the BBC in the decades following the success of *All That Fall* in 1957—these requests often being made very close to the time of publication of his new works. As the BBC WAC files reveal, the producers of the Third Programme were acutely aware of the great literary value of Beckett's writings across all genres and media, and were therefore willing to broadcast even his most difficult works, at the ever-present risk of alienating some listeners.[4] In a letter dated 20 April 1966, for instance, Martin Esslin, Head of Radio Drama from 1963 to 1977, asked for two copies of *More Pricks Than Kicks* (1934), long gone out of print, in preparation for a potential broadcast: "We want to explore the possibility of adapting the book or to produce readings of it for the Third Programme."[5] Despite Beckett's claim to Barbara Bray in 1959 that he "[w]ouldn't open More Pricks for a king's ransom,"[6] he must have given his approval eventually, as "Dante and the Lobster" was later broadcast in a program dedicated to Beckett's works in honor of his birthday, first aired in April 1976 and repeated in 1979. This two-part program contained a variety of recordings of live readings given at the National Theatre, featuring the following works: *From an Abandoned Work, Malone Dies,* "Dante and the Lobster," *Murphy, Watt, Molloy, Still, The Unnamable, Cascando,* "First Love," *Mercier et Camier, Texts for Nothing,* as well as a selection of Beckett's poems. This program, among others like it, illustrates the wide range of works deemed suitable for broadcast and likely to appeal to the audience, including early texts written in a more "obscure" and referential style or stage plays conceived, by definition, to be seen as well as heard. Some lesser-known texts were also broadcast, such as "The Drunken Boat," Beckett's translation of "Le Bateau ivre" by Arthur Rimbaud, broadcast on Radio 3 in 1977 with an introduction by James Knowlson.[7] *How It Is*, however, is conspicuous by its absence from these records.

This chapter proposes to investigate this curious absence from the BBC archive, starting with a retrospective of documented recordings and broadcasts of *Comment c'est / How It Is*, in order to question and explain Beckett's statement to his American editor, Barney Rosset, about six months after starting work on the book: "Struggling on with new work which as you rightly surmise has nothing to do with theatre or radio. I hear their siren voices and tell them to stick it up."[8] My aim is to re-examine Beckett's last "novel" as the prose counterpart of a wider-ranging enterprise of voice and sound exploration in the 1950s, by studying the influence of Beckett's engagement with the radio medium in *How It Is* in order to delineate particular issues of performance and broadcasting inherent to what Beckett once called "a microphone text, to be murmured."[9]

"Recorded None the Less":[10] A Chronology of Recordings and Broadcasts of *Comment c'est / How It Is*

After the publication of *L'image* in *X: A Quarterly Review* in November 1959, the ongoing prose work that would become *Comment c'est* was first introduced to the world through a public reading from "a new and as yet unfinished 'novel' by Mr. Samuel Beckett"[11] by Patrick Magee on 5 April 1960 at the Royal Festival Hall in London, as part of the third installment of the "Music Today" concert series organized by Mark Wilkinson. Beckett had tentatively agreed to contribute a piece of writing, which he would translate into English for the occasion, though as the event approached he remained dissatisfied with the text and reluctant to see his friend attempt to perform it: "Translated beginning of III, but not satisfactory. Shall try and have something for them by March. Poor Pat, get up on his hind legs and read that!"[12] To Magee, who was indeed nervous about the event, he wrote: "I have made the writing as clear as…circumstances permit, but I intend also to have the goodness to point the copy I shall be sending you in a fortnight or three weeks from now …. I have never committed anything—I trust—so exhausted and unpalatable and shall not be in the least offended if you refuse to have anything to do with it."[13]

On 2 February 1961, less than a month after the publication of *Comment c'est* by Les éditions de Minuit in France, Barbara Bray presented her laudatory review of the book on the BBC Third Programme, for which Beckett returned her praise: "You have 'understood' the book as no one so far."[14] On 11 October, during an evening program "entirely devoted to the works of Samuel Beckett," Bray briefly discussed words and language in *Comment c'est* in her presentation of the novels: "The voice that murmurs into the mud in COMMENT C'EST, the latest novel, is all too certain that 'tout est trop dire'[15]—words must always either fall short or go too far."[16] There are no more documented readings or recordings from the work before 1964, the year of its publication by John Calder in Beckett's English translation. In preparation for the release of the book on 30 April, Calder organized an event dedicated to Beckett at the Criterion Theatre: "The Novels and Plays of Samuel Beckett / an afternoon of readings and debates under the chairmanship of Martin Esslin / Readings by Jack MacGowran and Patrick Magee."[17] The debates and performances were recorded by Calder—perhaps with a view to editing them for broadcast, as Esslin's involvement would suggest—including another breathless, urgent reading by Magee of a short excerpt from part III of *How It Is*.[18] According to Zillacus, "John Calder, stimulated by the BBC readings of the trilogy, was inventive enough to send out his review copies of *How It Is* in 1964 with a record attached of Magee reading a passage from the book. The idea met with unstinted praise."[19] While Calder did send a tape of Magee's reading to P. H. Newby (then Chief of the Third Programme) on 7 April, the BBC WAC archive indicates that the latter in fact turned it down:

> The readings are, of course, excellent, but we have already arranged an hour long program drawn from Comment C'est which Patrick Magee and Jack McGowran are going to read for us. The extracts have been chosen by Mr Beckett himself and we have, of course, already broadcast the plays and readings from the trilogy .... I think we should start from the beginning with the special requirement of radio in mind and try to devise broadcasts that really do stand by themselves.
>
> The discussion was, of course, interesting and lively but a lot of it was conducted off-mike and the interventions from the audience were inaudible. We have ourselves already recorded a discussion between Barbara Bray, Patrick Magee and Jack McGowran, which we shall be broadcasting just before End Game [*sic*] opens at the Royal Court Theatre.

With these considerations, coupled with the thought that the tape would need an enormous amount of editing, I think I must say we would rather not make use of it for broadcasting.[20]

Although no evidence has been found that this "hour-long program" on *Comment c'est/How It Is* was ever broadcast or indeed recorded, this letter draws attention to the inherent specificity of radio performance, which, just like Magee's public deliveries, is not reducible to a simple "staged reading." Thanks to his readings of other works by Beckett, in public or on the Third Programme, Magee was highly regarded as a Beckett actor and the 1964 Criterion recording of *How It Is* has since become a somewhat iconic audio counterpart to the novel, occasionally played in place of a live performance at events featuring *How It Is*[21]—though such events have remained relatively rare.

It therefore appears that, as hinted by its notable absence from Zilliacus' list of works broadcast by the BBC until 1973,[22] *How It Is* never made it to the radio in Great Britain. The only copyright clearing for this work by the BBC occurred in February 1974, for a televised reading from its first 12 pages by Nicol Williamson, a celebrated Scottish actor who took a keen interest in Beckett's works and became a friend of his following a successful run of *Waiting for Godot* in 1964 at the Royal Court Theatre. On 11 July 1973, Beckett wrote to Barney Rosset that "Williamson used parts of *How It Is* in a one-man show without first getting Beckett's approval, but Beckett decided not to intervene because he considered Williamson as a friend after having worked with him in London."[23] Williamson had indeed already shown his affinity for *How It Is* by electing to give a reading of its last few paragraphs[24] on the set of the "Frost on Saturday" television show on 30 October 1968, to illustrate his own feelings of apprehension toward death. His performance was as electrifying as Magee's, with more of a manic quality to his voice and brutal, terrifying outbursts—reminiscent in this respect of his rendering of Vladimir a decade earlier, which, according to Calder, prompted Beckett to declare: "there's a touch of genius in that man somewhere."[25] Williamson continued to include live readings from *How It Is* in his shows until the late 1980s at least, to the distress of some critics: "He emits some hair-raising yelps, like a fox in a trap, in a passage from Beckett's novel 'How It Is' but the words are so rushed that the piece doesn't build."[26]

Another acclaimed thespian who was sensitive to the dramatic potential of *How It Is* as uttered speech was American actor-turned-director Joseph

Chaikin, whom Beckett met and befriended in 1980 in Paris while Chaikin was involved in a production of *Endgame* at the American Center. Beckett gave his consent for a one-man stage adaptation of *Texts for Nothing* and *How It Is*, even proposing a title idea borrowed from Virgil, "*Inania Verba*" (empty words), but Chaikin went for the more sober "Texts" and had successful runs in Paris, London and New York, touring till November 1981. According to Knowlson, "[t]his was praised for its sharply comic qualities and the high standard of its acting by the theatre critic of *Le Monde*, 22 Feb. 1980."[27] Beckett, who was sent a tape,[28] "was not unhappy with the results,"[29] though he wrote to Chaikin: "I listened to it with much interest. I thought the utterance too brisk and lively, especially end of *How It Is*, for such consternation and extremity. But you know what authors are."[30]

It is worth noting that these three documented adaptations in English involved friends of Beckett's. This could indicate that he was more inclined to overcome his initial reticence at the prospect of *How It Is* being forced out of its original written form to please those close to him. However, the absence of broadcasts on the Third Programme is especially confounding, since Bray, who admired the novel, was keen for it to be adapted by the BBC. Even though she had moved to Paris by then, she wrote to Esslin on 18 September 1961:

> The author would be very pleased for you to do the English translation of THE END as a reading; also the translation of COMMENT C'EST, when there is a definitive passage ready. So far there's only the section Magee read at the Festival Hall, and that will have to be amended. It could be done as it is en attendant, if you wished; but perhaps by the time you'd done THE END the final text of the other would be there. Who were you thinking of as reader?[31]

The BBC WAC collection being entirely non-digitized, the idea that missing documents might account for the apparent lack of programs featuring *How It Is* cannot be dismissed. However, it is significant that the French Radiodiffusion-Télévision Française/Office de Radiodiffusion-Télévision Française (RTF/ORTF) archive presents the exact situation,[32] with the notable exception of a two-part program entitled "Anthologie Vivante" dedicated to Beckett and broadcast by the RTF on 3 April 1963 (repeated 11 June 2008 and 20 October 2010[33]). Here too, the main host, writer and critic Alain Bosquet, was an admirer of Beckett's works and a good friend of his. The program features a commentary on language and Beckett's Irishness and an introduction to the novels (both by Bosquet) as well as five readings from *Molloy* (19"50, by Jean Martin), *Malone Meurt* (10", by Lucien Raimbourg), *L'innommable* (26", by Michel Bouquet), *Textes pour rien* (10"36, by Alain Cuny) and *Comment c'est* (8"40, by Michel Bouquet), selected by Beckett himself. Bosquet describes *Comment c'est* as "one of the great post-war masterpieces, because of the tension, the richness, the variety of this thing which, as a genre, is quite unnameable" (my translation).[34] The excerpt from *Comment c'est*, which Bosquet also calls a "prose poem," "perhaps a litany—entitled 'novel', but incorrectly" (my translation)[35] is again drawn from its final pages.[36] Bouquet's reading is slow and imprecatory, at times not unlike Magee's whispers in tone, but overall fails to acknowledge the peculiar typography of the original, restoring the coherence of entwined propositions through his intonations, from which one wouldn't necessarily infer a complete absence of punctuation. It is difficult to speculate on Beckett's own views as to how *Comment c'est/How It Is* should be performed, if it had to be performed at all. After over two years of tedious labor, by the time the book came out, he was simply tired of it: "Total indifference to its coming into world and reception. Never look at it again."[37] He did, nevertheless, mark Magee's script for easier deciphering and offer some advice—and this, despite his initial claims that this troublesome piece had "nothing to do with the radio," strongly indicates that the work does in fact have ties to the world of sound and the dynamics of radio diffusion. In fact, as already mentioned, Beckett was quite specific about this: "I think it is a microphone text, to be murmured."[38]

"A Microphone Text, to Be Murmured": A Radiophonic Filiation

While there is an understandable tendency to consider Beckett's engagement with the radio medium exclusively in terms of the six radio plays written between 1956 and 1962, his progressive awakening to the artistic and aesthetic possibilities of the radio in the late 1950s influenced his writings for other media in such a way as to make his well-known tirade from 1957 easy to overread into: "If we can't keep our genres more or less distinct, or extricate them from the confusion that has them where they are, we might as well go home and lie down."[39] Firstly, it should be recalled that this remark was prompted by Beckett's irritation at receiving news of an obviously unauthorized stage production of *All That Fall* in New York, as well as at having to explain why he couldn't conceive of *Act*

Without Words, which to him is "primitive theatre, or meant to be,"[40] as a film. Much has been made of Beckett's legendary aversion to cross-genre (or cross-medium) adaptations, but this is largely due to his particularly strong feelings about the specificity of writing for the stage: "I have perhaps an exaggerated sense of what separates the two media [radio and theatre], but there it is."[41] This somewhat undermines Beckett's previous statement that genres should be kept "distinct," which could also be read as an admonition to himself not to yield too easily to the "siren voices" of radio and aggravate the "confusion" of the genres. In that case, Beckett was not very true to his word since, as we shall see, the strategies inherent to radio scriptwriting seeped copiously into his creative process on the tortuous journey toward *How It Is*.

After *All That Fall*, written for the BBC in 1956 and broadcast for the first time in January 1957, Beckett's next two plays were *Krapp's Last Tape* (1958) for the stage and *Embers* (1959, written 1957) for the radio. Both were evidently influenced by his discovery of the radio medium— the former being a radio play and the latter a theater play inspired by Magee's recording of *Molloy* for the BBC and revolving around the on-stage use of a tape recorder. Pim Verhulst[42] makes a case for a late 1958 dating for the abandoned radio play *Pochade radiophonique* (translated as *Rough for Radio II*), currently uncertainly bunched with *Esquisse radiophonique* (*Rough for Radio I*) and the other radio plays written between 1960 and 1962; this would make *Pochade* closer chronologically to the beginnings of *Comment c'est* (December 1958) than either *Krapp's Last Tape* or *Words and Music* (first broadcast in 1962, written in 1960). I want to suggest that *Comment c'est*, which Beckett kept working on till August 1960, should be considered as an extension of this exploration of sound technique across genres in the late 1950s.

In *The Art of Radio* (1959), "[w]riting that 'the affinity between stage drama and radio drama is superficial,' McWhinnie aligns radio drama more directly with genres relying primarily on words – whether spoken or written – than with the stage and other media with strong visual components."[43] McWhinnie's stance is in keeping with the presence of a number of echoes between *Pochade* and *Comment c'est*. In spite of the genre gap, the thematic premise of *Rough for Radio II* stands close to that of *How It Is*: in both texts, for instance, torture is used as a means to elicit language. Fox is repeatedly flogged with a pizzle, while Pim is scratched, stabbed, beaten and carved into. This reflects a progressive systematization of the theme of torture in Beckett's aesthetics over the course of the

1950s, largely due, I argue, to his rediscovery of the Marquis de Sade in 1950–1951, which involved thorough research and translation work[44] and resulted in an abandoned, unpublished short story entitled "On le tortura bien" (1952)[45] as well as what is perhaps Beckett's most Sadean work: *How It Is* itself.[46] As Verhulst comments, "[a] common trait that…marks *Pochade* and *Comment c'est* as works written in the late 1950s is their reference to moles, which were wreaking havoc on Beckett's lawn at his country retreat in late 1957 and early 1958."[47] Dante can also be mentioned as a shared connection between the two works, as Beckett was rereading the *Divina Commedia* "out of sheer boredom"[48] in the spring of 1958. *Rough for Radio II* contains an overt reference to Dante ("Have you read the Purgatory, miss, of the divine Florentine?"[49]) and "the premise of the play does indeed sound like some infernal or purgatorial contrivance."[50] The Dantesque resonances of *How It Is*[51] are reflected in Beckett's dejected comments about its composition: "[T]he hole I have got myself into now is as 'dumb of all light' as the 5th canto of HELL and by God no love."[52]

Daniel Albright convincingly describes *How It Is* as a "parody of Dante based on modern technology" as well as "a sort of meditation on radio."[53] Indeed, the fragmented utterance re-enacts and dramatizes the three distinct roles taken on by scriptwriter, actor and listener, in a kind of parable of the radio transmission: "I hear it…I learn it I quote."[54] For Lea Sinoimeri, "[t]he novel plays with the equivocal exchange between the narrator…and the listener of a radio play, whose reception of the broadcast is being disturbed."[55] Sinoimeri also writes that, in France, the early 1950s marked "a return to an idea of radio as a *machine à rêver* (a dream machine): a place where a theatre of the mind, inhabited by invisible shadows and ghosts, takes its place and where the listener becomes the true protagonist of a radio play."[56] In that sense, *How It Is* a true "heir" to *Krapp's Last Tape* or, rather, a "post-Krapp *Krapp's Last Tape*," where Krapp, his human memories, and the stage are gone, and the recording alone remains, droning on (printing on) blindly without him. We, as the audience, are left to read/listen from this printed recording, effectively replacing the protagonist. No wonder, then, that, faced with the unappealing perspective of public readings of the text, Beckett sought to experiment further with this technological metaphor, asking Magee and McWhinnie separately to make use of a microphone, "notwithstanding the liveness of the occasion."[57]

It is easy to see how Beckett's experience with the radio could have influenced the conception of *How It Is*. According to Zilliacus, "radio provides a suitable medium for blurring the distinction between internal and external reality."[58] Blurring distinctions is certainly something that Beckett was very thorough about in composing the text. O'Reilly[59] and Cordingley[60] describe how the language was "eroded" over the many successive drafts, progressively losing its "'healthy', graphical normality" and "grammatical, fully punctuated sentences."[61] In May 1959, about halfway through the genesis of the work, Beckett refers to this characteristic process of deletion, which S.E. Gontarski called the "intent of undoing,"[62] in a letter to Barney Rosset: "I rely a lot on demolishing process to come later and content myself more or less with getting down elements and rhythms to be knocked hell out of when I'm ready .... All a problem of rhythm and syntax and weakening of form, nothing more difficult."[63] This comment confirms that the sheer phonogeny of *How It Is* is central to the work as well as an intended result of Beckett's drastic revisions. In January 1960, Beckett completed the first draft of *Comment c'est* and began his "demolishing" and fragmenting process, writing to Bray: "Pim: trying to break up into short units the continuum contrived with such difficulty."[64] Alongside this, even though the book was not finished, Beckett had to set about translating two excerpts: one would become Magee's script for the Festival Hall reading, the other, drawn from Part I, would be published as "From an Unabandoned Work" in the September-October issue of Rosset's *Evergreen Review* in America.[65] The intent behind Beckett's merciless blurring process is made clearer in his letter to Magee in preparation for the reading: "What will meet your disgusted eye is a series of short paragraphs (average of 4 or 5 lines) separated by pauses during which panting cordially invited and without as much punctuation as a comma to break the monotony or *promote the understanding*"[66] (emphasis mine). O'Reilly speculates on whether this early dip into translation might be responsible for the layout of *How It Is* as we know it:

> This partial reconstruction gives rise to the tantalizing idea that the fragmentation, so defining both stylistically and semantically, may have taken place in English. That having finally got through the as yet untitled *Comment c'est* in a prose similar to that of *Textes pour rien*, it may have been in switching to English that the idea of giving the text a formal discontinuity dawned on Beckett.[67]

Albright notes that "the radio voices [came] to Beckett in English rather than French."[68] While this statement should be approached with caution, the brief English "episode" preceding the completion of *Comment c'est* clearly constituted an integral step in the genesis of the work, and may have provided Beckett with the perspective he needed to proceed with its writing and amplify the phonogenic and radiogenic qualities of its language. It follows that *Comment c'est/How It Is* may rightly be viewed as an offspring of Beckett's engagement with radio and the BBC, as well as the prose counterpart to the radio plays—just as *Krapp's Last Tape* in the theater, where a representation of the dynamics of recording and listening serves the reflexion on memory and the divided self.

What I call the "phonogenic" qualities of *How It Is* have been discussed in a number of studies concerned with sound and aurality in this work. Recently, Sinoimeri and Cordingley have written about the text's "hybrid nature, suspended as it is between orality and literacy" and its "gradual sonorisation and oralisation…in the passage from the preliminary version of *L'Image* to *Comment c'est* …. The novel engages with modes of textual listening that insist both formally and thematically on diffusion, resonance and fluctuation."[69] These arguments are based on the observation that language in *How It Is* possesses rhythmic and sound patterns reminiscent of poetry, thus inscribing the work in a fabricated oral filiation, as suggested by the tireless repetition of "I say it as I hear it." Indeed, repetition—a major rhythmic device in *How It Is*—contributes to distancing the language from the realm of written words. As often as possible, assonances and alliterations are preserved (or increased) between the French and English versions: "mon sac une possession ce mot qui siffle tout bas"[70] becomes "my sack a possession this word faintly hissing"[71]; "je découpais aux ciseaux en minces rubans les ailes des papillons"[72] becomes "I scissored into slender strips the wings of butterflies."[73] The sibilants /s/ and /z/ here add stridency to the utterance, in a reptilian, predatory analogy echoing the primitive sadism that runs through the "novel," while the softer fricatives /f/ and /ð/ evoke Beckett's idea of a microphone murmur. This text also has the remarkable ability to be construed as sound or, rather, to be "evocalized" by the act of reading. As Sinoimeri puts it, "*Comment c'est/How It Is* develops a close affinity between reader and listener and between the inner, silent audition of a narrative text and radiophonic diffusion."[74] She adds:

> Like the translator, the listener is constantly on the edge of language, existing in that liminal space where fidelity to the original sound/text mingles with betrayal, transmission of that text in another language/medium. Thus reading *evocalises* the text as sound resonates into the reader's 'little chamber all bone-white,' imperceptibly changing and recreating it.[75]

As Cordingley has shown, Beckett's choice to do away with punctuation and logical connectives effectively allows him to control the reading speed: "The effect is to slow the reader's eye and allow the text to be heard, as if a reader were speaking it to himself, or reading it aloud."[76] Thus, the phonogenic text is further invested with self-performative properties, specially designed to be activated by its interaction with a reader.

Beckett's attempts to disencumber written language from its grounding formal conventions bring into question the gradual movement toward abstraction which, as Erik Tonning has argued, characterizes Beckett's later works. In his younger years, Beckett seemed to despise a strict poetics of abstraction in visual arts, denouncing them as "self-sufficient formalism of the 'abstractors of quintessence.'"[77] He did, however, Tonning claims, approve of "a use of an abstract language as long as this is conceived as a means of responding to the 'rupture of the lines of communication' between subject and object."[78] Tonning regards *Play* (written 1962–1963) as marking Beckett's turn toward abstract drama, and it is my view that this move had seminal roots in *How It Is*. Beckett's prose text stages just such a "rupture" through its narrator's relentless efforts to establish a form of communication with "Pim" based on violence—a creature whom he supposes he has encountered, but eventually claims to be his own fictional concoction, "all balls," like every story he has told and every image he has conjured:

> and all this business of above yes light yes skies yes…littles scenes yes all balls yes the women yes the dog yes the prayers yes the homes yes all balls yes
>
> and this business of a procession no answer this business of a procession yes never any procession no nor any journey no never any Pim no nor any Bom no never anyone no only me no answer only me yes so that was true yes it was true about me yes and what's my name no answer WHAT'S MY NAME screams good[79]

Here, whatever little was said about the universe of *How It Is* denied as fiction within the fiction, including the narrator himself, whose ontological integrity is from the outset at what can only be described as an advanced stage of dilapidation. His discourse is informed by "the fragmentary recollection of an extraneous voice once heard 'quaqua on all sides,'"[80] therefore he is never truly established as "subject" of his own rambling.

As Ruby Cohn comments, by 1959 Beckett was "[n]o longer wrestling with the subject-object conundrum."[81] This abstract quality of the language and diegetic set-up of *How It Is* evokes the theoretical discourse on radio in the twentieth century, in particular Rudolf Arnheim's view that

> the radio is the most abstract of media. If radio can incarnate a presence, the body of this presence is nevertheless imaginary, spectral .... For Arnheim, radio can create an 'acoustic bridge,' melding into a formal unity all the various phenomena of sound ... [R]adio causes the spoken word to lose its semantic aspect, even as its phonic force reaches new levels of intensity ....[82]

If one were to replace the word "radio" with "*How It Is*" in this passage, Albright's discussion of Arnheim's theory here would make for as accurate a description of the narrative strategies at work in Beckett's text as any other. The concept of an "abstract radio" was also appealing to other European thinkers: "Marinetti and Palitzsche also advocated a radiophony liberated from the word, and every movement to treat speech as the sound-equivalent of text-strips in a collage, stuck in at every angle, tended toward abstraction."[83] This experimental vision evokes the juxtaposition of propositions in the language of *How It Is*, deprived as it is from the convenience of logical connectives and, like orality, more prone to stutters, interruptions and repetitions. As put by Alain Bosquet in his broadcast on *Comment c'est*:

> [S]entences are embedded into one another, there is no punctuation – there are verses. Sometimes sentence A starts with three words, then gets interrupted by sentence B, then sentence C, then back to A and back to B. Well, this seems superficial for twenty lines, but after that it conveys an extraordinary rhythm, causing syllables to be repeated ... from sentence to sentence (one might pause at times and think: 'This is the end of a sentence, or perhaps the beginning of another,' but it is irrelevant) and we are left with an impression of implacable rhythm such as one rarely hears. (my translation)[84]

This lends some further support to the argument that Beckett discovered the radio medium at a time when it could provide him with much-needed tools and inspiration to return to prose writing. However, as often with Beckett, the problematic question of performance significantly complicates matters: Could a highly phonogenic text somehow be deemed utterly unsuitable for broadcast?

"That Kind an Image Not for the Eyes Made of Words Not for the Ears"[85]: *How It Is*, the Senses, and the Issue of Performance

In Barbara Bray's review of *Comment c'est* on the Third Programme, Beckett was most impressed by her point that "COMMENT C'EST isn't about anything. It is something …. It is a novel if the DIVINE COMEDY is a novel. Otherwise it's poetry, pure if not simple."[86] Bray was the first to acknowledge the indifference with which *Comment c'est* lets itself be labeled as a "novel" in the Minuit edition. Beckett was likely pleased that her approach differed from many others' in search, for instance, of a definitive interpretation of *Waiting for Godot* without necessarily trying to see the play for the "thing" that it is and what it does. Two years later, on the RTF, Bosquet also described *Comment c'est* as a "prose poem" or "prose narrative," adding: "After *L'innommable*, but especially after *Comment c'est*, one cannot tell the difference between tale and incantation" (my translation).[87] In terms of what *Comment c'est/How It Is* "does" as a literary "something" posing as a novel, Daniela Caselli efficiently sums up: "The main fiction of *How It Is/Comment c'est* is that of constructing itself as a voice while being a written text."[88] While it is true that the dynamics of sonority and aurality are central to *How It Is*, the merits of this particular achievement are precisely dependent on the text retaining its written form: to read it on the radio or, to a lesser extent, in public or on stage is to destroy, or negate, the complexity of its phonogenic powers, since the text is then delivered as vocalized speech by the actor in the first place. Relatedly, the main danger of reading *Comment c'est/How It Is* on the radio is to disrupt the carefully crafted equilibrium between ink and sound which makes the work "something" rather than "about something"—as Bray also says in her review: "This is a piece of total writing." In this final section, I want to examine *How It Is* and the issue of performance, in order to shed some light on Beckett's insistence that his "novel" has "nothing to do with theatre or radio" as well as on his complex stance on adaptations of his works.

Beckett's exploration of any given medium involves a great deal of attention to the effects achievable through sensory input or, alternatively, sensory deprivation. In *Waiting for Godot* and *Endgame* (1958), for instance, Pozzo and Hamm attest to his interest in blindness as a dramatic device, as does Dan Rooney in *All That Fall*—as Zilliacus writes: "Of the various afflictions imaginable in a Beckett moribund, blindness undoubtedly is the most radiogenic."[89] This in turn resonates with a 30 October 1980 letter from Jérôme Lindon, Beckett's French publisher, to the Société des Auteurs et Compositeurs Dramatiques (SACD), refusing permission to the Théâtre du Fil d'Ariane to stage *Tous ceux qui tombent* because it is "by definition a 'blind' play."[90] This is because radio may be considered a "blind" medium (strictly in terms of sensory input) relying exclusively on the evocative powers of aurality. In Martin Esslin's words: "Information that reaches [the listener] through other senses is instantly converted into visual terms. And aural experiences, which include the immense richness of language as well as musical and natural sound, are the most effective means of triggering visual images."[91] With regard to these considerations, the paradoxical feat of *Comment c'est/How It Is* is that of usurping the prerogatives of the radiophonic medium by simultaneously recreating a form of blindness for the reader while being "evocalized," functioning in effect like "printed sound." Very little is known of the universe in which the precarious "story" of *Comment c'est/How It Is* is supposed to take place, except that it is a muddy immensity plunged in total darkness. Up until the end of Part III, the narrator's laborious description of the world he imagines he inhabits is based on perceptions mediated through other senses than sight, as when he allegedly determines Pim's hair color by touching him: "Mass of hairs all white to the feel."[92] "Similarly to the radiophonic medium, mud in *Comment c'est/How It Is* involves a perfect blindness, where the only distinguishable images are images of the mind."[93] The decidedly internal focalization means that the reader can only "see" what the "characters" see, that is nothing at all, aside from images summoned by the narrator's memories or by his fragmented description of Pim's misfortunes in Part II—all brutally dispelled by his final avowal of fictionality. In short, the experience of reading *How It Is* relies on the same principles as those inherent to the process of listening to a radio play: a sustained effort of imagination is needed to counterbalance the perceived "ablation" of the sense of sight.

However, crucially, the "printed sound" crafted by Beckett in *How It Is* should not be mistaken for a radio script proper, nor with "poetic improvisation or even automatic writing," warns Cordingley: "There isn't the innocence of either spoken or indirect discourse but the theatricality of feigned speech."[94] As a textual, printed object, *How It Is* acts as a constant reminder of its own artificiality, of the fundamental failure of its linguistic stratagems to imitate life. Its performative nature lies more in this exercise in "feigned speech" than in the phonogeny itself.

This entire metatextual paradigm would be lost on the radio, erased at once by the very performance. Cordingley also writes: "The written condition of the word in *L'image* exhibits its desire to be heard as audible voice and not the grapheme of written culture"[95]; while this is still true of the final text, it may well be that this "desire" is precisely the tension which *How It Is* seeks to "incarnate," and that to vocalize it is to break it. On 18 February 1961, *Le Figaro Littéraire* published a scathing review of *Comment c'est* by Luc Estang, which Beckett sent to Bray with the note "Enclosed another cry of alarm."[96] After quoting from the book, Estang writes: "And on and on like this for another one hundred and seventy-five pages. But the lack of punctuation in the logorrhoea is the least of the impending headaches!...This flood of words which outruns conscious formulation demands to be 'spoken' and not just 'read' .... This isn't literature: it can't be."[97] It isn't hard to see why this review caught Beckett's eye (and perhaps amused him), since these comments only confirm that he succeeded in devising his "printed sound" hybrid. Therefore, we may say that *How It Is*, despite presenting itself as a reflection on radiophony, is disfigured by actual utterance and consequently ill-suited for broadcast, in an eminently Beckettian aporia of the genre, reminiscent of his well-known statement that "there is nothing to express, nothing with which to express, nothing from which to express, no power to express, no desire to express, together with the obligation to express."[98]

Beckett's attitude toward adaptations of his works for other media was complex and, at times, flexible. While he did not actively encourage readings of *How It Is*, we have seen that he would not object to them as firmly as he was known to oppose stagings of *All That Fall*, though he did express reservations: "To read that in private is asking too much of anyone, let alone in public. I simply had nothing else to offer them."[99] To Chaikin, Beckett gave "carte blanche to use the *Texts* as you please + end of *How It Is*," but asked later: "How stage that bodilessness? That groping vox-inanis (soulless voice)?"[100] Although there is no available evidence that Beckett ever instructed his publishers to automatically withhold performance rights for *How It Is*, Lindon's handling of the many requests to perform other works in French provides some insight into their stance on this matter. A 20 February 1984 letter from Lindon advises a director hoping to put up *Tous ceux qui tombent* to prepare himself for "the quasi-ineluctable perspective of a refusal" from Beckett:

This is…a radiophonic work, that is, by definition, a text intended solely to be heard. Any representation of speech could cause a painfully redundant effect. If certain things are said, it is precisely because, to Samuel Beckett, they are not being seen. He would never have written this text had it been a matter of showing them. (my translation)[101]

This illustrates Beckett's hostile views about his works being forced in or out of the theater, as mentioned previously, but also invites an interesting comparison between the radio play and *How It Is*, in which the situation is reversed: it is the text, as visual speech, that makes vocalization redundant.

Fortunately, the large proportion of such refusals in the Minuit archive also serves to highlight rare exceptions when permission was granted to adaptations that were felt to respect the integrity of the original work. In December 1960, Lindon agreed to a production of *Cendres* (1959) where "a curtain would be placed between the actors and the audience, so that the latter, without seeing anything, would listen to the play in 'live' audition" (my translation).[102] In February 1970, after opposing a project to set up *Paroles et Musique* (1966) for the stage because the work is "meant to be heard, not seen," Beckett consented to a "concert performance devoid of any theatrical manifestation" that would take place "in the dark or with minimum light" (my translation).[103] In March 1978, Beckett and Lindon agreed to a stage performance of *Tous ceux qui tombent* by Compagnie du Delta, Marseille, taking place "in the dark (in accordance with one of Beckett's wishes)" in order to "get as close as possible to the radiophonic aspect of the work" (my translation).[104] In November 1986, the Italian translator of *Comment c'est*, Franco Quadri, asked for permission to read two excerpts from *Como È* (1965) in Modena and Milan. The letter bears Lindon's marginalia: "d'accord" ("agreed"[105]). In March 1987, permission was granted to director Yvan Blanloeil of Compagnie Fartov in Bordeaux for a stage representation of *Cendres* described in the following terms:

> The dramaturgy of these productions is assigned to the sole vector of sound, as in radiophonic dramaturgies. However, this sound is conveyed by means of sophisticated technical spatial installations, which radiophonic broadcasting is unable to produce. The audition is therefore organised at a given place, where listeners gather. This is the only common trait between an audio-show and a show in the proper sense. Indeed the pieces are meant to be heard in a virtually neutralised space, in darkness most of the time, within the limits of the listeners' security. The presence of live, but invisible players,

uttering the text in microphones located near the audition site, doesn't amount to the set-up of a spectacle…but rather to an attempt to reunite with the dynamics created by live radio. (my translation)[106]

As we can see, it is possible for a dramatic production to meet radio halfway with performances that inform the meta-discourse instead of neutralizing it.[107] In the examples just cited, the visual input is obliterated in order to revisit the radiophonic medium. What, then, of live readings of *How It Is*? Assuming that Beckett would have opposed the performances had he thought the text entirely unsuitable for this type of delivery, it could be surmised that one reason they went ahead was that the introduction of a live, theatrical element partially reactivated the "textual tension" at work in the original. In performance, vision is restored, and the actor murmuring into his microphone before the audience becomes a sort of stand-in for the narrator of *How It Is* and for the text itself. This literalization of the dynamics of aurality evokes what Jean-Jacques Bloch's calls the "subjective style":

> We will call "subjective radio" any radio play in which the microphone corresponds to the ear of the main character. This basic principle implies many others: this microphone, which has become "all ears," hears everything, everything that is said by others, but it does not hear its own voice (we do not hear ourselves speak). On the other hand, we follow our own thought, 'we listen to ourselves think.' It follows that our main character is mute, and that only internal resonances will allow listeners to determine the main character's introspection.[108]

Transposed to a live reading of *How It Is*, this means that the entity consisting of the actor and his microphone on the stage becomes a monstrous self-contained allegory of radio transmission, where the "protagonist" murmurs into his own "ear" (the microphone) strings of words which he then hears again and repeats to himself indefinitely, so that the audience, despite seeing a man, cannot confirm that this utterance comes from a sentient being rather than a machine or the recorded spasms of a long-dead conscience. Only then, perhaps, at the crossroads of theater, oral poetry and radio, can performance return *How It Is* to its intended nature of "something."

The BBC WAC files offer a uniquely intimate perspective on an institution with which Beckett engaged closely during a decisive period in his development as a writer. It invites a consideration of the chronology of

Beckett's works as an aesthetic continuum and therefore also a reflection on works not originally intended for the aural medium in terms of their underlying discourse on radio. Without additional archival evidence, it is difficult to explain why *Comment c'est/How It Is*, as a major prose work written and published at a time when Beckett's works were highly sought after, features so rarely in national radio archives in England and France. It seems curious that this work in particular should have attracted comparatively little attention from radio producers, considering its marked preoccupation with sonority and Beckett's popularity at the time of its publication. While it is possible that the "novel" was thought too difficult for broadcast by the Sound Drama team under Esslin's directorship, the archive attests to the BBC's interest in most other published prose works by Beckett well into the 1990s. As we have seen, Beckett might have had grounds to object to certain adaptations involving *How It Is* due to the performative aurality of its peculiar language and the resulting risk of structural redundancy when this text is vocalized. In any case, the filiation between Beckett's works for the radio and *How It Is* evident in their respective exploration of the voice as a literary apparatus. Beckett's growing interest in the radio and the process of recording/transmitting as compositional devices inspired a number of formal experiments in the late 1950s, as part of the natural course of the evolution of his style since *L'innommable*. *How It Is* was influenced by the radio, then itself informed Beckett's later radio plays: "The same elements of language that dominated *How It Is* are at work [in *Cascando*], too: near-obliterated syntax, short phrases, images hectically panted forth."[109] Beckett would continue his creative research on the recorded/transmitted voice and disembodiment across genres up to his very last works, as with *What Where* (1984)/*Quoi Où* (1986), where the microphone, "v," effectively became a character in the play.

Notes

1. Clas Zillacus, *Beckett and Broadcasting: a Study of the Works of Samuel Beckett for and in Radio and Television* (Åbo: Åbo akademi, 1976), 18.
2. See *SW 63–67*.
3. James Knowlson, "The works of Samuel Beckett: a Discography" (*Recorded Sound*, January 1984), 19.
4. A December 1957 audience report on Magee's readings from *Molloy* and "From an Abandoned Work" shows mixed reactions to the broadcast: "sharp divisions of opinion characterised the response of the sample

audiences, ranging from intense disgust to great admiration and excitement." Some were put off by "the monotony and repetitiveness of these 'rambling reminiscences'" and by Magee's voice, whose "guttural intonation made [it] almost unintelligible" (*SW 53–62*).
5. See *SW 63–67*.
6. Beckett, *Letters III*, 249.
7. See *SCR 75–79*. "The Drunken Boat" was written in the early 1930s and published in 1976.
8. Beckett, *Letters III*, 229–30.
9. Ibid., 306.
10. Beckett, *How It Is*, 3.
11. Beckett, *Letters III*, 282.
12. Ibid., 285.
13. Ibid., 306. Beckett's "pointing" of the script refers to the addition of "marks to facilitate the understanding" (ibid., 315).
14. Ibid., 397.
15. "To say anything is to say too much." (my translation)
16. 'New Comment' no. 40, October 1961 (BBC WAC 'Talks Library' Sample Scripts).
17. University of Reading, Beckett International Foundation archives (hereafter UoR), mss BC MS 4392.
18. From "no more I'll hear no more" (92) to "stop panting let it stop" (94), with the omission of the paragraph starting "movements for nothing" (94).
19. Zillacus, *Beckett and Broadcasting*, 66.
20. Letter dated 17 April 1964, P.H. Newby to John Calder (*SW 63–67*).
21. There was, for instance, a production entitled "A celebration of the life and work of Samuel Beckett" at the National Theatre and Olivier Theatre in London (April 1990). The production comprised a compilation of readings from Beckett's drama, prose and poetry, including a diffusion of Magee's recording of *How It Is* (UoR, BC MS 3689).
22. Zillacus, *Beckett and Broadcasting*, 208–209.
23. Deirdre Bair, *Samuel Beckett: A Biography* (London: Vintage, 1990), 673.
24. From "and all this business of above" (*How It Is*, 127).
25. James Knowlson, *Damned to Fame: the Life of Samuel Beckett* (London: Bloomsbury, 1997), 526.
26. Review of "Nicol Williamson: An Evening With a Man and His Band" at the Hollywood Playhouse, Los Angeles, by Dan Sullivan: "Stage Review: Think Casual For Your Date With Williamson," *Los Angeles Times*, 27 August 1986, http://articles.latimes.com/1986-08-27/entertainment/ca-14394_1_nicol-williamson (accessed 12.11.15).

27. Knowlson, *Damned to Fame*, 824.
28. Letter to Ruby Cohn dated 27 April 1980 (UoR, BC MS 5100 [COH] COH/149).
29. Chris. J. Ackerley and Stan. E. Gontarski, *The Grove Companion to Samuel Beckett: a Reader's Guide to his Work, Life and Thought* (Grove Press: New York, 2004), 91.
30. Knowlson, *Damned to Fame*, 824
31. *BSW 53–62*.
32. See Zillacus 116–118 for details on the RTF/ORTF and why its context wasn't conducive to a more sustained promotion of Beckett's works on the French radio.
33. This program is available for consultation at http://www.ina.fr/audio/PHD88005593/samuel-beckett-2eme-partie-audio.html (accessed 12.11.15).
34. "un des grands chefs d'œuvre de la littérature d'après-guerre, par la tension, par la richesse, la variété de cette chose qui, en tant que genre, est tout à fait innommable."
35. "*Comment c'est*, c'est un poème [en prose], une litanie peut-être, intitulée roman mais faussement ...."
36. From "et si l'on peut encore à cette heure tardive" (*Comment c'est*, 222) becomes "and if it is still possible at this late hour" (*How It Is*, 125).
37. Beckett, *Letters III*, 389.
38. Ibid., 306.
39. Ibid., 64.
40. Ibid., 64.
41. Ibid., 281.
42. Pim Verhulst, "'Just howls from time to time': Dating Beckett's *Pochade radiophonique*," Samuel Beckett Today/Aujourd'hui 27, no 1 (2015), 143–158.
43. James Jesson, "'White World. Not a Sound': Beckett's Radioactive Text," *Texas Studies in Literature and Language, Vol. 51, No. 1, Samuel Beckett in Austin and Beyond* (Spring 2009), 50.
44. Beckett's correspondence with Georges Duthuit suggests that the two might have been working toward an (aborted) special issue of the journal *transition* dedicated to Sade (cf. entries under "Duthuit" in *Letters II*).
45. UoR MS 1656/3.
46. For an account of Sade's presence in *Comment c'est*, see Elsa Baroghel, "Samuel Beckett, lecteur de Sade: *Comment c'est* et *Les 120 Journées de Sodome*," in "Samuel Beckett" 4, *La violence dans l'œuvre de Samuel Beckett: entre langage et corps* (ed. Llewellyn Brown, Lettres Modernes Minard/Classiques Garnier, forthcoming in 2016), and Paul Stewart's

chapter "Sadism and Relation in *How It Is*" in *Sex and Aesthetics in Samuel Beckett's Works* (New York: Palgrave Macmillan, 2011), 117–132.
47. Verhulst, "'Just howls from time to time,'" 154.
48. Knowlson, *Damned to Fame*, 453.
49. *Samuel Beckett: The Complete Dramatic Works* (London: Faber and Faber, 2006), 278.
50. Albright, Daniel, *Beckett and Aesthetics* (Cambridge: Cambridge University, 2003), 116.
51. For an account of Dante's presence in *How It Is*, see Daniela Caselli's chapter "Staging the Inferno in *How It Is*" in *Beckett's Dante: Intertextuality in the Fiction and Criticism* (Manchester and New York: Manchester University Press, 2005), 148–82.
52. Beckett, *Letters III*, 252–53.
53. Albright, *Beckett and Aesthetics*, 120.
54. Beckett, *How It Is*, 3.
55. Lea Sinoimeri, "Ill-Told Ill-Heard": Aurality and Reading in *Comment c'est/How It Is*," *Samuel Beckett Today/Ajourd'hui* 24, no 1 (2012), 326.
56. Ibid., 323.
57. *Letters III*, 306.
58. Zillacus, *Beckett and Broadcasting*, 81.
59. Magessa O'Reilly, "Beckett's 'From an Unabandoned Work': On the Way to *Comment c'est*," in *Translation and Literature* 12, no. 1 (Spring 2003), 144–154.
60. Anthony Cordingley, "The Reading Eye from Scriptura Continua to Modernism: Orality and Punctuation between Beckett's *L'image* and *Comment c'est/How It Is*," *Journal of the Short-Story in English* vol. 47 (2006), 49–63.
61. Cordingley, "The Reading Eye," 59.
62. Gontarski, S. E., *The Intent of Undoing in Samuel Beckett's Dramatic Texts* (Bloomington, Ind: Indiana University Press), 1985.
63. Beckett, *Letters III*, 230.
64. Ibid., 282.
65. According to O'Reilly, this was finished by 17 March: "Beckett's 'From an Unabandoned Work,'" 146.
66. Beckett, *Letters III*, 306.
67. O'Reilly, "Beckett's 'From an Unabandoned Work,'" 147.
68. Albright, *Beckett and Aesthetics*, 106.
69. Sinoimeri, "Ill-Told Ill-Heard," 322–23.
70. Beckett, *Comment c'est*, 25–6.
71. Beckett, *How It Is*, 12.
72. Beckett, *Comment c'est*, 13.

73. Beckett, *How It Is*, 5.
74. Sinoimeri, "Ill-Told Ill-Heard," 323.
75. Ibid., 327.
76. Cordingley, "The Reading Eye," 60–61.
77. Erik Tonning, *Samuel Beckett's Abstract Drama: Works for Stage and Screen 1962–1985* (Bern; Oxford: Peter Lang, 2007), 26.
78. Ibid.
79. Beckett, *How It Is*, 127–28.
80. Beckett, *Letters III*, 327.
81. Ruby Cohn, *A Beckett Canon* (Ann Arbor: University of Michigan Press, 2001), 254.
82. Albright, *Beckett and Aesthetics*, 99–100.
83. Ibid., 100.
84. "[L]es phrases sont imbriquées les unes dans les autres, il n'y a pas de ponctuation – il y a les versets; parfois la phrase A commence par trois mots, est interrompue par la phrase B, puis une phrase C, puis on revient à la A et on revient à la B. Eh bien, ça a l'air artificiel pendant 20 lignes, et puis après il s'en dégage un extraordinaire rythme qui fait que les syllabes qui sont répétées ainsi de phrase en phrase (on peut d'ailleurs parfois s'arrêter, on se dit: 'c'est la fin d'une phrase, c'est peut-être le début d'une autre,' ça n'a pas d'importance) et on en retient une impression de rythme implacable comme il est rare d'en entendre."
85. Beckett, *How It Is*, 38.
86. Beckett, *Letters III*, 398. Bray's remark may be read as a nod to Beckett's own comments on James Joyce's *Work in Progress* in his 1929 essay "Dante... Bruno. Vico.. Joyce": "His writing is not *about* something; *it is that something itself.*" in *Disjecta: Miscellaneous Writings and a Dramatic Fragment*, ed. Ruby Cohn (London: Calder, 1983), 27.
87. "Après *L'innommable*, et surtout après *Comment c'est*, on ne voit plus la différence entre l'incantation et le récit."
88. Caselli, *Beckett's Dante*, 148.
89. Zillacus, *Beckett and Broadcasting*, 61.
90. "par définition une pièce 'aveugle'," IMEC/Fonds Samuel Beckett, Samuel Beckett 'Boîte 15': "SACD II 1979—*Tous ceux qui tombent*."
91. Martin Esslin, "Samuel Beckett and the Art of Radio," in *On Beckett: Essays and Criticism*, ed. S.E. Gontarski (New York: Grove Press, 1986), 278.
92. Beckett, *How It Is*, 46.
93. Sinoimeri, "Ill-Told Ill-Heard," 330.
94. Cordingley, "The Reading Eye," 59.
95. Ibid., 50.
96. Beckett, *Letters III*, 399.

97. Ibid., 400. Ironically, Bair, in her far more enthusiastic chapter on *Comment c'est*, echoes: "*Comment C'est* is a work which requires careful, slow reading, one which almost demands to be spoken, in order to savour the full flavour of the language" (*Samuel Beckett: A Biography*, 555).
98. Beckett, *Proust and Three Dialogues with Georges Duthuit* (London: Calder, 1965), 103.
99. Beckett, *Letters III*, 326.
100. Knowlson, *Damned to Fame*, 824.
101. "Il s'agit ... d'une œuvre radiophonique, c'est-à-dire, par définition, d'un texte destiné à être seulement entendu. Toute représentation du discours risque de provoquer un effet péniblement redondant. Si certaines choses sont dites, c'est précisément parce que, pour Samuel Beckett, on ne les voit pas. Jamais il n'aurait écrit ce texte-là s'il s'était agi de les montrer.... Je vous préviens sans attendre pour que vous puissiez vous préparer à la perspective quasi inéluctable d'un refus" (IMEC/Fonds Samuel Beckett 'Boîte 17': "SACD II 1984, *Tous ceux qui tombent*").
102. Letter from Mrs. Wildschitz (SACD) to Lindon, 23 December 1960: "il placerait un rideau entre les acteurs et les spectateurs, de sorte que ceux-ci, sans rien voir, écouteraient le jeu en audition 'directe'" (IMEC/Fonds Samuel Beckett 'Boîte 6': "*La dernière bande/Cendres*").
103. Letter from Arié Dzierlazka, 3 February 1970: "C'est une œuvre qui 'est faite pour être entendue et non vue' ... Monsieur Beckett ... me donne son accord pour que Paroles et Musique se donne à Royan dans une version concert qui exclut toute manifestation théâtrale, au point que l'idéal me semble-t-il serait que l'œuvre puisse se donner dans le noir ou avec une lumière minimum" (IMEC/Fonds Samuel Beckett 'Boîte 5': "S. Beckett Correspondance 1969–70"). Beckett also agreed to the ORTF recording the performance.
104. Letter from Eric Eychenne to Gérard Baby (SACD), February 1978: "interprétation du texte par des acteurs, dans l'obscurité, (selon un des désirs de Beckett) afin aussi, de se rapprocher le plus possible de l'aspect radiophonique de l'œuvre" (IMEC/Fonds Samuel Beckett, 'Boîte 15,': "*Tous ceux qui tombent*—1972–1978").
105. Letter from Xavier Buffet Delmas (SACD) to Lindon, 21 November 1986: (IMEC/Fonds Samuel Beckett, 'Boîte 18,' "SACD I 1984–1986—*Cendres*").
106. "Il s'agit de productions dont la dramaturgie est confiée au seul vecteur du son, à l'instar des dramatiques radiophoniques. Cependant, ce son est restitué par des moyens techniques sophistiqués de mise en espace, que la diffusion radiophonique n'est pas en mesure de produire. L'écoute est donc organisée dans un lieu donné, où les auditeurs se rassemblent. C'est là le seul point commun entre un audio-spectacle et un spectacle au sens

propre. En effet, les œuvres sont destinées à être entendues dans un espace virtuellement neutralisé, la plupart du temps obscur, dans les limites de la sécurité de l'auditeur .... La présence de comédiens vivants, mais non visibles, disant une partie du texte dans des micros à proximité du lieu d'écoute, ne signifie pas non plus, bien entendu, une mise en spectacle, mais une tentative de retrouver les rapports créés par le direct radiophonique" (IMEC/Fonds Samuel Beckett, 'Boîte 19': "SACD 1987–1988—*Cendres*").

107. Cf. Verhulst's discussion of the July 1958 broadcast of *Malone Dies* on the Third Programme: "Not only does the announcement efface the metafictional self-awareness of Beckett's novel as a written construct, it also ... relocate[s] it entirely inside the narrator's mind as a kind of geriatric *monologue intérieur*. The novel, in contrast, plays with the tension between Malone's thoughts and what he chooses to record of them" (Verhulst, "'Just howls from time to time,'" 153).
108. Quoted in Sinoimeri, "Ill-Told Ill-Heard," 325.
109. Zillacus, *Beckett and Broadcasting*, 138.

Fitting the Prose to Radio: The Case of *Lessness*

Paul Stewart

On 25 February 1971, BBC Radio 3 broadcast an adapted reading of Beckett's prose text, *Lessness*, as produced by Martin Esslin. For the producer, this was an occasion when medium and material came together in a form of near perfect synergy. In a broadcast introduction to the piece, Esslin argued that "'Lessness' [was] a text peculiarly suited to radio, and perhaps fully realisable *only* in radio."[1] This confidence in the medium was not entirely shared by Beckett, who was subsequently "deeply dissatisfied" with the results of the production,[2] despite his involvement with the adaptation almost from its conception. The adaptation of the highly abstract, repetitive text therefore raises many questions as to the suitability of radio as a medium for Beckett's later prose and as to the nature of *Lessness* itself. Ulrika Maude is surely correct to argue that throughout "his writing for the radio, Beckett [was] concerned with the distinctive nature of sonorous perception: the fragile, ghostly and discontinuous soundscapes it evokes."[3] The lingering question with adaptations of Beckett's prose for radio is whether the distinctive natures of the two media are entirely compatible or lead to the creation of unresolved tensions. This chapter will trace such

P. Stewart (✉)
Department of Languages and Literature, University of Nicosia, Nicosia, Cyprus

tensions through the archival record of the BBC's production, as well as of the promotion and reception, of *Lessness* for radio.

THE PRODUCTION OF *LESSNESS*

Esslin's forceful claim for the radio *Lessness* as potentially more effective than the prose version implicitly draws attention to the process that brought this adaptation to broadcast. In many ways, it was a complicated process conducted at surprising speed.

Beckett's translation of *Sans* appeared in the *New Statesman* on 1 May 1970. It was quickly seized on by Esslin with a view for radio adaptation, and the rights department was asked to get clearance for the piece as early as 8 June 1970. Due to some confusion as to who actually had the rights to *Lessness* in the UK, clearance was not confirmed until 11 October. In a copyright memo of 10 October, Eileen White of the Drama Department added an important handwritten note stating that "[t]his memo supercedes [*sic*] one of 20.7.70, owing to some argument between two agents: Beckett eventually directed that John Calder dealt with this."[4] Evidently, Beckett had had to intervene to clarify the issue.

Esslin quickly assembled the necessary six actors. Initially, Esslin had tried to recruit Jack McGowran to the project but he was "in exile from London" as he informed Beckett on 1 February 1971.[5] The actors, all described as Beckett "enthusiasts," had varying degrees of experience in dealing with Beckett's texts. Patrick Magee was already established as a leading Beckett interpreter, and Harold Pinter's suitability was also apparent. Nicol Williamson had been championed by Esslin as a possible reader for *Texts for Nothing* in a letter of 18 July 1967[6] and had reportedly made a great impression on Beckett as Vladimir in the 1964 Royal Court revival of *Waiting for Godot*, with Beckett apparently even going so far as to suspect that the actor had a "touch of genius" about him.[7] Williamson was considered to be friend enough to be allowed to use parts of *How It Is* in his one-man show from 1973, although he had not obtained prior permission.[8] Leonard Fenton would go on to play Willie opposite Billie Whitelaw's Winnie in the Royal Court production of *Happy Days* in 1979. Donal Donnelly had played Lucky in the first Irish production of *Godot* at the Pike Theatre in 1955. What is perhaps curious in the casting is the mix of accents—including Scottish, Irish (both North and South) and London ones—especially as the six voices were meant to convey a single consciousness.

Beckett was involved with the production from the beginning, and by 7 July 1970, he had gone so far as to provide a key to the six voices of the text, via his publisher John Calder, who wrote:

> I now enclose Beckett's key to Lessness together with the text for broadcasting. There are, as you can see, six voices. I think it is quite clear what he wants. He says in his letter to me "Suggest for broadcast 6 male voices corresponding to 6 groups. As close to one another in pitch and quality as possible. Cold. Low. Monotonous rhythm same for all. 2 seconds between sentences. 4 between paragraphs. Rhythm difficult to catch without me. An evening here with you and Martin?"[9]

Of course, Beckett and Esslin did meet and Beckett's reading of this difficult rhythm was recorded. Incidentally, Beckett's key was not complete—he had missed out a single line, which was duly corrected[10]—pointing to some of the potential dangers of adaptation by post.

Beckett's detailed key is not extant within the BBC files, but one can make a tentative reconstruction from the broadcast playscript,[11] supplemented with Rosemary Pountney's work on the *Lessness* manuscripts. The script as broadcast follows the printed text with just a few erroneous handwritten alterations that appear be a case of the eye slipping down the page to a lower line. Fortunately, these erroneous "corrections" did not make it into the final broadcast. Beside each line of the script is a legend such as for the first line: "1. A.3" The first number is the line number on that particular page; the letter denotes the speaker; the final digit seems to denote the number of the line within that speaker's recording. If this is correct, then the speakers did not record their lines sequentially in accordance with the published text. Each line was subsequently repeated later in the piece. On this basis, actor A (Nicol Williamson) would have been recorded according to a key such as the one below:

Speaker and line		Place in broadcast (page and line number)
A1	In four split asunder over backwards true refuge issueless scattered ruins	3.8/7.1
A2	Blacked out fallen open four walls over backwards true refuge issueless	1.4/5.13
A3	Ruins true refuge long last toward which so many false time out of mind	1.1/9.1
A4	Slow black with ruin true refuge four walls over backwards no sound	3.1/9.4

(continued)

(continued)

Speaker and line		Place in broadcast (page and line number)
A5	Four square true refuge long last four walls over backwards no sound	2.5/6.12
A6	True refuge long last issueless scattered down four walls over backwards no sound	3.10/10.2
A7	True refuge long last scattered ruins same gray as the sand	5.4/8.1
A8	Scattered ruins ash gray all sides true refuge long last issueless	3.13/8.10
A9	Scattered ruins same gray as the sand ash gray true refuge	1.5/6.11
A10	Blacked out fallen open true refuge issueless toward which so many false time out of mind	4.8/8.6

It is important to note that Beckett did not merely refer Esslin to the published version of the text. Rather, Esslin appears to have been working from a typescript of the original six image groups as they would have appeared prior to being structured by Beckett via a process of relative chance, as described by Rosemary Pountney.[12] The "key" then provided the necessary numerical annotations to structure the piece as it appeared in the published version. It is as if Beckett sent Esslin a version of *Lessness* that was halfway through its creative process, with the six image groups yet to be arranged in their final order. However, these image groups were not then subjected to a form of random selection, but were expected to conform to the already established published version.

For Esslin, this arrangement would have been extremely difficult to achieve as, in order to produce the final piece, each individual line would have to be edited into place while trying to ensure that they were as "close to one another in pitch and quality as possible" and conforming to the rhythm that had been dictated to Esslin by Beckett. The wild-track silences—those moments of recorded ambient sound between edits—would also have to be of the same quality. The intricacy of the necessary editing would no doubt have bolstered Esslin's sense that the meaning of the text only emerged through the painstaking editorial process that radio could provide. It also reinforces Esslin's claim that the radio production was itself an "intertwining" of strands of the text, as he claimed in his introduction.[13] This "intertwining" does not pertain to the published Beckett text itself—where the formal pattern might be discernible through the act of reading—but to radio as a medium for recreating the published text from the six image groups.

Esslin's contention that *Lessness* only achieved its fullest expression through radio was one he long held, claiming in *Beckett Remembering / Remembering Beckett* that the piece "was really for the radio,"[14] but from the outset there was a tension within the production's use of six voices to indicate the six image groups, at least as Esslin characterized the proposal in his introduction:

> When we were talking about a broadcast of the text, Mr Beckett indicated how he wanted six voices to share the reading. Not as different characters or persons, but as indicators of different groups of images.[15]

In other words, the six voices were not to be associated with six different individual consciousnesses and yet, no matter how much Esslin may have tried to equalize the disparate parts, the individuality of the voices remained. It is little wonder, then, that Esslin felt a little "trepidation" when sending Beckett tapes of the recording. In a letter of 23 February 1971, Esslin writes:

> I tried to follow the reading you gave as closely as possible but of course each voice retains its individuality. I personally was very moved by the piece as it is now. Please let me know what you think even if it is devastating.[16]

Beckett was indeed unhappy with the result and for reasons that Esslin seemed to have already intuited: "He [Beckett] felt that the voices were too strongly differentiated, that the reading seemed too slow (we had rigidly adhered to the tempo he himself had adopted when reading a sample to me) and thus too sentimental."[17]

The problem was in part a technical one: how to indicate change in image aurally while maintaining some sense of a single consciousness. According to Esslin, Beckett with "his usual kindness and courtesy ... took the blame upon himself and confessed that the idea of using six different voices might have been a mistake."[18] If Beckett had not suggested the six-voice solution, perhaps a single voice recorded at different levels or in different ambient conditions might have achieved the required effect. One should note, perhaps, that this effect is achieved on the stage in *That Time* when a single voice, differentiated through "source and context" or "pitch,"[19] indicates different groups of image and mood and yet is clearly from the same consciousness. No doubt this is helped visually by having one's focus directed to the head of the Listener that is actually present on stage. It may be that Beckett learnt from his mistakes in radio to achieve a greater success in theater. Perhaps, then, the solution was ultimately a theatrical, rather than a radiogenic, one.

The Promotion and Reception of *Lessness*

As was customary with any radio drama on the BBC, *Lessness* was trailed prior to broadcast and publicized via the *Radio Times*. These texts—as documented in the BBC archive—demonstrate how *Lessness* was framed for the first audience and might go some way to suggest how the text and broadcast were regarded within the organization.

The original press release, on which the trails and other promotional material were based, seems merely informative in its opening remarks:

> Six distinguished actors will read Samuel Beckett's short prose work 'Lessness' on Thursday, February 25 at 10.05 p.m. on Radio 3. It was first published in France under the title 'Sans'. Beckett's own translation into English appeared first in the New Statesman last May. Beckett himself has indicated how the work should be distributed among the six readers, who are Nicol Williamson, Harold Pinter, Donal Donnelly, Patrick Magee, Denys Hawthorne, and Leonard Fenton, all Beckett enthusiasts. Producer Martin Esslin will also introduce the work with a short foreword.[20]

Of course, information is the prime goal here, but even such an apparently objective text reveals certain assumptions regarding the broadcast. Firstly, the recent nature of the text is highlighted; the radio broadcast comes just two years after initial publication in French and just seven months since it first appeared in English, suggesting that Radio 3 is keen to stress that it is fulfilling its remit to bring the most current developments in the arts to its audience. More importantly, perhaps, Beckett's involvement in the adaptation is emphasized, although with a certain omission. It is only mentioned that Beckett indicated how the work should be distributed among the voices, but omits to mention that Beckett was very precise in his instructions regarding the tone, timbre and pace of those voices. Nevertheless, Beckett's involvement is seen to be a positive attribute that is duly emphasized. Finally, the six actors involved are accorded due recognition: they are "distinguished" in their field and "enthusiasts" of Beckett. While these two terms need not necessarily go together, they are meant to indicate the quality of the radio production.

When the press release describes the nature of the text adapted, the language becomes much more evocative and reveals many more critical and interpretive assumptions apparently held by the production team:

'Lessness' unfolds, in poetry, a grey desolation, and a desperate human situation with no hope, no faith, no refuge left. Its effect is cumulative, through key phrases which constantly return in kaleidoscopic permutations, as in the paragraph:

> "Little body same grey as the earth sky ruins only upright. No sound not a breath same grey on all sides earth sky body ruins. Blacked out fallen open four walls over backwards true refuge issueless."[21]

The first assumption is one of genre: the text conducts itself in "poetry" rather than in prose. The inclusion of the term "poetry" in the press release could be informed by a desire to prepare the audience for the density of the words and imagery that the broadcast will contain. The removal of prosaic elements of syntax in *Lessness* that indicate a clear relation between aspects of a single sentence as well as between sentences would make the experience of listening to the adaptation very different from listening to a more conventional narrative. One might go further to argue that the very issue of whether there is a narrative element to the text is highlighted by this apparent preference for poetry over prose.

Although one might be willing to accept the contention that there is "no faith, no hope" apparent in *Lessness*, one might quibble about "no refuge," not least as the text repeatedly uses the phrase "true refuge" throughout and, indeed, the sample paragraph contains that very phrase. Here is not the place to question whether *Lessness* asserts that there is no refuge, or whether it suggests that the featureless waste among the ruins *is* the true refuge at last. However, it is important to note that what is offered as a description of the broadcast already contains elements of interpretation. Similarly, the press release also emphasizes the "human situation" of the piece, hinting that a certain subjectivity lurks beneath the dense prose rhythms and vasts of gray earth and sky. Again, this reading of *Lessness* may or may not be correct, but it certainly serves to guide the audience toward a particular understanding of the piece while listening. These instances—poetry rather than prose, no true refuge, the human situation—may also indicate the guiding assumptions behind the adaptation itself.

The descriptive paragraph of the press release went through at least one draft. What one assumes to be the prior draft reads as follows:

> "Lessness" unfolds, in sheer poetry, a grey desolation, and a desperate human situation (Beckett's own, perhaps) with no hope, no faith, no refuge left. Its effect is cumulative, through key phrases which constantly return in kaleidoscopic permutations ....[22]

The "sheer" and "Beckett's own, perhaps" are visible in the manuscript beneath the deletions in blue biro. Of obvious concern is that the human situation of the text is tentatively described as being Beckett's own condition. (Elsewhere in the archive in a "Copy of Promotion Note"—the title inscribed by hand in pen—it is said that Beckett "explores his personal vision" in *Lessness*.[23] The phrasing is ambiguous as to how "personal" that vision might be.) Therefore, in order to make an apparently cold, objective text palatable, there is a desire to relate this to a human subject and to then further identify this subject as the author.

Many of these aspects recurred in the *Radio Times* article of 18 February, yet some new elements now emerge. For the first time, the manner in which the work is divided between the six voices is made public: "Each voice is assigned a group of sentences in which one particular image prevails: ruin, exposure, wilderness, mindlessness, past and future denied and affirmed."[24] Esslin then justifies the rather complex manner in which the voices were recorded and the production was edited:

> although the text itself consists of an intricate weaving of these images (each sentence occurring twice), each group of images was recorded separately by the speaker concerned, so that the actual tapestry of the interweaving images only emerged in the tape cutting room. Thus the rhythmic pattern and the finely calculated structure of paragraphs and pauses demanded by the author could be far more accurately realised than if the whole piece had been recorded in the conventional way.[25]

The passage is quoted at length because it highlights a major concern: the role of the production business of radio in the creation of an audio *Lessness*, and the claims that one can make for the medium of radio. There is a paradox within the article in that a published text that is already said to be an "intricate weaving" is then re-woven by the radio production, although the "actual tapestry" of the piece "only emerged" through the editing process. A prior draft of the article shows that Esslin sought to emphasize the crucial role radio production played. In what seems to be blue fountain pen, Esslin makes some key emendations: "the tapestry" becomes "the *actual* tapestry; "the interweaving images *only emerged*" replaces the more neutral "had to be produced"; and the rather prosaic "more accurately achieved" is deleted in favor of "*far more* accurately *realised*."[26] These emendations may seem trivial, but they appear to have a coherent rationale behind them: it is only through the medium of radio that the true nature of *Lessness* can be revealed. So, the latent meaning of the original text only emerges in the *actual* tapestry of the radio adaptation. Also noticeable is the preference for the organic-sounding "emerged" over the more clinical, if more accurate, "produced." As such, the radio production is for Esslin an act of realizing the full potential of the text that had remained latent within the prose.

A further emendation from draft to published article highlights another recurring motif. The draft reads: "Thus the rhythmic pattern and structure of paragraphs and pauses demanded by the author ...." Again in his blue pen, Esslin adds the phrase "finely calculated" to characterize the structure of paragraphs and pauses.[27] While in one sense a simple acknowledgement of Beckett's craftsmanship, this emphasis on the "calculated" structure of the piece also omits any consideration of the elements of chance and partially random selection that were part of the process of assembling the original text of *Sans*. Indeed, across the press release material there is no mention of the role of relative chance in the creation of the text. Instead, the rhetorical emphasis is upon the careful intricacies of the arrangement of *Lessness* and radio's ability to realize this arrangement for its audience.

Such press release material acts as a framework for those audience members listening to *Lessness* for the first time, and was designed to prepare the listener for a difficult broadcast. What one might regard as a sophisticated group of listeners—the reviewers in the newspapers—also seem to have been influenced by this material to varying degrees. The archive contains a single A4 page of cuttings from newspaper articles from *The Guardian*, *The Times*, *The Sunday Times* and *The Telegraph* that include both reviews and previews.[28]

When *The Telegraph* came to review the production, it was clear that it was not entirely to the reviewer's taste. Sylvia Clayton wrote that as "read by a distinguished group of actors ... the sound was titally [*sic*] and chillingly depressing," but then worries as

> "Lessness" began to sound much of a muchness. Since it was concerned with eternity, was there any reason why it should ever end? But after half an hour a correct B.B.C. voice, possibly a recorded angel, cut off the flow of potent melancholy.[29]

The tone might be somewhat sneering, but Clayton rightly identifies one of the implications of the piece: an almost infinite set of permutations could logically be constructed on the basis of the limited variation of the 60 sentences as repeated in the text. Certainly, Clayton suggests that listening to *Lessness* was not exactly pleasurable. Indeed, the description in the headline of "Beckett work's depressing word cadence" at once recognizes the hypnotic quality of the production and conveys an undoubtedly pessimistic reading of its overall meaning.

Indeed, pessimism and nihilism run throughout the cache of newspaper reviews. David Wade in *The Times* argues that Beckett "appeals to the pessimist in us which is satisfied to find 'reality' every whit as ghastly as it had dared hope," and seems to suggest that an audience would have been conditioned to expect this "remembering Beckett's reputation."[30] In *The Sunday Times*, Jeremy Rundall identifies Beckett as a "poet of nihilism," before adding that this itself is a "contradictory notion" that Beckett manages to maintain with "bitter force."[31] In the most evocative description of the broadcast, Rundall speaks of it as "a kind of requiem madrigal, funeral oration to an empty coffin."[32] In a *Guardian* piece on the same day as the initial broadcast, Gillian Reynolds also ably conveys the impression made upon the audience, without, however, really suggesting what the piece might mean: "It is as if the mind of the listener is being painted in individual strokes, with each phrase, each image, falling separately on the ear yet being received as part of an accumulating whole by the mind."[33] Indeed, save for general impressions of the effects, there is little attempt at interpreting the piece across the newspapers. Reynolds perhaps comes closest to this as she suggests that the "blue celeste of poetry" must surely have been ironic in the context and, further, that there is "horror and desolation but the listener hears also of a particular kind of blank calm."[34]

Many of the newspaper articles bear the traces of the press release that Esslin penned prior to broadcast; an indication of how far such a release can condition a response. For example, *The Times, Telegraph* and *The Guardian* all dutifully note that *Lessness* is not a play (despite the headline for *The Guardian* speaking of "Beckett's play") in accordance with Esslin's press release and article in the *Radio Times*, sections of which reappeared in the broadcast introduction. The *Radio Times* article is directly quoted in Rundall's piece, which also reflects the press material's focus on the human dimensions of *Lessness*: "[H]e [Beckett] has become progressively less articulate, more tormented by the human condition, obsessed—as the Radio Times neatly put it—with the 'landscape of desolation.'"[35]

It is clear from the articles that the critical framing of *Lessness* through press releases and trails had an important influence on the immediate reaction in the newspapers. It might perhaps strike one as odd, then, that the more overt attempt at providing a critical gloss for the adaptation—Martin Esslin's introduction, aired immediately before *Lessness* itself—is twice criticized in the reviews. Gillian Reynolds in *The Guardian* worries that Esslin's introduction might discourage the listener due to its "rather possessively didactic tone" but reassures her readers that the "content is scholarly and sympathetic."[36] If anything, Sylvia Clayton is even more displeased with Esslin's introduction, describing it as a "lengthy and aggressive" speech, which "nearly suffocated [her] interest from the start."[37] The criticisms seem to be leveled more at Esslin's delivery than at the content itself, for, as we shall see, his introduction performed an important role in the reception of the work, while also revealing the possible critical assumptions underpinning the adaptation.

On 1 February, Esslin wrote to Beckett in part to ask for permission to introduce *Lessness*, saying, "I hope you won't have any objection to me mentioning the structural principle of the piece, i.e. that there are six groups of ten sentences and that each sentence occurs twice, etc."[38] Esslin seems concerned to make clear that he will be making no interpretative comments on the piece, yet he still apparently fears that Beckett would object to even so much. However, Esslin's introduction does not confine itself to the machinery of the text and the distribution of the images among the six voices. Indeed, some important interpretative remarks are made.

Firstly, Esslin places *Lessness* within the context of Beckett's most recent prose and drama works. "Thematically," he argues, "*Lessness* belongs to a group of short texts which have appeared in the last few years and which seem to form part of a larger whole, a work yet in progress."[39] "Imagination Dead Imagine", "The Lost Ones"—described as a "fragment"—and "Ping" are said to be the other works within this work in progress. With hindsight, one can clearly say that Esslin was wrong in this assumption as no "larger work" was forthcoming, but his claim does raise the issue of the status of *Lessness*. Perhaps Esslin was concerned that so slight a piece—it is, after all, only 120 sentences long—might seem insubstantial and so need bolstering by framing it as an insight into the next major Beckett work. One should bear in mind, of course, that *How It Is* was the last novel-length piece of prose and that, in its English translation, was almost a decade prior to *Lessness* being broadcast. Yet Esslin is correct when he relates *Lessness* to these texts in terms of the new "objective" style that Beckett had adopted and on equally sure ground when relating *Lessness* to "Ping," writing that "*Lessness* seems to show the same little body at a later stage."[40] In this, Esslin is supported by Beckett's comments on the dust jacket of the Calder edition of *Lessness*, as reported by John Pilling: "*Lessness* has to do with the collapse of some such refuge as that last attempted in *Ping* and with the ensuing situation of the refugee."[41] This would certainly seem to suggest a continuation of theme and, for want of a better word, person between the two texts. However, Esslin chooses to emphasize that the texts are related thematically, rather than only stylistically, and the theme he adduces is that "[a]ll these texts describe, as it were, landscapes of the soul,"[42] which is to suggest a distinctly humanistic, almost essentialist, reading of those texts.

The introduction also compares *Lessness* to *Play* in terms of the use of repetition and time. It is pointed out that the stage and later radio production of *Play* incorporated variations in the order of the repeated sentences, suggesting that in

> eternity the same things occur in endless permutation, ever the same and yet ever changing: after all, in infinite time every combination, every change must recur an infinite number of times and a mind, capable of being aware of these all at once, would therefore see this infinite number of changes as a totally static, unchanging rigidity.[43]

This paradox, Esslin tells his audience, "is also the image which *Lessness* is designed to convey."[44]

Esslin goes on to lay out the structural use of the six voices which appear not "as different characters or persons, but as indicators of different groups of images."[45] It is clear that Esslin believes that radio is uniquely placed to bring out the interplay of these voices and hence the structural principle on which *Lessness* is built:

> These groups of statements are intricately woven: in a rhythmical structure; and the different voices serve to bring out the pattern; each voice is a strand of colour intertwining to form this web of sounds and images. It is thus only by *hearing Lessness* that we can become fully aware of its structure and indeed of its full meaning which is expressed by its formal pattern.[46]

Esslin's confidence in the radio adaptation of *Lessness* seems to go beyond that of creating a version of the prose text that would be suitable for a listening audience. Indeed, he claims that radio is the proper home for the text, as if the prose had been waiting for radio to reveal its true nature. Throughout the introduction, the trope of expressing the text's latent or "full" meaning through the business of radio adaptation and broadcast is emphasized, making one wonder if "adaptation" would be the term Esslin would have preferred. For the producer of the radio *Lessness*, the process of adaptation was rather more a process of "realization."

***

The history of the production and promotion of *Lessness* raises a number of issues about Beckett's working relationship with the BBC at this stage, the business of radio adaptation and the nature of the text itself.

As was clear from the outset, Beckett was deeply involved in the radio production of *Lessness* to such a degree that the nature of the adaptation was Beckett's own. It was his decision, for good or ill, to divide the text into six voices and it was his voice that the actors were trying to match in terms of pace and tone. Rather than Esslin's claim that Beckett taking the blame for the unsatisfactory result of the broadcast was an example of his habitual "kindness and courtesy" one might argue that Beckett recognized the fault as his own quite correctly. One notices that at no point did Esslin question the proposed scheme for the adaptation; his primary concern was always to match his radio production to the vision that Beckett had delineated in very specific terms. One could speculate as to why, then, Beckett felt so dissatisfied with the results. It could be that Beckett's vision was itself at fault, or Esslin's execution failed to match that vision. Alternatively, it may be that Beckett did not fully appreciate the inevitable changes that would ensue in a radio adaptation, no matter how faithful. As noted above, the tension implicit within the adaptation for six voices coalescing about a single consciousness was there from the start and never properly resolved.

This tension might be attributed to the media differences between prose and radio. When reading *Lessness*, the groups of images coalesce in the single consciousness of the reader. Logically, this could also occur in the consciousness of the radio listener if a single voice—perhaps with subtle differences in pitch or pace—had been employed. One must weigh against this, however, the need for some diversity in a purely aural piece, which by its very nature is highly repetitive. In such a case, the six voices could be seen as a concession to the medium that compromises the overall effect of the piece.

Although the change from prose to radio undoubtedly effected the nature and possible meaning of *Lessness*, it should be noted that Beckett's proposed scheme for the adaptation is in many ways similar to his intervention in the critical responses to the text. When reviewing the critical discourse surrounding *Lessness*—including Ruby Cohn, and Rosemary Pountney—Dirk van Hulle and Lars Bernearts argued that, whether or not the critics used the term, the predominant approach was in effect that of Genetic Criticism. With the notable exception of John Pilling in *Frescoes of the Skull*, a knowledge of how the text of *Lessness* was created—with the relatively random selection of six groups or families of image—has largely informed the critical debate and the focus on the six image groups was sanctioned by Beckett himself: Cohn (on whom J.E. Dearlove largely bases her account) claimed to have been told of the groups by Beckett,[47] and for the single volume edition of *Lessness* Beckett outlined the six groups on the dust jacket:

> Ruin, exposure, wilderness, mindlessness, past and future denied and affirmed, are the categories, formally distinguishable, through which the writing winds, first in one disorder, then in another.[48]

While one may be accustomed to uncovering structural principles through genetic analysis of drafts and differing versions of a Beckett text, the case here is rather different as Beckett effectively promoted a form of genetic awareness. Van Hulle and Bernearts correctly note in the case of Cohn that "[w]ithout her knowledge of the genesis, it would have been hard to discern the patterns of numbers in the finalized text."[49] In other words, the identification of the permutations of the sentence groups and, quite possibly, that there are six groups at all may only have been possible through Beckett's intervention.

This guiding of critical reactions through revealing the creative history of the piece might find its apotheosis in J.E. Dearlove's claim that in order to come to terms with *Lessness* it has to be "unmade" according to the six image groups: "In order to read the work at all the reader must reverse Beckett's creative process and break the piece back down into groups of sentences and into permuted phrases within those groups."[50] By sending Esslin the key rather than merely referring him to the published version, Beckett effectively had already "unmade" the text which was then reconstituted through the medium of radio, as if the radio production mimicked the creative process through which the original text was made, albeit with the random selection of sentences and paragraphs now replaced by the finalized text as published. In such a way, the radio adaptation falls between two stools: on the one hand following the initial creative process, while on the other adhering to a fixed conception of the text itself. Rather than a possible opening of *Lessness* to an almost infinite series of permutations, the finalized text and the identification of the six image groups curtails such possibility. By way of contrast, J.M Coetzee, without any knowledge of the six image groups, suggested that one could infer that "there are millions of other possible re-orderings…and nothing to indicate that any one is more or less valid as fiction than the ordering published."[51] Elizabeth Drew and Mads Haar, while respecting the six image groups, have taken this principle further by creating a computer program that generates new versions of the text, noting that the "published version of *Lessness* is one of the 1.9×10^{176} possible arrangements."[52] Rosemary Pountney also "restructured" *Lessness* into an alternative arrangement, arguing that each "reordered text develops its own strengths from a new juxtaposition of sentences …."[53]

This opening up to permutation in the creative process of the text makes the role of a central consciousness—dispersed among the six voices in Esslin's production—even more crucial, as Coetzee suggests: "The residue of the fiction is then *not* the final disposition of the fragments but the motions of the consciousness that disposes them according to the rules …."[54] John Pilling—who felt no compunction to be "hidebound by the known circumstances of composition"—argues that "to get the most out of *Lessness* … we have to revert to a 'naïve realist' linear approach."[55] Such an approach posits a consciousness—that of the reader—in which the text can take shape. It is precisely this consciousness that the radio adaptation as based on Beckett's scheme jeopardized, leaving Beckett dissatisfied—possibly as much with his own scheme for adaptation as with the radio production itself.

Notes

1. SS.
2. Martin Esslin, "Samuel Beckett and the Art of Radio," in *On Beckett: Essays and Criticism*, ed. S.E. Gontarski (New York: Grove Press, 1986), 374.
3. Ulrika Maude, "Working on Radio," in *Samuel Beckett in Context*, ed. Anthony Uhlmann (Cambridge: Cambridge University Press, 2013), 189–90.

4. *SW 68–72.*
5. Ibid.
6. *SW 63–67.*
7. James Knowlson, *Damned to Fame: The Life of Samuel Beckett* (London: Bloomsbury, 1996), 526.
8. Deirdre Bair, *Samuel Beckett: A Biography* (London: Vintage, 1990), 673.
9. *SW,* 68–72.
10. Ibid.
11. SS.
12. Rosemary Pountney, *Theatre of Shadows: Samuel Beckett's Drama, 1965-76: From All That Fall to Footfalls* (Gerrards Cross: Colin Smythe, 1988), 15–26.
13. SS.
14. Martin Esslin, "Martin Esslin on Beckett the Man" in *Beckett Remembering / Remembering Beckett*, ed. James Knowlson and Elizabeth Knowlson (London: Bloomsbury, 2006), 150.
15. SS.
16. *SW 68–72.*
17. Martin Esslin, "Samuel Beckett and the Art of Radio," in *On Beckett: Essays and Criticism*, ed S.E. Gontarski (New York: Grove Press, 1986), 374.
18. Ibid., 374.
19. Samuel Beckett, *That Time* in *The Complete Dramatic Works of Samuel Beckett* (London: Faber and Faber, 1990), 387.
20. CL.
21. Ibid.
22. Ibid.
23. Ibid.
24. Ibid.
25. Ibid.
26. Ibid. Italics are my emphasis.
27. Ibid.
28. Ibid.
29. Ibid.
30. Ibid.
31. Ibid.
32. Ibid.
33. Ibid.
34. Ibid.
35. Ibid.
36. Ibid.
37. Ibid.
38. Ibid.

39. SS.
40. Ibid.
41. Quoted in James Knowlson and John Pilling, *Frescoes of the Skull: The Later Prose and Drama of Samuel Beckett* (London: John Calder, 1979), 172.
42. SS.
43. Ibid.
44. Ibid.
45. Ibid.
46. Ibid.
47. Ruby Cohn, *Back to Beckett* (Princeton: Princeton University Press, 1973), 265.
48. Quoted in Knowlson and Pilling, *Frescoes*, 173.
49. Lars Bernarts and Dirk Van Hulle, "Narrative across Versions: Narratology Meets Genetic Criticism," *Poetics Today* 34:3 (2013), 309.
50. J.E. Dearlove, *Accommodating the Chaos: Samuel Beckett's Nonrelational Art* (Durham N.C.: Duke University Press, 1982), 118.
51. J.M. Coetzee, "Samuel Beckett's *Lessness*: An Exercise in Decomposition," *Computers and the Humanities* 7:4 (1973), 198.
52. Elizabeth Drew and Mads Haar, "*Lessness:* Randomness, Consciousness and Meaning." Accessed July 2014. http://www.cs.tcd.ie/publications/tech-reports/reports.03/TCD-CS-2003-07.pdf 2.
53. Pountney, *Theatre of Shadows*, 155.
54. Coetzee, "Beckett's *Lessness*," 198.
55. Knowlson and Pilling, *Frescoes of the Skull*, 176.

"My comforts! Be friends!": Words, Music and Beckett's Poetry on the Third

Melissa Chia

Samuel Beckett's radio play *Words and Music* (1962) was first broadcast on the BBC's Third Programme on 13 November and received a polarized reception.[1] Its earliest reviews reflect this: two days after its second relay on 7 December, in a review program titled "The Critics" which aired on the Home Service—in a bid to reach a wider, more "general"[2] audience—the critic Karl Miller said of the radio play: "We mustn't regard it as a totally satisfactory piece of art so to speak."[3] The broadcast, which featured a number of critics in discussion over the piece, was led by Barbara Bray,[4] who gave a synopsis of the radio play and generally praised it, albeit indicating minor exceptions which she attributed to its "interpretation."[5] This was in stark contrast to Miller, who openly voiced his dissent and deemed *Words and Music* "unimpressive"[6] and unrewarding. However, he was willing to concede one of its strengths. In a transcript of the broadcast, located at the BBC Written Archives Centre (WAC) at Caversham, Miller's judgment is noteworthy:

M. Chia (✉)
Faculty of English, University of Cambridge, Cambridge, UK

© The Author(s) 2017
D. Addyman et al. (eds.), *Samuel Beckett and BBC Radio*,
New Interpretations of Beckett in the 21st Century,
DOI 10.1057/978-1-137-54265-6_11

> I would merely say that the poetry itself when you come down to it is undeniably strong, there are two poems, embedded in the text, and those two poems are heralding it as it were and the heralding is [*sic*] made the stuff of the half-hour's radio programme. When you come to the verse itself, you're getting something.[7]

Retrospectively, Miller's comments could be seen as a prophetic statement heralding an era that would see a marked change in the listening expectations of the BBC's audiences, helped and shaped by executive decisions within the Corporation. Beckett's poetry, not least the two poems tucked away in *Words and Music*, was one of the seeds of this phenomenon. Just as *All That Fall* was a springboard for the BBC's Radiophonic Workshop,[8] this play was the catalyst for a program featuring a commingling of poetry and music, which would begin in 1968 on the Third: it too would be called "Words and Music."

It took three years for the seed to germinate. Martin Esslin, then the Head of BBC Radio Drama, was keen to keep radio in step with print and to promote Beckett as poet and critic. By late 1965, the Third had broadcast a range of Beckett's works, from radio drama to stage plays as well as some of his early prose, but nothing of his poems or his critical essays. In addition, several editions of Beckett's poetry had appeared in print between 1961 and 1964,[9] and in 1965 Esslin was launching his edited volume of critical essays on Beckett, which included the author's *Three Dialogues with Georges Duthuit*.[10] Internal BBC correspondence dated 6 October 1965 indicates a directive from "H.D. (S)"—Head of Drama (Sound)—referring to Esslin, requesting copyright clearance of *Three Dialogues* and noting the launch of Esslin's volume, which was due that same month.[11] By that time, obstacles had been removed to make way for a broadcast of the poems: copyright for ten of Beckett's poems had been cleared with the author's publishing firm several days earlier.[12] However, while Beckett gave the green light for broadcasts of his poetry, he was not keen to allow *Three Dialogues* on the air, and held back the rights to the piece. Representatives at Curtis Brown replied apologetically on Beckett's behalf, refusing permission to broadcast the piece.[13] Esslin was eager to explain his position and immediately wrote to Beckett in an attempt to persuade him otherwise, and outlining the impetus for promoting the roles of Beckett as poet and as critic in tandem:

[W]e also want to broadcast an anthology of your poems with a critical commentary by John Fletcher (similar to the essay published in the American volume I edited). This led Third Programme to the idea that we might associate with these broadcasts of some other works of yours which have not yet been done on the air.[14]

The *Duthuit Dialogues*, Esslin argued, seemed "to be excellent radio,"[15] but Beckett held fast in his rejection of the idea.[16] This did not deter Esslin from recording a commentary, also by Fletcher, titled "Beckett as Critic," which was broadcast on 9 March 1966, a day after a selection of Beckett's poems was read for the first time on air. The *Radio Times* listing for the program on these poems concurrently advertizes the transmission of Fletcher's commentary of the author as critic.[17] In addition, *The Listener*—a weekly magazine by the BBC, launched as a counterpart to the listings in the *Radio Times* for more "intellectual" readers—had featured on 25 November 1965 a two-page spread titled "Samuel Beckett as Critic," written by John Fletcher.[18] But while a quarter of Fletcher's article was dedicated to a discussion on *Three Dialogues*, the impact of the idea of Beckett as a literary critic—Beckett having kept the critical piece off the air—was perhaps considerably smaller than Esslin had desired among listeners.

What then of Beckett as poet? Thanks to Fletcher and Esslin, one of the earliest commentaries on Beckett's poetry was made public in 1965 via broadcast and print. As Esslin stated in his letter to the author, the idea of transmitting the poems on air can be traced to Fletcher's critical essay, "The Private Pain and the Whey of Words: A Survey of Beckett's Verse," which in turn had its genesis as a lecture delivered at Durham University in November 1964.[19] Esslin published it that same year along with the *Three Dialogues*. In contrast to his disapproval of broadcasting the critical piece, Beckett appeared to have taken a positive, even active role, in the dissemination of his poetry over the airwaves. Recording of the poems for the 8 March broadcast occurred over January and February 1966.[20] They were read by Jack MacGowran and Denys Hawthorne, the latter being familiar to listeners of the Third, having performed in Beckett's radio play *Cascando*, which shares its title with one of Beckett's poems, the year before. According to a BBC Production Details Report, Beckett was present at the recording of MacGowran's reading and even "in some cases amended the text, which therefore differs slightly from the published version."[21] These alterations[22] attest to Beckett's perspective on the performative aspect of his poems which echoes the changes he made to his theatrical texts when he occupied the director's seat. The recording of the broadcasts took place at the BBC's Broadcasting House, where, on the first of these occasions, Fletcher adjourned for lunch with Beckett, MacGowran and Esslin "in hallowed Third Programme style"[23] to a pub nearby. The broadcast, "Poems by Samuel Beckett," aired on the Third at 9.55 pm for 35 minutes along with an introduction by Fletcher, who was to uncover the "personal" references to Beckett's life in the "difficult"[24] poems. Listeners of the Third were encouraged to approach Beckett not as a newly minted poet, but to see him as an established wordsmith, a literary architect with whom they were already familiar, presented in a new light. The *Radio Times* listing for the program acknowledged that Beckett was "relatively little known as a poet, if the sense of the word poet is taken to mean a writer of poetry"[25] but went on to position his poetry on a continuum with works previously broadcast:

> In fact, of course, in a wider sense all Beckett's writing is that of a poet. His plays, novels and stories are highly precise structures of sound and sense where not a single word can be removed without doing damage to the total structure.[26]

Indeed, poetry is to be found within his radiogenic work, as was observed with the radio play *Words and Music*. The poetry program was introduced by Fletcher, whose commentary was aimed at "uncovering" the references in these poems to Beckett's "life in Dublin, London, and Paris"[27]—a suggestion that perhaps to know the man was to know the poet. The selection of Beckett's pre- and post-war poems included "Whoroscope," "Eneug I," Serena II," "Malacoda," "Alba," "Cascando," "Saint-Lô," and the untitled poems beginning with "my way is in the sand flowing," "what would I do without this world, faceless, incurious," and "I would love my love to die."[28] Repeat broadcasts took place on 14 and 24 November later that year.[29] The latter broadcast included an additional poem, "Gnome," titled erroneously by its first line in later BBC production reports as "Span [*sic*] the years of learning."[30] As John Pilling has pointed out, this was probably an administrative mistake, since MacGowran clearly pronounces, "Spend."[31] The reports, written in 1976 when extracts of the original broadcasts were repeated as part of BBC festivities to commemorate Beckett's seventieth birthday (aired on 14 April and 5 June 1976),[32] also incorrectly state that the poem was unpublished, although it had appeared in an issue of the *Dublin Magazine* in 1934.[33] However, this inaccuracy did not occur in the programming of the 1966 broadcasts, when the *Radio Times* for 24 November appropriately noted, "a short poem which has not been republished since it appeared in a magazine more than thirty years ago."[34]

Esslin's proposal of a radio program of Beckett's poems appears to have led to a unique development: the release of a long-play (LP) record, *MacGowran Speaking Beckett* (1966), on which MacGowran can be heard performing a variety of Beckett's works across genres, including prose, plays for the radio and stage, and poetry. What was unique about this record was the way Beckett and MacGowran, with the help of John and Edward Beckett, wove together words from Beckett's works with the music of Schubert's *Quartet in D minor*,[35] a move that was as uncommon as it would have been unwelcome by many listeners of the Third. Recording for the vinyl took place in the same month as Esslin's production, in January 1966, at a studio in London, where it was, as the back cover of the re-released compact disc (CD) album boasts, "recorded under the personal supervision of Samuel Beckett."[36] Malcolm Eade of Pye Studios—who later recorded the vinyl *Round the Horne* (1969) by Kenneth Horne as a BBC radio series—was responsible for recording the LP.[37] It seems MacGowran was particularly active in various projects of different media that involved Beckett during that period. Besides the poetry reading for the BBC radio and the vinyl album, both actor and author were busy with the BBC television program *Monitor* for a televised version of *Beginning to End* which was underway in January. The WAC archives indicate that MacGowran met with Beckett on the 31st in Paris, along with the director of *Beginning to End*, Patrick Garland, and the editor of *Monitor*, Jonathan Miller, to discuss the production.[38] These multiple projects did not appear to dim Beckett's enthusiasm for the work on the gramophone record. He even ventured to the other side of the studio's glass window to play the gong, alongside cousin John on the harmonium and nephew Edward on his flute, for the recording.

The details of Beckett's gong recital might sound like a frivolous aside, but his mallet-wielding, together with the unique interlacing of words and music on the LP, may have far greater resonances that touch on sound montage and its place in both Beckett's work and BBC radio production. The stroke of the gong, which sounds at the beginning of each audio track and precedes each passage read by MacGowran on the more contemporary recording medium, the CD, would have had more impact as an acoustic frame in the playback of the LP. Since an LP record does not consist of separate audio "files" like a CD but forms one continuous track on the vinyl, it appeared necessary to introduce a type of aural barrier to mark the transition from one reading to the next. In *MacGowran Speaking Beckett*, for example, the gong sounds between the passages of *Embers* and *Molloy*, and even between extracts that share the same source, as in the interval between two passages from *Endgame*. In the LP's continuous, non-segregated unfolding of sound, the gong-toll frames the spoken text, acting as both divider and link between the different works and genres that otherwise formed a steady stream of words intertwined with music. Early radio theorist Rudolf Arnheim mentions the use of the gong for radio broadcasting in general and calls it a type of "acoustic curtain."[39] In his seminal work, *Radio* (1936), he sets out the perimeters of writing a radio play and suggests the clearest manner to change scenes, or to signal the end of the play, is to introduce the sound of a gong. An interval of silence, Arnheim indicates, might do as well but does not differentiate a change in space and/or time as well "as lowering a curtain on an open stage,"[40] whereas a distinguishable sound does.

MacGowran Speaking Beckett does something very unique with words and music, combining the two to form a type of sound montage. Beckett was no stranger to theories of montage, especially in the cinematic arts. His early interest, apparent in the thirties, occurred at a time when the debate on film montage and the introduction of sound to cinema were ongoing, a spillover from the late twenties. This passion for montage appears to have stayed with him beyond the decade and informed his later work.[41] James Knowlson points out Beckett's keen interest in the subject.[42] As is well known, before the war, Beckett's interest in film montage led him to write to the Soviet Russian filmmaker Sergei Eisenstein to apply to his film school. In May 1934, Beckett wrote to Nuala Costello about feeling "the trucs of montage and photography, very keenly, very keenly indeed"[43] after viewing the documentary film *Man of Aran* (1934); his phrase, echoing the French idiom "les trucs du métier" (the tricks of the trade), suggests both familiarity with and eagerness to employ the method.[44] Two years later, he spoke with some derision to Thomas McGreevy of his meeting with a "cinematography expert," Fitzgerald, who seemed to "know a lot about the actual tricks of phot[o]graphy" but has "no interest in montage."[45] In the same letter, Beckett told McGreevy he had "borrowed a lot of works on cinema from young Montgomery, who is certainly a curious little card: Pudovkin, Arnheim & back numbers of Close Up with stuff by Eisenstein,"[46] referring to Arnheim's *Film*.[47] Beckett was certainly familiar with Arnheim's monograph. Gaby Hartel points out that Beckett wrote to McGreevy a week later on 6 February, quoting Arnheim's treatise nearly verbatim on the future of the two-dimensional silent film as art alongside the development of sound and color film in *Film*.⁴⁸ In addition, as the editors of *The Letters of Samuel Beckett* have noted, Beckett's correspondence to Arland Ussher closely follows a description by Arnheim in *Film* on the technique of simultaneous montage.⁴⁹ Beckett's knowledge of *Film* would have given him some insight into sound. While it is uncertain whether Beckett later read Arnheim's monograph, *Radio*, published three years after *Film*, the earlier publication contains a chapter titled "Radio Plays." In this chapter Arnheim illustrates the concept of sound montage using the example of Dziga Vertov's film, *Enthusiasm*.⁵⁰ Here, as in *Radio*, Arnheim compares aural montage to its visual counterpart, inevitably using the language of cameras and film cutting techniques to discuss his theories on acoustics. Montage in sound—like film montage, Arnheim argues—is achieved by a "cutting" of sections of sound in the production room, where disparate elements of sound are edited and spliced, juxtaposed to form a composition on a shared theme.⁵¹

Viewed through this lens, Beckett's gong recital appears to attempt a more complex task in order to place disparate text and music side by side, positioning them to create a montage of sound. Rather than introduce a change in space or suggest a lapse of time, as a scene change is meant to achieve, the repetition of the musical stroke throughout the reading connects the ten extracts to craft a single piece orchestrated for voice and instruments. The gong joins the flute, the harmonium and the sole, consistent voice, MacGowran's, to form an ensemble performing a tapestry of words and music. As such, the title of the work, *MacGowran Speaking Beckett*, could be said to be misleading in its emphasis on the spoken element. The LP ends with the poem, "Echo's Bones," and a few bars from Schubert's *Quartet No. 14 in D minor* (1824), also known as *Death and the Maiden*, which features in Beckett's first radio play, *All That Fall* (1957). This musical fragment threads through the recording and can be heard at its beginning, middle and end.

The same fragment is played by a string quartet in the BBC's first broadcast of *All That Fall* in 1957 produced by Donald McWhinnie.⁵² It derives from the opening bars of the second movement of Schubert's chamber music, marked as "Andante con moto," (moderately slow or at a walking pace). The music overlaps with the sound of Maddy Rooney's footsteps and soon fades and "dies,"⁵³ a part of the backdrop to her journey. It acts as a signpost that signals Maddy's approach and retreat from the "poor woman" hidden "in that ruinous old house."⁵⁴ In contrast, the fragment on the vinyl stands apart from the voice and appears as a distinct entity. At no point does it act as mere "background" music to the words.

In fact, the music itself derives from poetry. The extract from the Quartet's (1824) second movement, which dwells on the words of Death, coincide with the opening of a lied composed by Schubert several years earlier, titled *Der Tod und das Mädchen* (1817), D. 531 (*Death and the Maiden*).[55] The Romantic German lied in the nineteenth century was a musical setting that consisted of ideas suggested by words, usually poetry, and composed for piano and voice.[56] This was no exception; the lied is based on a poem by Matthias Claudius, similarly titled. There is no doubt Beckett knew Claudius' poem—Knowlson points out the author's near obsession with it later in his life, which speaks of death "as a comforter, welcoming the maiden into its arms."[57] In *MacGowran Speaking Beckett*, the music of *Death and the Maiden* stands alongside companion pieces that echo its textual genesis. The fragment qualifies as part of a unified soundscape; combined with words from Beckett's work, they form a meditation on moments of the breath (and breadth) before death, a hastening and hesitating toward the end. A snatch of Clov's monologue in *Endgame* (1957), voiced in the final sections of the recording, best exemplifies this:

> Good, it'll never end, I'll never go. (*Pause*.) Then one day, suddenly, it ends, it changes, I don't understand, it dies, or it's me, I don't understand that either. I ask the words that remain – sleeping, waking, morning, evening. They have nothing to say.[58]

BLACK, BECKETT AND LISTENERS OF THE THIRD

Shortly after the repeat broadcasts of Beckett's poems on the Third in November 1966, a peculiar radio program incorporating Beckett's poetry was transmitted on the Music Programme. Titled "Music Making," the poems were aired on 9 December 1966 at 11.38 am, with the *Radio Times* listing promising "a sequence including music by Handel and Mozart, and three poems by Samuel Beckett, who is sixty this year."[59] The poems—listed rather carelessly in files at the Third as "Cascando," "my way is in the sand [flowing]," and "what should [*sic*] I do? [*sic*]"[60]— formed only a fraction of the entire "Music Making" broadcast. More than half of the program consisted "purely" of music by Mozart, Haydn and Handel. The portion fusing poetry with music, which subsequently met with opposition within the Corporation, was obviously an early experiment by the Music service, but one that was to become a prototype of a program with a much longer legacy. This was the only appearance of

Beckett's poems on the Music Programme, but the one-off broadcast[61] was to become the predecessor of a program that ran for more than four decades on the Third, titled "Words and Music."

Leo Black, who was responsible for devising this particular "Music Making" broadcast, found that further plans to develop this combination of poetry and music featuring Beckett's poems met with strong opposition from the BBC management. The reason, he was told by P. H. Newby, Controller for the Third Programme, was "that people tended to listen either for speech or for music and would find an alternation of the arts within a single programme puzzling."[62] Embedded in this observation is an ambiguity that raises a number of questions: was Newby referring to his audience's radio-listening habits, their tuning in to regular programming in expectation of encountering either words or music, as they preferred, or to some physiological or psychological limitation likely to make any listener unable to pick out words from music or vice versa were both to be played at the same time? Either option indicates the listener's being at the mercy of the machine, left to a dismal selection between "the two knobs,"[63] limited to the "I switch off,"[64] and volume control. The Music Programme was a service on the same radio frequency as the Third, and while both programs fell under the umbrella of Network Three, also called the Third Network, the two were not perceived in the same way as broadcast programs on the same channel are viewed today. Then, each program occupied a particular time slot within a consistent weekly schedule. For example, in 1966, the Third ran on weekdays from 7.30 pm to the "close down"[65] of transmission at 11.20 pm and had a different timetable over the weekends. On the other hand, the Music Programme took up a larger proportion of airtime in the day, beginning at 7 am and broadcasting until the late afternoon, when a series of educational programs broadly categorized as the Study Session formed an interlude between the Music Programme and the Third in the evening. When the Music Programme had been launched on 30 August 1964, it was with the intention "to consider the special problems of broadcasting to a daytime audience,"[66] including listeners' inability "to give the concentrated attention that they would naturally bring to evening programmes,"[67] such as broadcasts later in the day on the Third. A cursory glance at the layout of the weekday schedules in the *Radio Times* at that that, which clearly differentiates between the broadcasts of each service with a definitive line demarcating a cut-off mark at 7.30 pm, supports the perception of segregation.

Black's plans for the new series, however, focused on the "mingling"[68] of poetry and music, and he thought Beckett's poems were suitable material for it. When this met with opposition and "communication broke down," with the series "finally ruled ineligible"[69] in 1967, Black's secretary wrote to Calder, who at that time held the rights to Beckett's poetry, to say that plans for the broadcast of a program "including poems by Samuel Beckett"[70] on 2 October 1967 had fallen through. According to Black, the program would not take off as "its unsuitability was diagnosed by the Controller of the Home Service and Music Programme."[71] Black took pains to point out this did not refer to William Glock, who was the Controller of Music.

This letter, dated just over a week before the launch of BBC Radio 3 on 30 September, gives an insight into the programming decisions that led to the cancelation of this crucial, ground-breaking endeavor by Black. The switch from Network Three to Radio 3 was intended to bring the Third and Music services under one roof. Although the replacement was perceived as a mere change in name in the eyes of the public,[72] an internal BBC report claimed that listeners preferred a more "specialized" radio channel which transmitted "a continuous stream of one particular type of programme, meeting one particular interest"[73] and proposed a more focused network. Black's program—a combination of music and poetry –would have seemed at odds with this proposal. The report, titled "Broadcasting in the Seventies," was only made public in 1969 and the Third was fully absorbed into Radio 3 shortly after in 1970. However, such threats were already close at hand as early as 1966 within the Corporation and plans for the future of broadcasting had begun, albeit in secrecy.[74] It seemed that despite the implementation of the UK's Marine Broadcasting Offences Act in 1967,[75] which considered offshore and "pirate" radio transmissions to the territory illegal, listeners were still tuning in to these competing radio stations which played rock or popular music throughout the day.[76] In a bid to stay competitive, the BBC set up a Policy Study Group in 1968, a four-man team sworn to secrecy and responsible for writing "Broadcasting in the Seventies."[77] The chair of this group was Gerard Mansell, the same Controller Black had referred to in his letter to Calder. Black did not name him in the correspondence, although he hinted at one who "is what the BBC calls a Planner."[78] At the time, programmers like Black would have been in the dark about the ongoing internal study.[79] Despite the push from the upper echelons to "specialize" in the station's output, both departments, the Music and the Third, appeared to desire a continued segregation in their output. The case for distinguishing between the two services, even after both were subsumed under Radio 3, is hinted at in Black's letter to Calder:

There is a faint possibility that this and similar programmes <u>might</u> by [*sic*] broadcast in the <u>Third</u> Programme at a later date, but Mr. Black feels that in any case he should communicate the news to you, not to mention his embarrassment at having to do so.[80]

Moreover, the case for a separation of music and words was compounded by fears prominently voiced in the early sixties that music had already been devalued by its ready availability on the radio. Black points out that Benjamin Britten's Aspen Lecture in 1964 presented a case against the growing availability of music as unnerving and undesirable, a view which gained some foothold even within the Corporation.[81] On the other hand, the Third had already broadcast poetry mixed with music by the mid-sixties. Jack Kerouac had read his poems to piano jazz on a Third broadcast as early as 9 January 1960.[82] But these experiments with poetry and more contemporary tunes, such as popular music and jazz, were not concerned with the construction of montage and were more closely related to the performance of poetry on the air.[83] The focus of these programs was primarily on the spoken word.

Another reason for the opposition faced by Black was the listeners. Black admitted that Newby had been right in predicting the reaction of audiences when tuning in to a program mixing music and poetry.[84] Even after the series "Words and Music" eventually took flight on the Third in 1968, poet Philip Larkin, whose works were combined with Mussorgsky's song-cycle *Sunless* in the variegated program, wryly wrote to Black, "I can see that lovers of music 24 hours in the day might be upset if they found poetry coming at them instead."[85] The expectations of listeners go some way to explaining the criticism Beckett's *Words and Music* had received six years earlier; Clas Zilliacus notes that the BBC Audience Research Report conducted on the broadcast indicated a poor score of 43, the lowest recorded figure for a production of Beckett's work on the Third.[86] In contrast, *All That Fall* achieved an index of 58 after its premier broadcast, while the first transmission of *Embers* scored 50.[87] While unwise production choices and outcomes may have contributed to the poor response, as Zilliacus and Bray note,[88] the opinion of the listening majority indicated satisfactory acting and production, which meant their dissatisfaction lay elsewhere. Given the listening climate experienced by Black and the comments made in the review program of Beckett's *Words and Music*, it appeared that many listeners and critics alike were not enthusiastic about the combination of the two arts, with Miller in "The Critics" review show complaining that the result was "not art, but a process of art recorded in a documentary way."[89]

This would also explain the programming decision to single out one of the poems from Beckett's *Words and Music* and include it in the repeat broadcast of Beckett's poetry on 24 November 1966. The poem, which begins "Age is when to a man" recited by Words/Joe, was extracted from the radio play and featured alongside pieces of the same genre. Seán Lawlor and John Pilling's edition of Beckett's *Collected Poems* includes this poem in the post-war section of the collection and note, alongside examples of its appearance in print, its inclusion in that broadcast.[90] If the penchant among audiences of the Third was to listen out for either poetry or music, then a separation of the poetry in the "uncomfortable" drama of *Words and Music* from its musical counterpoint could have been thought more satisfactory to the general listener. It is ironic that the Third had earlier proclaimed, when Beckett's poetry first went on air, that his "plays, novels and stories are highly precise structures of sound and sense where not a single word can be removed without doing damage to the total structure."[91] Extracting the poem from its original sound architecture results in an abridgement, a process that undoes the montage of sound in the radio play in order to avoid the puzzling "alternation of the arts" Newby had opposed.

Nine months after Black's note to Calder explaining the canceled broadcast on the Music Programme, Black successfully negotiated the transmission of his six-part program, "Words and Music," on the Third. The frontman was Beckett. His "Alba" and "Dieppe," read once again by MacGowran, launched the first of the six installments. On 24 May 1968, Black,[92] the "deviser devising it all for company,"[93] introduced the half-hour program, which mingled the poems with songs by Frank Bridge, Liszt, and Debussy.[94] Beckett was also the only poet featured twice in the six episodes. The fourth installment aired on 28 July for 40 minutes and combined the poems "Cascando," "Malacoda," and "my way is in the sand," read by Denys Hawthorne with music by Mozart, Schoenberg and Schubert.[95] In a *Radio Times* article by Black that ran in the same issue as the scheduling of the first program, the devisor—as the *Radio Times* states—humbly shied away from the term "creator," but emphasized the possibility of building something creative, such as a montage:

> But these programmes use existing material: here the creators meant their work to stand on its own, so it shouldn't be messed about by the traders, the uncreative. And yet the divisions *can* be broken down, in a different way. Just as programmes of music can be 'built', to convey a pattern (meaningful to the

builder, and, he hopes, to others), so could programmes of words and music. For poetry and music both communicate the texture of exceptional lives, each in its own way; both have 'poetic' content, express a truth, re-create a mood.[96]

Here, Black refers to the musical definition of "programme" of which counterpart terms in literature and the other arts include "subject, theme, or idea."[97] A musical program refers to "a sequence of scenes or events intended to be conveyed by a piece of music, or serving as the inspiration or basis for a composition."[98] Before Black's series, other one-off BBC programs had been given the title "Words and Music," ranging from song recordings with piano and voice on the Home Service since 1940, to the playback of musical reviews on the same service from 1945 onwards, especially by Noël Coward, as well as broadcasts of gramophone records originating from the Second World War. Black's proposal was different, in that the union of words and music, wisely and artistically wrought, was to communicate an underlying theme much in the same way cinematic montage juxtaposes disparate images to evoke a subject.

A return to Beckett's *Words and Music*, auscultated with these ideas of musical programming and montage in mind, yields echoes of a certain, recurring theme. In Arnheim's theory of cinematic montage, the yoking of dissimilar, even contrasting, elements, usually achieved through the process of post-production film editing, evokes a particular subject that is not apparent when each element is viewed separately. Similarly, the radio play suggestively resonates with a particular foundational theme when its seemingly distinct parts are regarded as a unit. In Bray's synopsis of *Words and Music* in "The Critics" program (9 December 1962), she speaks of Croak as an animator or producer who "issues themes upon which Joe and Bob must improvise."[99] The first theme, Bray explains, is love, and the second, age. The two poems in the play—the lyrical culmination of Words, both as character and as linguistic constituent—are respectively concerned with the concepts. What is often forgotten is Music's part in prompting Words to articulate both poems, and the significance of Music's accompaniment while the poems are uttered. Even without a score for Music's lines, the published play-text clearly indicates that both servants elaborate on the proposed concepts. Music's role is significant since it is he who "invites" Words to articulate the poem on age and who delivers a "discreet suggestion" that Words may continue to the play's climax of the "wellhead" poem.[100] However, these perennial concepts of love and age should not be mistaken for the themes that cinematic montage and music programs aspire to weave. The combined efforts of Words and Music postulate each idea, but their contributions are not to be taken severally. While their offerings initially create a simple form of montage, like that of a series of shots from various camera perspectives depicting a single event, it is only by perceiving the images "not *next* to the other, but on *top* of the other,"[101] as film theorist Sergei Eisenstein explained, that the montage builds toward the theme. In *Words and Music*, this *leitmotiv* is the face.

This is the face that delays Croak's arrival at the beginning of the play, the face, for love of which, that inspires Croak's anguished interjections, and "the face in the ashes" which causes Croak to unravel and murmur repeatedly, "The face. (*Pause.*) The face. (*Pause.*) The face. (*Pause.*) The face."[102] Music follows this echo with a "*rap of baton and warmly sentimental*";[103] is Music the maestro, a master in his own right? Croak's words are taken as further instruction, to which Words responds. The poem on the "wellhead" arises from this, accompanied "very softly"[104] by Music. Verse and music, resplendent in their completion, are too much for Croak to endure, resulting in his abrupt departure. The "wellhead," referring at once to a source (of a stream or river) and a structure built at the top of a well,[105] ostensibly points to the overarching and/or originating subject of a visage. Zilliacus, in his milestone study on Beckett's broadcasting activities with the BBC, accurately indicates that Croak leaves because he is overwhelmed, in contrast to proposals by Alec Reid and John Fletcher, who suggest Croak's departure stems from disappointment in their underachievement.[106]

While Zilliacus does not employ the term "montage," he likewise points to a "variation on a single theme"[107] in the radio play. He designates the play as a "mock opera,"[108] citing the prominent employment of music in the aural performance while hesitating to identify it as a full opera, given Beckett's unequivocal aversion to operatic art expressed in his early critical work, *Proust*. It would be more appropriate to call *Words and Music* a sound montage that moves beyond a simple collage utilizing different genres and concepts to form a new type of radio drama. In an interview with Zilliacus on 5 September 1966, Michael Bakewell, the producer of the first *Words and Music* broadcast in 1962, said he believed "this play pioneered the role of music as an autonomous member of a cast."[109] This form brought music to a level on par with words and made Music "a dramatis persona, a character in its own right."[110] If words have priority in radio drama, as Zilliacus asserts, then words certainly had a greater footing on the Third in the sixties, while music was given pole position on the other, eponymous program. Beckett's radio play presented a different platform where both elements could meet with equity. As one reviewer described, it was a play that employed "music in much less conventional ways"[111] than was common in the sixties.

The devisors, Beckett and Black, have shaped the mingling of poetry and music on the radio, and their legacy has lasted beyond the dissolving of the Third. One of the first programs to face the axe, a year before the Third closed down, was the weekly arts discussion, "The Critics," on the Home Service, which ended its run of 22 years in 1969.[112] The program "Words and Music" continues to this day on the BBC Radio 3, with each broadcast founded on a different theme, presenting montages of sound through the yoking of poetry with classical music. Meanwhile, Beckett's radio play and poetry have inspired music. The Swedish composer Ingvar Lidholm wrote his *Poesis per orchestra* (1963) after listening to a broadcast of *Words and Music*, while Marcel Mihalovici's Fifth Symphony, Opus 94 (published in 1972) features a soprano solo based on Beckett's poem which begins, "*que ferais-je sans ce monde sans visage sans questions*" ("what would I do without this world faceless incurious").[113] Significantly, Beckett's poetic lines, the "only one theme"[114] in Beckett's life, formed the musical program of Morton Feldman's similarly titled opera, *Neither* (1977). Later, on Beckett's recommendation, Feldman composed the music for Everett Frost's production of *Words and Music*.[115] Perhaps somewhere, in each journey "between unattainable self and unattainable non-self,"[116] is the ever-present cry for conciliation: "My comforts! Be friends!"[117]

Notes

1. I thank Deborah Bowman and Matthew Feldman for their invaluable advice and support in the writing of this chapter.
2. Kate Whitehead, *The Third Programme: A Literary History* (Oxford: Clarendon Press, 1989), 11–12. In a March 1943 memorandum, early plans for the Third Programme differentiated it from the Home Service by designating broadcasts on the latter as "general," in the words of Richard Maconachie, Controller of Home Programmes. On the other hand, the establishment of the Third was aimed to reach "the ready intelligent section of the public" (Quoted in Whitehead, 12).

3. Broadcast transcript. BBC WAC, "The Critics," *Words and Music*. I am grateful to Samantha Blake at the BBC WAC and Pim Verhulst for their generosity in sharing this manuscript.
4. In 1960, Bray suggested to Beckett the idea of a collaborative piece with John Beckett. The composer, Beckett's cousin, eventually wrote the score to *Words and Music*. See Beckett, *Letters III*, 375, n.6.
5. Broadcast transcript. BBC WAC, "The Critics," *Words and Music*.
6. Ibid.
7. Ibid.
8. Desmond Briscoe and Roy Curtis-Bramwell, *The BBC Radiophonic Workshop: The First 25 Years: The Inside Story of Providing Sound and Music for Television and Radio 1958–1983* (London: British Broadcasting Corporation, 1983).
9. Refer to Raymond Federman and John Fletcher, *Samuel Beckett: His Works and His Critics: An Essay in Bibliography* (Berkeley, Los Angeles and London: University of California Press, 1970), 33–34.
10. Esslin's volume published by the American firm Prentice-Hall features Beckett's *Three Dialogues* in full for the first time since it appeared in a 1949 issue of the literary magazine, *transition*. See *Samuel Beckett: A Collection of Critical Essays*, ed. Martin Esslin (Englewood Cliffs, N.J.: Prentice-Hall, 1965).
11. BBC internal memo, 6 October 1965, in BBC WAC, *Samuel Beckett Copyright File* (1965–1969).
12. BBC copyright form, signed and dated by Calder and Boyars, 2 October 1965, in ibid.
13. Curtis Brown to the BBC, 27 October 1965; see BBC WAC SB Copyright 65–69 (Part I)
14. Martin Esslin to Samuel Beckett, 3 November 1965, in *SW 63–67*.
15. Ibid.
16. Samuel Beckett to Martin Esslin, 9 November 1965, *Letters III*, 677–678.
17. *Radio Times* 170, no. 2208, 3 March 1966, 34.
18. John Fletcher, "Samuel Beckett as Critic," *The Listener* 74 (1965), 862–863.
19. Federman and Fletcher, 122.
20. Correspondence, 16 February 1976, in *RCON 73–79*.
21. BBC Production Details Report for the broadcasts of "Jack MacGowran Reads Poems by Beckett," produced by Martin Esslin, 14 April 1976 and 5 June 1976, in *RCON 73–79*.
22. The changes are detailed in Beckett's poetry collection edited by Seán Lawlor and John Pilling: *The Collected Poems of Samuel Beckett*, ed. by Seán Lawlor and John Pilling (London: Faber and Faber, 2012).
23. John Fletcher, *About Beckett: The Playwright & the Work* (London: Faber and Faber, 2006), 182.

24. *Radio Times* 170, no. 2208, 3 March 1966, 34.
25. Ibid.
26. Ibid.
27. Ibid.
28. See *SBS 910*.
29. *Radio Times* 173, no. 2244, 10 November 1966, 26 and *Radio Times* 173, no. 2246, 24 November 1966, 54.
30. Correspondence, 16 February 1976, in *RCON 73–79*; Production Details Report, 14 April 1976, in *RCON 73–79*.
31. Lawlor and Pilling, *The Collected Poems of Samuel Beckett*, 55 and 349.
32. Production Details Report, in *RCON, 73–79*.
33. *Dublin Magazine*, IX, n.s. (July–September, 1934), 8. Refer to Federman and Fletcher, 15.
34. *Radio Times* 173, no. 2246, 24 November 1966, 54.
35. *MacGowran Speaking Beckett*, LP converted to 1 CD, back cover. Recorded by Malcolm Eade of Pye Studios, London. January 1966 for Claddagh Records Ltd.
36. *MacGowran Speaking Beckett*, back cover.
37. Pye Studios was located at Great Cumberland Place in the sixties, a mere 1.5 kilometers from the Broadcasting House.
38. Samuel Beckett to Patrick Magee, 24 January 1965. *Letters III*, 648–649.
39. Rudolf Arnheim, *Radio*, trans. Margaret Ludwig and Herbert Read (London: Faber and Faber, 1936), 115.
40. Ibid., 114.
41. Refer to Jean Antoine-Dunne, "Beckett, Eisenstein, and the Image: Making an Inside an Outside," in *The Montage Principle: Eisenstein in New Cultural and Critical Contexts*, ed. Jean Antoine-Dunne with Paula Quigley (Amsterdam and New York: Rodopi, 2004), 191–214; Jonathan Bignell, *Beckett on Screen: The Television Plays* (Manchester and New York: Manchester University Press, 2009), 131.
42. James Knowlson, *Damned to Fame: The Life of Samuel Beckett* (London: Bloomsbury, 1996), 226.
43. Samuel Beckett to Nuala Costello, 10 May 1934, *Letters I*, 207.
44. In a footnote, the editors of *Letters I* indicate that "trucs" may also point to "*truca*," a method which uses footage from two different cameras to create effects (210).
45. Samuel Beckett to Thomas McGreevy, 29 January 1936, ibid., 307.
46. Ibid., 305.
47. *Close Up* is a periodical with issues containing essays by Russian filmmaker Sergei Eisenstein on his cinematic approaches.
48. Gaby Hartel, "Emerging Out of a Silent Void: Some Reverberations of Rudolf Arnheim's Radio Theory in Beckett's Radio Pieces," in *Journal of Beckett Studies* 19, no. 2 (2010), 218–227.

49. Samuel Beckett to Arland Ussher, 25 March 1936, *Letters I*, 328.
50. Rudolf Arnheim, *Film*, trans. L.M. Sieveking and Ian F.D. Morrow (London: Faber and Faber, 1933), 225. Space and time have always been important elements in definitions of montage, as proposed by early film directors Eisenstein, Vertov and Vsevolod Pudovkin, but Arnheim makes them its backbone.
51. Arnheim, *Radio*, 106.
52. Samuel Beckett, *All That Fall*, produced by Donald McWhinnie, a recording of the BBC broadcast, 1957, British Library C1398/0257.
53. Samuel Beckett, *All That Fall*, in *The Complete Dramatic Works* (London: Faber and Faber, 2006), 169–200, 172.
54. Ibid.
55. Walter Wilson Cobbetts, *Cobbetts Cyclopedic Survey of Chamber Music Vol. II* (London: Oxford University Press, H. Milford, 1930), 359.
56. *Grove Music Online*, 8th ed., s.v. "lied," entry last revised 26 October 2011, *Grove's Dictionary of Music and Musicians*, http://libsta28.lib.cam.ac.uk:2969/subscriber/article/grove/music/16611?q=lied&search=quick&pos=1&_start=1#firsthit.
57. Knowlson, *Damned to Fame*, 626.
58. *MacGowran Speaking Beckett*, 57 minutes 43 seconds into the recording; Samuel Beckett, *Endgame*, in *The Complete Dramatic Works* (London: Faber and Faber, 2006), 89–134, 132.
59. *Radio Times*, 173, no. 2248, 8 December 1966, 66.
60. See SBS 910.
61. This excludes another broadcast on the Music Programme which fused Empson's poetry with music. Leo Black's secretary to John Calder, 21 September 1967 (see *SW 63–67*).
62. Leo Black, *BBC Music in the Glock Era and After: A Memoir*, ed. Christopher Wintle and Kate Hopkins (London: Plumbago Books and Arts, 2010), 36.
63. Samuel Beckett, *Rough for Radio I*, in *The Complete Dramatic Works* (London: Faber and Faber, 2006), 265–271, 268.
64. Samuel Beckett, *What Where*, in *The Complete Dramatic Works* (London: Faber and Faber, 2006), 467–477, 471.
65. *Radio Times* 173, no. 2246, 24 November 1966, 54.
66. "The BBC's Music Policy," February 1963, a report by William Glock on the Corporation's music policy, quoted in Humphrey Carpenter, *The Envy of the World: Fifty Years of the BBC Third Programme and Radio 3, 1946–1996* (London: Weidenfeld & Nicolson, 1996), 226.
67. Ibid.
68. Leo Black's secretary to John Calder, 21 September 1967, in *SW 63–67*.
69. Ibid.
70. Leo Black's secretary to John Calder, 21 September 1967, in *SW 63–67*.

71. Ibid.
72. Whitehead, *The Third Programme*, 232.
73. Ibid.
74. Whitehead, *The Third Programme*, 228.
75. UK Legislation. "Marine (Etc.) Broadcasting Offences Act (1967)," accessed 16 January 2015, http://www.legislation.gov.uk/ukpga/1967/41/contents.
76. Refer to Kimberley Peters, "Sinking the Radio 'Pirates': Exploring British Strategies of Governance in the North Sea, 1964–1991," *Area* 43: 3 (2011), 281–287.
77. Whitehead, *The Third Programme*, 228; Carpenter, *The Envy of the World*, 251.
78. Leo Black's secretary to John Calder, 21 September 1967, in *SW 63–67*.
79. Carpenter, *The Envy of the World*, 249.
80. Leo Black's secretary to John Calder, 21 September 1967, in *SW 63–67*. Emphasis by Black.
81. Black, 42. Refer also to Carpenter, *The Envy of the World*, 225, for William Glock's private views in the early sixties, which were similar to Britten's.
82. Whitehead, *The Third Programme*, 164.
83. Whitehead's monograph on the Third includes a chapter on "Poetry Programmes" which details the development of poetry as performance, helped by broadcasting at the Third.
84. Black, 36.
85. Ibid. Elsewhere, Larkin remarked that he did not approve of poetry readings and thought poetry should be read on the page, going on to claim—perhaps not entirely seriously—that "I don't like hearing things in public, even music." Robert Phillips, "Philip Larkin: The Art of Poetry No. 30", *Paris Review* 84 (1982), available online at: www.theparisreview.org/interviews/3153/the-art-of-poetry-no-30-philip-larkin.
86. Clas Zilliacus, *Beckett and Broadcasting: A Study of the Works of Samuel Beckett for and in Radio and Television*, Acta Academiae Aboensis 51, no. 2 (Åbo: Åbo Akademi, 1976), 115.
87. Ibid., 209.
88. Ibid., 115; Broadcast transcript. BBC WAC, "The Critics," *Words and Music*.
89. Broadcast transcript. BBC WAC, "The Critics," *Words and Music*.
90. Lawlor and Pilling, *The Collected Poems of Samuel Beckett*, 111 and 394–395.
91. *Radio Times* 170, no. 2208, 3 March 1966, 34.
92. See *SBS 910*.
93. Samuel Beckett, *Company*, in *Samuel Beckett: The Grove Centenary Edition*, Vol. IV (New York: Grove Press, 2006), 427–450, 443.

94. *Radio Times* 179, no. 2323, 16 May 1968, 61.
95. *Radio Times* 180, no. 2333, 25 July 1968, 15.
96. *Radio Times* 179, no. 2323, 16 May 1968, 41. Emphasis by Black.
97. *Oxford English Dictionary Online*, 3rd ed., s.v. "programme, n.," entry last revised June 2007, Oxford University Press, http://libsta28.lib.cam.ac.uk:2072/view/Entry/152225?rskey=HA6jGm&result=1&isAdvanced=false#eid.
98. Ibid.
99. Broadcast transcript. BBC WAC, "The Critics," *Words and Music*.
100. Samuel Beckett, *Words and Music*, in *The Complete Dramatic Works* (London: Faber and Faber, 2006), 291, 293, 294.
101. Sergei Eisenstein, *Film Form and The Film Sense: Essays in Film Theory*, ed. Jay Leyda (Cleveland and New York: The World Publishing Company, 1957), 49. Emphasis by Eisenstein.
102. Beckett, *The Complete Dramatic Works*, 291.
103. Ibid.
104. Ibid., 293.
105. *Oxford English Dictionary Online*, 3rd ed., s.v. "wellhead, n.," entry last revised December 2014, Oxford University Press, http://libsta28.lib.cam.ac.uk:2072/view/Entry/227334?redirectedFrom=wellhead#eid.
106. Zilliacus, *Beckett and Broadcasting*, 111.
107. Ibid.
108. Ibid., 103.
109. Ibid., 101. Zilliacus indicates Bakewell's extensive "Script Unit experience of what had and what had not been tried in radio drama." Ibid.
110. Ibid.
111. Margaret Stenström, "Häxan med värmekruset," *Svenska Dagbladet*, Oct. 1963, quoted in Zilliacus, *Beckett and Broadcasting*, 116.
112. Carpenter, *The Envy of the World*, 250.
113. Zilliacus, *Beckett and Broadcasting*, 116; James Knowlson, *Samuel Beckett: An Exhibition Held at Reading University Library, May to July 1971* (London, Turret Books, 1971).
114. Knowlson, *Damned to Fame*, 631.
115. Everett Frost, "The Note Man on the Word Man: Morton Feldman on Composing the Music for Samuel Beckett's *Words and Music* in The Beckett Festival of Radio Plays," in *Samuel Beckett and Music*, ed. Mary Bryden (Oxford: Clarendon Press, 1998), 47–55.
116. From Beckett's poetic lines entitled "Neither." Knowlson notes that Beckett never called it a poem (*Damned To Fame*, 631).
117. Beckett, *The Complete Dramatic Works*, 291.

Meditations and Monologues: Beckett's Mid-Late Prose on the Radio

Steven Matthews

One of the stranger aspects of Samuel Beckett's presence on the BBC from the 1950s onward has to be the radio broadcast of unabridged versions of the post-*Trilogy* prose. Even more startlingly, this happened in programs which sometimes (and more often latterly) went out on air at around the time each new short Beckett prose work appeared in the UK, as a kind of promotional drive for attention and sales. Indeed, the BBC archives reveal how frequently John Calder, as Beckett's UK publisher, was involved in alerting the BBC to the imminent appearance in print of new (or republished) Beckett writings, and in organizing broadcast readings from them. These broadcasts from the middle- and later-period prose began with "From an Abandoned Work" in 1957 and continued through to Barry McGovern's rendering of *Stirrings Still* in 1989. They included along the way (an excerpt from) *How It Is* (1964), "Imagination Dead Imagine" (1967), "Lessness" (1971), "The Lost Ones" (1973), all 13 of the "Texts for Nothing" (1975), and "For to End Yet Again" (1976). The whole of the later "trilogy"—*Ill Seen Ill Said* (1982), *Worstward Ho* (1983), and *Stirrings Still*—was broadcast as these novels appeared in print.

S. Matthews (✉)
Department of English Literature, University of Reading, Reading, UK

Until these last broadcasts of the 1980s, the works were largely performed by Patrick Magee (Jack MacGowran's "Imagination Dead Imagine" was an exception), and produced by Martin Esslin. Esslin's broadcast introductions to the prose works for radio audiences are held in the Caversham archives, and raise important questions about the nature of the constraint in, and ambition of, Beckett's thinking from the 1960s onwards particularly. The presentation of this later prose on the radio clearly became a regular part of the publication of the later prose texts in the UK, and a facet of this publication that Beckett was aware of and in which he often collaborated. The recovery of this particular context from the BBC archive focuses important issues about the later prose which this chapter will consider in detail. In particular, what is it about the later texts that offers them for presentation as *radio* texts—as works which, without alteration (the scripts in the BBC archive repeat word for word the published UK text in each case), can be broadcast?

The Caversham records provide testimony to Esslin's energy, diligence and persistence, and to his concern to present Beckett's later prose sympathetically in this medium. Esslin's firm belief throughout is clearly that these *are* in some sense already texts for radio; often, beyond all other media, this is considered the proper mode for their dissemination. Esslin's determination in this regard is demonstrated by the fact that these texts were broadcast even if it took a span of years to achieve that goal. The Magee performance, across four programs in 1975, of all of "Texts for Nothing," for example, seems to originate eight years earlier. In a letter of 18th July 1967, Esslin approached another actor, Nicol Williamson, to record either a selection, or all, of the "Texts" with a view to putting them out over the airwaves in some version.[1] Beckett's more enigmatic, often quite abstract and experimental, mid-late prose writings, therefore, through Esslin's efforts, received a surprisingly strong representation from the BBC. As mentioned, these broadcasts also derived from the culture of collaboration between the BBC and Beckett's major publisher across this period. The Caversham files show that John Calder would send new collections of Beckett's reprinted shorter prose, such as the 1967 *No's Knife*, on publication, to the BBC, with a view to interesting them in broadcasts of the newer work. The files also cover such matters as copyright for the dissemination of the work in the radio medium.

The traffic of paperwork around the potential Williamson recording of "Texts for Nothing" reveals a considerable tension, however, surrounding the broadcast of the texts which is related to the form and nature of

Beckett's later work, as well as to its linguistic difficulty. This tension is especially revealing, since it throws up significant questions about what it was that the later prose of Beckett was seeking to achieve, and about the kinds of formal practice which it was, both implicitly and explicitly, measuring itself against, and dissenting from. This whole issue derives from Esslin's particular sense that the later prose which he wanted to see broadcast was alien to what the BBC audience might be taken to expect an arts program to offer them. In effect, the BBC radio broadcasts of later Beckett, when taken to include the "framing" materials associated with them—the radio announcements advertising them, and the introductions given before the works themselves were read—cast the Corporation as an important mediator of Beckett's avant-garde practice to the broader UK public. In this lies much of the materials' interest and significance, and much of this "framing" matter is recoverable from the Caversham archive.

The "framing" which BBC mediation of these texts felt must be brought to bear for their broadcast was considerable, and yet at the same time it also in many senses goes to the heart of some of those texts' actual complexity. There was, in other words, a necessity for Esslin and the BBC to achieve some textual, even frequently some generic, transformation of Beckett's original work, in order for such seemingly "difficult" writing actually to be put out by the Corporation. But it is a transformation which, this chapter will argue, is also inherent as a potential in the writings themselves—their own generic and vocal instability offers them as possible texts and forms for this kind of translation into another medium. Esslin's uncertainty around his negotiations with Nicol Williamson, about whether all of the "Texts" might be broadcast, or whether a selection of them might be put together, is reflected in several telling ways in the Caversham files. Esslin, in the end, recommends that the actor record all of the pieces over four days, and that the decision might be made as to completion or excerption at a later date. But the Samuel Beckett Scriptwriter File II (1963–1967) at Caversham also contains a letter from Esslin to Beckett dated 9 June 1967, in which he asks whether Beckett might make a selection of the "Texts" himself, "which would look like a sequence with a progression"—a request to which, later correspondence seems to suggest, Beckett acceded. Esslin *and* Beckett, then, felt that such a "sequence" might be discernible within "Texts for Nothing," even if that sequence was not immediately evident in their published form. Strikingly, as mentioned, with regard to the prose of Beckett's last years, and its broadcast, no such process of unearthing and excerption was deemed necessary.

It is as though those texts were considered always already somehow broadcastable radio works *in their current form*, provided they be properly "framed" by the mediating material which Esslin and later producers provided for them.

In fact, in the event, this excerpted format for a broadcast of "Texts for Nothing" was abandoned through circumstances not revealed either in the archive materials, or in Esslin's own essays on his time as a radio drama producer at the BBC. Magee was broadcast reading all of the "Texts" across two evenings eight years later. Yet the attempt to mine something that could at least "look like a sequence with a progression" out of "Texts for Nothing" tells us something of the broad approach Esslin adopted in order to transpose Beckett's later prose to the radio medium. The ways in which Esslin mediated the intractabilities and inscrutabilities of Beckett's later prose, and framed it, in order to present the works to the audience, reveals much about the formal and generic instabilities of the writing itself, its frequent existence *between*, or *outside* of, accepted genres or modes of prose writing—a unique aspect of Beckett's later practice which enabled their translation into other media.

With regard to his ponderings about the possible versions through which "Texts" might have been put out, Esslin, as in other instances, seeks the imposition of a more traditional, and identifiable, generic possibility out of Beckett's recalcitrant material (something which makes Beckett's seeming acquiescence in making his own "narrative" selection from the pieces the more striking). The call for a selection which is not just a sequence, but which shows "progression," hints at the need to discover some thread of plot, and plot moving toward some culmination, from the otherwise scattered and fragmentary situations of the "Texts." "Plot" was needed, presumably in order to engage an audience hearing the pieces for the first time, but an audience which was taken to be resistant to the radical practice of dislocation and abstraction which the prose otherwise presents. This is a persistent feature of Esslin's procedure with these later prose works, particularly when he presents them personally through his spoken introductions before the various performances. In his "Introduction to Jack MacGowran's reading of IMAGINATION DEAD IMAGINE," for example, Esslin assured the listener that

> if you're looking for a plot, all that you can say is that it tells how a vision of a tiny white rotunda three feet across and three feet high, with the recumbent figure of a man and woman inside, is discovered by chance in the midst of a surrounding, seemingly cosmic whiteness ....[2] Esslin's words perform a

neat mediation here, anticipating that "plot" might be just what an average listener might "look for," and then providing them with one as a way of framing the ensuing abstraction of "Imagination Dead Imagine" itself. Arguably the "plot" provided here resonates with sci-fi; that "by chance" carries something of the edge and risk of a space voyage; and such rendering familiar of the unfamiliar in a contemporary generic idiom presumably provides another hook for an audience.

But it is also clear from his introductions to these later works that Esslin is cleverly smuggling in a more complex, and personal, version of what he thinks Beckett's art is really about. Therefore, some sense of Esslin's own purpose in so pursuing the production and broadcast of these later prose texts is revealed, through the generic mutations he puts them through in his broadcast preambles. Esslin's speaking, with regard to "Imagination Dead Imagine," of a "vision" of "a tiny white rotunda" "discovered" in Beckett's prose ties in with his sense that what Beckett is involved in is some existential quest about "being." Earlier in this introductory talk, he stated that the bareness of Beckett's recent work is nothing other than "an approach to 'being' itself." His phrase "seemingly cosmic whiteness," regarding the situation in which the "drama" takes place, is nicely poised, suggesting in addition to an alertness to the popular science of contemporary sci-fi books and TV, the possibility of an existential blankness which carries metaphysical resonance ("seemingly" pivots the two). Later on in the piece, Esslin projects this into a broader representativeness, claiming that "since the artist's function is to dream chaos into order, the resulting visions make our truth." "Vision" is a word which strikingly also appears in Esslin's direct comparison of Beckett with Heidegger in his essay "Samuel Beckett—Infinity, Eternity," for Enoch Brater's *Beckett at 80* volume.[3] The word "vision" recurs in Esslin's framings of these abstract Beckett texts—the Billing Announcement for the broadcast of "Lessness" in 1971, for instance, spoke of the work as "one of a group of short prose pieces in which Samuel Beckett explores his personal vision." Further, in what seems to be another announcement or "Billing" for "Lessness," that text is described as "unfolding" "in poetry, a grey desolation, and a desperate human situation with no hope, no faith, no refuge left. Its effect is cumulative, through key phrases which constantly return in kaleidoscopic permutations."[4] Once again, the presentation of the text is given descriptive, proto-narrative "sense" in the framing for radio of what is to be heard, but "faith" or its lack remains something that Esslin looks for in mid- to late Beckett.

There is a slippage here, then, between the seeming need to mediate Beckett's later work through the attribution of "plot," and the hermeneutic claim which then Esslin makes for the *nature* of this work, one which needs to dispel the enigma by discovering within it metaphysical intensity and perspective. Both the first and second parts of this enterprise are, of course, particularly ironic when sought for in relation to "Imagination Dead Imagine," with its self-canceling second sentence "Islands, waters, azure, verdure, one glimpse and vanished, endlessly, omit."[5] The continual rejection in this Beckett piece of mere "glimpses" of such standard furniture of the imagination does not, however, in the original, unlike Esslin's rendering of it, guarantee access necessarily to "vision." Although Beckett's text dallies with metaphysics when speaking of its own origin, it does not ensure that metaphysics provide the sole means to an understanding of his text. Of the "return sooner or later to a temporary calm" which can exist between the raising and lowering of the temperature within the rotunda in "Imagination Dead Imagine," we are told that "rediscovered miraculously after what absence in perfect voids it is no longer quite the same, from this point of view, but there is no other."[6] The piece, in other words, when considered in detail, is about perspectives upon the primal scene of encounter and meaning, as upon some primal scene of writing, not upon some fixed "visionary" potential. Esslin's attribution of a religious potential to Beckett's rebarbatively modernist self-canceling text presumably mediates it, however, in ways congenial to the higher cultural and spiritual purpose of the BBC Third Programme via which Beckett's later prose was broadcast.[7]

Attribution of cumulative and progressive "plot," apparently as a way of making these late texts less difficult, in fact assumes a considerable further charge in the BBC presentation. It is as though the sense that the audience must be helped to "get" the Beckett text on its one-off performance via radio enabled Esslin to further his own understanding of these texts as repositories of visionary or Heideggerian purpose. With the text alongside us, however, the text slowed down as it were by the process of reading it on the page, we can see the self-undoing intricacies of the prose which might otherwise be passed over in its immediate aural performance. Esslin's understanding and mediation is "right" within one context in which the text might have its being—the immediacy of radio performance—but "wrong" if we consider the text as text. One strain or strand of the complexity is unpicked by Esslin, but it is this strand alone that furthers his "reading" of Beckett's career. It is a strand which, as we shall see, Esslin was particularly preoccupied by, as it appears from the Caversham materials.

Esslin's promotional purpose for—but also his philosophical and religious belief around these late Beckett texts seems typically represented in the BBC materials relating to "Imagination Dead Imagine." It is a purpose which might be described as the conferral of singularity upon texts which, on the page, delight precisely in their lack of syntactical or vocal consistency. The creation of such an aura around these late Beckett texts has a curious effect in casting Beckett as a central upholder of the BBC's cultural mission, as a religiose presence uniquely able to "dream chaos into order." He embodies a (traditional) representation of the artist, and fulfills art's function, even in work which seems otherwise to trouble and resist such status. In a world presumably perceived to be troubled and unbelieving (and of which he creates excoriating images in texts such as "Lessness"), Beckett is held up through the BBC materials as a singular but also representative version of late modernist writing, one whose difficult work, paradoxically, is ultimately reassuring. Esslin's phrase "dream chaos into order" echoes T.S. Eliot's famous contention that the modern artist such as Joyce must deploy myth "simply as a way of controlling, of ordering, of giving a shape and a significance to the immense panorama of futility and anarchy which is contemporary history."[8]

It is worth noting here that, in spite of his unique situation as producer of these radio works, Esslin's perspective upon them is not in itself now particularly distinctive, although in some ways it does pre-empt the strategies of critics writing on Beckett, and the vital significance of radio to his development, several decades later. For what Esslin's pioneering response shares with that later strain of Beckett criticism is a conviction that *radio* is essential to the innovation and achievement of Beckett's later prose work. Enoch Brater, for instance, in a study which foregrounds the connection between Beckett's "late fiction" and his "fascination with the art of radio," claims that

> in this mechanized medium, dedicated to the art of embodying rather than analysing, the musicality which has always been inherent in [Beckett's] "text" achieves a rare spontaneity in what he once called the "rhythm of a labouring heart."

Under such an ethics of embodiment, or singularity, the primacy of a performative presence in the text is inevitable for Brater, who continues with the assertion that "Beckett's real energy as a writer of prose is based on a single assertion: the line is written primarily for recitation, not recounting."[9]

The connection which Brater makes between Beckett's later prose and the radio medium, with its "mechanized" but "evocative acts of enunciation,"[10] seems to render inevitable, in other words, those tropes of immediacy, presence, and consistency which Esslin otherwise confers; a kind of aural actuality is realized through the speaking voice. This is something which runs through much of the criticism about what Beckett might have been fascinated by in the radio medium. Katherine Worth, herself a producer of Beckett's plays for the medium, cast this as an identifying feature of Beckett's style in his works which were specifically written for radio. It is a feature of his writing which

> necessarily involves closer listening ... make[s] demands for very close listening indeed, listening such as the artist himself must practise, in order to distinguish the right tones, the natural from the affected, the true from the false, the half realised from the fully realised.[11]

Underlying such views is the idea that the radio medium in Beckett's writing—both in those works which he wrote for radio *and* in those works which seem particularly to offer themselves for radio performance—conferred a kind of co-creativity between audience and artist, one in which listening in to oneself, listening in to the tones of one's language, are uniquely engaged. There is a sense that radio *is* a direct means of communication, but one which involves from both sides, as it were, the creative imagination as an essence being turned toward the language written/spoken and read/heard (this will be explored further below). The "live" speaker from the radio set, even when speaking words which make no immediate sense, is on this view a full presence at the moment of speaking, a presence which demands a reciprocal fullness of response from the auditor (we might think of the scene prescribed for *Not I* as in some sense a trope for the radio "experience," as we witness the auditor's repeated gestures "of helpless compassion" in response to Mouth's stream of language[12]).

It has to be said, though, that this possible reading of the metaphysics, as it were, of radio production with regard to Beckett's later works, is something which their mediation via the BBC also promoted. The Billing Announcement for Patrick Magee's reading of the full *Ill Seen Ill Said* on 31st October 1982, for instance, described the text as "A Monologue for Radio," just as the next year's rendition of *Worstward Ho* was to do. Once again the BBC gave, in its Billing for *Ill Seen Ill Said*, a "narrative" hook:

> By recalling the last months of the life of an old lady encased in a frail body, we come to have a perception of the end of life and the meaning of what has come and gone to bring us to this point. There emerges a fear that all our perception is ill seen and ill expressed.[13]

That "recalling" is symptomatic, I think: it is not obvious from the text itself that it is an account of "the last months" of a life, nor is it clear that any "perception" of "meaning" is achieved through the text. Do we in fact gain the sense that it is "all our perception" which is "ill seen and ill expressed" (an odd translation of the title's simple word "said") from the novella itself? The idea that, from "the end of life," there is encapsulated here some kind of narrative about life itself, seems alien to the actual text, and the attribution of an emergent "fear" across the text anticipates just that congruence between speaker and auditor which Katherine Worth and Enoch Brater attribute to the effect of radio within Beckett's later creativity. Yet "fear" is precisely something absent in the third-person descriptive tone of the "narrator" (or speaker) in the text itself.

Again, we seem to be left with a kind of double-take, where the consideration of this late text as a "work for radio" troublingly seems to involve *Ill Seen Ill Said* in a form of transposition which lessens its formal and verbal distinctiveness, in order to make it conform to accepted tropes which render it "legible" to an audience's conventional expectations. Yet, on the other hand, the transference of the text into this more conventional genre and idiom does in some sense emerge from the preoccupations flickering within the text. That word "recalling," from the BBC Billing Announcement, for instance, has an inevitable presence in the text, especially as the female character perceived through the text increasingly "vanishes" from it, as she (and it) approaches the end:

> Suddenly enough and way for remembrance. Closed to that end the vile jelly or opened again or left as it was however that was. Till all recalled. First finally by far hanging from their skirts the two black greatcoats. Followed by the first hazy outlines of what possibly a hutch when suddenly enough. Remembrance! When all worse there than when first ill seen.[14]

One could say that the BBC's conventionalizing of such moments ("we come to have a perception of the end of life") both captures something about the text in conferring narrative and presence, and also eradicates much of what is visible on the page. We might receive, for example, a general sense of the rhythmic and repetitive sounding of the text from the radio performance of it, but can only *see* the bases for that sounding when, once again, the process is slowed on the page by the careful structuring which Beckett inheres in his version: "Suddenly enough…suddenly enough"; "first finally…first ill seen." The fine vowel distinctions of "Till all recalled." The half rhyme of the Shakespearian "vile jelly" with that "first finally." And so on. We recognize the typical Beckettian paradox that ill saying is rendered in well-said, poetic prose; we need to see well the text on the page, and the white spaces around and through it, to fully experience how well things are seen ill. Radio performance inevitably deprives us of sight, especially in a movie and televisual age; yet it also partly deprives the text of its sounding properties as they are visible in the book.

And of course in these later works from the 1960s onwards, the concept of "ill saying" seems to become dominant through the grammatical and syntactic contortions and distortions of the text. Our attention is drawn, in other words, not so much to what is said, but to the contrivances through which the saying occurs, and to the difficulties of saying itself. We might claim that these later texts in fact draw more attention to their textuality *per se* than to the fact of their being said by some present speaker. Heard as a piece of text taken from a page, even the sole sentence from "Imagination Dead Imagine" quoted above might seem to undermine such relatively easy assumptions of (human) reciprocity: "Rediscovered miraculously after what absence in perfect voids it is no longer quite the same, from this point of view, but there is no other." The word "it" here is a floating signifier. The poetic inversion seems oddly to confer legitimacy upon the self-undoing of the phrase "after what absence in perfect voids," which is itself passed over by the reversion to a seemingly identificatory "it," that (however tenuously it may relate to the dome's "calm") does in context also refers to the nothing (or everything) contained by the text. Words and grammatical markers on the page in late Beckett, in other words, do more work than they could possibly do through the "presence" of voice on the radio; yet they also yield the possibility of that presence through their preoccupation with such things as "saying" and "speaking," as by their undoing in the original text (that odd sense of their being, in the phrase above from "Imagination Dead Imagine," only "this point of view, but there is no other").

"Saying," we realize, is the dominant trope in late Beckett, where writing might have been the most obvious scene of difficulty in the early *Trilogy*, from the collection of the pages at the start of *Molloy*, to the report of Jacques at the end of it, thence to the notebooks of Malone, and the signage on *The Unnamable*. The often unidentified speakers or "characters" in the later work are palpable and of the point: as it enjoins us near the beginning of *Worstward Ho*:

> Say a body. Where none. No mind. Where none. That at least. A place. Where none. For the body. To be in.[15]

The peculiar absence of perception, the narrowing of sense to one only, the aural, conferred by radio, both opens this prospect for saying, or for joining in with the said, and delimits it at the same time.

Critics who emphasize the textuality of these later prose works typically see such non-sequential and non-teleological syntactical sequences as consonant with Beckett's only strategy to enable him to "go on" after the impasse at which he had arrived with *The Unnamable*. Susan D. Brienza's stylistic study of the post-1950s prose, for example, casts it simply as an attempt to continue in this sense:

> Beckett uses several tricks of language which enable him to multiply the number and variety of words and phrases without having them add up to a narrative expression.

Among the "tricks" (odd word!) which Brienza considers Beckett to have developed for this purpose is precisely that kind of syntactical and temporal confounding to be found in the sentence from "Imagination Dead Imagine," the repetitions of *Ill Seen Ill Said* and all of the late prose, or the brokenness of such text as *Worstward Ho*. These are "tricks" for which Brienza, on the basis of a study of the manuscripts, sees "Texts for Nothing" as being a particular breeding ground:

> The rapid switching of tenses expands the text because it permits repetition of similar clauses with different verb phases, thus obviating continuity of plot or story line.[16]

Beckett, in other words, after the *Trilogy*, discovered a mode of writing which was strangely self-generating, expanding from within from out of the syntactic facets of language itself. Evidence for this view might be adduced from the first "Text":

> All mingles, times and tenses, at first I only had been here, now I'm here still, soon I won't be here yet, toiling up the slope, or in the bracken by

> the wood, it's larch, I don't try to understand, I'll never try to understand any more, that's what you think, for the moment I'm here, always have been, always shall be, I won't be afraid of the big words any more, they are not big.[17]

From phrase to phrase the perspective is adjusted again, and the "I"s and the "you" sit alongside the other "information" ("it's larch") in ways which are difficult to weigh. For Brienza, such a passage would be proof that an "I" in Beckett's later prose signals a discontinuity, a lack of ground for being, amidst a welter of text which miraculously keeps reproducing itself. It is the very irregularity of the prose that guarantees its ceaselessness.

Derrida's delineation of the disparity between the spoken and the written clearly shadows the critical disagreements of such as Brater and Brienza about the very nature of Beckett's late prose. Yet, in this context, it is perhaps the more striking that the framing of the BBC broadcast of readings from Beckett's prose, such as Magee's four programs of "Texts for Nothing," should confront a similar dilemma with a different solution. Perhaps startlingly for the original audience of the 1975 broadcasts, the Opening Announcements for each program put "Texts" in a convenient narrative of Beckett's writing career, by explaining that they were written after the completion of the *Trilogy*, which was an exploration of man's self which had led to a point at which it seemed to the author that no more could be said, that the resources of language were exhausted.

Typically, in terms of the broadcasts of the middle and later period of Beckett's prose, after what seems like a pronouncement of authorial self-reflection here, the opening announcement finds a generic possibility within the "Texts" which might "explain" the nature of their escape from this silence: "The 13 meditations of 'Texts for Nothing' were thus an attempt by Beckett to find his way out of that dead end."[18]

The generic categorization of Beckett's post-*Trilogy* prose as "meditation" had, in fact, been a remarkable feature of it from the very first broadcast, of "From an Abandoned Work" in 1957, which the BBC cover sheet simply describes as "A Meditation by Samuel Beckett."[19] The cover sheets for the "Texts for Nothing" broadcasts make another generic leap:

> These prose poems are meditations on the nature of the self and the burden of being. The voice we hear has reached a state detached from a world which has become unreal. It is from this vantage point that the speaker looks back at existence.[20]

"Unreal" again strikes a kind of modernist high note for its belated 1970s audience, resonating with the "Unreal cities" of T.S. Eliot's *The Waste Land* (1922). But it is remarkable that the continuing presumed existentialism of this explanation expands once more upon the issue of a "vantage point" from which the "world" is being perceived. Presumably also it is the presentation of the "Texts" as "prose poems" which licenses them as such grandly significant works; the cross-generic definition again pushes the sheer abstraction of these works ("detached") as the more revealing to a concerted listener. "Meditation," of course, carries something of that religious aura that the term "vision" elsewhere acquires in Esslin's vocabulary about the later works: it is as though radio performance provides a unique space for contemplation in an otherwise hectic "unreal" world, something which enables us to measure our distance from the world in a private sphere of possibility. What emerges consistently, then, is a sense that in this prose as broadcast we are privileged witnesses to a process of self-communing ("personal vision") which lays bare the mechanisms of "self" or "being."

It is clear that Esslin wrestled with various facets of the implications of such readings, and that he tried to mount his own narrative of development in Beckett's work which accounted for some tension between spoken presence and pure unmediated textual event. The BBC files at Caversham, and Esslin's various commentaries on his time as a producer for radio of Beckett's work, suggest that it was the production of "Lessness" in 1971 which was crucial in this regard. The production had Beckett's full backing: he provided, via John Calder, a typescript suggesting how he wanted the various 60 sentences in his original prose text distributed between the voices of six actors. Those six actors hired for the work were well known—they included Pinter, Magee and Nicol Williamson. As Esslin's introduction to the broadcast of the work shows, however, the distinguished cast list for the production led to misunderstandings about the nature of "Lessness," and "the press" had presumed that what was to be transmitted *was* a new Beckett "play." In trying to explain in his introduction, however, what is actually about to be broadcast, Esslin makes some telling statements about Beckett's development. He sees "Lessness" as part of a group of recent Beckett texts which include "Imagination Dead Imagine" and "Ping" which will form "a larger whole, a work yet in progress"—once again Esslin's instinct is against fragmentation, toward integration. "All these texts describe, as it were, landscapes of the soul," he told the audience of 1971. In "Lessness," however, the scene for this landscape has shifted, and we "are in a landscape of ruins."[21]

This, for Esslin, involves a shift in the nature of Beckett's work. He characterizes the early "great narrative trilogy," *Texts for Nothing*, and the early radio works as "internal monologues, voices which emerged from the depths of consciousness telling us—and their narrator—stories." The early work, in other words, is about communion, and, implicitly, in Esslin's rendering, is therefore especially appropriate for the radio medium. With a 1966 radio production of *Play*, however, Esslin said in introducing "Lessness," Beckett's writing began to shift away from "internal monologue." What the radio version brought out was that the repeat of the text of *Play* indicated its infinite and purgatorial situation: "in eternity the same things occur in endless permutation, ever the same and ever yet changing: after all…a mind, capable of being aware of these [combinations] all at once, would therefore see this infinite number of changes as a totally static, unchanging rigidity."[22] "Lessness" is a kind of repeat then of *Play*: its voices act "not as different characters or persons, but as indicators of different groups of images." "Lessness" is musical, "a rhythmic structure." Esslin concludes, therefore, that "[i]t is only by *hearing* 'Lessness' that we can become fully aware of its structure and indeed of its full meaning which is expressed by its formal pattern." In Esslin's view, then, the absence of character, the dropping of that "internal monologue" which he had claimed to define Beckett's work into the 1950s, does not mean the loss of "meaning" or "expression," simply a re-organization of it on different terms—and it is those different terms, the inclusion and predominance of "hearing," which marks the "radio possibility" of the text. [23]

This prioritization of "hearing" occurs despite Beckett's seeming insistence on the seeming *in*expressiveness of the piece. As Esslin recounted in his later writing about the productions of both *Play* and "Lessness," Beckett insisted that the one thing that radio recording could achieve was precisely the destruction of that communion between characters and actors which might have hampered the former text when it was staged. In the radio production of "Lessness," Esslin tells us, Beckett

> wanted each group of sentences to be recorded separately by their speaker, so that the final production would consist of exactly the same sentences recombined in a different sequence by mechanical reproduction and editing, which would make it possible for the intervals to be exactly the same length, down to a tenth of a second.[24]

The BBC Caversham archives show the complex bureaucratic procedure within the organization of obtaining at the right time for the production something called a "Zeit-Dehner Machine"—obviously the editing device necessary to obtain that "tenth of a second" accuracy for the timings of the voices in the production of "Lessness." It is notable in this regard, however, about Beckett's intentions for the production, that Esslin notes that he was "deeply dissatisfied" with it: he found the voices to be "far too strongly differentiated," and the readings of the sentences too slow. The effect rendered, in Beckett's view, was "thus too sentimental."

That imputation of *faux*-humanity to the performance (and thence the response) to this late text points up the further tension which underlies these works' equivocal relation to radio. These works are both particularly "suited" to radio, but also, somehow, not amenable at all to the constrictions upon the understanding of the text which the medium inevitably makes. Of course, in grindingly practical terms, what makes these texts— even the last novellas—amenable to radio is their sheer brevity. The resistance to redacting them nonetheless meant that the late work could be given in handy program lengths. *Ill Seen Ill Said*, for instance, was given by Magee in a first broadcast on 31 October 1982 and was repeated on 20 March 1983: it ran to one hour and ten minutes. To be sure, a hefty period of listening and concentration, but not out of kilter, say, with the duration of orchestral pieces by such as Mahler, often performed on Radio 3 at the time. It is clear that, for Esslin himself, this progressive abbreviation of the length of a completed text was another "way" that Beckett navigated out of the "impasse" of the *Trilogy*. The monologue centerd qualities of that work were now being adapted to a more deliverable (and bearably receivable) form.

Once more, Esslin's introductory talk before Jack MacGowran's reading of "Imagination Dead Imagine" is the place where he most strikingly formulates this possibility. He points out that Beckett's earlier works, including the so-called *Trilogy*, and even *How It Is*, are roughly the same length as conventional novels, and, daringly, he suggests that these texts contain "a sort of plot with a beginning, middle and end." What has happened otherwise in recent Beckett, for Esslin, however, is a countermovement, and this he feels is where the trajectory of Beckett's work is to move forwards. "Form as well as content has become ever more stripped and quintessential," he avers:

> This progression in Beckett has sometimes been mistaken for an obsession with mutilation. But that's the opposite of the truth. The gradual whittling away of externals, although of course like every element in Beckett it has a comic aspect, is primarily a way of making, and marking, an approach to "being" itself, with everything extraneous as far as possible eliminated.

The "comic aspect" of all of this is reassuring to an audience who might otherwise be disturbed by suggestions of mutilation; but it is clear that, for Esslin, this "stripping away" had specific generic implications which perhaps rendered this later prose especially amenable to radio performance.

What he sees presented as a possibility in the later prose work is the retention of a singular speaking voice with whom the audience might commune, but, at the same time, a detachment of that speaking voice from any specific person. For him, in elaboration of the stance later to be adopted by academic critics such as Brienza or Brater, the presence conferred in these later texts is paradoxically the presence of something other than a "self":

> While Pim in the mud and The Unnamable in his jar could still speak of themselves in the first person, here [in "Imagination Dead Imagine"] even the "I" has been got rid of, and the actions of the imaginer are conveyed by means of the imperative. The writing is now approaching as near as he can get to imagination unalloyed.

We might note that this sense of "the imperative" is a notable feature of even later texts quoted in this chapter, as in the opening moments of *Worstward Ho*.

Imagination seems the particular facet of human possibility surprisingly enjoined by other late Beckett texts, which are otherwise focused upon alerting audiences to the limitation of the medium for which they are created. As part of the punishment enacted by the voice of the "absent" female character upon the sensibility of the male protagonist in the 1965 television piece *Eh Joe*, the drama moves toward its culmination on precisely these grounds. Responsible, so the female claims, for the death by suicide of one of his lovers, Joe is ordered "Now *imagine*" the scene of her death; "*Imagine* the hands" in the stones as she dies, "*Imagine* the hands."[25] "The imperative," of course, is addressed as much to the viewer as it is to Joe himself. By this stage in *Eh Joe*, the viewer is confronted with nothing but the blank, staring, silent face of Joe in extreme close-up.

We are involved with his situation by *imagining* what he has done along with him. The typical hiatuses in the voice's spoken text here give us space and time for that sympathy.

Esslin's exuberant harnessing of the title of the work he was introducing in 1967, "Imagination Dead Imagine," tells us something, then, of the space into which Beckett's later work, with its self-undoings and absences, was, crucially, to enter. "Say a body. Where none," as *Worstward Ho* was (still) to have it. When introducing the 1967 broadcast, Esslin came up with an interesting trope for all of this, one which subtly gains authority through its suggestion of his own closeness to Beckett as a person, while also enhancing what he means by "imagination," as the bringing of a kind of motion to a seemingly static set of propositions:

> In ordinary life Beckett is a great walker. In his work, imagination has always been a kind of place—a place where there's an imperative need to walk around. Just as someone whose physical faculties are failing may limit his movements to a house or a room or a little garden, which he knows and where he feels at home, so the poet, finding "given" space insupportable, must organise a special, autonomous space in which to move around.

We note here the slip into the characterization of Beckett as "poet": there is a play here, in speaking of the "space" as a "room, or a little garden," upon the etymology of the word "stanza." We might feel, though, that there is another kind of slippage being undertaken here, in the discussion of physical restriction, and assertion of the homely "special, autonomous space." Esslin is almost claiming that the "home" of even such abstract work as "Imagination Dead Imagine," *because* it, like the other late writing, offers "imagination unalloyed," *is* radio, that box before which we do not often move far, but in which we can witness the particular "movement" of a voice which needs participatory imagination in order to effect its scenes. This, he is saying, is the avant-garde in Beckett, the shift away from the "given" spaces of novels and narrative into that new space which liberates everything and everyone: the radio.

These various documented exchanges and "framings" of Beckett's texts, retrievable from the BBC archival material, and from Esslin's otherwise published accounts, point to a real tension, therefore, at the heart of Beckett's later work, one which its performance on radio brings out. Beckett himself seems to have been interested in the "voice" as a kind of "mechanical reproduction," to point up the Benjamin term echoed by Esslin himself; for Beckett, radio could best reveal the mechanics of that fact. For Esslin, with his emphasis on the "musical structure" that radio could display between voices, and within the internal monologue of the voice, radio could bring out the kinds of pattern and narrative which exist always beneath "being" or "meaning." Radio is the ultimate medium to say something about that purgatory which seems, for Esslin, to preside as the dominant revelation of Beckett's work. Reading the materials in Caversham alongside the original texts, and seeing the interchanges between Beckett and the various radio producers and technicians, offers greater understanding of the fact that it is part of the uniqueness of Beckett's later work that *both* possibilities—shall we call them the Beckett "take" on his later writing, and the Esslin "take" on it—remain plausible ones.

NOTES

1. *SW 63-67*.
2. *SW 63-67*.
3. Martin Esslin, "Samuel Beckett—Infinity, Eternity," in *Beckett at 80*, ed. Enoch Brater (Oxford: OUP, 1986), 114. Esslin's introductions on radio to these Beckett works do not seem to have received universal approval; Sylvia Clayton's review of the broadcast of "Lessness" in February 1971, held in the BBC file, complained that Esslin's lengthy introduction had nearly put her off the performance which she disliked anyhow (*Daily Telegraph*, 26 February 1971).
4. *SW 68-72*.
5. Samuel Beckett, "Imagination Dead Imagine" *The Complete Short Prose 1929-1989*, ed. S.E. Gontarski (New York: Grove Press, 1995), 182.
6. Ibid, 184.
7. For a discussion of the relation between late modernism and the BBC mission, see, for instance, Michael Coyle's "T.S. Eliot on the Air: 'Culture' and the Challenges of Mass Communication," in *T.S. Eliot and Our Turning World*, ed. Jewel Spears Brooker (London: Macmillan, 2001), 148.
8. T.S. Eliot, "*Ulysses*, Order, and Myth," in *Select Prose of T.S. Eliot*, ed. Frank Kermode (London: Faber, 1975), 177.
9. Enoch Brater, *The Drama in the Text: Beckett's Later Fiction* (New York: Oxford University Press, 1994), ix, 5.
10. Ibid,. ix.

11. Katherine Worth, "Beckett and the Radio Medium," in *British Radio Drama*, ed. John Drakakis (Cambridge: Cambridge University Press, 1981), 195.
12. Samuel Beckett, *The Complete Dramatic Works* (London: Faber, 1986), 375.
13. *SW 73-82*.
14. Samuel Beckett, *Ill Seen Ill Said*, in *Company etc.*, ed. Dirk Van Hulle (London: Faber, 2009), 73–74.
15. Ibid, 81.
16. Susan D. Brienza, *Samuel Beckett's New Worlds: Style in Metafiction* (Norman and London: University of Oklahoma Press, 1987), 20, 41.
17. Beckett, *The Complete Short Prose*, 102–3.
18. *SW 73-82*.
19. *SW 53-62*.
20. *SW 73-82*.
21. *SW 68-72*.
22. Ibid.
23. *SW 68-72*.
24. Martin Esslin, *Mediations: Essays on Brecht, Beckett, and the media* (London: Methuen, 1980), 140–141. In his account of the recording of *Play* in another essay, Esslin notes that he thought that Beckett "was intrigued by one of the opportunities sound recording provides for such a work, namely, that the speeding up and softening down [of the voices] could, on tape, be done mechanically and with the utmost exactitude – something that would be quite outside the capability of live actors during a live performance." See Martin Esslin, "Samuel Beckett—Infinity," 116–117.
25. Samuel Beckett, *Eh Joe*, in *The Complete Dramatic Works* (London: Faber, 1986), 366–367.

"None But the Simplest Words": Beckett's Listeners

Natalie Leeder

On 29 November 1962, Asa Briggs, the English historian, contributed a "talk"—the scare quotes will take on relevance presently—to the BBC magazine *The Listener* on the topic of "BBC Programmes and their Audiences." He notes:

> The word "listener," indeed, was endowed with special significance when the periodical The Listener was founded in 1929. One medium, the older and the more established, the medium of words, written words, was to reinforce the other .... Significantly, according to its first editor, there were critics who felt that the title lacked force and suggested passivity or furtiveness: they were perhaps stretching back in time to the notion of listeners eavesdropping, rather than looking forward to the idea of viewers hypnotically glued to the screen.[1]

Two important and interrelated matters arise in this passage. First, listening is depicted as a less authoritative medium than reading for the transmission of information. Not only does Briggs note critics' fears at the magazine's

N. Leeder (✉)
Department of English, Royal Holloway, University of London,
Egham, Surrey, UK

launch in 1929 that the term "lacked force and suggested passivity or furtiveness," but he also indicates his belief in a hierarchy of language modalities by suggesting that "written words," as "older and ... more established," are required to "reinforce" listening itself. This leads us neatly to the second point, implied, in fact, by the fact that Briggs' article, originally broadcast on the Third Programme, is still referred to as a "talk": there is a tension-filled, unstable relationship between listening and reading, writing and speaking here, and the very emergence of *The Listener*, as a print magazine explicitly conceived for *listeners*, testifies to this uneasy relationship.

Beckett's radio plays, alongside what Matthew Feldman elsewhere in this volume describes as his "non-canonical radio adaptations," were not infrequently discussed in *The Listener* by critics and the general public alike. Moreover, these plays disclose a self-conscious interest in the tension-filled interplay between speaking, or performing more generally, and writing. Even the supposedly transparent correlation between speaking and listening is upset: as Maddy Rooney notes, "I use none but the simplest words, I hope, and yet I sometimes find my way of speaking very... bizarre."[2] Her uneasy awareness of being split in two discloses a fundamental non-alignment between the self as speaker and the self as listener. Words in Beckett have a tendency to morph as they are transposed—or translated, perhaps—from one medium to the next. In a radical extension of Molloy's observation that "there could be no things but nameless things, no names but thingless names,"[3] not only does name refuse to correspond to thing, but name, or word, refuses to correspond to itself when uttered, or written, or heard. This chapter will consider Beckett's radio plays in light of this jarring relationship between the modalities of language. Far from prompting a simple retreat into a world of pure sound, Beckett's radio plays are finely attuned to the complex relationship between a text and its reproduction, and the effect this has on the listener-*cum*-reader.

***

Beckett's one-time sparring partner,[4] Theodor W. Adorno, offers a persuasive theoretical perspective on this very subject in his posthumously published collection of notes written sporadically through the 1940s and 1950s, *Towards a Theory of Musical Reproduction*. In these notes, Adorno tackles what Henri Lonitz describes as "the scene of the confrontation ... between the forces upon which musical form is based,"[5] that is, the complex yet inextricable relationship between live (or recorded) performance and written score. To appreciate the full significance of this relation, we need to return to the origins of notation itself. For Adorno, the "seemingly natural, reasonable attitude that musical notation arose as an aid to memory"[6] is fundamentally flawed. Instead, he argues, notation represents "not so much the preservation of something already present in tradition as the disciplinary function of the traditional exercise."[7] That is, in what he describes as "primitive music,"[8] no notation is required because the music is in a constant state of flux, not a finished product that is fixed and repeated. The "rational element" of notation is the objectification and concomitant reification of such music, "the spatialization of experience for the purpose of controlling it."[9] According to this theory, notation emerged precisely as a method of preservation and control and precipitated the decline of memory: once something has been conserved in the form of writing, memory itself becomes redundant. This spatialization of the apparently fleeting and ephemeral in the form of notation qualitatively changes music and inaugurates a peculiar situation in which it exists, simultaneously, in two distinct yet related forms. This narrative may seem to bespeak a kind of nostalgic longing for this primitive, wholly temporal period in music's history, but Adorno is actually finely attuned to the contradictory nature of the development of notation. The paradox is, as Andrew Bowie neatly encapsulates it, that "this form of repression of memory is also what makes possible modern Western music culture."[10] Musical notation, which on the one hand "regulates, inhibits, and suppresses whatever it notates and develops,"[11] is on the other a precondition for the development of music: "[a]utonomy and fetishism are two sides of the *same* truth."[12]

Adorno's account emphasizes the paradox that the musical score, as an auxiliary to the lived performance, simultaneously enhances and replaces it. For Adorno, this takes on the form of a negative dialectic, which identifies the inner contradictions of supposedly stable identities. For the uncomprehending eye (or ear), the relationship between score and performance is unremarkable—indeed, identical. Adorno's interest lies in what he terms the "non-identical" element that interrupts any seeming identity—in this case that stubborn disconnect between notation and performance. Far from aiming to diffuse this tension, Adorno's aim is to exemplify it, to bring it to consciousness and hence to learn from it. In this case, the lesson works on three levels. First, Adorno is writing from the perspective of an accomplished musician. He notes that "the practising musician is incessantly confronted by his texts with questions that cannot easily be resolved, either through recourse to the works or to the requirements of his own playing, but only through recognizing the fundamental relationship between the two."[13] This aesthetic perspective is one that Beckett, as a writer, would share: the often frustrating grapplings with the contradictions inherent in one's own chosen medium, and the productive negotiations—or, indeed, failures—that ensue. Second, Adorno is concerned with the epistemological ramifications of negative dialectics—the abstract problem that there is a fundamental contradiction between two things that are logically equivalent (A = A), or between a concept and its referent. Finally, and perhaps most importantly, Adorno is troubled by the ethical implications of what he terms identity thinking: the compulsion to whitewash those irritating non-identical remnants that leads directly to segregation, intolerance and even genocide. These levels of critique cannot easily be disassociated in Adorno.

In the case of the negative dialectic between a musical score and its performance, the score is seen to be a direct consequence of domination, spatialization of the temporal, and repression of memory. Nonetheless, in a unique and inexplicable moment, the mastery of aesthetic material through the mechanism of notation leads not to a regressive and cold performance, but to "aesthetic freedom."[14] The disciplinary function of notation undoes itself, precipitating a productive tension between performance and text, in which no originary or authentic music can be stipulated. In this section of his notes, Adorno really only expands on the relationship between notation and performance, but elsewhere he considers, separately, the roles of the listener and reader in musical reproduction. Both, he emphasizes, form part of the interpretive structure, but his concept of listening bears particular relevance to our discussion. Listening, Adorno suggests, is "the first stage of internalization, of spiritualization—in 'listening to' the sound, listening is already posited as *imagination*, as the means of fixing it, of identifying it."[15] For this reason, in a slightly counter-intuitive move, he situates listening as "[t]he complement to writing: the more writing there is, the more necessary listening becomes."[16]

Nonetheless, however convincing this may be in relation to music, it still may seem an abstraction from the situation of radio. Indeed, Elissa S. Guralnick goes so far as to claim that radio, "[c]onceived as a species of electronic music, in which phonemes take the place of notes ... can neither be written nor scored: it exists, by definition, solely in performance";[17] that is, radio simply does not include a written component. This claim is, however, somewhat surprising given Guralnick's general attentiveness to radio's affinity with music: "Might not radio plays," she speculates, "at least some proportion of them, be akin to chamber music?"[18] It is ultimately this kinship between radio and music—of which Beckett, as so many critics have shown, was acutely conscious[19]—that Guralnick fails to exploit. The tension inherent in music's simultaneous expression via score and performance is intriguingly thematized in Beckett's radio plays.

Notation, therefore, provides a provocative concrete model through which Beckett's radio plays can be considered, in order to tease out the intricate relationship between the modalities of language presented in these plays. This relationship is most immediately apparent in *Words and Music*, in which Croak's attempts to summon the memory of the elusive "Lily"[20] are predicated on the harmony (musical and interpersonal) of his two servants, Joe and Bob, or "Words" and "Music" respectively. The pathos of musical notation for Adorno is that "'[a]ll reification is a forgetting'—making available what has passed at once makes it irretrievable."[21] Notation preserves that which has temporally passed, but in so doing loses music's original protean quality. It has methodically constrained it into semibreves and crotchets; the most complex rhythms are rendered neatly into black-and-white symbols, beamed according to the time signature. It is perhaps less sentimental than it sounds to claim, with Adorno, that "[a]ll music-making is a *recherche du temps perdu*,"[22] a desperate yet impossible endeavor to salvage that which has been constrained and repressed by notation. However, as we must remember, the music that expresses this nostalgia would not even be possible without the dominating force of notation:

> [T]his reification through notation, the central aspect of musical rationalization, is not *merely* external to the composition ... but rather seeps into it as an aspect in itself, as the frictional coefficient of its externality, so to speak, the resistance that strengthens it. And interpreting therefore means not simply allowing the idea to crystalize, but making this force field visible.[23]

With this in mind, Croak's instructions to his servants can be seen as a rudimentary form of notation: literal enactments of the "force field" Adorno describes. He offers them themes, indicates dynamics and controls their relation to each other, directing them to come "[t]ogether."[24][25] He uses his servants instrumentally, undermining his original address of "My comforts!" with his "*Violent thump of club*" and brutal exhortation: "Together, dogs!"[26] Music-making in *Words and Music* is quite literally a "*recherche du temps perdu*"—one which cannot unequivocally succeed. Like Orpheus, the archetypal musician, Croak is unable to gaze upon his beloved, to "retrieve the irretrievable." Adorno's Proustian allusion is of particular relevance given Beckett's own enduring and well-documented interest in the distinction between voluntary and involuntary memory, overtly considered in his monograph *Proust*. While Kevin Branigan, however, claims that Croak "remains open to the impact of painful involuntary memory,"[27] which is unleashed through the collaboration of Words and Music, I would suggest that Croak's efforts cannot be seen through the lens of a simple opposition between voluntary and involuntary memory. He indeed hopes to prompt an involuntary remembrance through a particular combination of words and music, but he attempts to do so by an act of will, namely in his instrumental control of his servants. He therefore only succeeds in objectifying the music by means of a primitive form of notation. Nonetheless, as Adorno observes, it is possible for such domination of musical material to have a surprising effect. In *Words and Music*, Croak's unbending will eventually leads to a moment of revelation, painful though it may be, as he glimpses the lost Lily.

The script for *Words and Music*, along with two other radio plays, *Rough for Radio I* and *Cascando*, is inherently incomplete; that is, it lacks precisely that which is so central to its thematic concern: music. In his script, Beckett, like Croak, offers a form of basic musical notation, particularly indicating variances in tone, as, for example: "*Soft music worthy of foregoing, great expression*" and "*warmly sentimental.*"[28] These rudimentary indications are, in themselves, insufficient; as Morton Feldman, the composer for the 1987 American radio production of *Words and Music*, explained: "I know what [a particular emotional characterisation] is in terms of Puccini. If Beckett says he wants something sentimental, I have no idea what that means."[29] The music is therefore notated for a second time by the composer, based on Beckett's own version but crucially new. Musical notation, then, can be seen as synonymous with Beckett's own exacting stage directions and notoriously precise written and verbal performance instructions.[30] Although these are conspicuous in all of Beckett's plays, radio offers a particularly appropriate medium for an absolute control of material. Thomas Mansell suggests that Beckett's dissatisfaction with performances of his theater plays could be attributed to the "messy aspects of theatrical work"[31]—to those human elements that cannot be strictly controlled, since the very nature of theater is its repetition under different conditions. This messiness is, if not eliminated, significantly reduced in radio work: the performance can be edited before it is broadcast; there are considerably fewer competing performances; and, with visual distractions stripped away, radio supposedly operates in a world of pure sound—a world that, arguably, Beckett was intent upon perfecting throughout his career. As Ruby Cohn elucidates:

> Midway during the rehearsal period [of *Endgame*] ... Beckett held a rehearsal for tone, pitch, rhythm. Especially in the last two weeks, he tended to comment in musical terms—legato, andante, piano, scherzo, and a rare fortissimo. Often he spoke of "reine Spiel," pure play.[32]

Beckett's idiosyncratic and even anachronistic use of musical vocabulary in a theatrical setting has hardly escaped attention. Mansell argues that Beckett's envy of "what he considered the greater subtlety and precision of musical notation"[33] in comparison to stage directions was due to a subconscious desire for authenticity that would render all subsequent performances of his plays inadequate. He suggests that "Beckett's envy of the alleged accuracy of musical notation bespeaks a desire to fix performances of his plays to the specifications of their texts."[34]

Mansell's is not an uncommon view and seems to accord with Beckett's modernist propensity for exacting direction—in the script and in person. *Contra* Mansell, however, I would suggest that Beckett's extreme attentiveness to sound and his indisputable attraction to musical vocabulary bespeaks an appreciation of the complex relation between a text (or score) and its reproduction: a relation that is itself dependent on an understanding of the score as inherently and necessarily liberating through its restrictions. Indeed, Mansell even gets close to this point himself; he refers to a conversation between Beckett and the neoclassical composer Igor Stravinsky on the possibility of "notating the tempo of the performance of his plays"[35] and concludes that "Stravinsky's point is that both words and music are inevitably transformed in the transposition from text to performance—a practical truth Beckett was reluctant to acknowledge."[36] What Beckett's radio plays attest to, I argue, is precisely this "practical truth": that, as Bowie explains, "in the writing down of music, the difference of what is written from what is performed is '*constitutively* established at the same time.'"[37] There is necessarily a gap between score and performance (a gap that did not exist before the emergence of notation), and this gap cannot be overcome either by viewing the score as a rigid set of instructions to be adhered to, or the performance as the true and liberated expression of the work. The nonidentity between written score and sounded reproduction must be acknowledged and accentuated so as to preserve the work's objectivity from weak subjective expression, on the one hand, and subjective freedom from the score's rigidity—"its brittle shell"[38]—on the other. When Adorno suggests that successful artworks "rescue over into form something of the amorphous to which they ineluctably do violence,"[39] he is referring to this nonidentical element.

The layers of notation in *Words and Music*, I suggest, demonstrate Beckett's fascination with what Adorno would term the negative dialectic between score and performance. By incorporating a composer figure into the play itself, Beckett discloses not, as Mansell argues, a prioritization of either a definitive script that can never be truly reproduced or an authentic yet unattainable performance, but an intense preoccupation with the relationship between—to adapt Adorno's famous phrase—these "torn halves" of one whole music, "to which, however, they do not add up."[40]

The significance of Croak's role was not lost on the play's first listeners; shortly after its BBC broadcast on 13 November 1962, the "Drama" writer of the "Critic on the Hearth" column in *The Listener* noted that "like Marlowe's Faustus he was calling the universe up before him." Like Faustus and Shakespeare's Prospero after him, Croak is a magician figure, able to manipulate the tools at his disposal to create something extraordinary; a composer contained within the orchestration of the play itself. Beyond this, however, he is also a listener. Indeed, a striking particularity of Beckett's radio plays is the proliferation of listeners within them. Once again, this attests to Beckett's musical influences, for the presence of music within a radio play, rather than as a mere accompaniment, necessitates the presence of an active listener.[41] Beckett's first two radio plays, *All That Fall* and *Embers*, incorporate music—and its concomitant listener—into the dramatic action through the use of a gramophone as an invisible stage prop. The music emanating from the gramophone is heard by and commented upon by Mrs Rooney at the beginning of *All That Fall* and finally identified by Mr Rooney near the end of the play as Schubert's "Death and the Maiden."[42] In *Embers*, the gramophone never appears, but Henry draws attention to his habit of carrying it around in order to drown out the sound of the sea: "I forgot it today."[43] These tentative movements toward incorporating music, and, indeed, listeners, into the radio plays are soon superseded by more striking and experimental efforts. *Rough for Radio I* and *Rough for Radio II* are self-reflexively concerned with the nature of radio. In both texts, the increasingly desperate—and in *Rough for Radio I*, addictive—attempts by resigned listeners to control sound ultimately lead to an *impasse* of dependence and anguish: a conclusion far from the liberatory if anguishing vision of Lily in *Words and Music*. Governed purely by the impulse of self-preservation, the protagonists of these plays exert a tortuous control over their material that radically backfires as their own subjective freedom dissolves. In *Cascando*, on the other hand, the use of repetition acts as a principle of constraint by which the play can rigorously control and curtail its material in a way that does not result in repression. The listener here, the enigmatic Opener, offers an alternative to a purely instrumental domination of material as he submerges himself, this time depersonalized, in words and music.

A number of critics have noted that Beckett's six radio plays get progressively shorter and more oblique. Guralnick argues that "the more conspicuously [Beckett's] radio plays aspired to the condition of music, the shorter they grew"[44]; narrative is gradually (but never completely) ousted from the texts in an attempt to suppress the referential quality of language. This is certainly a persuasive reading, in keeping with Beckett's widely acknowledged preoccupation with stories and their ends; however, it glosses over the particularly musical nature of this drive toward constraint, and the concomitant paradox whereby aesthetic freedom is attained not despite but because of domination.

Rough for Radio I and *Rough for Radio II* occupy an ambiguous position within Beckett's radio canon; they are treated variously by critics as works in and of themselves and as "preliminary sketches"[45] for *Words and Music* and *Cascando*. Their equivocal status is only heightened by the incomplete nature of *Rough for Radio I*, which is not only lacking a musical score but also, more fundamentally, the text of one of the four characters, Voice. These short texts share a preoccupation with power and control, which, though more overt in *Rough for Radio II*, is explicitly tied to the nature of radio technology in *Rough for Radio I*. The plot of the latter is, characteristically for Beckett, at once simple and oblique. A woman, known only as She, visits a man, He, who reluctantly demonstrates a contraption consisting of "two knobs"[46] that, when twisted, emanate music and words respectively. These, to the woman's great shock, emerge from different sources. Having witnessed the phenomenon, She departs, leaving He to phone the doctor's surgery with the anxious claim that "they're ending."[47] With the doctor unable to attend until the following day, the play ends with He alone with his contraption. This machine, though described so sparingly, bears an unmistakable resemblance to a radio set, with its transmission of sound that "goes on all the time,"[48] only to be rudimentarily controlled by twisting the knobs. Marle Tönnies suggests that Beckett's radio plays establish a "hierarchical instability" in depicting an "'elicitor,' whose apparent control over others turns out to be a sham":

> The listeners to the radio plays, who are structurally made to share the thoughts of the "elicitor," then become implicated in the slipping away of control, as it becomes obvious that the master is as dependent on his servants as they are on him.[49]

In *Rough for Radio I*, He certainly possesses the power to turn the knobs and thus control, to a certain extent, the transmission of sound. However, this power is presented as purely nominal.[50] He is a self-confessed addict, who is crucially unable to control his "need" to listen.[51] The demonstration of the machine's workings gives way to an insight into the compulsive behavior of He and the effect this has had on his life: "who? ... but she's left me ... ah for God's sake ... haven't they all left me?" Moreover, Tönnies' recognition of the structural similarity between the listeners outside the play and the elicitors within the play (Croak, He, Animator and Opener) positions these latter characters precisely as listeners. The shifting modes of these dual roles are among the most interesting moments in the radio plays, and the capacity or incapacity of the characters to truly *listen* has an enormous impact on their success as composers or, in Tönnies' words, elicitors.

Rough for Radio II is far more overtly concerned with questions of control and domination, presenting as it does the torture of a prisoner, Fox, at the hands of Animator, Dick and Stenographer. Animator is nominally in charge and directs the torture that is carried out by the mute Dick, while Stenographer transcribes Fox's every word. Despite its apparent dissimilarities with *Rough for Radio I*, the radio play, as Esslin's early reading suggests, is intimately related to its medium:

> The Animator with his ruler and stenographer and additional acolyte reproduces the team of producer, secretary, and technician which Beckett must have encountered in his contacts with production teams at the BBC or the French radio. (In French *animateur* is a term used for a radio or television producer).[52]

Within this structure, Fox, with his incoherent babbling, can be seen to play the part of the radio sound itself. Refining Fox's corporeal being into pure sound, Stenographer, at the request of her mysterious superiors, omits the transcription of "mere animal cries" and the "play of feature."[53] Beckett's listeners, however, eavesdrop on this editorial process, witnessing the sound of the "*Swish and thud of pizzle on flesh*" and Fox's cries of pain. Animator and Stenographer relentlessly analyze every syllable of Fox's output, but they are blind to anything beyond their own (admittedly obscure) instrumental purposes.[54] The torturers exhibit a dispassionate and coldly rational attitude throughout.[55] Animator enquires if "Dick functioned?"[56] as a euphemism for his lashing; the mysterious employers "note yet again with pain that these dicta ... are totally inacceptable"[57]—the dead language of Latin serving to distance them from the embodied screams and cries issuing from Fox; and both Animator and Stenographer register confusion at how to record Fox's "weeping." Moreover, the division of labor, most evident in the ironic inclusion of Dick who, being mute, is fundamentally redundant as a radio character, serves to abstract the torturers from the corporeal reality of their actions. They are like workers on a production line, utterly detached from the complete picture.

The fusion of physical torture and semi-aesthetic expression is repeated in the roughly contemporaneous *How It Is*, in which the narrator plays upon Pim like an instrument:

> table of basic stimuli one sing nails in armpit two speak blade in arse three stop thump on skull four louder pestle on kidney
> five softer index in anus six bravo clap athwart arse seven lousy same as three eight encore same as one or two as may be.[58]

Noting the radiophonic resonances of this moment, Daniel Albright argues that in the novel "the notion of phonic control exuberates far beyond a mere on/off switch: the human body simulates a whole electronic console or mixing-board. Each mud-crawler with his can opener treats the man in front of him as if he were a radio."[59] The analogy, however, goes both ways: Animator, for all the radiophonic associations of his name, becomes a composer figure not unlike Croak, attempting to orchestrate the sound production of Fox with his team supporting him.

Albright compares the disparate "vision[s] of radio"[60] held by Beckett and Brecht, with the latter, not unlike the readers of *The Listener*, demonstrating concerns at the passivity inspired by radio's one-way dissemination. For Beckett, on the other hand, "meaning is fragile, easily overwhelmed by doubt: assertions carry little weight, but counter-assertions carry great weight."[61] Far from radio permitting a direct transmission of power, *Rough for Radio II* demonstrates the ways in which "speech is destroyed in the very act of broadcast, dissemination, recording."[62] In re-imagining and staging the editorial process of radio, Beckett discloses the manipulation of sound. Animator—listener as well as composer—is fundamentally unhappy with what he hears. For this reason, Albright paints him as representing "a preposterously critical audience that not only rejects everything it hears, but also flogs the speaker for the inadequacy of his speech."[63] However, this implies that the floggers have control over the situation—an assumption that by the end of the play has been strongly undermined. The desperation of Animator and Stenographer to uncover the right word from Fox's incomprehensible stream of consciousness reveals their own unfreedom as helpless listeners—embodiments of the passivity feared by Brecht and early readers of *The Listener*. Like He in *Rough for Radio I*, they are compelled to listen, this time by an external agency that provides scathing reports and inspires such fear that the Animator himself amends the record of Fox's words, angrily demanding: "What the devil are you deriding, miss? My hearing? My memory? My good faith? (*Thunderous*) Amend!"[64] Animator's wistful hope that "[t]omorrow, who knows, we may be free"[65] offers a final and decisive insight into the ultimate dependence of these composer figures, undermined by the very activity that purports to empower them.

In these drafts, then, the extreme control exerted first by He over the knobs that nonetheless dominate his life, and second by Animator, Stenographer and Dick over Fox, who supposedly holds the key to their freedom, only serves to bind those who are supposedly in command. Crucially, excessive constraint cannot lead to freedom within these texts, because in neither is the control exerted aesthetic: it is purely technological. This is apparent in the miserable futility of the knob-turning in *Rough for Radio I* and the inhuman, instrumental torture in *Rough for Radio II*. This control is exerted for the sake of self-preservation alone, whether due to the addict's insistence that the control is necessary, or the employees' fear of the repercussions of failure. And, just as Adorno predicts in *Minima Moralia*, "self-preservation forfeits itself."[66] The very self that these characters attempt to preserve disintegrates:

He has become a lonely husk confined to his own home, while Animator, Stenographer and Dick remain in the Dantean Purgatory Animator alludes to, in which "all sigh, I was, I was."[67] While Croak's embodied composition allows him to return, if momentarily, to the past in the form of the lost Lily, the dispassionate torture of Fox confines Animator and his colleagues to the eternal present of a purgatorial existence.

Beckett's final radio play, *Cascando*, is in many ways a recapitulation of the major themes and devices of *Rough for Radio I* and *II* and *Words and Music*. However, while, as before, Beckett includes a composer figure who acts simultaneously as a listener, he also implements the composer's mechanisms of control within the very structure of the text, closing the gap between his own role and that of his character. The plot, such as it is, follows Opener, who "open[s]" and "close[s]." Voice and Music in a manner reminiscent of the knob-twisting in *Rough for Radio I*. However, while *Cascando* contains echoes of the addiction that controls He in *Rough for Radio I*—namely the suggestion that the Opener "live[s] on"[68] the sound he elicits—I suggest that the prevailing tone of the play is quite different. A number of critics, including Clas Zilliacus in his seminal 1976 text, *Beckett and Broadcasting*, have noted the musical quality of the text spoken by Voice. This is usually attributed to the disintegration of an already perfunctory narrative, or, as Zilliacus describes it, the ascendancy of the "*élément soi*"[69]—Voice's metatextual musings about the need to finish the "right" story[70]—over the "*élément histoire*"[71]—the narrative that follows Woburn. Zilliacus also notes Beckett's indications that Voice should speak extremely quickly, supporting the primacy of sound over content.[72] What, however, is neglected in such arguments is the prevailing feature of Voice's text: repetition. Voice's text is clearly divided into short phrases, which are separated by ellipses. Over 30 % of these phrases are repeated at least once, some up to seventeen times. Repetition therefore accounts for an overwhelming proportion of the text; indeed, so much so that when Opener opens Voice for the final time, the passage is comprised almost entirely of recycled phrases, the only original material being the slightly revised "a few more" and "it was him,"[73] even these seen previously in slightly varied form: "just a few more" and "it's him."[74] The incessant repetition within *Cascando* is, I suggest, what renders it truly musical. Music, unlike the more expansive quality of language,[75] is necessarily limited to a finite quantity of notes that can be combined in various ways. Though unable to imitate harmony, Voice's text has an affinity to a musical score in its combinations of a limited number of phrases.

This sense is encapsulated in Adorno's concrete image of "a child at the piano searching for a chord never previously heard": "This chord, however, was always there; the possible combinations are limited and actually everything that can be played on it is implicitly given in the keyboard. The new is the longing for the new, not the new itself."[76] Adorno specifically utilizes this image to explore his claim that utopia must be a determinate negation of the already existing. However, the musical nature of the image has a resonance beyond its explicit purpose: it indicates the broader dialectic of constraint and freedom that characterizes music. The child has to learn that freedom must necessarily be accessed through the constraint of musical form—here evident in the very concrete restriction of a finite number of notes on a piano.[77] In *Cascando*, the musical quality of repetition acts as a mechanism by which Beckett controls his text, forcing it to restrict itself to progressively fewer new words and phrases. Beckett's very choice of title attests to the increasing constraint of the text. Zilliacus notes the musical associations of the Italian term—"calando, diminuendo, decrescendo"—and remarks that all "concern volume as well as tempo."[78] The word *Cascando* therefore signifies not only the necessary control involved in a gradual reduction of sound, but also more broadly the inherent constraint derived by diminishing.

In this final radio play, Beckett is experimenting with constraint in a way that brings his work closer to the sphere of music—the culmination of his manifest interest in the incorporation of music into his plays. A number of critics have noted Voice's typically Beckettian quest to reach the end of all storytelling by completing the "right one"[79]—the story that will set him free. Zilliacus, for example, suggests that:

> *Cascando* is paradigmatic insofar as the play, in model form, expresses a desire which pervades the entire Beckettian oeuvre: the desire not merely to finish a story but to find that story which, when finished, and being the right one, would absolve its teller of the need to go on, and thus make peace possible.[80]

This is hardly a controversial claim: Voice admits that "…if you could finish it…you could rest … sleep…not before."[81] However, what is more interesting is Beckett's parallel attempt to achieve, in this case, *aesthetic* freedom, through the very same mechanisms of constraint that Voice uses in order to continuously refine his narrative into the correct one. That is, in an imitation of the structural quality of music, Beckett forces his text to work with ever less material. Far from inducing the expected effect of boredom, this move encourages a different kind of listening—one in line with that experienced by Opener himself, who actively exhorts himself—and, indeed, us—to "[l]isten."[82]

Throughout the text, the control exerted by Opener is qualitatively different to that of *Rough for Radio I*, *Rough for Radio II* and even *Words and Music*. He "open[s]" and "close[s]" Voice and Music in a far less authoritative way than the other texts, and seems to have a more nuanced relationship with his material:

> What do I open?
> They say, He opens nothing, he has nothing to open, it's in his head.
> They don't see me, they don't see what I do, they don't see what I have, and they say, He opens nothing, he has nothing to open, it's in his head.
> I don't protest any more, I don't say any more,
> There is nothing in my head.
> I don't answer any more.
> I open and close.[83]

The Opener here takes on the role of the modernist musician, whose compositions are incomprehensible to others: "they don't see what I do." More significantly, his being is utterly caught up with his role as "Opener": "They say, That is not his life, he does not live on that. They don't see me, they don't see what my life is, they don't see what I live on."[84] Opener does not understand his nature as qualitatively distinct from the material he manipulates, though he is careful to separate subject and object by insisting that "[t]here is nothing in my head." He is not intent upon achieving a specific, instrumental goal—unlike He, Animator and even Croak—but upon bringing Voice and Music to fruition: "From one world to another, it's as though they drew together."[85] While the question of Voice's success or failure in reaching the right narrative is ultimately suspended in the silence, or dead air-time, that finishes the play, Beckett's achievement is evident in *Cascando* itself. Just as the development of Western music exceeds the rational control inaugurated by notation, the freedom gestured to by *Cascando* emerges from the gradual curtailment of possibilities within its very form.

* * *

"Our world is full of lonely people conversing with the tape-recorders," is the observation of Christopher Ricks in *The Listener* on 17 December 1964, a few months after the BBC broadcast of *Cascando*. Ricks is impressed by this supposed fidelity to reality: "It was a stroke of genius that led Beckett to incorporate this craze or craziness, this evidence of solitude. But our world is not full of Hamms with their dustbins, except in the imagination of Beckett. Or, of course, in the lunatic asylum." Ricks' observation is, I believe, sound, even if the conclusions he draws from it are somewhat trite. The image of a lonely person conversing with technology is hardly confined to *Krapp's Last Tape*, the direct object of Ricks' scrutiny, and it is perhaps more interesting when considered in relation to radio, that supposedly one-way street.

I began this chapter by considering the launch of *The Listener* as a written supplement to the more ephemeral BBC broadcasts—a supplement that, like all writing, simultaneously enriches and replaces spoken discourse. This, I argued, bore resemblances to Adorno's narrative of musical notation, in which the emergence of a score through a process of aesthetic domination and mastery permits, paradoxically, the possibility of aesthetic freedom. In the negative dialectic between score and performance, neither can be secured as the true location of music; rather, it lies in the relationship between the two: the objective claim of notation and the subjective experience of its reproduction. Beckett, as we have seen, populates his radio plays with composers, in the loosest sense, and listeners—very often performing both roles simultaneously. He incorporates into the space of radio a dialogue that relies on multimodality, mimicking the mechanisms of writing so as to stage the tension between text and performance—the "force field,"[86] as Adorno describes it, in which these elements coexist. Most interestingly, this very tension is couched in musical terms: from the incorporation of music into the dramatic action of his early radio plays to its role in the very structure of *Cascando*. From *Rough for Radio I* onwards, Beckett explores the control of aesthetic—predominantly musical—material and its success or failure.

In closing, I would like to return to the three levels within which Adorno's negative dialectics takes on significance: the aesthetic, the epistemological and the ethical. Indeed, if Beckett's radio plays share an ethics, it would seem to lie in their very exploration of these aesthetic and epistemological questions. In staging the tension between text and performance through various composer-listener figures, Beckett moves beyond the aesthetic problematic of musical reproduction, touching on mastery and domination in their broader forms. Amidst the inhumanity of *Rough for Radio II* and the desperation of *Rough for Radio I* there are traces of more valuable and productive relationships with material, aesthetic or otherwise. If, as Bowie argues, Adorno's fragments, which only ever take us *toward* a theory of musical reproduction, offer a "glimpse of a way of being both beyond mere technical domination and beyond a failure to live up to human creative possibilities—possibilities which necessarily involve technical command,"[87] then Beckett's radio plays can be seen as variations on this very theme.

Notes

1. Asa Briggs, "BBC Programmes and their Audiences," *The Listener*, 29 November 1962.
2. Samuel Beckett, *The Complete Dramatic Works* (London: Faber and Faber, 2006), 173.
3. Samuel Beckett, *Molloy*, ed. Shane Weller (London: Faber and Faber, 2009), 29.
4. Beckett's confrontation with Adorno at a lecture in Frankfurt on 27 February 1961 has been well documented by James Knowlson in his biography of Beckett (James Knowlson, *Damned to Fame* [London: Bloomsbury, 1996], 478), and has since entered Beckett lore, with Adorno cast as the "'critic' who failed to listen to Beckett" (Dirk van Hulle, "Adorno's Notes on Endgame", *Journal of Beckett Studies* 19 [2010], 199). Since this chapter is not primarily concerned with the empirical relationship between these figures, I gloss over this incident in passing, noting only that van Hulle's account offers a thoughtful and nuanced rereading of it.
5. Lonitz, p. xi.
6. Theodor W. Adorno, *Towards a Theory of Musical Reproduction: Notes, a Draft and Two Schemata*, ed. Henri Lonitz, trans. Wieland Honban (Cambridge: Polity, 2006), 52.
7. Ibid., 171.
8. Ibid., 172.
9. Ibid., 53.
10. Andrew Bowie, *Music, Philosophy and Modernity* (Cambridge: Cambridge University Press, 2007), 319.
11. Adorno, *Theory of Musical Reproduction*, 53.
12. Ibid., 53.
13. Ibid., 163.
14. Ibid., 53.
15. Ibid., 65.
16. Ibid., 65.
17. Elissa S. Guralnick, *Sight Unseen: Beckett, Pinter, Stoppard, and Other Contemporary Dramatists on Radio* (Athens: Ohio University Press, 1996), p. xi.
18. Ibid., p. x.

19. See, e.g., Catherine Laws, "Music in *Words and Music*: Feldman's Response to Beckett's Play," *Samuel Beckett Today/Aujourd'hui* 11 (2000), 279–90, and Kevin Branigan, *Radio Beckett: Musicality in the Radio Plays of Samuel Beckett* (Oxford: Peter Lang, 2008).
20. Beckett, *Complete Dramatic Works*, 292.
21. Adorno, *Theory of Musical Reproduction*, 53.
22. Ibid.
23. Ibid., 140.
24. Ibid., 53.
25. Beckett, *Complete Dramatic Works*, 289.
26. Ibid., 287–9.
27. Branigan, *Radio Beckett*, 145.
28. Beckett, *Complete Dramatic Works*, 288, 291.
29. Quoted in Laws, "Music in *Words and Music*," 282.
30. Knowlson notes Beckett's reputation as a "tyrannical figure, an arch-controller of his work, ready to unleash fiery thunderbolts onto the head of any bold, innovative director, unwilling to follow his text and stage directions to the last counted dot and precisely timed pause," and although he insists that "the truth of his position was more complex" (*Damned to Fame*, 691), it is certainly the case that Beckett insisted on metronomical precision from his actors.
31. Thomas Mansell, "Beckett's Theatrical Conduct," *Samuel Beckett Today/Aujourd'hui* 15 (2005), 229.
32. Ruby Cohn, *Just Play: Beckett's Theater* (Princeton: Princeton University Press, 1980), 241.
33. Mansell, "Theatrical Conduct," 220.
34. Ibid., 230.
35. Quoted in ibid., 230.
36. Ibid., 230.
37. Bowie, *Music, Philosophy and Modernity*, 320.
38. Adorno, *Theory of Musical Reproduction*, 164.
39. Ibid., 65.
40. Theodor W. Adorno and Walter Benjamin, *The Complete Correspondence: 1928–1940*, ed. Henri Lonitz, trans. Nicholas Walker (London: Polity, 1999), 130.
41. Indeed, it is not inconceivable that this accounts for Beckett's objections to the use of background music in JoAnne Akalaitis' 1984 production of *Endgame* (Knowlson, *Damned to Fame*, 692). Background—or "incidental" (Beckett, quoted in Knowlson, *Damed to Fame*, 692)—music eliminates the role of the listener, not only because it encourages a kind of passive listening in its audience, but also because the characters themselves are supposed to be oblivious to it.

42. Beckett 2006, 197. Branigan (2008) argues that in *All That Fall*, "Beckett assimilates musical models from the composer Franz Schubert's *Leider* for thematic, structural and autobiographical reference" (83), though he acknowledges that "The framework of Schubert's sonata cannot be drawn too rigidly" (98).
43. Beckett, *Complete Dramatic Works*, 261.
44. Guralnick, *Sight Unseen*, 80.
45. Martin Esslin, "Beckett's *Rough for Radio*," *Journal of Modern Literature* 6 (1977), 100.
46. Beckett, *Complete Dramatic Works*, 268.
47. Ibid., 270.
48. Ibid., 267.
49. Marle Tönnies, "Players, Playthings and Patterns: Three Stages of Heteronomy in Beckett's Drama," *Samuel Beckett Today/Aujourd'hui* 11 (2001), 198–99.
50. Beckett, *Complete Dramatic Works*, 270.
51. Ibid., 269.
52. Esslin, "Beckett's *Rough for Radio*," 99.
53. Beckett, *Complete Dramatic Works*, 276, 275.
54. Ibid., 277.
55. Ibid., 279.
56. Ibid.
57. Ibid., 276.
58. Samuel Beckett, *How It Is* (London: Calder & Boyars, 1964), 76.
59. Daniel Albright, *Beckett and Aesthetics* (New York: Cambridge University Press, 2003), 120.
60. Ibid., 216.
61. Ibid.
62. Ibid.
63. Ibid.
64. Beckett, *Complete Dramatic Works*, 284.
65. Ibid.
66. Theodor W. Adorno, *Minima Moralia: Reflections From Damaged Life*, trans. by E. F. N. Jephcott (London and New York: Verso, 2005), 230.
67. Beckett, *Complete Dramatic Works*, 278.
68. Ibid., 300.
69. Clas, Zilliacus, *Beckett and Broadcasting: A Study of the Works of Samuel Beckett For and In Radio and Television* (Abo: Abo Akademi, 1976), 129.
70. Beckett, *Complete Dramatic Works*, 297.
71. Zilliacus, *Beckett and Broadcasting*, 129.
72. Ibid., 128.
73. Beckett, *Complete Dramatic Works*, 304.

74. Ibid., 300, 301.
75. It is certainly the case that a remarkably small number of distinct words are actually utilized in any given text; nonetheless, the deliberate patterning and unusual amount of repetition is distinct enough in *Cascando* for my claim to be valid.
76. Theodor W. Adorno, *Aesthetic Theory*, ed. Gretel Adorno and Rolf Tiedemann, trans. Robert Hullot-Kentor (London: Continuum, 1997), 41.
77. Adorno suggests as an aside that piano-playing "in a certain sense is also a "writing" of music, its imitation through the accents of the keys," and therefore a form of the spatialization of time that, as seen in notation, "is by its nature controllability" (Adorno, *Theory of Musical Reproduction*, 175, 173).
78. Zilliacus, *Beckett and Broadcasting*, 123.
79. Beckett, *Complete Dramatic Works*, 299.
80. Zilliacus, *Beckett and Broadcasting*, 119.
81. Beckett, *Complete Dramatic Works*, 297.
82. Ibid., 300.
83. Ibid.
84. Ibid.
85. Ibid., 301.
86. Adorno, *Theory of Musical Reproduction*, 65.
87. Bowie, *Music, Philosophy and Modernity*, 314.

Bibliography

BBC Written Archives Centre Files (with Abbreviations in Parentheses)

RCont. 1: Samuel Beckett, Scriptwriter file I, 1953-1962. (*SW 53–62*)
RCont. 12: Samuel Beckett, Scriptwriter file II, 1963-1967. (*SW 63–67*)
RCont. 12: Samuel Beckett, Scriptwriter file III, 1968-1972. (*SW 68–72*)
RCont. 15: Samuel Beckett, Scriptwriter file IV, 1973-1982. (*SW 73–82*)
RCont. 1: 910, Samuel Becket Source file, n.d. (*SBS 910*)
Rcont 18: Samuel Beckett, Copyright file, n.d. (*CR n.d.*)
RCont. 18: Samuel Beckett, Copyright file, 1970-1974. (*CR 70–74*)
RCont 20: Samuel Beckett Solicitors and Copyright Registry, n.d. (*SCR n.d.*)
RCont 21: 8/00263, Samuel Beckett Solicitors and Copyright Registry, 1975–1979. (*SCR 75–79*)
RCont 22: Samuel Beckett Solicitors and Copyright Registry, 1980-. (*SCR 80–*)
T48: Samuel Beckett, Drama Writer's file, 1960-1974. (*DW 60–74*)
RCont. 1: Barbara Bray, Personal file I, 1960-1962. (*BP 60–62*)
RCont. 1: Barbara Bray, Scriptwriter file I, 1955-1962. (*BSW 55–62*)
RCont. 12: Barbara Bray, Scriptwriter file II, 1963-1967. (*BSW 63–67*)
Rcont. 12: Barbara Bray, Talks file I, 1960-1962. (*BT 60–62*)

Works by Samuel Beckett (Individual Editions Cited by Chapters)

Beckett, Samuel. *All That Fall and Other Plays for Radio and Screen.*
———. *The Collected Poems of Samuel Beckett.*
———. *Comment C'est.*
———. *Company.*
———. *The Complete Dramatic Works of Samuel Beckett.*
———. *The Complete Short Prose 1929-1989* (ed. S. E. Gontarski).
———. *Disjecta: Miscellaneous Writings and a Dramatic Fragment* (ed. Ruby Cohn).
———. *Dream of Fair to Middling Women.*
———. *How It Is.*
———. *Malone Dies.*
———. *Molloy.*
———. *Murphy.*
———. *Proust* and *Three Dialogues with Georges Duthuit.*
———. *The Unnamable.*
———. *Watt.*

Letters by Samuel Beckett (with Abbreviations in Parentheses)

———. *No Author Better Served: The Correspondence of Samuel Beckett & Alan Schneider.* Edited by Maurice Harmon. Cambridge: Harvard University Press, 1998.
———. *The Letters of Samuel Beckett Volume 1: 1929-1940.* Edited by Martha Dow Fehsenfeld and Lois More Overbeck. Cambridge: Cambridge University Press, 2009. (*Letters I*)
———. *The Letters of Samuel Beckett Volume 2: 1941-1956.* Edited by George Craig, Martha Dow Fehsenfeld, Dan Gunn and Lois More Overbeck. Cambridge: Cambridge University Press, 2011. (*Letters II*)
———. *The Letters of Samuel Beckett Volume 3: 1957-1965.* Edited by George Craig, Martha Dow Fehsenfeld, Dan Gunn and Lois More Overbeck. Cambridge: Cambridge University Press, 2014. (*Letters III*)

Secondary Literature

Ackerley, C. J. and Gontarski, S. E. *The Grove Companion to Samuel Beckett: a Reader's Guide to his Work, Life and Thought.* Grove Press: New York, 2004.

Adeney, Elizabeth. *The Moral Rights of Authors and Performers: An International and Comparative Analysis.* Oxford: Oxford University Press, 2006.
Adorno, Theodor W. *Aesthetic Theory.* Edited by Gretel Adorno and Rolf Tiedemann. Translated by Robert Hullot-Kentor. London: Continuum, 1997.
———. *Current of Music: Elements of a Radio Theory.* Edited by Robert Hullot-Kentor. Cambridge: Polity, 2009.
———. *Minima Moralia: Reflections From Damaged Life.* Translated by E. F. N. Jephcott. London and New York: Verso, 2005.
———. *Towards a Theory of Musical Reproduction: Notes, a Draft and Two Schemata.* Edited by Henri Lonitz. Translated by Wieland Honban. Cambridge: Polity, 2006.
Adorno, Theodor W. and Walter Benjamin. *The Complete Correspondence: 1928–1940.* Edited by Henri Lonitz. Translated by Nicholas Walker. London: Polity, 1999.
Albright, Daniel. *Beckett and Aesthetics.* Cambridge: Cambridge University Press, 2003.
Antoine-Dunne, Jean. "Beckett, Eisenstein, and the Image: Making an Inside an Outside." In *The Montage Principle: Eisenstein in New Cultural and Critical Contexts*, edited by Jean Antoine-Dunne with Paula Quigley, 191–214. Amsterdam: Rodopi, 2004.
Arnheim, Rudolf. *Film.* Translated by L. M. Sieveking and Ian F. D. Morrow. London: Faber and Faber, 1933.
———. *Radio.* Translated by Margaret Ludwig and Herbert Read. London: Faber and Faber, 1936.
Avery, Todd. *Radio Modernism: Literature, Ethics and the BBC, 1922-1938.* London: Ashgate, 2006.
Bair, Deirdre. *Samuel Beckett: A Biography.* London: Vintage, 2002 [1978].
Bann, Stephen. "Robert Pinget," *London Magazine* 4:7 (1964), 20–5.
BBC Publications. *From the Third Programme: A Ten-Years' Anthology. Imagination, Argument, Experience, Exposition* Edited by John Morris. London: Nonesuch Press, 1956.
Bently, Lionel, and Brad Sherman. *Intellectual Property Law.* 4th ed. Oxford: Oxford University Press, 2014.
Ben-Zvi, Linda. "Samuel Beckett's Media Plays." *Modern Drama* 28. 1 (1985), 22–37.
Beplate, Justin. "Samuel Beckett, Olympia Press and the Merlin Juveniles." In *Publishing Samuel Beckett*, edited by Mark Nixon, 97–109. London: The British Library, 2011.
Bernarts, Lars and Dirk Van Hulle. "Narrative across Versions: Narratology Meets Genetic Criticism." *Poetics Today* 34:3 (2013), 281–326.
Bignell, Jonathan. *Beckett on Screen: The Television Plays* (Manchester: Manchester University Press, 2009).

———. "Performing Right: Legal Constraints and Beckett's Plays on BBC Television." In "'Beginning of the murmur': Archival Pre-texts and Other Sources." *Samuel Beckett Today/Aujourd'hui* 27, edited by Conor Carville and Mark Nixon, 129–42. Amsterdam: Rodopi, 2015.

Black, Leo. *BBC Music in the Glock Era and After: A Memoir*. Edited by Christopher Wintle and Kate Hopkins. London: Plumbago Books and Arts, 2010.

Bostridge, Ian. *Schubert's Winter Journey: anatomy of an obsession*. London: Faber, 2015.

Bowie, Andrew. *Music, Philosophy and Modernity*. Cambridge: Cambridge University Press, 2007.

Bowles, Patrick. "How to Fail." *PN Review* 96. 20.4 (1994), 24–38.

———. "Patrick Bowles on Beckett in the Early 1950s." In *Beckett Remembering/Remembering Beckett: Uncollected Interviews with Samuel Becket & Memories of Those Who Knew Him*, edited by James and Elizabeth Knowlson, 108–115. London: Bloomsbury, 2006.

Boyce, Brynhildur. "Tuning In/Tuning Up: The Communicative Efforts of Words and Music in Samuel Beckett's *Words and Music*." In *Beckett and Musicality*, edited by Sara Jane Bailes and Nicholas Till, 63–83. Farnham: Ashgate, 2014.

Branigan, Kevin. *Radio Beckett: Musicality in the Radio Plays of Samuel Beckett*. Peter Lang, Oxford: 2008.

Brater, Enoch. *The Drama in the Text: Beckett's Later Fiction*. New York: Oxford University Press, 1994.

Brienza, Susan D. *Samuel Beckett's New Worlds: Style in Metafiction*. Norman and London: University of Oklahoma Press, 1987.

Briggs, Asa. "BBC Programmes and their Audiences." *The Listener*, 29 November 1962.

———. *The History of Broadcasting in the United Kingdom, Volume 4: Sound and Vision*. Oxford: Oxford University Press, 1979.

———. *The History of Broadcasting in the United Kingdom, Volume 5: Competition*. Oxford: Oxford University Press, 1995.

Briscoe, Desmond and Roy Curtis-Bramwell. *The BBC Radiophonic Workshop: The First 25 Years: The Inside Story of Providing Sound and Music for Television and Radio 1958-1983*. London: British Broadcasting Corporation, 1983.

Broadcasting in the Seventies. London, BBC Publishing, 1969.

Bryden, Mary. "Beckett's Reception in Great Britain." In *The International Reception of Samuel Beckett*, edited by Mark Nixon and Matthew Feldman, 40–54. London: Bloomsbury, 2009.

Burns, Tom. *The BBC: Public Institution and Private World*. London: Macmillan, 1977.

Campbell, Julie. "'A Voice Comes to One in the Dark. Imagine': Radio, the Listener, and the Dark Comedy of *All That Fall*." In *Beckett and Death*, edited by Steven Barfield, Matthew Feldman and Philip Tew, 147–68. London: Bloomsbury, 2009.

———. "Bunyan and Beckett: *The Legacy of Pilgrim's Progress* in *Mercier and Camier.*" In "Samuel Beckett: Debts and Legacies", *Samuel Beckett Today/Aujourd'hui* 22, edited by Erik Tonning, Matthew Feldman, Matthijs Engelberts and Dirk van Hulle, 209–22. Amsterdam: Rodopi, 2010.

———. "Beckett and the BBC Third Programme." In *Samuel Beckett Today Aujourd'hui* 24, edited by Sjef Houppermans and Angela Moorjani, 109–22. Amsterdam: Rodopi, 2012.

Carey, John. *The Intellectuals and the Masses*. London: Faber and Faber, 1992.

Carpenter, Humphrey. *The Envy of the World: Fifty Years of the BBC Third Programme and Radio 3*. London: Weidenfeld & Nicolson, 1997.

Caselli, Daniella. *Beckett's Dantes: Intertextuality in the Fiction and Criticism*. Manchester: Manchester University Press, 2005.

Chabert, Pierre. "Rehearsing Pinget's Hypothesis with Beckett." In *As No Other Dare Fail* London: John Calder, 1986.

Cobbetts, Walter Wilson. *Cobbetts Cyclopedic Survey of Chamber Music Vol. II*. London: Oxford University Press, H. Milford, 1930.

Cohn, Ruby. *Back to Beckett*. Princeton: Princeton University Press, 1973.

———. *Just Play: Beckett's Theater*. Princeton: Princeton University Press, 1980.

———. *A Beckett Canon*. Ann Arbor: University of Michigan Press, 2001.

Coe, Richard N. *Beckett*. London: Oliver and Boyd, 1964.

Coetzee, J.M. "Samuel Beckett's *Lessness*: An Exercise in Decomposition." *Computers and the Humanities* 7:4 (1973), 195–98.

Collini, Stefan. *Absent Minds: Intellectuals in Britain*. Oxford: Oxford University Press, 2006.

Connor, Steven. "I Switch Off: Beckett and the Ordeals of Radio." In *Broadcasting Modernism*, edited by Debra Rae Cohen, Michael Coyle and Jane Lewty, 274–93. Gainesville: University of Florida Press, 2009.

Cordingley, Anthony. "The reading eye from scriptura continua to modernism: orality and punctuation between Beckett's *L'image* and *Comment c'est/How It is*." *Journal of the Short-Story in English* 47 (2006), 2–11.

Coyle, Michael. "'T. S. Eliot on the Air': 'Culture' and the Challenges of Mass Communication." In *T. S. Eliot and Our Turning World*, edited by Jewel Spears Brooker, 141–54. London: Macmillan, 2001.

Dearlove, J.E. *Accommodating the Chaos: Samuel Beckett's Nonrelational Art*. Durham: Duke University Press, 1982.

Derrida, Jacques. *Of Grammatology*, trans. Gayatri Chakravorty Spivak. Baltimore and London: John Hopkins University Press, 1997.

Dilks, Steven. *Samuel Beckett in the Literary Marketplace*. Syracuse: Syracuse University Press, 2011.

Drew, Elizabeth and Mads Haar. "*Lessness:* Randomness, Consciousness and Meaning." Accessed July 2014. http://www.cs.tcd.ie/publications/tech-reports/reports.03/TCD-CS-2003-07.pdf

Driver, Tom. "Beckett by the Madeleine." *Columbia University Forum* 4.3 (1961), 21-5.

Eisenstein, Sergei. *Film Form and The Film Sense: Essays in Film Theory*. Edited by Jay Leyda. Cleveland and New York: The World Publishing Company, 1957.

Eliot, T. S. "*Ulysses*, Order, and Myth." In: *Selected Prose of T.S. Eliot*, edited by Frank Kermode. London: Faber, 1975.

———. "Baudelaire." In *Selected Essays*. London: Faber and Faber, 1999, 419-30.

Ellmann, Richard. *James Joyce*. New and revised ed New York: Oxford University Press, 1982.

Esslin, Martin. "Beckett's *Rough for Radio*." *Journal of Modern Literature* 6 (1977), 95-103.

———. *Mediations: Essays on Brecht, Beckett and the Media*. London: Abacus, 1983.

———. "Samuel Beckett and the Art of Radio." In *On Beckett: Essays and Criticism*, edited by S.E. Gontarski, 273-91. New York: Grove Press, 1986.

———. "Samuel Beckett—Infinity, Eternity." In *Beckett at 80*, edited by Enoch Brater. Oxford: Oxford University Press, 1986, 110-123

———. "Martin Esslin on Beckett the Man." In *Beckett Remembering/Remembering Beckett: Uncollected Interviews with Samuel Beckett & Memories of Those Who Knew Him*, edited by James and Elizabeth Knowlson, 146-51. London: Bloomsbury, 2006.

———. ed. *Samuel Beckett: A Collection of Critical Essays*. Englewood Cliffs, NJ: Prentice Hall, 1965.

Federman, Raymond, and Fletcher, John. *Samuel Beckett: His Work and His Critics*. Berkeley: University of California Press, 1970.

Feldman, Matthew. "Beckett's Trilogy on the Third Programme." In "Revisiting *Molloy, Malone meurt/Malone Dies, L'Innommable/The Unnamable*." In *Samuel Beckett Today/Aujourd'hui* 26, edited by David Tucker, Mark Nixon and Dirk Van Hulle, 41-62. Amsterdam: Rodopi, 2014.

———. "Beckett and the BBC Revisited." In *Falsifying Beckett: Essays on Archives, Philosophy, and Methodology in Beckett Studies*. Stuttgart: Ibidem/Columbia University Press, 2015, 153-73.

Feldman, Matthew, Erik Tonning and Henry Mead, eds. *Broadcasting in the Modernist Era*. London: Bloomsbury, 2014.

Fletcher, John. "Samuel Beckett as Critic." *The Listener* 74 (1965), 862-863.

———. *About Beckett: The Playwright & the Work*. London: Faber and Faber, 2006.

Fordham, Finn. "Early Television and Joyce's *Finnegans Wake*: New Technology and Flawed Power." In *Broadcasting in the Modernist Era*, edited by Matthew Feldman, Erik Tonning and Henry Mead, 39-56. London: Bloomsbury, 2014.

Fraser, G. S. [Published anonymously.] "They Also Serve." *Times Literary Supplement*, 10 February 1956, 84.

Frost, Everett. "Fundamental Sounds: Recording Samuel Beckett's Radio Plays." *Theatre Journal* 43.3 (1991), 361–76.

———. "The Note Man on the Word Man: Morton Feldman on Composing the Music for Samuel Beckett's *Words and Music* in The Beckett Festival of Radio Plays." In *Samuel Beckett and Music*, edited by Mary Bryden, 47–55. Oxford: Clarendon Press, 1998.

———. "The Sound is Enough: Beckett's Radio Plays." In *The Edinburgh Companion to Samuel Beckett and the Arts*, edited by S. E. Gontarski, 251–65. Edinburgh: Edinburgh University Press, 2014.

Gilliam, Laurence. *BBC Features*. London: Evans, 1950.

Gontarski, S. E. "Bowdlerizing Beckett: The BBC *Embers*." *Journal of Beckett Studies* 9.1 (1999), 127–31.

———. "Greying the Canon: Beckett in Performance." In *Beckett after Beckett*, edited by S. E. Gontarski and Anthony Uhlmann, 141–57. Gainesville: University Press of Florida, 2006.

Gray, Ronald. "Waiting for Godot: A Christian Interpretation." *The Listener* 57 (1957), 160–61.

———. "Waiting for Godot" (letter to the editor). *The Listener* 57 (1957), 239.

Gribben, Darren. "Beckett's Other Revelation: 'The Capital of the Ruins.'" *Irish University Review*, 38.2 (2008), 263–73.

Guralnick, Elissa S. *Sight Unseen: Beckett, Pinter, Stoppard, and Other Contemporary Dramatists on Radio*. Athens: Ohio University Press, 1996.

Hartel, Gaby. "Emerging Out of a Silent Void: Some Reverberations of Rudolf Arnheim's Radio Theory in Beckett's Radio Pieces." *Journal of Beckett Studies* 19.2 (2010), 218–27.

———. "'Cher ami'—'Lieber Samuel Beckett': Beckett and his German Publisher Suhrkamp Verlag." In *Publishing Samuel Beckett*, edited by Mark Nixon, 131–37. London: The British Library, 2011.

Hullot-Kentor, Robert. "Second Salvage: Prolegomenon to a Reconstruction of 'Current of Music.'" *Cultural Critique* 60 (2005), 134–69.

Jackson, Kevin. *Constellation of Genius, 1922: Modernism and all that Jazz*. London: Windmill Books, 2013.

Jesson, James. "'White World. Not a Sound': Beckett's Radioactive Text." *Texas Studies in Literature and Language, Vol. 51, No. 1, Samuel Beckett in Austin and Beyond* (Spring 2009), 47–65.

Johnson, Nicholas. "Samuel Beckett: Radio head." *The Irish Times*. 5 February 2016.

John-Steiner, Vera. *Creative Collaboration*. Oxford: Oxford University Press, 2000.

Jones, David. "Art and Democracy." In *Epoch and Artist*, 85–96. London: Faber and Faber, 1959.

———. "Religion and the Muses." In *Epoch and Artist*, 97–106. London: Faber and Faber, 1959.

Joyce, James. "Communication de M. James Joyce sur le Droit Moral des Écrivains." In *XVe Congrès International de la Fédération P.E.N.* Paris: P.E.N., 1937, 24.
———. *The Critical Writings of James Joyce*. Edited by Ellsworth Mason and Richard Ellmann. New York: The Viking Press, 1959.
———. *Letters of James Joyce*. 3 vols. Edited by Stuart Gilbert (vol. 1, reissued with corrections) and Richard Ellmann (vols. 2–3). New York: The Viking Press, 1966.
Kalb, Jonathan. "The Mediated Quixote: The Radio and Television Plays, and *Film*." In *The Cambridge Companion to Beckett*, edited by John Pilling, 124–44. Cambridge: Cambridge University Press, 1994.
Kavanaugh, Jacquie. "BBC archives at Caversham." *Contemporary British History* 6.2 (1992), 341–49.
Kenner, Hugh. "The Cartesian Centaur." *Perspective* 2.3 (1959), 132–41.
Knowlson, James. *Samuel Beckett: An Exhibition Held at Reading University Library, May to July 1971* 1971. London: Turret Books.
———. "Introduction to the Works of Samuel Beckett: A Discography." *Recorded Sound: Journal of The British Library National Sound Archive* 85 (1984), 17–30.
———. *Damned to Fame: The Life of Samuel Beckett*. London: Bloomsbury, 1997.
Knowlson, James and John Pilling. *Frescoes of the Skull: The Later Prose and Drama of Samuel Beckett*. London: John Calder, 1979.
Kurlberg, Jonas. "The Moot, the End of Civilisation and the Re-birth of Christendom." In *Modernism, Christianity and Apocalypse*, edited by Erik Tonning, Matthew Feldman and David Addyman, 222–35. Leiden: Brill, 2015.
Laws, Catherine. "Music in *Words and Music*: Feldman's Response to Beckett's *Play*." In *Samuel Beckett Today/Aujourd'hui* 11, edited by Angela Moorjani and Carola Veit, 279–90. Amsterdam, Rodopi, 2000.
———. *Headaches Among the Overtones: Music in Beckett/Beckett in Music*. Leiden: Brill, 2013.
Leventhal A. J. "Samuel Beckett: Poet and Pessimist." *The Listener*, 1957.
Levin, Thomas Y., and Michael von der Linn. "Elements of a Radio Theory: Adorno and the Princeton Radio Research Project." *Musical Quarterly* 78 (1994), 316–24.
Lonitz, Henri. "Editor's Foreword." *Towards a Theory of Musical Reproduction: Notes, a Draft and Two Schemata*. Cambridge: Polity, 2006.
Mansell, Thomas. "Beckett's Theatrical Conduct." In *Samuel Beckett Today/Aujourd'hui* 15, edited by Marius Buning, Matthijs Engelberts, Sjef Houppermans Dirk Van Hulle and Danièle de Ruyter, 225–39. Amsterdam, Rodopi, 2005.
Matthews, Steven. "Beckett's Late Style." In *Beckett and Death*, edited by Steven Barfield, Matthew Feldman and Philip Tew, 188–205. London: Bloomsbury, 2009.

Maude, Ulrika. *Beckett, Technology and the Body*. Cambridge: Cambridge University Press, 2009.
———. "Working on Radio." In *Samuel Beckett in Context*, edited by Anthony Uhlmann, 183–191. Cambridge: Cambridge University Press, 2013.
McGovern, Barry. "Beckett and the Radio Voice." In *Samuel Beckett: 100 Years: Centenary Essays*, edited by Christopher Murray, 132–44. Dublin: New Island, 2006.
McMullan, Anna. *Performing Embodiment in Samuel Beckett's Drama*. Abingdon: Routledge, 2010.
McWhinnie, Donald. "*All That Fall*". *The Listener*, 9, 1957, 25.
———. *The Art of Radio*. London: Faber and Faber, 1959.
Melnyk, Davyd. "Never been properly Jung." In *Samuel Beckett Today/Aujourd'hui* 15, edited by Marius Buning, Matthijs Engelberts, Sjef Houppermans Dirk Van Hulle and Danièle de Ruyter, 355–62. Amsterdam, Rodopi, 2005.
Mintz, Samuel I. "Beckett's *Murphy*: A Cartesian Novel." *Perspective* 2.3 (1959), 156–65.
Moorjani, Angela. "En attendant Godot on Michel Polac's Entrée des Auteurs." Samuel Beckett Today Aujourd'hui 7, edited by Marius Buning, Danielle de Ruyter, Matthijs Engelberts and Sjef Houppermans, 47–56. Amsterdam: Rodopi, 1998.
Morin, Emilie. "Beckett's Speaking Machines: Sound, Radiophonics and Acousmatics." *Modernism/Modernity* 21.1 (2014), 1–24.
———. "Beckett, Samuel Johnson and the 'Vacuity of Life.'" In *Beckett/Philosophy*, edited by Matthew Feldman and Karim Mamdani, 238–59. Stuttgart: Ibidem/Columbia University Press, 2015.
Murphy, Peter and Pawliuk, Nick. "Addenda: Beckett Cetera: A Pop Cultural Miscellany." In *Beckett in Popular Culture: Essay on a Postmodern Icon*, edited by P.J. Murphy and Nick Pawliuk. Jefferson: McFarland & Company, 2016, 124–145.
Newby, P. H. *The Third Programme*. London: BBC Publications, 1965.
Niebur, Louis. *Special Sound: The Creation and Legacy of the BBC Radiophonic Workshop*. Oxford: Oxford University Press, 2010
Nixon, M. "Beckett's Manuscripts in the Marketplace." *Out of the Archive*, special issue of *Modernism/Modernity* 18.3-4 (2011), 823–32.
———. "Introduction: 'Silly Business'—Beckett and the World of Publishing." In *Publishing Samuel Beckett*, edited by Mark Nixon, 1–9. London: The British Library, 2011.
———. ed. *Publishing Samuel Beckett*. London: The British Library, 2011.
Ojrzyńska, Katarzyna. "Music and Metamusic in Beckett's Early Plays for Radio." In *Beckett and Musicality*, edited by Sara Jane Bailes and Nicholas Till, 47–62. Farnham: Ashgate, 2014.
O'Reilly, Magessa. "Beckett's 'From an Unabandoned Work': On the Way to *Comment c'est*." *Translation and Literature* 12, no. 1. (Spring, 2003), 144–54.

Owen, Lynette, ed. *Clark's Publishing Agreements: A Book of Precedents.* 9th ed. Haywards Heath: Bloomsbury Professional, 2013.

———. *Selling Rights.* 7th ed. London: Routledge, 2014.

Perloff, Marjorie. "The Silence That Is Not Silence: Acoustic Art in Samuel Beckett's *Embers.*" In *Samuel Beckett and the Arts: Music, Visual Arts, and Non-Print Media*, edited by Lois Oppenheim, 247–68. New York: Garland Publishing, 1999.

———. "Beckett in the Country of the Houyhnhms: The Transformation of Swiftian Satire." In "Samuel Beckett: Debts and Legacies", *Samuel Beckett Today/Aujourd'hui* 22, edited by Erik Tonning, Matthew Feldman, Matthijs Engelberts and Dirk van Hulle, 17–38. Amsterdam: Rodopi, 2010.

Peters, Kimberley. "Sinking the Radio 'Pirates': Exploring British Strategies of Governance in the North Sea, 1964-1991." *Area* 43: 3 (2011), 281–7.

Phillips, Robert. "Philip Larkin: The Art of Poetry No. 30." *Paris Review* 84 (1982), at:www.theparisreview.org/interviews/3153/the-art-of-poetry-no-30-philip-larkin.

Pilling, John. *A Samuel Beckett Chronology.* Basingstoke: Palgrave, 2006.

———. "The Predator and his Prey: Strategies and Strangeness in Beckett's Early Poems." *Journal of Beckett Studies* 24.1 (2015), 18–31.

———. "Changed Modalities in *Malone Dies*: putting Sapo in his place." In *Revisiting* Molloy, Malone meurt/Malone Dies *and* L'Innommable/The Unnamable, *Samuel Beckett Today/Aujourd'hui* 26, edited by David Tucker et al, 121–35. Amsterdam: Rodopi, 2014.

Porter, Jeffrey Lyn. "Beckett and the Radiophonic Body: Beckett and the BBC." *Modern Drama* 53.4 (2010), 431–46.

Pountney, Rosemary. *Theatre of Shadows: Samuel Beckett's Drama, 1956-1976: From All That Fall to Footfalls.* Gerrards Cross: Colin Smythe, 1988.

Quigley, Megan M. "Justice for the 'Illstarred Punster': Samuel Beckett and Alfred Péron's Revisions of 'Anna Lyvia Pluratself.'" *James Joyce Quarterly* 41:3 (2004), 473–80.

Richardson, Stanley and Hale, Jane Alison. "Working Wireless: Beckett's Radio Writing." In *Samuel Beckett and the Arts: Music, Visual Arts, and Non-Print Media*, edited by Lois Oppenheim, 269–94. New York: Garland Publishing, 1999.

Ricks, Christopher. "The Roots of Samuel Beckett." *The Listener*, 17 1964.

Robinson, Michael. *The Long Sonata of the Dead: A Study of Samuel Beckett.* New York: Grove Press, 1969.

Sandison, Garry. "Beckett's *Embers* and the Modernist Ovid: A Tiresian Poetic?" *Journal of Beckett Studies* 22:2 (2013), 180–200.

Schaeffer, Pierre. "Acousmatics." Translated by Daniel W. Smith. In *Audio Culture: Readings in Modern Music*, edited by Christoph Cox and Daniel Warner, 76–81. New York and London: Continuum, 2004.

Searle, Humphrey. *Quadrille with a Raven*, 1982. Accessed 4 November, 2013. http://www.musicweb-international.com/searle/titlepg.htm.

Shloss, Carol Loeb. "Privacy and Piracy in the Joyce Trade: James Joyce and *Le Droit Moral.*" *James Joyce Quarterly* 37:3–4 (Spring-Summer 2000), 447–57.

Silvey, Robert. *Who's Listening? The Story of BBC Audience Research.* London: Allen & Unwin, 1974.

Sinoimeri, Lea. "'ILL-TOLD ILL-HEARD': Aurality and Reading in *Comment c'est/How It Is.*" In *Samuel Beckett Today/Aujourd'hui* 24, edited by Sjef Houppermans and Angela Moorjani, 321–34. Amsterdam: Rodopi, 2012.

Smart, Marie. "New Novel, Old Tune: Beckett and Pinget in Postwar France." *Modernism/modernity* 21:2 (2014), 529–46.

Stewart, Paul. "Sterile Reproduction: Beckett's Death of Species and Fictional Regeneration." In *Beckett and Death*, edited by Steven Barfield, Matthew Feldman and Philip Tew, 169–87. London: Bloomsbury, 2009.

Stuckenschmidt, H. H. "The Third Stage: Some Observations on the Aesthetics of Electronic Music." Translated by Hans G. Helm. *Die Reihe* 1, 11–13.

Sullivan, Dan. "Stage Review: Think Casual For Your Date With Williamson." *Los Angeles Times*, 27 1986. http://articles.latimes.com/1986-08-27/entertainment/ca-14394_1_nicol-williamson (accessed 12.11.15).

Thompson, John B. *Merchants of Culture: The Publishing Business in the Twenty-First Century.* 2nd ed Cambridge: Polity Press, 2012.

Tönnies, Marle. "Players, Playthings and Patterns: Three Stages of Heteronomy in Beckett's Drama." *Samuel Beckett Today/Aujourd'hui* 11, edited by Angela Moorjani and Carola Veit, 294–301. Amsterdam: Rodopi, 2001.

Tonning, Erik. *Samuel Beckett's Abstract Drama: works for stage and screen 1962-1985*; Bern Oxford: Peter Lang, 2007.

———. *Modernism and Christianity.* Basingstoke: Palgrave, 2014.

———. "David Jones: Christian Modernism at the BBC." In *Broadcasting in the Modernist Era*, edited by Matthew Feldman, Henry Mead and Erik Tonning, 113–34. London: Bloomsbury Academic, 2014.

———. "Beckett's Unholy Dying: From Malone Dies to The Unnamable." In *Beckett and Death*, edited by Steven Barfield, Matthew Feldman and Philip Tew, 106–27. London: Bloomsbury Academic, 2009.

Tucker, David. "'Oh Lovely Art': Beckett and Music." In *The Edinburgh Companion to Samuel Beckett and the Arts*, edited by S. E. Gontarski, 373–85. Edinburgh: Edinburgh University Press, 2014.

Uhlmann, Anthony. *Samuel Beckett and the Philosophical Image.* Cambridge: Cambridge University Press, 2006.

Van Hulle, Dirk. "Adorno's Notes on Endgame." *Journal of Beckett Studies* 19 (2010), 196–217.

———. *The Making of Samuel Beckett's* Krapp's Last Tape/La Dernière Bande. London and Brussels: Bloomsbury and University Press Antwerp, 2015.

Van Hulle, Dirk and Shane Weller. *The Making of Samuel Beckett's* L'Innommable/The Unnamable. London: Bloomsbury, 2014.

Van Laan, Thomas F. "*All That Fall* as 'a Play for Radio'." *Modern Drama* 28.1 (1985), 38–47.

Verhulst, Pim. "'There are differences': Variants and Errors in the Texts of Beckett's Radio Plays." *Journal of Beckett Studies* 24 (2015), 57–74.

———. "'Just howls from time to time': Dating *Pochade radiophonique*." In "'Beginning of the murmur': Archival Pre-Texts and Other Sources." *Samuel Beckett Today/Aujourd'hui* 27, edited by Conor Carville and Mark Nixon, 147–62. Amsterdam: Rodopi, 2015.

Walker, Roy. "It's Tragic, Mysterious and Wildly Funny." *Tribune*, 18, 1957: 8.

Weller, Shane. "Beckett's Last Chance: *Les Éditions de Minuit*." In *Publishing Samuel Beckett*, edited by Mark Nixon, 111–30. London: The British Library, 2011.

———. "The Tone of Displacement: Samuel Beckett, Robert Pinget and the Art of Adaptation." In *On In Their Company: essays on Beckett, tributes and sketches*, edited by. Mark Nixon and John Pilling, 21–41. Reading: Beckett International Foundation, 2015.

Whitehead, Kate. *The Third Programme: A Literary History*. Oxford: Clarendon Press, 1989.

Wood, James. "Cold-Shouldered." *London Review of Books*, 8, 2001, 13–15.

Worth, Katharine. "Beckett and the Radio Medium." In *British Radio Drama*, edited by John Drakakis, 191–217. Cambridge, Cambridge University Press, 1981.

Zilliacus, Clas. "Scoring Twice: Pinget's *La Manivelle* and Beckett's *The Old Tune*." *Moderna Språk* LXVIII: 1 (1974), 1–10.

———. *Beckett and Broadcasting: A Study of the Works of Samuel Beckett for and in Radio and Television*. Åbo: Åbo Akademi, 1976.

———. "*All That Fall* and Radio Language." In *Samuel Beckett and the Arts: Music, Visual Arts, and Non-Print Media*, edited by Lois Oppenheim, 295–310. New York: Garland, 1999.

INDEX[1]

A

Adet, Georges, 6, 22
Adorno, Theodor W., 15, 270–4, 276, 280, 282, 284, 285n4, 285n6, 285n11, 286n21, 286n38, 286n40, 287n66, 288n76, 288n77, 288n86
Albery, Donald, 66
Alighieri, Dante, 9, 10, 19n33, 19n41, 30, 193, 206n51
Arnheim, Rudolf, 108, 116, 118, 119, 133n30, 137n127, 197, 234–5, 241, 245n39, 246n50, 246n51
Ashcroft, Peggy, 38
aurality, 195, 198, 199, 202, 203
autonomy, 60, 61, 117, 121, 130, 144, 265

B

Bakewell, Michael, 6, 22, 25, 88, 90–2, 94, 101n99, 182n35, 242, 248n109
BBC WAC Caversham, 1, 11–12, 20n47, 21, 105, 109, 124, 128, 172, 174, 186, 188, 190, 202, 229, 233
Beadsmore, Richard, 39
Beckett, John, 9, 13, 22–4, 54, 55, 89–91, 105, 174, 183n49, 233, 244n4
Beckett, Samuel
  Acte sans paroles I, 66
  "Age is when to a man" [from Words and Music], 27, 240
  "Alba," 11, 26, 232, 240

[1] Note: Page numbers followed by "n" refer to notes.

Beckett, Samuel (*cont.*)
  All that Fall [*Tous ceux qui tombent*], 2, 4, 6–8, 13, 18n30, 21, 22, 41n4, 49, 51, 55, 63, 67–70, 81–3, 86, 105, 106, 108–10, 112–16, 118, 121, 123–5, 127–30, 132n17, 136n99, 138n150, 142, 146, 148–51, 159, 166n61, 173, 174, 178n5, 178n6, 179n14, 186, 191–2, 198–201, 230, 235, 239, 276, 287n42
  ...but the clouds..., 21
  Cascando, 2, 10, 13, 21, 26, 30, 91–3, 104, 134n44, 139, 155, 163n10, 174, 186, 203, 231, 232, 236, 240, 274, 277, 281–4, 288n75
  Collected Poems in English and French, 35
  Company, 38, 161
  "Dante and the Lobster," 38, 186
  "Da Tagte Es," 27
  "Dieppe," 240
  "The Drunken Boat" [*Le Bateau ivre*], 35–7, 161, 187, 204n7
  "Echo's Bones," 5, 11, 27, 235
  Eh Joe, 8, 21, 93, 264
  Embers, 2, 7, 13, 21, 50–3, 81–6, 95, 97, 99n38, 118, 135n80, 148, 153, 174, 179–80n14, 192, 234, 239, 276
  Endgame [*Fin de partie*], 7, 12, 25, 43, 48–54, 68, 73, 76, 86, 149, 150, 154, 182n35, 190, 198, 234, 236, 275, 286n41
  "Enueg I," 26
  "First Love," 32, 159, 174, 186
  "For to end yet again," 11, 34, 160, 249
  From an Abandoned Work, 2, 4, 14, 23, 38, 50–4, 83, 112, 113, 149, 152, 161, 170, 174–6, 186, 203n4, 249, 260
  Ghost Trio, 8, 21, 103, 104, 108
  How It Is [*Comment c'est*], 7, 9, 12, 14, 27, 30, 55, 88, 89, 97, 170, 174, 179n10, 180n14, 181n27, 185–203, 208n97, 212, 221, 249, 263, 279
  Ill Seen Ill Said, 38–9, 161, 174, 249, 256, 257, 263
  "Imagination Dead Imagine," 8, 27–30, 158, 221, 249, 250, 252–5, 258, 259, 261, 263–5
  "I would like my love to die," 26, 38
  Krapp's Last Tape [*La Dernière bande*], 9, 12, 43, 45, 53–6, 84, 103, 181n27, 182n36, 182n38, 192, 193, 195, 284
  "Lessness," 14, 16n2, 29–31, 93, 142, 149, 158, 174, 211–25, 249, 253, 255, 261–3, 266n3
  "The Lost Ones," 32, 142, 159, 221, 249
  "Malacoda," 26, 232, 240
  Malone Dies, 2, 10, 23, 38, 49, 52, 54, 83, 149, 152, 170, 174, 175, 177, 183n47, 183n49, 186, 209n107
  Mercier and Camier, 38
  Molloy, 2, 6, 7, 10, 22–3, 45, 46, 49–54, 57n9, 70, 83, 84, 106, 112, 113, 147, 149, 151, 170, 174–6, 186, 191, 192, 203n4, 234, 258
  More Pricks than Kicks, 5, 27, 38, 180, 182n31, 186
  Murphy, 5, 27, 28, 38, 50, 146, 170, 180n19, 186

"My way is in the sand flowing," 38, 232, 236, 240
No's knife, 30, 250
Old Tune, The, 10, 21, 148, 153, 169–74, 178n3, 178n5, 178–9n8, 179n10, 180n14, 180n19, 182n34
A Piece of Monologue, 11, 39, 40, 162
"Ping," 30, 221, 222, 261
Play [*Comedie*], 7, 8, 11, 14, 26, 31, 89, 93, 145, 146, 156, 178n5, 196, 222, 262, 267n24
radio productions; "Beckett at the National," 37–8; "*Embers, Molloy, Endgame*" (by Samuel Beckett), 21–3, 25; "MacGowran reads poems by Beckett," 34; *MacGowran Speaking Beckett* (vinyl record), 147, 233–6; "Poems by Samuel Beckett" (broadcast on the Third Programme), 26–7, 156, 232; "Words and Music" (devised by Leo Black), 30, 230, 237, 239–41, 243, 273
Rough for Radio I, 21, 192, 274, 276–8, 280, 281, 283, 284
Rough for Radio II, 11, 13, 21, 192, 193, 276–8, 280, 283, 284
"Saint-Lo," 26, 232
"Sanies I," 11, 27
"Serena I," 11, 27
"Serena II," 11, 26, 232
"Serena III," 27, 182n32
"Spent the years of learning" ["Gnome"], 27
"Still," 38, 186
"Stirrings Still," 40, 249

Texts for Nothing, 6, 15, 30, 32–4, 160, 174, 186, 190, 212, 249–52, 259, 260, 262
That Time, 215
Unnamable, The [*L'Innommable*], 2, 6, 19n33, 24, 38, 50–4, 83, 84, 106, 114, 149, 152, 169, 170, 174, 176, 177, 183n47, 186, 191, 198, 203, 259
"The Vulture," 27
Waiting for Godot [*En attendant Godot*], 2, 7–8, 10, 12, 24, 43, 46–8, 51, 56, 57n10, 68, 70, 82, 110, 153, 174, 175, 178n8, 182n32, 189, 198, 212
Watt, 4, 5, 7, 27, 38, 47, 51, 173, 180n19, 186
"Watt will not" [from Watt], 27
"What would I do without this world, faceless, incurious," 26, 232, 243
"Who may tell the tale" [from Watt], 27
"Whoroscope," 5, 11, 26, 232
Words and Music, 2, 7, 13, 15, 21, 27, 55, 81, 83, 88–92, 100n70, 104, 149, 154, 174, 192, 229, 230, 232, 239–43, 273, 274, 276, 277, 281, 283
Worstward Ho, 39, 162, 249, 256, 259, 264, 265
Wrth Aros Godot, 25, 155
Bernearts, Lars, 224
Black, Leo, 237–41, 243, 246n62, 246n68, 246n70, 247n78, 247n80, 247n81, 247n84
Blake, William, 62
blasphemy, 12, 60, 63, 69–76
Blin, Roger, 6, 22, 44, 56, 57n5, 110
Bowles, Patrick, 7, 10, 19n38, 19n39, 22, 23

B

Brambell, Wilfrid, 24
Brater, Enoch, 253, 255–7, 260, 264, 266n9
Bray, Barbara, 7–9, 19n33, 27, 47, 49, 78n37, 82, 84–91, 93, 94, 97, 99n30, 99n35, 99n36, 100n55, 100n57, 100n69, 100n73, 101n76, 101n85, 101n86, 101n89, 101n103, 101n104, 121, 124, 150, 165n34, 166n58, 167n75, 170–4, 176, 177, 178n6, 178n7, 180n20, 181n24, 181n26, 183n45, 186, 188, 190, 194, 198, 200, 207n86, 229, 239, 241, 244n4
Brienza, Susan D., 259–60, 264, 267n16
Brunius, Jacques, 6, 22

C

Campbell, Julie, 5, 17n15, 18n30, 19n41, 67, 78n43, 104, 108, 110, 115, 133n25, 134n70, 135n72
Carey, John, 75, 79n68
Chaikin, Joseph, 189–90, 200
Christianity, 12, 60, 61, 70–3, 76, 77n4, 144, 145
Coetzee, J.M., 225, 227n51, 227n54
collaboration, 9, 12, 13, 22, 23, 29, 47, 56, 61, 62, 64, 67, 76, 84, 89, 91, 93, 94, 105, 109, 115, 128, 130, 138n150, 143, 147, 150, 170, 250, 274
Collini, Stefan, 59, 77n1
commodification, 141, 143
composers, 91, 93, 94, 105, 119–22, 243, 274–6, 278–81, 284, 287n42
consciousness, the depiction of, 225
constraint, 250, 277, 280, 282

control, 63, 97, 105, 139, 271, 273, 274, 277–84
copyright, as human right, 139
Cotterell, Ian, 38
Cranham, Kenneth, 38
Crow, Barbara, 32, 34, 35

D

Davies, Anthea, 32
Dearlove, J.E., 224, 227n50
Denham, Maurice, 25
Dixon, John, 35
Donnelly, Donal, 24, 29, 31, 212, 216
Drew, Elizabeth, 225, 227n52
droit moral, 143
Dunstone, Esther, 29, 32

E

École Normale Supérieure, 35
editorial intervention
Eliot, T. S., 59, 61, 71–3, 77n1, 77n4, 79n56, 255, 261, 266n8
Emery, Jack, 38
Esslin, Martin, 2, 9, 13–15, 26, 27, 29, 32–5, 67, 78n43, 81, 88–96, 98n1, 101n81, 101n83, 101n95, 102n108, 102n114, 102n117, 102n125, 112, 133n31, 142, 145, 146, 165n35, 165n36, 165n37, 165n40, 165n47, 165n49, 165n50, 170, 174, 178n5, 183n50, 186, 188, 190, 199, 203, 207n91, 211–16, 218–25, 225n2, 226n14, 226n17, 230–3, 244n10, 244n14, 244n16, 244n21, 250–6, 261–6, 266n3, 267n24, 278, 287n45, 287n52

F

Feldman, Morton, 243, 274
Felton, Felix, 24
Fenton, Leonard, 29, 31, 212, 216
Fforde, Arthur, 75
Fletcher, John, 7, 8, 11, 15, 18n27, 26, 37, 183n89, 231, 232, 242, 244n9, 244n18, 244n19, 244n23, 245n33
Foxrock, Ireland, 36, 57n9, 68
Fraser, G. S., 7, 69, 71, 72, 79n49, 79n55
freedom, 82, 86, 143, 272, 276, 277, 280, 282–4

G

genetic criticism, 224
Gielgud, Val, 46–9, 62, 68, 85–8, 90, 98n4, 114, 116–18, 129, 134n66, 135n80
Goldschmidt, Bertold, 22
Goolden, Richard, 25
Grainger, Gawn, 38
Gray, Ronald, 7, 8, 18n31, 70–2, 77, 79n51, 79n53
Griffith, Kenneth, 25
Grisewood, Harman, 61, 71

H

Haar, Mads, 225, 227n52
Hall, Peter, 47, 64–6, 110
Handley, Tommy, 62, 63
Harwood, Peter, 40
Hawthorne, Denys, 16n2, 24, 26, 29, 31, 92, 216, 231, 240
Heppenstall, Rayner, 1, 61
Hobson, Harold, 64
Hodgson, Brian, 26
Holmes, Robin, 34
Hunger, Julienne, 39

I

integrity, 60, 74, 76, 121, 143, 144, 177, 196, 201
interference, 13, 103–38
imagination, 8, 13, 27–30, 76, 103–38, 158, 198–9, 221, 249, 250, 252–6, 258, 259, 261, 263–5, 272, 280, 284
Ireland, 8, 37, 47, 64, 69, 70, 170, 173, 178n6, 182n33, 190, 212

J

Jameson, Pauline, 26
Jones, David, 3, 61, 71, 72, 79n58
Jones, Haydn, 25

K

Kafka, Franz, 62
Kassel, Germany, 35
Keeffe, Bernard, 23, 24
King Bull, E. J., 46, 47, 61–5, 69, 77
Knowlson, James, 6, 9, 18n22, 19n34, 19n35, 19n42, 35, 40n1, 41n2, 56n1, 57n9, 57n12, 57n20, 63, 77n8, 78n19, 78n29, 79n48, 99n21, 99n24, 100n74, 101n92, 101n102, 106, 132n16, 182n38, 186, 187, 190, 203n3, 204n25, 205n27, 205n30, 206n48, 208n100, 226n7, 227n41, 227n48, 227n55, 234, 236, 245n42, 246n57, 248n113, 248n114, 248n116, 285n4, 286n30, 286n41
Kustow, Michael, 38

L

Leaver, Philip, 25
licensing , 5, 73, 75, 140, 141–4, 147–50, 261

Lindon, Jérôme, 61, 93, 94, 140–2, 167n70, 199–201, 208n102, 208n105
Listener, The, 8–11, 15, 18n30, 18n31, 70, 79n51, 137n116, 215, 231, 269, 270, 276, 280, 283, 284
listening expectations of the BBC's audiences, 4, 5, 15, 83, 92, 112–15, 121, 123, 125, 230, 239, 269–88
live reading, 186, 189, 202

M

MacLeod, Donald, 40
MacGowran, Jack, 8, 11, 14, 27, 29, 30, 34, 92, 95, 188, 231–3, 235, 240, 250, 252–3, 263
MacGreevy (McGreevy), Thomas, 5, 17n19, 35, 97, 101n91, 165n41, 182n31, 234, 245n45
Magee, Patrick, 2, 8, 9, 14, 15, 22–4, 29, 31–4, 38, 46, 50, 51, 53–6, 83, 84, 91, 92, 94, 96, 114, 173–7, 182n35, 182n36, 182–3n38, 187–94, 203–4n4, 204n21, 212, 216, 245n38, 250, 252, 256, 260, 261, 263
Mansell, Gerard, 238, 274–6, 286n31, 286n33
Marriot, R. D'A, 74, 76
Martin, Jean, 6, 22, 191
Mason, Ronald, 38, 39
mass communication, 12, 16, 60, 68, 71, 73, 75–7, 176
Maude, Ulrika, 17n4, 104, 132n22, 211, 225n3
Maxwell, Bennett, 26
McGovern, Barry, 16n4, 40, 249
McKay, Canon Roy, 74
McWhinnie, Donald, 6, 8, 18n23, 18n30, 22–4, 46, 47, 49–51, 53–6, 62, 67, 77, 79n44, 79n47, 82–8, 90, 91, 97, 98n5, 98n12, 98n16, 99n40, 105, 109–15, 117–119, 121–9, 131, 133n34, 133n36, 133n42, 134n50, 134n51, 134n61, 134n62, 134n64, 134n66, 135n91, 135n96, 136n99, 136n112, 137n117, 137n119, 137n122, 137n127, 137n128, 137n132, 138n144, 138n147, 150, 166n61, 167n73, 170, 174–7, 183n42, 183n43, 186, 192, 193, 235, 246n52
memory, 68, 106, 133n23, 193, 195, 199, 271, 272–4
Midgley, Robin, 24
Mihalovici, Marcel, 91, 92, 97, 243
Miller, Arthur, 74
Miller, Karl, 7, 229–30, 239
modernism, 12, 59–79, 108, 145, 193, 254, 255, 261, 271, 275, 283
moral rights, 139–67
Morris, John, 4, 17n13, 46–9, 51–5, 66, 67, 78n32, 79n46, 82–4, 86–8, 98n4, 98n10, 108–10, 115, 117, 118, 129, 133n41, 134n60, 134n69
music, 3, 4, 9, 12, 13, 15, 51, 54, 65, 66, 83, 88–92, 103–5, 116, 119–28, 131, 132–2n23, 137n127, 173, 174, 187, 229–48, 262, 266, 270–7, 281–5, 286n41, 288n77
music and poetry, 15, 65, 229–48
Music Programme, 236–8, 240, 246n61

N

negative dialectics, 271, 272, 276, 284
Network Three, 26, 237, 238

INDEX   307

Newby, Howard [P.H.], 6–7, 13, 18n26, 87–9, 91, 101n94, 146, 172, 188–9, 204n20, 237, 239, 240
Nietzsche, Friedrich, 75
notation, 122, 271–6, 283, 284

O

O'Farrell, Mary, 25, 166n33
Office de Radiodiffusion-Télévision Française (RTF/ORTF), 44, 56, 91, 92, 113, 119, 121, 124, 134n44, 190, 198, 205n32, 208n103
"Oirish" and English localities, 170, 173
Oram, Harold, 63

P

Paris, France, 1, 5, 36, 44, 56, 91, 109, 110, 112, 114, 115, 119, 190
paternity, 143, 144
performance, 6, 7, 14, 22, 44, 73, 85, 124–30, 174, 175, 181n24, 182–3n38, 185–209, 239, 242, 247n83, 250, 254, 256, 258, 261, 263–5, 270–6, 284
phonogeny, 185, 194–9
Pickup, Ronald, 35, 37, 39, 40
Pilling, John, 14, 17n10, 19n40, 41n2, 57n11, 57n13, 57n16, 58n25, 101n93, 101n98, 131, 138n152, 165n51, 169–83, 222, 224, 225, 227n41, 227n48, 227n55, 232, 240, 244n22, 245n31, 247n90
Pinget, Robert, 10, 14, 21, 41n2, 87, 89, 100n52, 100n66, 100n68, 150, 169, 170–3, 178n3, 178n4, 178n6, 179n8, 179n10, 179–80n14, 180n17, 180n22, 181n24, 181n27, 181n28
Pinter, Harold, 2, 29, 31, 86, 96, 118, 212, 216, 261
Plowright, Piers, 38
Polac, Michel, 44, 45, 56n2
positioning, 141, 235
Pountney, Rosemary, 20n48, 104, 132n17, 213, 214, 224, 225, 226n12, 227n53
programming decisions, 238, 240
property right, 139

Q

Quilley, Dennis, 38

R

radio diffusion, 191
radio plays, 13–15, 30, 41n2, 48, 51, 55, 66, 70, 76, 81–102, 104, 106, 108, 118, 122, 132n10, 134n44, 148, 149, 186, 191–3, 199, 201, 203, 229, 231, 232, 234, 235, 240–3, 270, 273–8, 281, 282, 284, 285
Radio Three (Radio 3), 6–7, 11, 14, 15, 16n2, 21, 22, 29, 32, 34, 35, 37–40, 95, 166n61, 166n63, 187, 211, 216, 238, 243, 263
Raikes, Raymond, 48, 65, 66
Raven, Terry, 25
recording, 85, 92, 105, 107, 109, 111–16, 119–21, 123, 125, 127, 128, 134n44, 146–8, 170, 183n49, 186–93, 195, 203, 213, 215, 231–3, 235, 236, 241, 250, 262, 267n24
Reeves, Cecilia, 1, 46–9, 61, 64, 66, 67, 78n38, 82, 87, 110, 113, 114, 134n60, 134n65

revisionary evaluations, 84–5, 194
Rigby, Cormac, 32
Rimbaud, Arthur, 35–7, 187
Rodway, Norman, 39
Rosset, Barney, 6, 18n20, 51, 63, 83, 84, 97, 141, 149, 157, 163n6, 163n8, 167n70, 177, 178n5, 179n14, 187, 189, 194
Ruthven, Malcolm, 39

S
Sachs, Andrew, 25
Sade, Marquis de, 193, 205n44, 205n46
Searle, Humphrey, 93, 94, 102n111
Silverthorne, Lloyd, 34
sound montage, 233–5, 239–43
sound production, 13, 14, 95–6, 103–38, 173, 181n27, 186, 187, 192, 195, 199, 200, 214, 219, 233–5, 240, 257–8, 267n24, 277–82
soundscape, 13, 67, 105–8, 118, 122, 124, 126, 129, 134n53, 172, 211, 236
Spurrier, Libby, 32
Stephens, Robert, 26
Stock, Nigel, 25
subsidiary rights, 140, 149
Sutcliffe, Tom, 38

T
Télévision Française. *See* Office de Radiodiffusion-Télévision Française (RTF/ORTF)
Third Programme, The, 1–15, 16n2, 22–7, 34, 43, 46, 48–51, 53–6, 59–79, 82–8, 90, 95, 108–19, 121, 123, 124, 128–9, 145, 146, 149, 150, 169–83, 185, 186, 188–90, 198, 229–48, 254, 270
Tophoven, Elmar, 29

Trinity College, Dublin, 35, 37, 82, 99n28
Tsingos, Christine, 6, 22
Tynan, Kenneth, 64

V
Van Hulle, Dirk, 12, 43–58, 82, 84, 98n14, 98n15, 98n18, 110, 224, 227n49, 285n4
Vocalization, 126, 198, 200, 201, 203, 251, 255
volume rights, 140

W
Ward, Jeremy, 24
Warmington, Anne Marie, 40
Warrilow, David, 38
Wellington, Lindsay, 53, 74–5
Westwood, Susan, 40
Whitehall, John, 34
Whitelaw, Billie, 26, 96, 212
Williamson, Nichol, 29, 31, 189, 212, 213, 216, 250, 251, 261
Wolfit, Donald, 25
Wood, Helena, 46, 47, 64–5, 69
Wood, James, 75, 79n69
Worth, Katherine, 16n4, 256, 257, 267n11

Z
Zilliacus, Clas, 40n1, 57n19, 83, 98n13, 99n39, 102n107, 102n131, 107, 132n13, 132n19, 132n20, 167n74, 169, 170, 177n1, 177–8n3, 182n37, 183n39, 183n47, 189, 193–4, 198–9, 239, 242–3, 247n86, 248n106, 248n109, 248n111, 248n113, 281, 282, 287n69, 287n71, 288n78, 288n80